VISIT US AT

www.syngress.com

Syngress is committed to publishing high-quality books for IT Professionals and delivering those books in media and formats that fit the demands of our customers. We are also committed to extending the utility of the book you purchase via additional materials available from our Web site.

SOLUTIONS WEB SITE

To register your book, visit www.syngress.com/solutions. Once registered, you can access our solutions@syngress.com Web pages. There you may find an assortment of value-added features such as free e-books related to the topic of this book, URLs of related Web sites, FAQs from the book, corrections, and any updates from the author(s).

ULTIMATE CDs

Our Ultimate CD product line offers our readers budget-conscious compilations of some of our best-selling backlist titles in Adobe PDF form. These CDs are the perfect way to extend your reference library on key topics pertaining to your area of expertise, including Cisco Engineering, Microsoft Windows System Administration, CyberCrime Investigation, Open Source Security, and Firewall Configuration, to name a few.

DOWNLOADABLE E-BOOKS

For readers who can't wait for hard copy, we offer most of our titles in downloadable Adobe PDF form. These e-books are often available weeks before hard copies, and are priced affordably.

SYNGRESS OUTLET

Our outlet store at syngress.com features overstocked, out-of-print, or slightly hurt books at significant savings.

SITE LICENSING

Syngress has a well-established program for site licensing our e-books onto servers in corporations, educational institutions, and large organizations. Contact us at sales@syngress.com for more information.

CUSTOM PUBLISHING

Many organizations welcome the ability to combine parts of multiple Syngress books, as well as their own content, into a single volume for their own internal use. Contact us at sales@syngress.com for more information.

SYNGRESS®

How to Cheat at

Configuring Exchange Server 2007

Including Outlook Web, Mobile, and Voice Access

Henrik Walther

Microsoft
Most Valuable
Professional

KEY	SERIAL NUMBER
001	HJIRTCV764
002	PO9873D5FG
003	829KM8NJH2
004	7934GNBCS3
005	CVPLQ6WQ23
006	VBP965T5T5
007	HJJJ863WD3E
008	2987GVTWMK
009	629MP5SDJT
010	IMWQ295T6T

PUBLISHED BY
Syngress Publishing, Inc.
800 Hingham Street
Rockland, MA 02370

How to Cheat at Configuring Exchange Server 2007: Including Outlook Web, Mobile, and Voice Access

Printed in the United States of America
3 4 5 6 7 8 9 0

ISBN-13: 978-1-59749-137-2
ISBN-10: 1-59749-137-3

Publisher: Andrew Williams
Acquisitions Editor: Gary Byrne
Technical Editors: Rodney Buike, Kirk Vigil
Cover Designer: Michael Kavish
Page Layout and Art: Patricia Lupien
Copy Editors: Mike McGee, Darlene Bordwell, and Judy Eby
Indexer: Richard Carlson

For information on rights, translations, and bulk sales, contact Matt Pedersen, Commercial Sales Director; email m.pedersen@elsevier.com.

Lead Author

Henrik Walther (Exchange MVP, MCSE Messaging/Security) is a senior consultant working for Interprise Consulting A/S (a Microsoft Gold Partner) based in Copenhagen, Denmark. Henrik has more than 14 years of experience in the IT business, where he primarily works with Microsoft Exchange, ISA Server, MOM, IIS, clustering, Active Directory, and virtual server technologies.

In addition to his job as a senior consultant, Henrik runs the Danish Web site Exchange-faq.dk. He is also the primary content creator, forums moderator, and newsletter editor at the leading Microsoft Exchange site, MSExchange.org. Henrik is the author of *CYA: Securing Exchange Server 2003 & Outlook Web Access* (Syngress Publishing), and he has been a reviewer on several other messaging books (including another Exchange 2007 book).

This book is dedicated to his beautiful wife, Michella, whose love, support, and patience he could never be without. And to his wonderful little son, Benjamin, who turned one just before the deadline.

Contributors

Twan Grotenhuis (MCT, MCSE NT4, 2000 and 2003, MCSE+messaging 2000 and 2003, MCSE+security 2000 and 2003, CCNA) is a consultant with Sylis Netherlands. He currently provides strategic and technical consulting to several customers of Sylis in the Netherlands. His specialties include Microsoft Exchange and ISA architecture, design, implementation, troubleshooting, and optimization. Twan has been involved in several major Exchange implementation and migration projects where designing the new messaging infrastructure was his main focus.

Twan wrote Chapter 11.

Technical Editors

Rodney Buike (MCSE) is an IT Pro Advisor with Microsoft Canada. As an IT Pro Advisor, Rodney spends his day helping IT professionals in Canada with issues and challenges they face in their environment and careers. He also advocates for a stronger community presence and shares knowledge through blogging, podcasts, and in-person events.

Rodney's specialties include Exchange Server, virtualization, and core infrastructure technologies on the Windows platform. Rodney worked as a LAN administrator, system engineer, and consultant and has acted as a reviewer on many popular technical books. Rodney is also the founder and principal content provider for Thelazyadmin.com and a former author for MSExchange.org.

Rodney enjoys all his personal and professional activities and is up-front about the support he gets from his family and especially his wife, Lisa. Without her support, what he does would not be possible.

Kirk Vigil (MCSE, MCSA), coauthor of *MCSA/MSCE Exam 70-291: Implementing, Managing, and Maintaining a Windows Server 2003 Network Infrastructure* and How *to Cheat at Managing Windows Server Update Services* is a senior systems consultant for NetBank, Inc. in Columbia, SC. He has worked in the IT integration industry for over 13 years, specializing in Microsoft messaging and network operating system infrastructures. He has worked with Microsoft Exchange since its inception and continues to focus on its advancements with the current release of Exchange 2007 as well as its integration with the Windows Server line of products.

Kirk holds a bachelor's degree from the University of South Carolina. He also works as an independent consultant for a privately owned integration company, lending technical direction to local business practices. He is a contributing author to *Microsoft Certified Professional Magazine*. Kirk would first like to thank God, for without Him nothing is possible. Kirk would also like to thank his beautiful girlfriend, Kimberley Paige, for her continued and loving support as Kirk's takes on more "bookwork" as she likes to call it. She is irreplaceable and loved very much. Kirk thanks his family for their unconditional love and support. Lastly, Kirk is grateful to the owners, editors, and writers of Syngress/Elsevier Publishing for the opportunity to continue working with them as a technical writer/editor.

Robert J. Shimonski (MCSE) is an Entrepreneur and best-selling author and editor of hundreds of published books and thousands of magazine and industry articles. Rob consults within today's most challenging business and technology environments and brings front-line industry knowledge to the reader in every page he writes. Rob is always on top of the latest trends and reporting the state of the business and technology industry from a real-world perspective. As of the writing of this book, Rob is currently on assignment testing and developing secure Vista images and designing a Longhorn upgrade for a large global firm.

For Syngress, Rob has written many cutting-edge "in demand" titles, including *The (ISC)2 SSCP Study Guide and DVD Training System* (ISBN 1931836809), *The Best Damn Firewall Book Period!* (ISBN 1931836906), *Designing and Building Enterprise DMZs* (ISBN 1597491004), *Nokia Network Security Solutions Handbook* (ISBN 1931836701), *Sniffer Pro Network Optimization and Troubleshooting Handbook* (ISBN 1931836574), *Configuring and Troubleshooting Windows XP Professional with CD-ROM* (ISBN 1928994806), *Configuring Symantec Antivirus Corporate Edition* (ISBN 1931836817), and the *Network+ Study Guide & Practice Exams: Exam N10-003* (ISBN 1931836426). Rob also helped to develop the first DVD video with Syngress for the launch of *The Security + Study Guide and DVD Training System* (ISBN 1931836728), which has become a best seller.

Rob owns and operates Sound Room Studios Inc, a media development company in Long Island, NY. His role there is to produce and engineer audio and video content for TV, radio, and digital distribution.

Rob assisted with the technical editing of Chapter 6.

Contents

Preface

Welcome to *How to Cheat at Configuring Exchange Server 2007: Including Outlook Web, Mobile, and Voice Access*. I hope you will enjoy reading this book as much as I enjoyed writing it, although it was a tough journey!

I first got the idea for this book in December 2005, the month when I received my first installment of E12 (beta 1). E12 was the codename for Exchange 2007 until the name change announcement in April 2006.

I've never been as involved in a beta program as I have with this one. Besides doing intensive testing of the product in my lab environment, I also had the opportunity to attend the first global series of technical training on the product, the "The E12 Ignite Training Tour," which was held in April/May 2006. I attended the E12 Ignite Training Tour in Amsterdam, and during this event, I became aware of the Exchange 12 Rapid Deployment Program (RDP). The RDP lets you plan, prepare, and deploy E12 beta 2 into a specifically selected client's corporate production environment. I already knew about the E12 Technology Adoption Program (TAP), but unfortunately, I didn't have any clients of the required size that were interested in participating in the TAP. However, the RDP matched the environment of two of my clients perfectly. So when I returned to Denmark, it was time for me to recommend them for an RDP. Fortunately, one of them was awarded an RDP! My involvement with this client provided me with an incredible amount of hands-on experience with the product, resulting in a lot of real-world experience that was necessary to write a book about Exchange Server 2007 at such an early stage.

I would not have been able to write this book without help (in one way or another) from the following people:

Andrew L. Williams, Managing Editor at Syngress Publishing, for believing in my idea for this book.

Gary Byrne, my Acquisitions Editor at Syngress Publishing, who did a great job putting everything together and shepherding the book through final production.

Rodney Buike and Kirk Vigil, my two technical editors, both of whom provided many great tips and suggestions. Thanks, guys, I appreciate it!

Twan Grotenhuis, who wrote Chapter 11 on Unified Messaging.

Henrik Damslund, former Exchange Technology Specialist at Microsoft Denmark, who nominated one of my clients for the Exchange RDP.

Jens Trier Rasmussen (Microsoft Services Denmark), who was my primary contact during the Exchange RDP.

Frank Nielsen, one of my good colleagues at Interprise Consulting, for the project management work he did for our client in the Exchange RDP.

KC Lemson, Exchange Program Manager, for doing a fantastic job as the lead program manager on the Exchange 2007 RDP team.

Sean Buttigieg, Michael Vella, and the rest of the MSExchange.org team for letting me be such a big part of the leading Microsoft Exchange server site, MSExchange.org. Since 1996 this site has been an essential companion guiding Exchange administrators in their quests to get the most out of their Microsoft Exchange environments.

I also want to thank Tim McMichael (Microsoft Support Professional, Charlotte, NC), Kadar M. Saadani (Exchange Beta Engineer, India), and Satguru Sharma (Exchange Beta Engineer, India).

—*Henrik Walther*
Copenhagen, Denmark
February 7, 2007

Chapter 1

Introducing Exchange Server 2007

Solutions in this chapter:

- **What Is Exchange Server 2007?**
- **Exchange 2007 Themes**
- **Architectural Goals with Exchange Server 2007**
- **Role-Based Deployment and Server Roles**
- **New Management Approach**
- **High Availability (HA) Improvements**
- **Exchange Server 2007 Services**
- **Exchange Server Permissions**
- **64-Bit Support Only**
- **Active Directory-Based Routing Topology**
- **De-emphasized Features**
- **Discontinued Features**

Introduction

This chapter provides you with a basic understanding of what Exchange Server 2007 is as well as an overview of the new features and improvements included in the product. Exchange Server 2007 now uses a role-based approach, which makes it much simpler to deploy different server roles to match the topology of your organization. In addition, Exchange Server 2007 has moved to being a true 64-bit application. Exchange Server 2007 also takes advantage of Windows PowerShell, making it possible to do complex tasks in a simple and automated way using scripts. Most complicated tasks that used to consist of several hundred lines of code can now typically be done with one line of code using the EMS.

Finally, this chapter lists the features that have been de-emphasized and discontinued in this version of Exchange Server 2007.

What Is Exchange Server 2007?

Exchange Server 2007 is Microsoft's new version of the industry's leading server software for e-mail, calendaring, and unified messaging. Exchange Server 2007 is considered the biggest upgrade in the history of the Exchange Product group. It has been totally reengineered, and most of the code has been completely rewritten. In addition, Exchange Server 2007 is the first released Microsoft product to take advantage of the new Windows PowerShell (formerly known as Monad) called the EMS. The "2007" indicates the close alignment of this release with the Microsoft Office 2007 wave of products, which together deliver a best-in-class enterprise messaging and collaboration solution.

Exchange 2007 Themes

In 2003, the Exchange Product group came up with three Exchange themes aimed at reflecting the different types of Exchange situations. Since their introduction, the themes have stayed constant, having played an important role during the development of Exchange Server 2007. Following is an overview of all three themes.

IT Pro Situation

The *IT Pro Situation* theme focuses on making sure that Information Technology (IT) professionals get what they need. The Exchange product team knows that e-mail is mission-critical, and that without it, there will be a loss of productivity and revenue. They also know that current systems are too complex and expensive, and that many of the day-to-day tasks would be better suited to scripted automation rather than tedious manual configuration. With Exchange Server 2007, the Exchange product team was able to give us this control.

Info Worker Situation

The *Info Worker Situation* theme focuses on availability. IT professionals need access to e-mail, voicemail, and faxes. Today, people are mobile and require access to all kinds of messaging data. With Exchange Server 2007, the Exchange Product team can make things easier for IT professionals.

Organizationwide Situation

The *Organizationwide Situation* theme focuses on security and control throughout the organization's messaging environment. Today, e-mail needs to be secure. Filtering out spam and removing viruses in order to provide a clean message stream needs to be a core design goal for any messaging system. The Exchange Product group began their road to e-mail security using Exchange Server 2003 Service Pack 2, which greatly improved overall security by introducing Sender ID filtering and version 2 of the SmartScreen-based Intelligent Message Filter (IMF). With Exchange Server 2007, security has improved. Anther requirement is that the messaging environment conform to legal and corporatewide policies, requiring us to journal, archive, and search through large amounts of messages. Luckily, these requirements have also been improved upon and have been added to Exchange Server 2007.

Architectural Goals with Exchange Server 2007

When the Exchange Product group developed Exchange Server 2007 they had four main architectural goals:

- **Simplicity** Deliver a product with a simple and intuitive user interface
- **Flexibility** Make the product flexible, especially regarding deployment and management
- **Trustworthiness** Secure all communication by default (OWA uses secure sockets layer [SSL], Hub Transport Server uses Transport Layer Security [TLS], and so forth)

Scalability

Scalability is achievable by using 64-bit code (reduced input/output [I/O], more data in address space, and so forth). The Exchange Server 2007 Product group delivered these goals. Many are of the opinion that too many management tasks must be accomplished by running the respective *cmdlets* in the EMS. Many of the management tasks missing from the Exchange Management Console (EMC) user interface will be added into the release of Exchange Server 2007 Service Pack 1.

Role-Based Deployment and Server Roles

Unlike previous versions of Exchange, Exchange Server 2007 is easy to deploy. Although you could dedicate an Exchange 2000 or 2003 server as either a front-end, back-end, or bridgehead server, you always had to install all of the Exchange binaries and services even if they were not required. Although it was possible to disable some of the Exchange Services that weren't required, this monolithic approach forced you to use valuable resources, disk space and/or Exchange components you didn't necessarily need to install.

This has all changed with Exchange Server 2007, which has a great new role-based setup wizard, allowing you the ability to deploy individual server roles (see Figure 1.1).

Figure 1.1 Exchange Server 2007 Setup Wizard

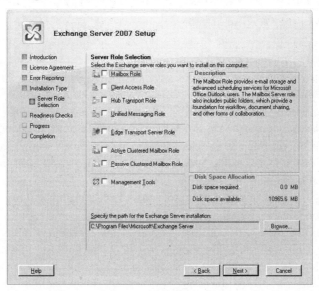

Based on the new server role-based approach, you can now select what server role(s) you want to install on a given server, thus deploying Exchange Server 2007 in a more flexible way. Exchange Server 2007 provides five distinct server roles that include specific features and functionality, thereby providing the messaging functionality you want.

NOTE

A server role is a unit that logically groups the required features and components that are required to perform a specific function in your messaging environment.

The server roles are as follows: Client Access Server, Hub Transport, Mailbox, Unified Messaging, and Edge Transport. All server roles except the Edge Transport server can be installed on the same physical server (typical scenario for a small organization), or distributed across multiple servers (typical for large organizations). It depends on your organizational requirements and sometimes on your budget.

The following sections give a short overview of each server role included in Exchange Server 2007.

Mailbox Server Role

The Exchange 2007 *Mailbox Server role* hosts mailbox databases where user and resource mailboxes are stored. This server role hosts the Public Folder database, used by organizations for the sharing of documents, calendar, contact, and task data, as well as for archiving distribution lists. As you will see in chapter 3, a legacy Outlook client (that is Outlook 2003 and earlier) requires a public folder database in order to connect to Exchange Server 2007.

In addition to hosting mailbox and public folder databases, the Mailbox Server also provides rich calendaring functionality, resource management, and offline address book downloads. The Mailbox Server role also provides services that calculate e-mail address policies (called recipient policies in Exchange Server 2000 and 2003) as well as address lists for recipients. Lastly, this server role enforces managed folders.

The Exchange Product group also improved the high availability (HA) and recovery features for the mailbox Server. Exchange Server 2007 includes a new continuous replication mechanism that can be used with both non-clustered and clustered mailbox Servers. Using Structured Query Language (SQL) technology, the new continuous replication feature uses log file shipping. Log file replay makes it possible to replicate any changes done in the active databases to a passive copy. When speaking about non-clustered mailbox Servers, this feature is more specifically known as Local Continuous Replication (LCR), making it possible to switch to the passive copy of the database using a manual switch. The continuous replication feature combined with Windows clustering is known as Cluster Continuous Replication (CCR) and provides automatic failover to the passive database should the active database fail or shutdown unexpectedly

Client Access Server Role

The *Client Access Server (CAS) role* replaces the front-end. This means that the CAS provides mailbox access for all types of Exchange clients, with the exception of Outlook MAPI clients. In a nutshell, the CAS accepts clients accessing their mailbox using Post Office Protocol version 3 (POP3), Internet Messaging Access Protocol 4 (IMAP4), Outlook AnyWhere (formerly known as Remote Procedure Call [RPC over HTTP], Outlook Web Access (OWA) and Exchange ActiveSync (EAS).

> **NOTE**
>
> The Outlook Mobile Access (OMA component is no longer a part of the Exchange Server product.

In addition to providing client access, the CAS is also responsible for providing access to the Offline Address Book (if using a Web-based distribution method), the AutoDiscover service, and the Availability service.

The Availability service is a new Web-based service providing access to the Offline Address Book (OAB) and free information (housed in a public folder). In addition, Out Of Office (OOF) messages and several Unified Messaging features such as Play on phone are accessed using this service.

The AutoDiscover service makes is easier to configure Outlook 2007 and Exchange ActiveSync clients, as end users only need to provide their e-mail address and password in order to configure an Outlook or EAS profile. If Outlook 2007 is configured on a workstation part of the Active Directory domain, you don't need to provide any information; instead you simply click **Next** a couple of times and the Outlook profile is created, using the cached credentials of the current logged on user. (For more information about the Client Access Server role, see Chapter 5.)

Hub Transport Server Role

The *Hub Transport Server* role is deployed inside your organization's Active Directory. This server role handles all internal mail flow and is also responsible for applying transport rules as well as journaling policies to the respective messages flowing through your organization. In addition, the Hub Transport Server delivers messages to the recipient mailboxes stored on the Mailbox Server. Messages sent from one user to another user that have their respective mailboxes stored on the same Mailbox server, use the Hub Transport Server in order to deliver a message. This means that a Hub Transport Server must be deployed in each Active Directory site that contains a Mailbox Server.

NOTE

Message routing in Exchange Server 2007 is no longer based on Exchange routing groups and routing groups are no longer part of the Exchange product. Instead, Exchange Server 2007 uses your Active Directory site topology.

A Hub Transport Server is typically only used for internal mail flow; however, this depends on whether you have deployed an Edge Transport server as the Internet-facing Simple Mail Transfer Protocol (SMTP) server in your demilitarized zone (DMZ). If you use an Edge Transport Server, all inbound and outbound e-mail will pass through the Edge Transport Server. If you don't want to deploy an Edge Transport Server, you can let the Hub Transport Server act as the Internet-facing SMTP server in your organization, although this isn't recommended. (For more information about the Hub Transport Server role, see Chapter 6.)

Unified Messaging Server Role

The *Unified Messaging Server role* is new to the Exchange product line. This server role combines voice messaging, fax, and e-mail into one single unified inbox, making it possible to access all of this information from a host of client solutions: Outlook 2007, Outlook Web Access 2007, Windows Mobile 5.0, and so forth.

Unified Messaging gives your end-users features like the following:

Auto Attendant

An *auto attendant* is a set of voice prompts that gives external users access to the Exchange 2007 Unified Messaging system. An auto attendant lets the user use either the telephone keypad or speech inputs to navigate the menu structure, place a call to a user, or locate a user and then place a call to that user. An auto attendant gives the administrator the ability to:

- Create a customizable set of menus for external users.

- Define informational greetings, business hours greetings, and non-business hours greetings.

- Define holiday schedules.

- Describe how to search the organization's directory.

- Describe how to connect to a user's extension so external callers can call a user by specifying their extension.

- Describe how to search the organization's directory so external callers can search the organization's directory and call a specific user.

- Enable external users to call the operator.

Call Answering

Call answering includes answering an incoming call on behalf of a user, playing their personal greeting, recording a message, and submitting it for delivery to their inbox as an e-mail message.

Fax Receiving

Fax receiving is the process of submitting a fax message for delivery to the Inbox.

Subscriber Access

The subscriber access feature enables dial-in access for company users. Company users or subscribers who are dialing into the Unified Messaging system can access their mailbox using Outlook Voice Access. Subscribers who use Outlook Voice Access can access the

Unified Messaging system by using the telephone keypad or voice inputs. By using a telephone, a subscriber or user can:

- Access voicemail.

- Listen, forward, or reply to e-mail messages.

- Listen to calendar information.

- Access or dial contacts stored in the global address list or a personal contact list.

- Accept or cancel meeting requests.

- Set a voicemail Out-of-Office message.

- Set user security preferences and personal options.

The Unified Messaging Server role integrates Exchange Server 2007 with your organization's existing telephony network and brings the features found in Unified Messaging to the core of the Exchange Server product line. (For more information about the new Unified Messaging role, see Chapter 11).

Edge Transport Server Role

The Exchange Product Group developed the Edge Transport Server to give enterprises powerful out-of-the-box protection against spam without needing to invest in a third-party solution. The messaging hygiene features in the *Edge Transport Server role* are agent-based and consist of multiple filters that are frequently updated.

Although the primary role of the Edge Transport Server is to route mail and perform message hygiene, it also includes features that allow you to rewrite SMTP addresses, configure transport rules, enable journaling, and associate company disclaimers.

The Edge Transport Server can also be used to set up a business-to-business domain security relationship, thereby reducing management overhead that might otherwise be required to provide domain security between two business partners. Domain security enables message-level encryption and digital signatures, and ad hoc business-to-business and partner-to-partner message security.

The Edge Transport Server uses Active Directory Application Mode (ADAM) to store the required Active Directory data, including Accepted Domains, Recipients, Safe Senders, Send Connectors, and a Hub Transport Server list (used to generate dynamic connectors so that they don't have to be created manually). The Active Directory data is replicated to the Edge Transport Server using an EdgeSync service that runs on the Hub Transport Server on the internal network. Since the EdgeSync service uses Lightweight Directory Access Protocol (LDAP) for replication, you only need to open two additional ports (besides port 25 used for SMTP) for Edge Server to internal Hub Transport Server communication (default ports 50389 and 50636, respectively). (For more information about the Edge Transport Server role, see Chapter 7.)

New Management Approach

Exchange Server 2007 will make your job as Exchange administrators much easier and more effective than in previous versions of Exchange.

EMC Console

The Exchange Management Console (EMC) is one of the most notable additions to Exchange Server 2007. The EMC is a complete rewrite of the Exchange System Manager user interface navigation tree. The Exchange Product group needed to organize the eight levels of tree navigation in Exchange Server 2003, so they developed the console with the goal of making it simple, intuitive, and more organized, using less nesting in hopes of reducing the learning curve, and effectively organizing all actions while maintaining strict consistency. In order to accomplish this goal, the Exchange Product group developed a new graphical user interface (GUI) using MMC 3.0, and divided the EMC into four different work areas: *Console* tree, *Work* pane, *Result* pane, and *Action* pane (see Figure 1.2). In addition, the Console tree is divided into four different work centers, making navigation much easier. Lastly, the entire console is built on top of the Windows PowerShell, making all user interface commands visible in shell *cmdlets* for noting and future scripting.

Figure 1.2 Exchange Server 2007 Work Centers

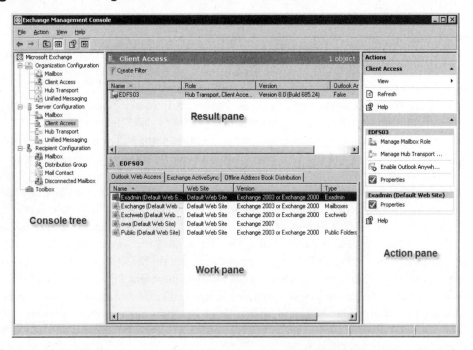

The following are short descriptions of each of the work panes available in the Exchange 2007 Management Console.

Console Tree

The purpose of the *Console tree* (located on the left side of the EMC) is to organize nodes based on the types of server roles that have been deployed in the Exchange Server 2007 organization.

Work Pane

The *Work* pane (located on the bottom of the EMC) is designed to display objects based on the server role subnode selected beneath the Server Configuration work center.

Result Pane

The *Result* pane (located on the top of the EMC) contains various configuration tabs that display the different objects available based on the selected work center node or subnode in the Console tree.

Action Pane

The *Action* pane (located on the right side of the EMC) lists the various actions that are available for a selected object. The Action pane is an MMC 3.0 feature that can be hidden if you want to use context menus (i.e., right-click menus.

Four New Work Centers

The Console tree is divided into four work centers that directly map the type of data you need to manage in your organization.

Organization Configuration Work Station

The *Organization Configuration* work center contains any global or systemwide configuration data and settings in the organization. This is where you find features such as E-mail Address Policies (formerly Recipient Policies), Address Lists, Accepted Domains, and so forth). The Organization Configuration work center is categorized by server role, as configuration data can be both *server-level* based or *organizationally* based. By using this approach, it's easy for the Exchange Administrator to discover the configuration data for a particular server role. If the Organization Configuration work center is selected, you can manage the Exchange Administrator roles (formerly known as the Exchange Administration Delegation Wizard).

The *Server Configuration* work center contains server-level data such as Storage Group, Mailbox databases, client protocols, and receive connectors. Just like the Organization Configuration work center, the subnodes in this work center are based on server roles. When selecting the Server Configuration work center node, you get an overview of the Exchange

2007 Servers in your Exchange organization, where you can see the server name, the build version, and which server roles are installed on each Exchange server.

The *Recipient Configuration* work center node is used for recipient management. Here is where you see various recipient type nodes such as mailboxes, distribution groups, mail contacts, and disconnected mailboxes.

> **NOTE**
>
> With Exchange Server 2007, mail-enabled objects are no longer managed via the Active Directory Users and Computers snap-in; instead, they have to be managed via the EMC or the Exchange Management Shell (EMS) (See Chapter 3.)

The *Toolbox* work center can be considered a central repository for different Exchange tools that will help you diagnose and troubleshoot Exchange-related issues, in addition to giving you best practice recommendations in terms of properly configuring and optimizing the servers in your organization. As shown in Figure 1.3, tools such as the Best Practices Analyzer, Database Recovery Management, Database Troubleshooter, Mail Flow Troubleshooter, and a Performance Troubleshooter can be found here. In addition, the Toolbox center is also the place to track messages using the Message Tracking Queue Viewer, and to track performance using the Performance Monitor.

Figure 1.3 Exchange Toolbox Work Center

The following sections are short descriptions of each administrator tool available in the Toolbox work center.

Exchange Server Best Practices Analyzer

The Exchange Server Best Practices Analyzer (ExBPA) is a tool that is used for checking the configuration and health of the Exchange server topology. Every time you run the tool it checks for updated Extensible Markup Language (XML) files as best practices for Exchange Server are reviewed and updated.

Database Recovery Management

This tool is used to manage disaster recovery scenarios. It can help reduce recovery time and streamline the recovery process after database problems occur on production servers running Microsoft Exchange Server.

Database Troubleshooter

This tool is used to help troubleshoot store mounting and other database-related problems.

Mail Flow Troubleshooter

This tool is used for troubleshooting mail flow and transport-related problems.

Message Tracking

This tool is used for examining message tracking logs.

Queue Viewer

This tool is used for managing Exchange mail queues.

Performance Monitor

This tool is used for monitoring server performance and overall health.

Performance Troubleshooter

This tool is used for troubleshooting server performance problems.

NOTE

A cool thing about the Toolbox work center is that it's extensible; meaning additional tools can be added via the Microsoft Exchange Eeb site. It would have been cooler if 3rd party tools could have been added to the Toolbox center as well, but unfortunately it's limited to Microsoft's own Exchange tools.

New Wizards

The Exchange Product Group also included some new wizards in an effort to get rid of the older Exchange System Manager internally (see Figure 1.4).

Figure 1.4 Exchange 2007 Wizard

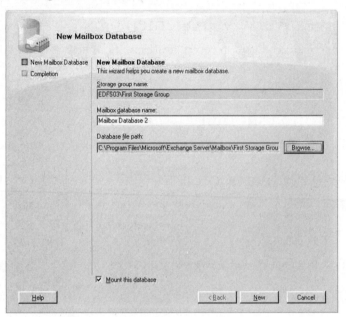

Exposed *CMDlet* Code

The EMC is built on top of the Windows PowerShell engine (formerly known as Monad), which ultimately means that the GUI wizards are just executing shell *cmdlets* in the background. Each executed wizard task in the user interface exposes the actual *cmdlet* code when the wizard has completed (see Figure 1.5). The cool thing about this is the fact that you can copy the exposed code to your computers clipboard, paste it to a text editor such as Notepad, edit it, and save it as a PS1script and/or paste it direct into the EMS to execute immediately.

Figure 1.5 Exposed CMDlet Code

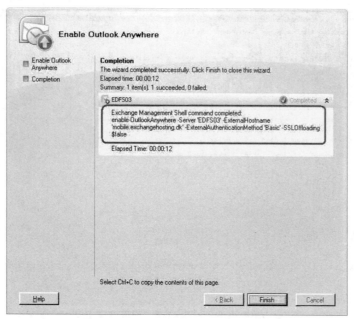

Here is the *cmdlet,* including the necessary parameters for enabling Outlook Anywhere:

```
enable-OutlookAnywhere -Server:'EDFS03'
-ExternalHostname:'mobile.exchangehosting.dk'
-ExternalAuthenticationMethods:'Basic' -SSLOffloading:'$false'
```

EMS

The Exchange Product Group included an EMS (see Figure 1.6) in order to make the Exchange Administrator's job easier. The new EMS is based on Windows PowerShell (formerly known as Monad). By using this new shell you can accomplish all of the tasks available in the EMC. The shell is there to make it easier to do bulk and/or repetitive administrative tasks.

Figure 1.6 EMS

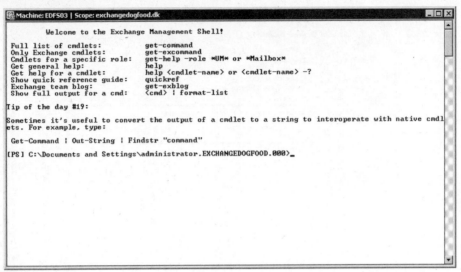

TIP

To get up to speed with the new EMS, I recommend you study the following two Microsoft PDF files, which give you a pretty good primer on use and functionality:

Introduction to the Exchange Management Shell: www.microsoft.com/downloads/details.aspx?familyid=1dc0f61b-d30f-44a2-882e-12ddd4ee09d2&displaylang=en

Exchange Management Shell Quick Reference: www.microsoft.com/downloads/details.aspx?familyid=01A441B9-4099-4C0F-B8E0-0831D4A2CA86&displaylang=en

Although we primarily use the Exchange 2007 Management Console throughout this book, we typically show you how that same task can be accomplished using the EMS.

HA Improvements

The availability requirements for messaging and collaboration servers have increased drasti-cally over the years, catapulting these servers to be amongst the most mission-critical servers in the datacenter. Several recent reports have concluded that e-mail is more important to end users than their phones. So, it's in your best interest as the Exchange Administrator to achieve as high an uptime as possible. Each of these facts played an important role when the Exchange Product Group developed Exchange Server 2007, so it should come as no surprise that HA and disaster recovery was of utmost concern, and the reason behind the many improvements and new functionality in the Exchange Server 2007 product. Most especially is the new continuous replication functionality, which uses log file shipping and replay to keep a second copy of a Mailbox database in sync with the production database.

LCR

LCR is a solution that uses the new continuous replication technology introduced in Exchange Server 2007. LCR is a new functionality that uses built-in asynchronous log ship-ping and log replay technology to create and maintain a replica of a storage group on a second set of disks that are connected to the same server as the production storage group. The interesting thing about LCR is that it only requires one Exchange Server 2007 with the Mailbox Server role installed. However, it does require that there only be one viable database in each storage group.

CCR

The most interesting new feature when it comes to HA is the CCR solution, which, like LCR, uses the new Exchange Server 2007 continuous replication technology. CCR is a clustered solution that eliminates the single point of failure that exists in traditional Exchange cluster setups. This is done by maintaining a copy of the database on the active node; in the event of a database corruption, this allows both services and databases to fail over to the passive node. CCR can only be deployed in a two-node active/passive cluster. (LCR and CCR are covered in more detail in Chapter 8.)

Exchange Server 2007 Services

The services used by the different Exchange Server 2007 roles are either completely new services or services that have changed since Exchange 2003. Table 1.1 lists each of the Exchange Server 2007 services along with a short description.

Table 1.1 Exchange Server 2007 Services

Service	Description
Exchange Active Directory Topology Service	This service provides Active Directory topology information to Exchange services. If this service is stopped, most Exchange services cannot start.
Microsoft Exchange ADAM	This service provides the ADAM directory service function to the Edge Transport Server.
Microsoft Exchange Credential Service	This service manages the credentials that the Hub Transport Server uses to authenticate to ADAM for a subscribed Edge Transport Server.
Microsoft Exchange EdgeSync	This service provides data replication and synchronization between Active Directory and ADAM for a subscribed Edge Transport Server.
Microsoft Exchange File Distribution	This service provides file distribution services.
Microsoft Exchange IMAP4	This service provides IMAP4 services to clients. If this service is stopped, clients cannot connect to the computer using the IMAP4 protocol.
Microsoft Exchange Information Store	The Microsoft Exchange Information Store service manages the Microsoft Exchange Information Store. This includes mailbox stores and public folder stores. If this service is stopped, mailbox stores and public folder stores on this computer are unavailable. If this service is disabled, any services that explicitly depend on it will not start.
Microsoft Exchange Mailbox Assistants	This service performs background processing of mailboxes in the Exchange store.
Microsoft Exchange Mail Submission Service	This service submits messages from the Mailbox server to the Hub Transport Servers.
Microsoft Exchange Monitoring	Microsoft Exchange Monitoring enables applications to call the Exchange diagnostic *cmdlets*.
Microsoft Exchange POP3	This service provides POP3 services to clients. If this service is stopped, clients cannot connect to this computer using the POP3 protocol.

Continued

Table 1.1 continued Exchange Server 2007 Services

Service	Description
Microsoft Exchange Replication Service	The Microsoft Exchange Replication Service provides replication functionality used by Local Continuous Backup (Replication) and CCR.
Microsoft Exchange Search Indexer	Microsoft Exchange Search Indexer drives indexing of mailbox content. This improves the performance of the content search.
Microsoft Exchange Service Host	Microsoft Exchange Service Host provides a host for several Microsoft Exchange services.
Microsoft Exchange Speech Engine	Microsoft Exchange Speech Engine provides speech processing services for Microsoft Exchange. If this service is stopped, speech recognition services will not be available to Unified Messaging clients.
Microsoft Exchange System Attendant	Microsoft Exchange System Attendant provides monitoring, maintenance, and Active Directory lookup services (e.g., monitoring of services and connectors, defragmenting the Exchange Store, and forwarding the Active Directory lookups to a global catalog server). If this service is stopped, monitoring, maintenance, and lookup services are unavailable. If this service is disabled, any services that explicitly depend on it will not start.
Microsoft Exchange Transport Log Search	This service provides remote search capability for Microsoft Exchange Transport log files.
Microsoft Exchange Transport Service	This service provides the SMTP to Exchange 2007 transport servers.
Microsoft Exchange Unified Messaging	This service enables Microsoft Exchange Unified Messaging features. This enables voice and fax messages to be stored in Microsoft Exchange and gives users telephone access to e-mail, voicemail, calendar, contacts, or an automated attendant. If this service is stopped, users will not be able use the Unified Messaging features.
Microsoft Search (Exchange)	Microsoft Search (Exchange) quickly creates full-text indexes on content and properties of structured data to enable fast linguistic searches on this data.

Exchange Server Permissions

In previous versions of Exchange, administrative groups were administrative boundaries that contained servers and other objects. Although these administrative groups could be used to segregate administration within your organization, they were far from flexible and thus have been discontinued in Exchange Server 2007. Instead, you can now delegate permissions from the organization down to the server. No matter whether your organization uses a centralized or decentralized administrative model, you can delegate permissions to more closely match that model and easily adapt to new models as your organization changes.

All permissions in an Exchange Server 2007 organization are configured by assigning administrative access roles to Active Directory users or groups. As can be seen in Figure 1.7, four different Exchange administrator roles exist in Exchange Server 2007.

In the next section, we briefly describe each role:

Figure 1.7 Adding an Exchange Administrator to an Administrator Role

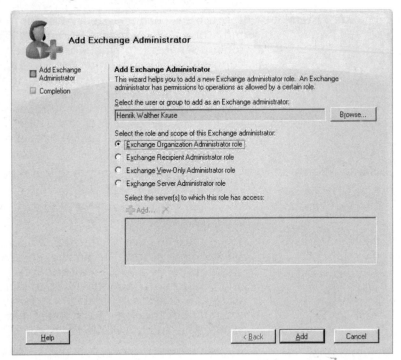

Exchange Organization Administrators Group

The Exchange Organization Administrators Group role provides administrators with full access to all Exchange properties and objects in the Exchange organization.

Exchange Recipient Administrators Group

The Exchange Recipient Administrators Group role has permissions to modify any Exchange property on an Active Directory user, contact, group, dynamic distribution list, or public folder object.

Exchange Server Administrators

The Exchange Server Administrators role has access to only local server Exchange configuration data, either in the Active Directory or on the physical computer on which Exchange Server 2007 is installed. Users who are members of the Exchange Server Administrators role have permission to administer a particular server, but do not have permission to perform operations that have global impact in the Exchange organization.

Exchange View-Only Administrators Group

The Exchange View-Only Administrators Group role has read-only access to the entire Exchange organization tree in the Active Directory configuration container, and read-only access to all of the Windows domain containers that have Exchange recipients.

64-Bit Support Only

One of the major architectural changes in the Exchange Server 2007 product is the shift to a true 64-bit environment. As you might be aware, previous versions of Exchange did support 64-bit processors, however they didn't take advantage of them since they were still only 32-bit applications under the hood. Exchange Server 2007 is a true 64-bit messaging platform, and thus gives significant database scalability creating larger mailbox and/or public folder stores in your environment. This is possible due to the fact that 64-bit processing allows you to store much more data in memory, causing a lot less I/O load on the disks.

In addition, there is support for much larger mailboxes (+2GB). The move to 64-bit also means you are no longer limited to the 4 GB memory limitation of Exchange 2003 in your servers. Exchange 2007 supports up to eight TB of memory, but at the time of this writing, the hardware limit is 64 GB of RAM, which should be sufficient.

The 64-bit Support Only heading is not 100 percent true, since a 32-bit version actually exists; however it is meant for evaluation and testing purposes only. The 32-bit version is a *time bombed* version in addition to not being supported in a production. There's only one exception to this rule, and that is using the 32-bit versions to install the Management Console and perform management tasks (using the EMC and Shell, extending the Active Directory and Schema with Setup, and so forth.)

Active Directory-Based Routing Topology

With Exchange Server 2007, the way messages are routed between the Hub Transport servers (known as *Bridgehead* servers in Exchange Server 2003) has changed considerably. You no longer need to set up routing group connectors between routing groups in the Exchange organization when you design your Exchange topology. The routing group functionality has been removed from the Exchange product (see the list of discontinued features later in this chapter). Why has this flexible way of routing messages throughout an Exchange organization been removed? It has been determined that routing groups actually have several drawbacks, one being long stretches of time where two servers disagree about a connection state, in many situations causing routing loops. Another is the difficulty in tracking why a message took a given route at a given point in time, because the link state table for the Exchange topology was never persistent and/or logged. Lastly, the routing groups and routing group connector concept forced Exchange administrators to recreate and mimic the underlying network, which can be a time-consuming task.

So, how do you set up your routing topology in Exchange Server 2007? You don't! Exchange Server 2007 is a site-aware application, meaning that it can determine its own Active Directory site membership and the Active Directory site membership of other servers by querying Active Directory. Instead of using its own routing group topology, Exchange uses the AD directory service site topology to determine how messages are transported in the organization. This means that the Hub Transport servers in your Exchange organization retrieve information from Active Directory in order to determine how messages should be routed between servers. You need to deploy a Hub Transport server in each site containing a Mailbox server, meaning when user A in one site sends a message to user B in another site, the Mailbox server contacts the Hub Transport server in its own site, and then routes the message to the Hub Transport server in user B's site, ultimately delivering the message to the mailbox server hosting user B's mailbox.

De-emphasized Features

The following legacy Exchange features have been de-emphasized in Exchange Server 2007. What does that mean? It means that these features are still included in the Exchange product, but they're not prioritized anymore, and will most likely disappear in the next Exchange release after Exchange Server 2007 (currently codenamed E14).

- Public Folders
- Proxy Address Generators
- CDO 1:21

- MAPI32
- CDOEX (CDO 3.0)
- Exchange WebDAV ex
- ExOLEDB
- Store Events
- Streaming backup AP
- Exchange Server Viru

Discontinued

Because of the major architec
and components included in
Exchange Server 2007. Disco
didn't make it into Exchange
features or because the Exch
supporting them in Exchang
didn't make it into Exchange Server 2007.

Architecture Features

Several architectural related features were removed or replaced in Exchange Server 2007.

- Routing Groups
- Administrative Groups
- Link State Routing
- Routing Objects
- IMF (replaced by Content Filter which can be considered IMF v3)
- Network Attached Storage (NAS)
- Exchange installable File System (ExIFS)
- Event Service

Recipient-Related Feat

- Exchange extensions in Activ
- Microsoft Exchange Serv
- Recipient Update Se

Mobile Feat

- Outlool
- Ou

e Directory Users and Computers MMC snap-in

er Mailbox Merge Wizard (ExMerge)

vice (RUS)

Mobile Access (OMA)

look Mobile Access Browse

Always-Up-To-Date version 1 (AUTD v1)

S/MIME (will be back when Exchange 2007 SP1 releases)

Outlook Web Access Features

- S/MIME Control component (will be back when Exchange 2007 SP1 releases)
- Rules, Notes, Post Forms, Monthly Calendar view
- Custom Forms
- Editing personal distribution lists
- URL commands except for free/busy, galfind, navbar, and contents
- Public folder access
- Exchange Web forms

Public Folder Features

- Public Folder Management via GUI (but will be back when Exchange 2007 SP1 releases)
- Non-MAPI top-level hierarchies in a public folder store
- Public folder access using NNTP
- Public folder access using IMAP4

Protocol Features

- Network News Transfer Protocol (NNTP)
- Management of POP3/IMAP4 via GUI (Will most likely be back when Exchange 2007 SP1 releases)
- X.400 Message Transfer Agent (MTA)
- SMTP Virtual Server Instances

Connector Features

- Connector for Novell GroupWise and migration tools
- Connector for Lotus Notes (an Exchange 2007 version is under development)

HA Features

- Active/Active (A/A) clustering

Exchange 5.5-Related Features

- Installing Exchange 5.5. into an Exchange 2007 organization
- Support for Exchange 5.5 in same forest as Exchange 2007
- Installing Exchange 2007 into an organization containing Exchange 5.5 servers (mixed mode)
- Active Directory Connector (ADC)
- Site Replication Service (SRS)

APIs and Development Features

- Transport Event hooks
- Workflow Designer (included in Exchange 2003 SDK)
- CDO for Workflow (on Exchange 2003 media)
- CDOEXM
- Exchange WMI classes
- MAPI Client on Exchange Server

Tools and Management Features

- Monitoring and Status Node
- Message Tracking Center Node and tracking mechanism
- Mailbox Recovery Center
- Mailbox Management Service
- Clean Mailbox tool
- Migration Wizard
- ExProfRe
- Inter-Organization Replication tool (InterORG)

Summary

Exchange Server 2007 is a huge product packed with many completely new features, as well as improvements to existing features from Exchange 2003. This chapter took a brief look at some of the more interesting new features such as the EMC and the EMS, as well as the new HA improvements. This chapter discussed the fact that Exchange 2007 is the first 64-bit version of Exchange ever released, and listed all the features that have been de-emphasized or even discontinued in Exchange Server 2007.

Chapter 2

Installing Exchange Server 2007

Solutions in this chapter:

- Exchange 2007 Server Editions and CAL Types

- Exchange 2007 Prerequisites

- Installing Exchange 2007 Using the Setup Wizard

- Installing Exchange 2007 Using Unattended Setup

- Verifying the Installation of Exchange Server 2007

- Licensing an Exchange 2007 Server

- Finalizing Deployment of Exchange Server 2007

- Adding and Removing Exchange 2007 Server Roles

- Uninstalling Exchange Server 2007

Introduction

In this chapter, we will go through the requirements of Exchange 2007. We'll look at what's required in terms of hardware and software, in addition to the Active Directory forest in which Exchange Server 2007 is to be installed. We'll then see, step by step, how you install Exchange 2007 Server into a clean Active Directory forest (that is, a forest that doesn't contain an Exchange organization or has had the schema extended with the Exchange attributes). We'll also take a brief look at the new Finalizing Deployment and End-to-End Scenario pages. Finally, you'll get an understanding of how you add and remove Exchange 2007 server roles on an existing Exchange 2007 server as well as how to remove an Exchange 2007 server from your organization.

This chapter does not cover transitions, coexistence, and other interoperability with Exchange 2000, 2003, and foreign messaging systems; it simply goes through the procedures of installing Exchange Server 2007 in a clean Active Directory environment. It also does not cover complex Exchange organizations distributed across multiple physical locations involving multiple Active Directory forests. The intention of the chapter is to get you started with the product.

Coexistence and Exchange 2007 transitions are covered in Chapter 10.

Exchange 2007 Server Editions and CAL Types

As is the case with previous versions of Exchange, Exchange Server 2007 exists in two different editions: a Standard Edition and an Enterprise Edition.

Standard Edition

Like previous Standard Editions of Exchange, Exchange 2007 Standard Edition has been designed to meet the messaging and collaboration requirements of small to medium-sized corporations and is aimed at meeting specific messaging server roles, such as branch offices. The Standard Edition has:

- Support for five storage groups
- Support for five databases
- No database storage limit
- Local Continuous Replication (LCR)

NOTE

Now that we are accustomed to referring to the EDB databases as Mailbox and Public Folder ìStoresî, the Exchange Product group thought they should be changed back to Mailbox and Public Folder ìDatabasesî, as they were prior to and including Exchange 5.5.

Enterprise Edition

So what extra benefits will you get out of deploying an Exchange 2007 Enterprise edition in your environment? The Enterprise edition of Exchange Server 2007 has been designed for large enterprise corporations. The Enterprise edition has support for:

- 50 Storage Groups
- 50 databases
- No database storage limit
- Local Continuous Replication (LCR)
- Exchange 2007 Clustering
  - Single Copy Clusters (SCC) using MSCS
  - Cluster Continuous Replication (CCR) using MSCS

Exchange Server 2007 Client Access Licensing

Exchange 2003 and earlier versions offered only one type of Exchange Client Access License (CAL), but with Exchange 2007 we now have two types: a Standard CAL and an Enterprise CAL.

Standard CAL

In addition to the features of Exchange 2003 CAL, the Exchange 2007 Standard CAL provides us with the following:

- Org-wide policy management
- Cross-org mailbox search
- Continuous Replication Technologies
- Mail-flow rules
- Server roles

Enterprise CAL

In addition to the features of Exchange 2007 Standard CAL, the Enterprise CAL provides us with the following:

- Unified messaging

- Per-user journaling

- Exchange Hosted Services Filtering

- Forefront Security for Exchange Server (Microsoft's antivirus product, formerly known as Antigen)

NOTE

Before you get too involved in planning the budget for a transition to Exchange 2007 in your organization, you should be aware of one very important thing. Many of you who have Exchange 2003 deployed in your organizations might very well be aware of the fact that each Exchange 2003 CAL included the right to install Outlook 2003 on the devices for which these CALs were obtained. You probably think this hasn't changed a bit with Exchange 2007 CALs. Think again, because Exchange Server 2007 Standard or Enterprise does not include the right to install Outlook on devices for which CALs are obtained! This means that your organization might have to wait to make the transition to Exchange 2007 until you're ready to deploy Office 2007 as well. To read more about this Exchange 2007 CAL change, visit www.microsoftvolumelicensing.com/userights/ProductPage.aspx?pid=111.

Exchange 2007 Prerequisites

Before you begin installing Exchange Server 2007, you should make sure that the computer on which you are installing the product meets the recommended hardware and software requirements. In addition, you should make sure that the Active Directory domain in which you are installing Exchange Server 2007 is configured with the correct functional level. The minimum Windows Active Directory functional level for Exchange 2007 is Windows 2000 native mode. If you are installing Exchange Server 2007 into an existing Exchange organization, it is also important to note that the organization should be running in native mode; however, since the purpose of this chapter is to show you how to install Exchange Server 2007 into a clean Active Directory forest, you really don't need to worry about this now.

Although the hardware and software requirements are the same, this chapter does not cover how to install an Exchange server into an existing Exchange organization. It also does not go into detail on how you transition from Exchange 5.5, 2000, or 2003 to Exchange 2007. Instead, these topics are covered in Chapter 10.

Hardware Requirements

The hardware requirements for a production Exchange 2007 server are described in the following sections.

Processor

Exchange Server 2007 exists in both 32- and 64-bit versions, but only the 64-bit version is supported in a production environment. This means that the server hardware on which you plan to install Exchange Server 2007 must have one of the following 64-bit processor types installed:

- An x64 architecture-based processor that supports Intel Extended Memory 64 Technology (Intel EM64T)

- An x64 architecture-based computer with AMD 64-bit processor that supports AMD64 platform

Note that the Intel Itanium IA64 processor is not listed, since it is not supported by Exchange Server 2007.

NOTE

If you are planning to use Exchange Server 2007 for either testing or evaluation purposes, you can use the 32-bit evaluation version. This simply requires an Intel Pentium or compatible 800 megahertz (MHz) or faster 32-bit processor. The Exchange 2007 Evaluation version can be downloaded from www.microsoft.com/exchange.

But it's important to understand that the Exchange Server 2007 32-bit evaluation version is meant to be used only in a test environment. It never should be used in a production environment because it is not supported by Microsoft. The only Exchange Server 2007 component you may use in a production environment is the Exchange 2007 Management Tools (more specifically, the Exchange Management Console, the Exchange Management Shell, the Exchange Help file, and the Exchange Best Practices Analyzer tool). These can be installed on a 32-bit machine running either Windows 2003 Server with Service Pack 1 (SP1) or Windows XP Professional with Service Pack 2 (SP2).

Memory

The memory requirements for a 64-bit Exchange 2007 server that is to be deployed in a production environment are 2 gigabytes (GB) of RAM per server. However, bear in mind that those are the minimum requirements. The recommend requirements are:

■   2GB of RAM per server plus approximately 5 megabytes (MB) of RAM per user mailbox located on the respective server

■   A paging file equivalent to the amount of server memory plus 10MB

Also be aware that it's recommended to add additional memory if you're planning to use more than four storage groups (approximately 2GB per three storage groups).

Disk Space

Disk space requirements are as follows:

■   At least 1.2GB of disk space on the drive on which Exchange Server 2007 is to be installed

■   200MB or more of disk space on the system drive

When installing the Unified Messaging role on a server, you will also need to allocate an additional 500MB for each Unified Messaging language pack that is installed.

Drives

A DVD drive isn't a real requirement, because you can install Exchange 2007 from an attached network drive or even a mounted ISO file.

Software Requirements

In addition to the hardware requirements, Exchange Server 2007 has some software requirements that need to be fulfilled before you can begin your install.

Operating System

When planning to install Exchange Server 2007 in a production environment, you will need Microsoft Windows Server 2003 64-bit version with Service Pack 1 or Windows Server 2003 R2 64-bit version.

Both Standard and Enterprise Editions are supported by the 64-bit version of Exchange Server 2007, but bear in mind that the Enterprise Edition is required if you are planning on deploying an Exchange 2007 cluster. (This goes for both Single Copy Clusters and Cluster Continuous Replication setups.)

If you plan on installing the Exchange 2007 32-bit version (for testing or evaluation purposes), you would need to install the 32-bit version of Microsoft Windows Server 2003 SP1 or Windows Server 2003 R2.

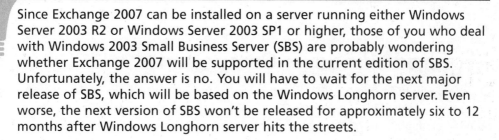

TIP

Since Exchange 2007 can be installed on a server running either Windows Server 2003 R2 or Windows Server 2003 SP1 or higher, those of you who deal with Windows 2003 Small Business Server (SBS) are probably wondering whether Exchange 2007 will be supported in the current edition of SBS. Unfortunately, the answer is no. You will have to wait for the next major release of SBS, which will be based on the Windows Longhorn server. Even worse, the next version of SBS won't be released for approximately six to 12 months after Windows Longhorn server hits the streets.

File Format

All disk partitions must be formatted with the NTFS file system. This means that all disk partitions holding any files or data in the following list should be formatted using NFTS:

- System partition
- Partition storing Exchange Server binaries
- Partitions containing transaction log files
- Partitions containing database files
- Partitions containing other Exchange Server files

Software Required

The following software is required for any of the five different Exchange 2007 server roles. Server roles were previously discussed in detail in Chapter 1.

- Microsoft .NET Framework Version 2.0
- Microsoft Management Console (MMC) 3.0 (bear in mind that MMC 3.0 is installed by default when you use Windows Server 2003 R2)

- Windows PowerShell V1.0

- HotFix for Windows x64 (KB904639)

> **NOTE**
>
> If you haven't installed .NET Framework 2.0, the MMC 3.0 snap-in, or Windows PowerShell when you launch the Exchange Server 2007 installation program, you will be provided with links to each respective piece of software so that you can install each separately.

Required Windows Components

Depending on the Exchange 2007 server roles you plan to install, different Windows components are required before doing so. This section lists each role as well as the required Windows components.

Mailbox Server

The following components are required for the Mailbox server:

- Enable network COM+ access

- Internet Information Services

- World Wide Web Service

Client Access Server

The following components are required for the Client Access server:

- World Wide Web Service

- Remote procedure call (RPC) over Hypertext Transfer Protocol (HTTP) Proxy Windows networking component (required only if you are deploying clients that will use the Outlook Anywhere functionality, previously called RPC over HTTP)

- ASP.NET v2.0

In addition, if you're planning to use OWA 2007 in an organization where you have non-English domain controllers, it's important you install the hotfix mentioned in MS KB article 919166 on all the respective domain controllers; otherwise, you'll experience issues in looking up recipients in the GAL using OWA 2007.

Hub Transport Server

No additional Windows components are required by the Hub Transport server; however, you must make sure that the SMTP and NNTP services are not installed.

Edge Transport Server

The following components are required for the Edge Transport server:

- ADAM
- Like the Hub Transport role, SMTP and NNTP must not be installed

NOTE

ADAM is an included Windows component of Windows Server 2003 R2. However, to install ADAM on a Windows 2003 server with SP1 or higher, you will need to download the ADAM installation package separately. You can download ADAM by clicking Active Directory Application Mode in the Downloads section of the following link: www.microsoft.com/windowsserver2003/adam.

As you might recall, Exchange Server 2000 and 2003 made extended use of the Windows Server 2000 or 2003 SMTP and NNTP protocol stacks, requiring that they be installed components (both subcomponents of IIS) prior to installing the Exchange Server product itself. Both the Hub Transport server and the Edge Transport server require NNTP not be installed, because it is one of the features that are not supported in Exchange Server 2007. Thus, you need to make sure this component isn't installed on the server, because the Exchange Server 2007 Readiness Check will fail if it is. In addition, because Exchange Server 2007 no longer uses the Windows Server SMTP protocol stack but instead uses its own, you also need to make sure that the Windows Server SMTP component isn't installed on the server. As with NNTP, the Exchange Server 2007 Readiness Check will fail if the SMTP component is found on the server.

NOTE

The SMTP engine included in Exchange Server 2007 has been written from the ground up using managed code within the Exchange Product group itself and not the Windows Server group. The Windows Server Group was responsible for the SMTP component of IIS in previous versions of Exchange.

Unified Messaging Server

The following components are required for the Unified Messaging server:

■ Microsoft Speech service (if Exchange 2007 setup doesn't find this component, it will install it automatically)

■ Microsoft Windows Media Encoder (the x64 edition can be downloaded from http://go.microsoft.com/fwlink/?LinkId=67406)

■ Microsoft Windows Media Audio Voice Codec (can be downloaded from http://support.microsoft.com/kb/917312)

■ Microsoft Core XML Services (MSXML) 6.0 (can be downloaded from http://go.microsoft.com/fwlink/?linkid=70796)

Server Requirements

As is the case with Exchange Server 2000 and 2003, Exchange Server 2007 relies on and is heavily integrated with Active Directory. So, before you install Exchange Server 2007 on a server, it is mandatory that the server be part of an Active Directory forest. The only exception to this rule is the Edge Transport Server role, which should instead be installed in a workgroup in your perimeter network. The server on which you plan to install Exchange 2007 should also be configured with a static IP address; in addition, you should verify that the DNS server settings are configured to point at the respective DNS servers in the Active Directory forest (see Figure 2.1).

Figure 2.1 Configuring TCP/IP Settings

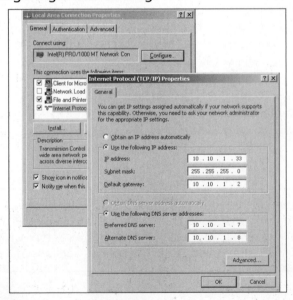

Active Directory Requirements

First, you want to make sure any domain controllers and global catalog servers in the Active Directory domain in which you're planning to install the Exchange 2007 server are running Windows Server 2003 SP1 or Windows Server 2003 R2. In addition, you need to set the Active Directory Domain functional level to at least Windows 2000 Native or Windows Server 2003 because these modes are required by the new Exchange 2007 Server Universal Groups.

To change the Active Directory functional level, you need to perform the following steps:

1. Log on to a Domain Controller in the respective Active Directory Domain.

2. Click Start | All Programs | Administrative Tools and then click Active Directory Users and Computers.

3. When the Microsoft Management Console (MMC) snap-in has launched, right-click the Active Directory domain in the left pane, then click Raise Domain Functional Level in the context menu, as shown in Figure 2.2.

Figure 2.2 Raising the Domain Functional Level

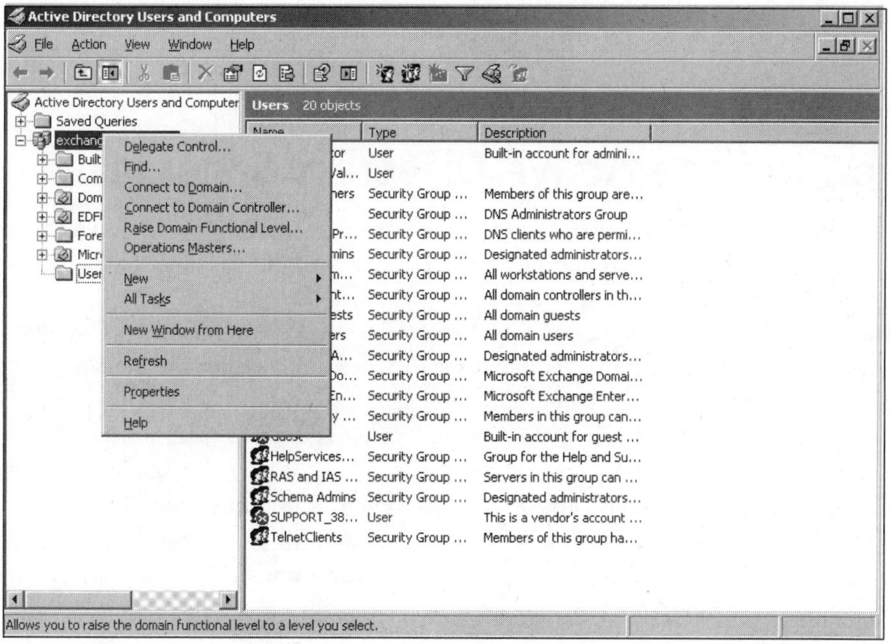

4. Now select Windows 2000 native or Windows Server 2003 in the domain functional level drop-down menu and click Raise (Figure 2.3).

Figure 2.3 Available Domain Functional Levels

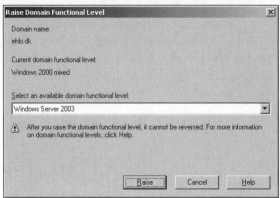

TIP

If you are planning to install Exchange Server 2007 into an Active Directory domain where an Exchange 2000 or 2003 organization already exists, you also need to make sure that the Exchange organization is running in native mode. This and more about installing Exchange Server 2007 into an existing Exchange organization can be found in Chapter 10.

Preparing the Active Directory Schema

Now that we have been through the hardware and software required by Exchange Server 2007, let's take a look at what we need to prepare before we can install an Exchange 2007 server into a clean Active Directory domain.

The first step is to prepare your Active Directory schema with new Exchange 2007 attributes by extending it using the Setup /PrepareSchema command-line switch. Exchange Server 2007 adds many new attributes and classes to the Active Directory schema (even more than Exchange Server 2003 did!) and makes additional modifications to the existing classes and attributes.

To be able to run the Setup /PrepareSchema switch, you must be logged on with an account that is a member of both the Schema Admins and the Enterprise Admins Active Directory groups. In addition, you must run this command from a machine that belongs to the respective Active Directory domain and is located in the same Active Directory site as the server holding the Schema Master role. The Setup /PrepareSchema command will connect to the server holding the Schema Master role and import the required LDAP Data Interchange Format (LDIF) files containing all the new Exchange 2007 specific classes and attributes.

NOTE

It is recommended that you run the Setup /PrepareSchema command-line switch on your Domain Schema Master server itself.

To prepare the schema, perform the following steps:

1. Log on to the server from where you want to run the command, with an account that is a member of both the **Schema Admins** and **Enterprise Admins** groups.

2. Now click **Start | Run** and type **cmd.exe**, followed by pressing **Enter** or clicking **OK**.

3. In the Command Prompt window, navigate to the folder in which the Exchange 2007 server setup files are located (for example, CD C:**Exchange Server 2007 RTM [64-bit]**).

4. Type **Setup /PrepareSchema** and press **Enter** (see Figure 2.4).

Figure 2.4 Running Setup with the PrepareSchema Switch

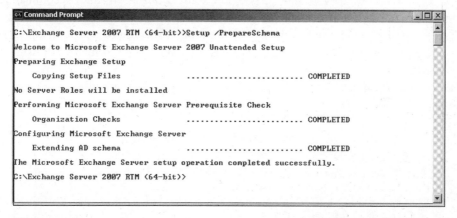

Since Setup /PrepareSchema needs to be run in the site holding the Schema Master, some of you might question what to do if you need to prepare the Active Directory schema in a site that doesn't have any 64-bit servers installed yet. You really don't have to worry about this, since you can just run this command using the 32-bit version of Exchange Server 2007. ¡What? Are you telling me to run Setup /PrepareSchema using the unsupported 32-bit version in a production environment?¡ we hear some of you grumble. To answer that question, yes. As a matter of fact, the 32-bit version of Exchange is supported in a production environment in terms of Exchange 2007 administration, which includes extending the AD.

NOTE

You do not necessarily need to run the *Setup /PrepareSchema* command prior to running the *Setup /PrepareAD* command, which is covered next. When *Setup /PrepareSchema* hasn't been run prior to running the *Setup /PrepareAD*, the Setup /PrepareSchema command will be run as part of the *Setup /PrepareAD* command. So, why would you want to run the *Setup /PrepareSchem* command before *Setup /PrepareAD*? Well, in most scenarios you would jump right to the *Setup /PrepareAD*, the exception being those environments using a split permission model, where different individuals might administer the Exchange Organization over the Active Directory forest.

Preparing the Active Directory

The next command you need to run is the Setup /PrepareAD command, which will prepare the current domain, configure global Exchange objects in Active Directory, and create the Exchange Universal Security Groups (USGs) in the root domain. To run this command you need to use an account that is a member of the Enterprise Admins group. (If you install Exchange 2007 into an existing Exchange organization, it also needs to be a member of the Exchange Admins group.) Next, go through the same steps you performed when you extended the schema, but replace Setup /PrepareSchema with Setup /PrepareAD /ON:<organizational name> (see Figure 2.5, where we use EHLO as the organization name).

Figure 2.5 Running Setup with the PrepareAD Switch

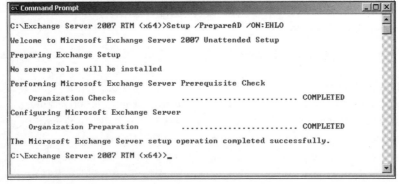

TIP

If you are running the *Setup /PrepareSchema* and */PrepareAD* commands in an organization with a large Active Directory topology, the replication time

could take quite a while. If you want to keep an eye on the replication process, you might want to use the Active Directory Replication Monitor tool
(replmon.exe), which is part of the Microsoft Windows Server 2003 Support
Tools Setup package. You can install the Support Tools directly off the
Windows Server 2003 CD media by navigating to the **Support | Tools** folder
and simply double-clicking the **SUPTOOLS.MSI** file. In the Windows Server
Support Tools Setup Wizard, click **Next**, accept the EULA, and click **Next** two
more times. Click **Install Now** and finally click **Finish**. When the Support Tools
have been installed, you can launch Replmon by clicking **Start | Run**, typing
ReplMon.exe, and clicking OK.

To verify that *Setup /PrepareAD* ran successfully, you can open the Active Directory
Users and Computers snap-in and confirm that a new Organizational Unit (OU) called
Microsoft Exchange Security Groups now exists and that the following Exchange Universal
Security Groups (USGs) exist beneath it:

- Exchange Organization Administrators

- Exchange Recipient Administrators

- Exchange View–Only Administrators

- Exchange Servers

- Exchange2003Interop

Preparing Any Additional
Active Directory Domains in a Forest

If you're dealing with an Active Directory forest consisting of multiple Active Directory
domains that contain either legacy Exchange server or mail-enabled users, you would also
need to prepare those domains for Exchange 2007. You can do this by running any of the
following commands (see Figure 2.6):

- Setup /PrepareDomain from the domain in question

- Setup /PrepareDomain:<FQDN of the additional domain you want to prepare>
  from any domain using the correct credentials

- Setup /PrepareAllDomains to prepare any and all domains in which you haven't
  run Setup /PrepareSchema or Setup /PrepareAD

Figure 2.6 Running Setup with the PrepareDomain Switch

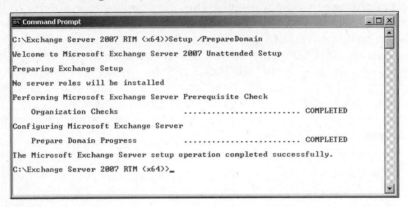

Installing Exchange 2007 Using the Setup Wizard

Because of the heavily improved and role-based setup wizard, installing Exchange 2007 is much easier than installing previous versions of Exchange. Because the Exchange 2007 Setup Wizard is role based, you can either select to install a typical Exchange Server installation, which will install the Hub Transport, Client Access, and Mailbox Server roles on the same server (which is what you typically want to do in an Exchange organization that will consist of one Exchange 2007 Server only), or you can do a custom Exchange Server installation, which lets you choose the server roles that should be installed on the respective servers. You would typically choose to do a custom Exchange Server installation in a large Exchange organization where you want to separate the various Exchange 2007 Server roles among different servers. Those of you who are dealing with large Exchange organizations probably have dedicated Exchange front-end servers, bridgehead servers, and back-end servers (Mailbox and/or Public Folder Servers) in place already. Because the Exchange 2007 Setup Wizard is role based, you have the option of selecting the server roles to be deployed on each server, and you can thereby design an Exchange topology matching your needs.

NOTE

Another benefit of a role-based approach is that Exchange 2007 Setup only installs the Exchange files and services necessary for the server role you deploy. This means that the respective servers won't waste disk space and resources on unnecessary files and services, as previous versions of Exchange did.

When all the mentioned hardware, software, and Active Directory requirements have been met, you can finally install Exchange Server 2007. You can do so using the GUI-based Exchange 2007 Setup Wizard or using unattended Setup (which gives you the option of creating command-line scripts for unattended installations using batch files). First, let's go through how installation is accomplished using the Exchange 2007 Setup Wizard.

After inserting the Exchange Server 2007 media in the DVD drive on the server or mapping to a share where the Exchange Server 2007 binary files are held, you can launch the installation by double-clicking the Setup.exe file (see Figure 2.7).

TIP

As most of you know, although it's generally avoided, you could install Exchange 2000 and 2003 on a server that also acted as domain controller. You might ask if Microsoft included support for this in Exchange Server 2007, since it was so widely discouraged in previous releases. It is supported to install Exchange 2007 on a domain controller, but Microsoft strongly recommends against it for security, performance, and availability reasons. The only situation where it would be okay to have Exchange 2007 installed on a server acting as a domain controller would be one in which you were dealing with a Small Business Server (SBS).

Figure 2.7 Running Exchange 2007 Setup

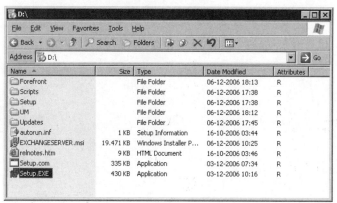

The Exchange 2007 Bootstrapper (a.k.a. the splash screen) will now appear and show you whether the required software has been properly installed on the server. As mentioned earlier in this chapter, you need to install .NET Framework 2.0, Microsoft Management Console (MMC) 3.0, and Windows PowerShell 1.0 before you can install Exchange Server 2007. If all three components have been properly installed, each link will be grayed out, allowing you to continue the installation process with step 4, installing Microsoft Exchange. If this is not the case, as in Figure 2.8, which shows we're missing the PowerShell component, you must click the link for each missing component in each step to download and install the needed Exchange 2007 prerequisites. (Since we used Windows Server 2003 R2 in our test environment, MMC 3.0 was already installed).

Figure 2.8 Exchange 2007 Setup Splash Screen

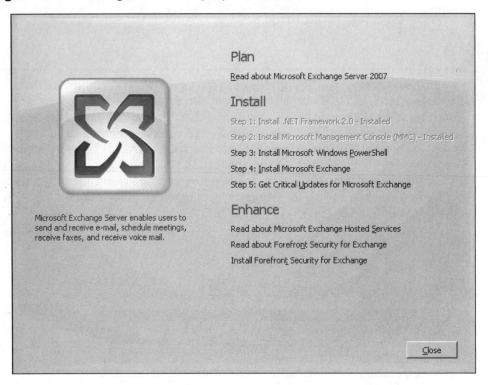

Setup will copy the necessary files and soon after begin initializing. After initialization completes, you will be taken to the first step in the Installation Wizard, the Introduction page. Click Next (see Figure 2.9).

Figure 2.9 Exchange Server 2007 Setup Wizard Introductory Page

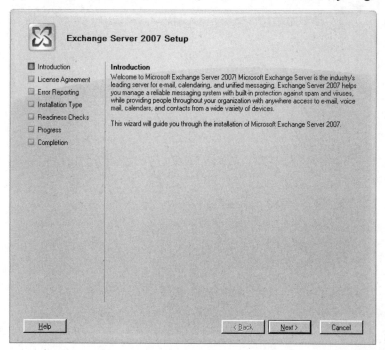

Next you will be presented with and need to accept the terms of the end-user license agreement (EULA). We know that reading the license agreement is not among the most exciting things in the world, but you should at least spend a couple of minutes skimming through it. When you have done so, select I accept the terms in the license agreement, and then click **Next**.

You now have the option of enabling error reporting, and we highly recommend you do so to help improve the quality, reliability, and performance of the Exchange Server 2007 product. Microsoft is very serious about every single error report it collects, and since all of us are interested in seeing the best messaging and collaboration product getting better and better, why not enable error reporting?

NOTE

Microsoft does not collect any personal information such as e-mail address, so you have nothing to worry about in terms of your privacy.

When you have enabled (or for some reason disabled) error reporting, you can click Next (see Figure 2.10).

Figure 2.10 The Error Reporting Page

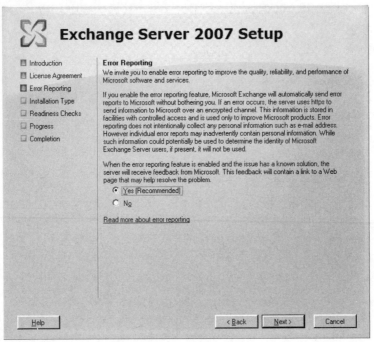

We have now reached the step where we need to choose the kind of Exchange roles we want to install and run. For the purpose of this chapter, we will do a Typical Exchange Server Installation, which installs the Hub Transport, Client Access, and Mailbox server roles. The Exchange Management Tools (Exchange Management Console and Shell) will, of course, also be installed when we choose this installation type.

Click **Typical Exchange Server Installation** and then **Next**, as shown in Figure 2.11.

NOTE

You have the option of specifying the path to which the Exchange Server files should be installed. The default path is C:\Program Files\Microsoft\Exchange Server, but best practice is to install the Exchange Server files on a dedicated partition instead of on the System partition.

Figure 2.11 Selecting Typical Exchange Server Installation

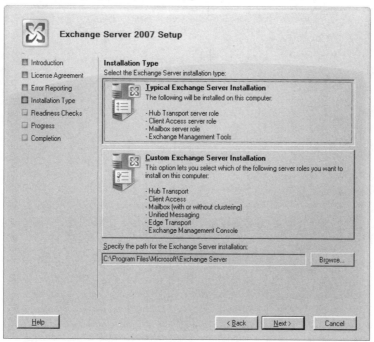

If you plan to deploy either a single Exchange 2007 server role or one including the Unified Messaging server or Edge Transport server roles, you should choose the Custom Exchange Server Installation type, which allows you to choose the specific roles you require in your environment. In addition, if you want to deploy a clustered mailbox server or perhaps only install one or two server roles on a given server, you also need to choose the custom installation type. When choosing a Custom Exchange Server Installation type, you'll see a screen similar to the one shown in Figure 2.12.

NOTE

Although this chapter focuses on just the Typical Exchange Server Installation type, fear not—we will also go through to the deployment steps for both an Edge Transport server role as well as a clustered mailbox server (both Clustered Continuous Replication and Single Copy Cluster setups) in Chapters 7 and 8.

Figure 2.12 Selecting Custom Exchange Server Installation

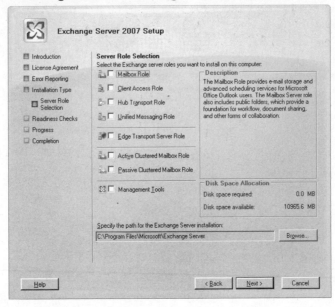

Since we are installing this server into a new Exchange organization, we will now be asked to enter the name of the new Exchange organization (see Figure 2.13).

Figure 2.13 Specifying the Name for the New Exchange 2007 Organization

When clicking **Next**, we'll be taken to the **Client Settings** page, where we need to specify whether there are any legacy clients (that is, Outlook 2003 and earlier) still in use in our organization. If this is the case, we need to select **Yes**, creating and mounting a Public Folder database on the server, because legacy Outlook clients use Public folders to retrieve free/busy calendar information. If you only have Outlook 2007 clients in the organization, you can safely select No, removing the need to create a Public Folder database on your Exchange 2007 server. The reason behind this is the ability for the Outlook 2007 client to use the new Exchange 2007 Web-based availability service (discussed more in Chapter 5) to retrieve free/busy information for other users.

NOTE

If you select **No** and Outlook 2003 and at a later time deploy Outlook 2003 and earlier clients into your environment, you can always go back and manually create a Public Folder database to house the Free/Busy calendaring information of these legacy clients.

Click **Yes** or **No**, depending on your scenario, then click **Next** (see Figure 2.14).

Figure 2.14 Specifying Whether Outlook 2003 or Earlier Is Used in the Organization

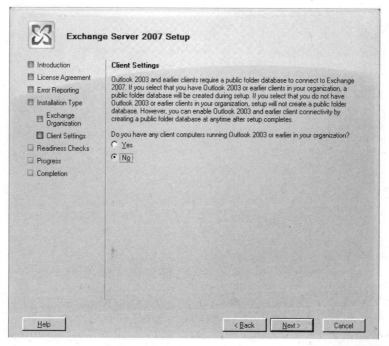

Next, the Exchange 2007 Installation Wizard will perform a readiness check to see whether the server itself, as well as the Active Directory forest, fulfils the prerequisites for the selected server roles.

NOTE

When the Exchange Server 2007 Setup Wizard checks whether Exchange is ready to be installed on the particular server, it uses the engine from the Exchange Best Practices Analyzer (ExBPA) tool to perform the necessary checks. Actually, the first thing that the Setup wizard will do is to download the latest version of the prereq.xml file from Microsoft.com (similar to when ExBPA download updates) so that the most up-to-date prerequisites information is always used.

If the prerequisite check for each server role completes without any errors or important warnings, we can click **Install** (see Figure 2.15), preparing the organization (if that is not already done), copying the necessary Exchange files, and installing each Exchange 2007 server role.

Figure 2.15 Exchange 2007 Readiness Check

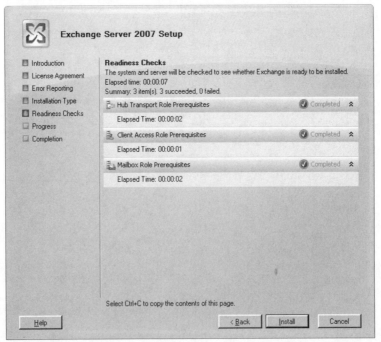

If you install the 32-bit version of Exchange or if a component required by Exchange Server 2007 hasn't been installed on the server, the particular server role check will give you a warning or fail, as shown in Figure 2.16. The cool thing about the checks is that we are given information about what causes the check to fail, and in most cases we're given a Recommend Action link that provides much more detail about what is actually causing the check to fail.

Figure 2.16 Readiness Check Failed

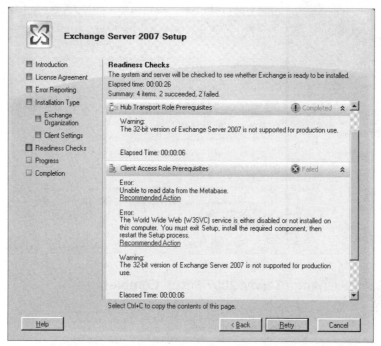

Clicking the link brings us to the Microsoft Exchange Server Analyzer Articles on the Microsoft TechNet Web site (see Figure 2.17). Depending on which components need to be installed before the Readiness Checks can complete successfully, it determines whether you can simply click the Retry button after the component has been installed. In most cases this will work, but with some components, such as the World Wide Web Service (W3SVC), it is required that you exit the Setup Wizard and run it again from the beginning.

When the installation process has completed, we can click Finish to exit the Exchange 2007 Installation Wizard. Note that you can launch the Exchange Management Console automatically after clicking Finish, so you can immediately begin finalizing your installation (see Figure 2.18).

Figure 2.17 Microsoft Exchange Server Analyzer Articles

Figure 2.18 Exchange Server 2007 Setup Completed

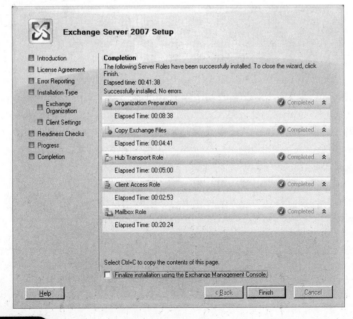

Installing Exchange 2007 Using Unattended Setup

Now that we have been through a typical installation of Exchange Server 2007 using the Setup Wizard, let's take a look at how you do a typical installation of Exchange Server 2007 using an unattended setup. This is done via the command prompt, and as in the case when doing a GUI installation, you need to insert the Exchange Server 2007 media in the DVD drive on the server, or map to a share containing the necessary Exchange Server 2007 binaries. Navigate to the DVD or mapped drive by typing **CD <letter of DVD drive>**:. You can install Exchange Server 2007 in unattended mode using Setup. Setup supports many different parameters and switches, so to whet your appetite, we recommend you type Setup /? to list all available parameters and switches, providing a short description of each. Because we are going to do a basic installation into an Active Directory forest that does not contain any existing Exchange organization, we need to use the following command:

```
Setup /mode:Install /roles:HT,CA,MB,MT /on:EHLO
```

First the command tells Setup that we want to install one or more server roles with the /mode:Install parameter. We then specify the roles we want to install using the /roles:<roles> parameter. Finally, we specify the name of the new Exchange organization with the /on:<Exchange organization> parameter (see Figure 2.19).

Figure 2.19 Running Setup in Unattended Mode

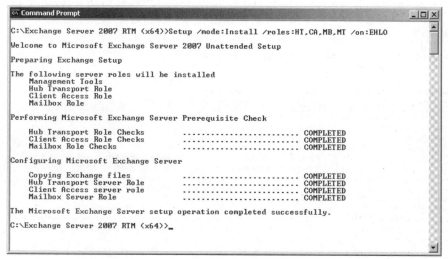

NOTE

If you have any legacy Outlook clients (Outlook 2003 and earlier versions) in your environment, you should also add /EnableLegacyOutlook to the command. /EnableLegacyOutlook makes sure that a Public Folder database is created on the Exchange 2007 server, which is necessary for the sharing of Free/Busy calendar information using the legacy Outlook client.

As with the Setup Wizard, Exchange 2007 unattended setup will do a set of prerequisite checks. If these are successful, setup will continue, copying the necessary Exchange files and finally installing the specified Exchange 2007 server roles.

Verifying the Installation of Exchange Server 2007

After Exchange Server 2007 has been installed, we recommend that you verify that the installation completed without any serious warnings or errors. If you didn't encounter any errors during installation, there's a good chance everything is in perfect shape, but you won't know for sure until you have checked the Windows event logs and the Exchange 2007 setup logs as well as doing a visual verification that each selected role has been installed. Start by examining both the application logs and the system logs for any warnings or errors related to the Exchange Server 2007 setup. If any are found, you can trace the problem using the information provided in the event URL, TechNet, or the troubleshooting section of the Exchange documentation. If everything looks good, move on and verify that no errors have been logged in the ExchangeSetup.log and ExchangeSetup.msilog, both located in the ExchangeSetupLogs folder located in the root of the system drive (typically C:).

In addition, you should check that all the respective Exchange 2007 services have been configured to start automatically and are indeed started (see Figure 2.20).

Figure 2.20 A List of Exchange 2007 Services

Name	Description	Status
Microsoft Exchange Active Directory Topology	Provides AD topology information to Exchange services. If this service is stopped, most Exchange services ar...	Started
Microsoft Exchange EdgeSync	The Exchange EdgeSync Service.	Started
Microsoft Exchange File Distribution	Microsoft Exchange File Distribution Service.	Started
Microsoft Exchange Hygiene Update	The Exchange Hygiene Update Service.	Started
Microsoft Exchange IMAP4	Provides Internet Message Access Protocol (IMAP4) Services to clients. If this service is stopped, clients are u...	
Microsoft Exchange Information Store	Manages the Microsoft Exchange Information Store. This includes mailbox stores and public folder stores. If t...	Started
Microsoft Exchange Mail Submission Service	Submits messages from the Mailbox server to the Hub Transport servers.	Started
Microsoft Exchange Mailbox Assistants	Performs background processing of mailboxes in the Exchange store.	Started
Microsoft Exchange Monitoring	Allows applications to call the Exchange diagnostic cmdlets.	
Microsoft Exchange POP3	Provides Post Office Protocol version 3 (POP3) Services to clients. If this service is stopped, clients are unable...	
Microsoft Exchange Replication Service	The Exchange Replication Service provides replication functionality used by Local Continuous Replication and ...	Started
Microsoft Exchange Search Indexer	Drives indexing of mailbox content, which improves the performance of content search.	Started
Microsoft Exchange Service Host	Provides a host for several Microsoft Exchange services	Started
Microsoft Exchange System Attendant	Provides monitoring, maintenance, and Active Directory lookup services, for example, monitoring of services ...	Started
Microsoft Exchange Transport	The Microsoft Exchange Transport Edge Service.	Started
Microsoft Exchange Transport Log Search	Provides remote search capability for Microsoft Exchange Transport log files.	Started

If a service that has been configured to start automatically is in a stopped state, try to start it. If you're unsuccessful, check the related error in the application log.

Tip

If the installation of Exchange 2007 completes the installation of one or more server roles but then fails at another one, you don't need to reinstall the server roles that were already installed. Instead, the Exchange 2007 Setup Wizard will start in maintenance mode the next time you launch it, and from there you can simply tick the server roles that failed the first time.

When the installation has been completed, it's a good idea to run the Exchange Best Practices Analyzer tool, now integrated into the Exchange Management Console (EMC) and found under the Toolbox node, as shown in Figure 2.21.

Figure 2.21 Opening the Best Practices Analyzer

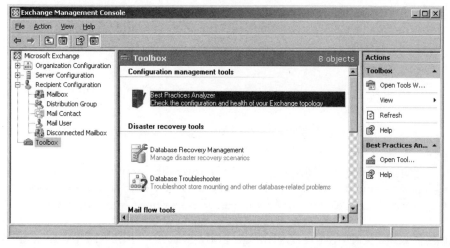

Licensing an Exchange 2007 Server

Unlike Exchange Server 2000 and 2003, you have to license Exchange Server 2007. By default, Exchange Server 2007 has a built-in time bomb (120 days). The first time you launch the Exchange Management Console you will be presented with a dialog box similar to the one shown in Figure 2.22.

If you have a Standard or Enterprise product key ready, now is a good time to license your Exchange 2007 server.

Figure 2.22 The License Warning

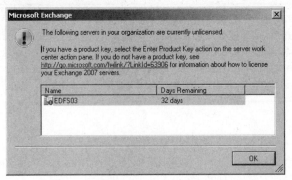

> **NOTE**
>
> You will not be able to license a 32-bit version of Exchange Server 2007 because this version is meant for testing and evaluation purposes.

To license an Exchange Server 2007 server, you will need to perform the following steps:

1. Open the Exchange Management Console, and then select the Server Configuration work center node.

2. You will be presented with a list of Exchange 2007 servers in your Exchange organization in the work pane. Select the server you want to license and click Enter Product Key in the Actions pane on the right (see Figure 2.23).

Figure 2.23 Selecting the Exchange 2007 Servers That Are to Be Licensed

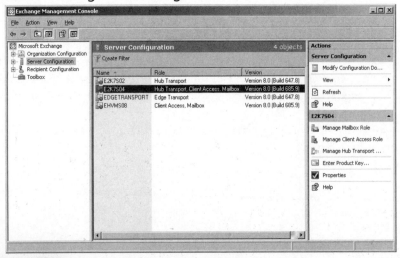

3. In the Enter Product Key Wizard, enter your product key license and click Enter (see Figure 2.24).

Figure 2.24 Entering the Product Key

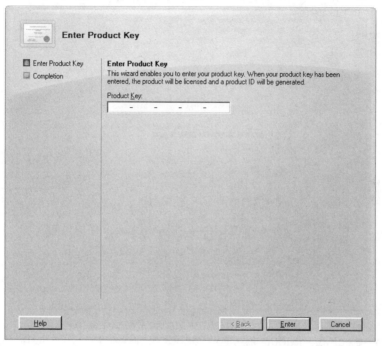

4. On the Completion page, click Finish (see Figure 2.25).

NOTE

If you're licensing an Exchange 2007 server with an Enterprise product key, and the server has the edition Mailbox server role installed, you need to restart the Microsoft Exchange Information Store service for the change to be reflected in the EMC.

To verify that an Exchange 2007 Server has been properly licensed, you can open the Properties page for the respective server. If the server is licensed, you'll see a Product ID number under the General tab, as shown in Figure 2.26. If it isn't licensed, it will show Unlicensed instead of a product ID number.

Figure 2.25 Exchange 2007 Server Successfully Licensed

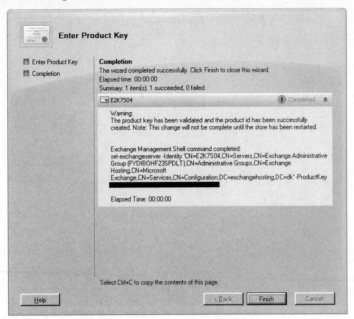

NOTE

Bear in mind that when you have licensed an Exchange 2007 server with an Enterprise edition product key, you cannot downgrade it to a Standard edition.

Figure 2.26 The Properties Page for a Licensed Exchange 2007 Server

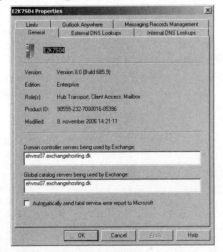

NOTE

You can also license an Exchange 2007 server using the Exchange Management Shell. To do so, run the following command: *Set-ExchangeServer –Identity* Servername *–ProductKey* <product key that consists of 25 digits>.

Finalizing Deployment of Exchange Server 2007

When you launch the Exchange Management Console for the first time, the Microsoft Exchange node will be selected. Under this node you'll find two new tabs: Finalize Deployment and End-to-End Scenario. The Finalize Deployment tab provides a list of recommended tasks you should perform (depending on the server roles installed on the server) to finalize the deployment of your Exchange 2007 server (see Figure 2.27).

Figure 2.27 The Finalize Deployment Tab

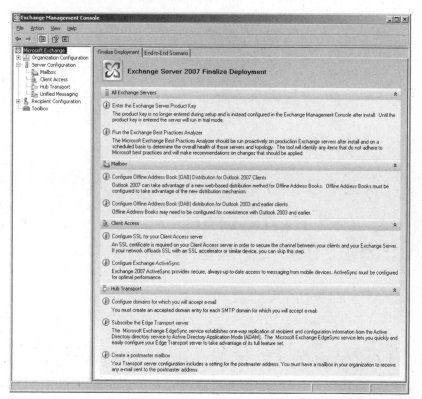

The tasks listed under this tab are applied to features that are enabled by default and need additional configuration. We highly recommend that you follow each task carefully so as not to overlook anything. However, don't rely 100 percent on this list; these are just Microsoft's attempt to show you the most basic configuration settings. Your environment could require additional configuration forethought and planning.

The End-to-End Scenario tab (see Figure 2.28) provides a list of tasks that are optional, but it's a good idea to review and complete them anyway.

Figure 2.28 The End-to-End Tab

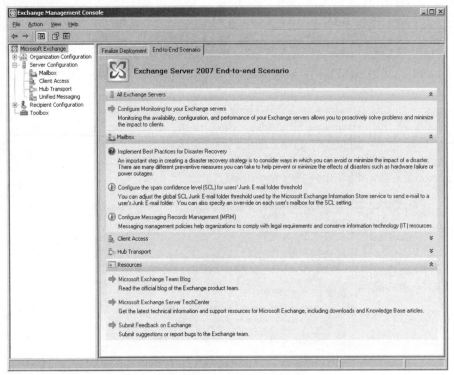

Adding and Removing Exchange 2007 Server Roles

After you have installed one or more Exchange 2007 server roles on a server, you have the option of adding roles later as required. This can be done using the GUI or command-line interface (CLI). Adding a server role using the GUI is done by following these steps:

1. Log on to the respective server with an account that has Exchange Organization Administrator rights.

2. Open the Control Panel.

3. Click Add or Remove Programs.

4. Select Microsoft Exchange Server 2007.

5. Click the Change button (see Figure 2.29).

Figure 2.29 Adding a Role to an Exchange 2007 Server

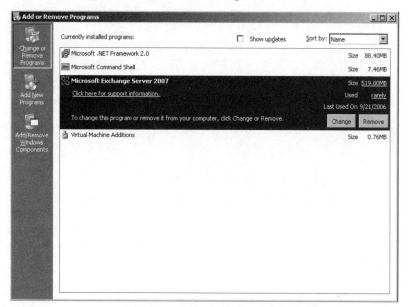

6. In the Exchange Server 2007 Setup Wizard, click Next (see Figure 2.30).

7. Now tick the roles you want to install on the server, and then click **Next** (see Figure 3.31).

8. When the Exchange Server 2007 Setup Wizard has installed the respective roles, click Finish.

To add one or more roles via the CLI, you need to use ExSetup.exe and not Setup.exe, as you might have thought. ExSetup.exe can be found in the C:\Program Files\Microsoft\Exchange Server\Bin folder. To add a role, perform the following steps:

Figure 2.30 Exchange Server 2007 Setup in Maintenance Mode

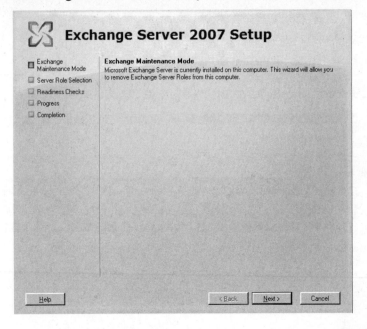

Figure 2.31 Selecting the Server Role to Be Added to the Exchange 2007 Server

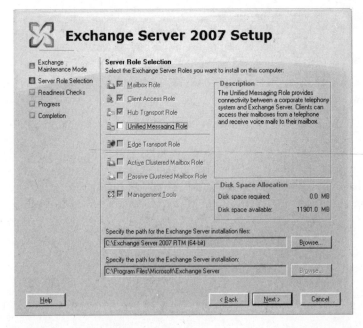

1. Log on to the respective server using an account that has Exchange Organization Administrator rights.

2. Click Start | Run, type CMD.exe and click OK.

3. Now change to the Exchange Bin folder by typing CD C:\Program Files\Microsoft\Exchange Server\Bin and press Enter.

4. Type ExSetup.exe /mode:Install /roles:<roles to be installed> as shown in Figure 2.32 (where we add the Hub Transport server role to an existing Exchange 2007 server) and press Enter.

Figure 2.32 Adding a Server Role Using Unattended Setup

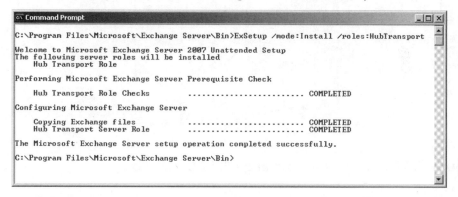

The process of removing a role from an Exchange 2007 server is very similar to that of adding a server role. To remove one or more roles from an existing Exchange 2007 server, do the following.

1. Log on to the respective server with an account that has Exchange Organization Administrator rights.

2. Open the Control Panel.

3. Click Add or Remove Programs.

4. Select Microsoft Exchange Server 2007.

5. Click the Remove button.

6. In the Exchange Server 2007 Setup Wizard, click Next (see Figure 2.33).

7. Clear the check boxes for the roles you want to remove and click **Next** (see Figure 2.34).

Figure 2.33 Exchange Server 2007 in Maintenance Mode

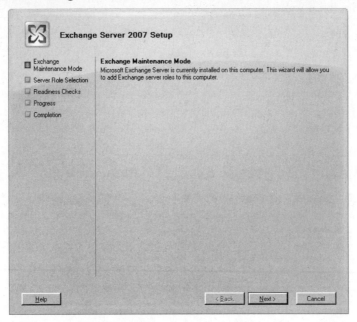

Figure 2.34 Removing an Exchange 2007 Server Role

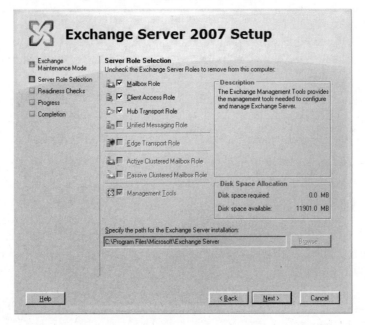

8. Let the readiness check complete, then click Uninstall. When the Exchange Server 2007 Setup Wizard has uninstalled the respective server roles, click Finish.

To remove one or more roles using the CLI, you must again use ExSetup.exe by performing the following steps:

1. Log on to the respective server using an account that has Exchange Organization Administrator rights.

2. Click Start | Run, type CMD.exe and click OK.

3. Now change to the Exchange Bin folder by typing CD C:\Program Files\Microsoft\Exchange Server\Bin and press Enter.

4. Type ExSetup.exe /mode:Uninstall /roles:<roles to be installed>, as shown in Figure 2.35.

Figure 2.35 Removing an Exchange 2007 Server Role Using Unattended Setup

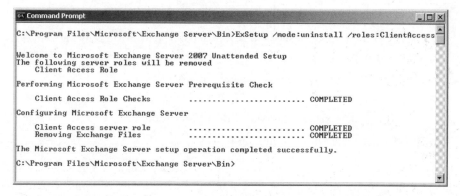

Uninstalling Exchange Server 2007

There might be situations in which you want to completely remove an Exchange 2007 server from your Exchange organization. This can be done using either the Exchange 2007 Installation Wizard or Setup.com.

Uninstalling Exchange 2007 using the Installation Wizard is done the following way:

1. Log on to the respective server with an account that belongs to the Enterprise Admins group.

2. Open the Control Panel.

3. Click Add or Remove Programs.

4. Select Microsoft Exchange Server 2007.

5. Click the Remove button.

6. Now clear the check box for each server role, including Management Tools, and click Next.

7. When the Readiness check has completed, click Uninstall.

NOTE

To remove the Mailbox server role, you'll need to make sure no mailboxes exist in the Mailbox database(s) on the respective server. In addition, if you have any Public Folder databases on the server, you'll need to move any existing offline address books to a Public Folder database on another server. Also, keep in mind that you will need to manually delete any EDB and transaction log files after you have uninstalled Exchange, because this is not done via the Exchange Server 2007 Setup Wizard.

Uninstalling Exchange Server 2007 using the CLI can be done the following way:

1. Log on to the respective server using an account that belongs to the Enterprise Admins group.

2. Click Start | Run, type CMD.exe and click OK.

3. Now change to the Exchange Bin folder by typing CD C:\Program Files\Microsoft\Exchange Server\Bin and press Enter.

4. Type ExSetup.exe /mode:Uninstall.

Removing all server roles from an Exchange 2007 server will also remove any installation files as well as the Exchange server object and all its child objects from the Active Directory forest.

Summary

In this chapter we focused on the hardware, software, and system requirements for an Exchange Server 2007 installation. We went through how you prepare a greenfield Active Directory forest (that is, an Active Directory forest without an existing Exchange organization) for an Exchange 2007 Server deployment. We also took a step-by-step walk through the process of installing a typical Exchange 2007 server into an Active Directory forest using both the GUI and the CLI. We touched on how to properly license an Exchange 2007 server and introduced the new Finalize Deployment and End-to-End Scenario task lists. Finally, we took a look at how you can add and remove Exchange 2007 server roles from an existing Exchange 2007 server with multiple server roles already installed, as well as how to completely uninstall Exchange 2007 from a server and ultimately from the Active Directory forest.

Solutions Fast Track

Exchange 2007 Server Editions and CAL Types

☑ As is the case with previous versions of Exchange, Exchange Server 2007 exists in two different editions: a Standard Edition and an Enterprise Edition.

☑ Exchange 2003 and earlier versions offered only one type of Exchange CAL, but with Exchange 2007 we now have two types: a Standard CAL and an Enterprise CAL.

☑ Before you get too involved in planning the budget for a transition to Exchange 2007 in your organization, you should be aware of one very important thing. Many of you who have Exchange 2003 deployed in your organization could very well be aware of the fact that each Exchange 2003 Client Access License (CAL) included the right to install Outlook 2003 on the devices for which these CALs were obtained. You probably think that this hasn't changed in regard to Exchange 2007 CALs. Think again because Exchange Server 2007 Standard or Enterprise does not include the right to install Outlook on devices for which CALs are obtained!

Exchange 2007 Prerequisites

☑ It's important that you examine the system hardware, software, and Active Directory requirements before you begin installing Exchange 2007 into a production environment.

☑ You'll need an x64 architecture-based processor that supports Intel Extended Memory 64 Technology (Intel EM64T) and an AMD 64-bit processor that supports the AMD64 platform, but bear in mind that the Intel Itanium IA64 processor isn't supported by Exchange Server 2007.

☑ The minimum Windows Active Directory functional level for Exchange 2007 is Windows 2000 native mode. If you are installing Exchange Server 2007 into an existing Exchange organization, it is also important to note that the organization should be running in native mode.

☑ Exchange Server 2007 exists in 32-bit and 64-bit versions; however, the 32-bit version is not supported in a production environment and is meant to be used for evaluation and testing purposes only. If you install the 32-bit version of Exchange 2007 in a production environment and experience an issue, you will not be able to get any support from Microsoft Support Services. There is one exception to the rule, though: The 32-bit version of the Exchange 2007 Management Tools (more specifically, the Exchange Management Console, the Exchange Management Shell, the Exchange Help file, and the Exchange Best Practices Analyzer tool) are supported for management tasks in a production environment.

☑ As most of you might recall, Exchange Server 2000 and 2003 made extended use of the Windows Server 2000 or 2003 SMTP and NNTP services, requiring that they be installed components (both subcomponents of IIS) prior to installing the Exchange Server product itself. Both the Hub Transport server and the Edge Transport server requires that both these services aren't installed, because NNTP support has been dropped in Exchange 2007 and Exchange 2007 now has its own SMTP service.

Installing Exchange 2007 Using the Setup Wizard

☑ Because of the heavily improved and role-based Setup Wizard, installing Exchange 2007 is much easier than was the case with previous versions of Exchange. Because the Exchange 2007 Setup Wizard is role based, you can either select to install a typical Exchange Server installation, which will install the Hub Transport, Client Access, and Mailbox Server roles on the same server (which is what you typically want to do in an Exchange organization that will consist of one Exchange 2007 Server only), or you can do a custom Exchange Server installation, which lets you choose the server roles that should be installed on the respective server. You would typically choose to do a custom Exchange Server installation in a large Exchange organization where you want to separate the various Exchange 2007 Server roles among different servers.

☑ A benefit of a role-based approach is that Exchange 2007 Setup installs only the Exchange files and services necessarily for the server role you deploy. This means that the respective server won't waste disk space and resources on unnecessary files and services the way previous versions of Exchange did.

☑ A typical Exchange Server 2007 installation will install the Hub Transport, Client Access, and Mailbox server roles and the Management Tools (more specifically, the Exchange Management Console, the Exchange Management Shell, the Exchange Help file, and the Exchange Best Practices Analyzer tool) on a server.

Installing Exchange 2007 Using Unattended Setup

☑ Setup.com supports many different parameters and switches that will let you install Exchange Server 2007 using unattended setup. To whet your appetite, we recommend that you type **Setup /?** to list all available parameters and switches, providing a short description of each.

Verifying the Installation of Exchange Server 2007

☑ After Exchange Server 2007 has been installed, we recommend that you verify that the installation completed without any serious warnings or errors. If you didn't encounter any problems during installation of Exchange Server 2007, there's a good chance everything is fine, but you won't know for sure until you have checked the Windows Event logs and the Exchange 2007 setup logs as well as do a visual verification that each selected role has been installed.

☑ If the installation of Exchange 2007 completes the installation of one or more server roles but then fails at another one, you don't need to reinstall the server roles that were already installed. Instead, the Exchange 2007 Setup Wizard will start in maintenance mode the next time you launch it, and from there you can simply tick the server roles that failed the first time.

Licensing an Exchange 2007 Server

☑ Unlike Exchange Server 2000 and 2003, you have to license Exchange Server 2007. By default, Exchange Server 2007 has a built-in time bomb (120 days), as you will notice the first time you launch the Exchange Management Console.

☑ You will not be able to license a 32-bit version of Exchange Server 2007, since this version is meant for testing and other evaluation purposes.

☑ If you're licensing an Exchange 2007 Enterprise Server with the Mailbox server role installed, you need to restart the Microsoft Exchange Information Store service for the change to be reflected in the EMC.

Finalizing Deployment of Exchange Server 2007

☑ When you launch the Exchange Management Console for the first time, the Microsoft Exchange node will be selected. Under this node you'll find two new tabs: Finalize Deployment and End-to-End Scenario. The Finalize Deployment tab provides a list of recommended tasks you should perform (depending on the server roles installed on the server) to finalize the deployment of your Exchange 2007 server.

☑ The tasks listed on the Finalize Deployment tab are applied to features that are enabled by default and that need additional configuration. We highly recommend you follow each task carefully so as not to overlook anything, but don't rely 100 percent on this list, since these are just Microsoft's attempt to show you the most basic configuration settings.

☑ The End-to-End Scenario tab provides a list of tasks that are optional, but it's a good idea to review and complete them anyway.

Adding and Removing Exchange 2007 Server Roles

☑ All Exchange 2007 server roles can be installed on a single server (except the Edge Transport server role, which must be installed on its own hardware in the perimeter network). So, if you're a small organization, you do not need to invest in more than one piece of hardware for your Exchange server. Bear in mind, however, that if you plan to cluster the mailbox server role, the mailbox server must run on its own hardware.

☑ You can add and remove Exchange server roles from an Exchange 2007 server as required using the Windows Control Panel's Add or Remove Programs function or the ExSetup.exe CLI.

Uninstalling Exchange Server 2007

☑ There might be situations in which you want to completely remove an Exchange 2007 server from your Exchange organization. This can be done using either the Exchange 2007 Installation Wizard or Setup.com.

☑ Removing all server roles from an Exchange 2007 server will also remove any installation files as well as the Exchange server object and all its child objects from the Active Directory forest.

Frequently Asked Questions

The following Frequently Asked Questions, answered by the authors of this book, are designed to both measure your understanding of the concepts presented in this chapter and to assist you with real-life implementation of these concepts. To have your questions about this chapter answered by the author, browse to **www.syngress.com/solutions** and click on the **"Ask the Author"** form.

Q: Which processors (CPUs) are supported by Exchange Server 2007?

A: This depends on whether we're speaking of the 32-bit version or the 64-bit version. The 32-bit version supports any Intel Pentium or compatible 800MHz or faster 32-bit processor. The 64-bit version supports Intel Extended Memory 64 Technology (Intel EM64T) and AMD 64-bit processor that supports AMD64 platform, but bear in mind that the Intel Itanium IA64 processor isn't supported by the 64-bit version of Exchange 2007.

Q: What are the memory requirements of the Exchange Server 2007 64-bit version?

A: The minimum requirements are 2GB RAM, but it's recommended that you install 2GB per server plus 5MB of RAM per mailbox. The more RAM, the better, since the 64-bit architecture allows Exchange 2007 to store much more data in the address space compared with previous versions of Exchange, which only existed in 32-bit versions. If we're talking about an Exchange 2007 Mailbox Server with more than four storage groups, it's recommended you install 2GB RAM per three storage groups (if you have between five and eight storage groups, you should install 4GB; if you have between nine and 12, you should install 6GB, and so on).

Q: Is it supported to use the 32-bit version of Exchange 2007 in a production environment?

A: No! Only the 64-bit version should be used in a production environment. The 32-bit version is meant to be used for evaluation and testing purposes. There is one exception to the rule, though: The 32-bit version of the Exchange 2007 Management Tools (more specifically, the Exchange Management Console, the Exchange Management Shell, the Exchange Help file, and the Exchange Best Practices Analyzer tool) is supported for management tasks in a production environment.

Q: Which operating systems does Exchange 2007 support?

A: You must install Exchange 2007 on a server running Windows Server 2003 with SP1 or Windows Server 2003 R2. Both the Standard and Enterprise Editions of these operating systems are supported, but bear in mind that you need to install the Enterprise Edition if you plan to use clustering features such as Cluster Continuous Replication (CCR) or Single Copy Clusters (SCC).

Q: I remember that Exchange 2000 and 2003 required the SMTP and NNTP Windows components to be installed before Exchange could be installed. Is this also the case with Exchange 2007?

A: No, this has changed with Exchange 2007. Exchange 2007 requires that you install neither the SMTP nor NNTP Windows components. The reason is that Exchange 2007 now includes its own SMTP service, which has been built from the ground up using managed code. The NNTP feature has been dropped in Exchange 2007.

Q: Should the Active Directory Forest and Domain(s) still be prepared using ForestPrep and DomainPrep, as was the case in Exchange 2000 and 2003?

A: The Active Directory forest as well as any domains should be prepared for Exchange 2007, but the ForestPrep and DomainPrep switches don't exist any longer. Instead you must use PrepareSchema and PrepareDomain or PrepareAD (which will run both PrepareSchema and PrepareDomain). But note that it's not mandatory that you run these switches before you start installing Exchange 2007, since they will be run automatically during the installation, if you have the appropriate permissions.

Q: Can I install Exchange 2007 in a Windows 2000 Active Directory?

A: No. Exchange 2007 can only be installed in a Windows 2003 Active Directory. In addition, each domain controller must be running Windows Server 2003 with SP1 applied.

Q: To what forest-level mode must the Active Directory be set to be able to install Exchange 2007?

A: The forest-level mode should be set to Windows 2000 Native mode or Windows 2003 Native mode.

Q: I heard that Exchange 2007 must be licensed with a product key. Could you confirm whether this is correct?

A: You heard right. Each Exchange 2007 server in an Exchange organization must be properly licensed using a 25-digit product key, which can be found on the DVD case or can be requested via the TechNet or MSDN sites. An unlicensed version of Exchange 2007 will expire after 120 days.

Chapter 3

Managing Recipients in Exchange 2007

Solutions in this chapter:

- **Managing Recipients Using the Exchange 2007 Management Console**

- **Managing Recipients in a Coexistence Environment**

- **Granting Access and/or *SendAs* Permissions to a Mailbox**

- **Creating a Custom Recipient Management Console**

- **Recipient Filtering in Exchange 2007**

☑ **Summary**

☑ **Solutions Fast Track**

☑ **Frequently Asked Questions**

Introduction

One of the things that have changed drastically in Exchange Server 2007 is the way in which you manage recipients. As most of us are aware, recipients were managed via Active Directory Users and Computers (ADUC) MMC snap-in in the Exchange 2000 and 2003 environments, but with Exchange 2007, the recipient management tasks have been integrated back into the Exchange Management Console and removed from ADUC, as was the case in Exchange versions prior to Exchange Server 2000. In addition to performing the recipient tasks using the Exchange Management Console, you also have the option of using the Exchange Management Shell, which is perfectly suited for performing bulk user changes using *one-liners* (single-line commands).

So, why did the Exchange Product group choose to move away from extending and using the ADUC MMC snap-in to manage recipients in Exchange 2007? There are several reasons. For one, the team wanted to attack the cost of managing recipient users by introducing automation. This automation has been introduced via PowerShell CMDlets, which, as mentioned, really shine when it comes to bulk user changes. For another, they wanted to truly support the split-permissions model, making it possible for an Exchange Administrator to do any relevant Exchange tasks from within a single console: the Exchange Management Console (EMC). Another goal was to simplify the management of the Global Address List (GAL) and recipient types from within the EMC. This goal was accomplished because only the objects and attributes that pertain to Exchange are shown in this console. Finally, the Exchange Product group wanted to have *explicit* recipient types instead of *implicit* ones. Exchange 2007 has a total of 14 different explicit recipient types, each with its own individual icon and recipient type details, lowering the overall administrative burden.

We'll be honest and say that there's been a lot of hype on the Internet about whether moving the management of recipients to the EMC was a good idea or not. During the Exchange 2007 Technology Adoption Program (TAP) and the Rapid Deployment Program (RDP), many Exchange Administrators, as well as independent consultants, expressed their opinion about this move. The majority of them think it's a bad decision, primarily because it leads to huge retraining costs (for help desk staff and others), and it means you suddenly have to administer users using two different consoles, the ADUC and the EMC. We think that the overall concern is valid, but at the same time we understand the Exchange Product group's decision to make the move. Since the group has no intention of changing this post-RTM, we'll have to live with it.

After reading this chapter, you will have a good understanding of what has changed since Exchange Server 2003. You will also be provided with step-by-step instructions on how you perform recipient management tasks using primarily the EMC but also some CMDlets in the Exchange Management Shell (EMS). In addition, we'll talk about how you should manage recipients when your systems are coexisting with an Exchange 2000 environment (where Exchange 2007 coexists with Exchange 2000 and/or 2003), how you create a custom recipient management console, and how to use recipient filters.

Managing Recipients Using the Exchange 2007 Management Console

As mentioned in the introduction to this chapter, the management of recipients in Exchange Server 2007 as well as their Exchange-related properties has been moved back into the EMC in addition to the EMS, both of which are based on Windows PowerShell. This means that all management of Exchange recipient objects should be modified from within the EMC or EMS, not using the ADUC snap-in.

In this first section of the chapter, we'll take a look at how you manage recipients using the EMC. Recipient management for all types of recipients, such as user mailboxes, mail-enabled contacts, and users and distribution groups, is done under the Recipient Configuration work center node, shown as selected in Figure 3.1. As you can see, we have four recipient type subnodes beneath this work center. In order, we have a Mailbox, Distribution Group, Mail Contact, and a Disconnected Mailbox node.

Figure 3.1 Recipient Work Center Node in the Exchange Management Console

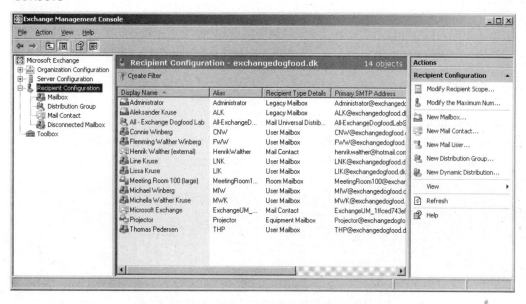

Also notice that when the Recipient Configuration work center node is selected, all types of recipient objects are listed in the Results pane, with the exception of disconnected mailboxes, since these aren't physically located in the Active Directory. If you take a closer look at the screenshot in Figure 3.1, you can also see that each type of recipient object has its own individual icon as well as recipient type description, due to the fact that they now are explicit and not implicit, as was the case in Exchange Server 2003. This is a nice addition because it makes it so much easier to differentiate the recipient types in Exchange 2007.

If you take a look at the tasks provided in the Action pane, you can see that it's possible to create any recipient type without having to specifically select the corresponding recipient type subnode beneath the Recipient Configuration work center node. If you select a recipient type subnode instead, you'll only see a list of the recipient types specific for that subnode. Furthermore, the available tasks in the Action pane are specific only to that particular recipient type.

Managing Mailboxes

All right, let's start by taking a look at the Mailboxes subnode, shown in Figure 3.2, which displays all mailbox user objects. *Mailbox user objects* are objects that have been mailbox enabled. Note that not only mail user objects created in Exchange 2007 are displayed, but also legacy (Exchange 2000 and 2003) mailbox user objects. You cannot see it in Figure 3.2, but there's also a *Server and Organizational Unit* column, which, as implied by the names, tells us the name of the mailbox server on which the mailbox is located and in which Active Directory OU the user object resides.

NOTE

Although legacy mailboxes are exposed via the Exchange Management Console, not all Exchange 2007-specific features apply to these types of mailboxes.

Figure 3.2 Mailbox Subnode in the Exchange Management Console

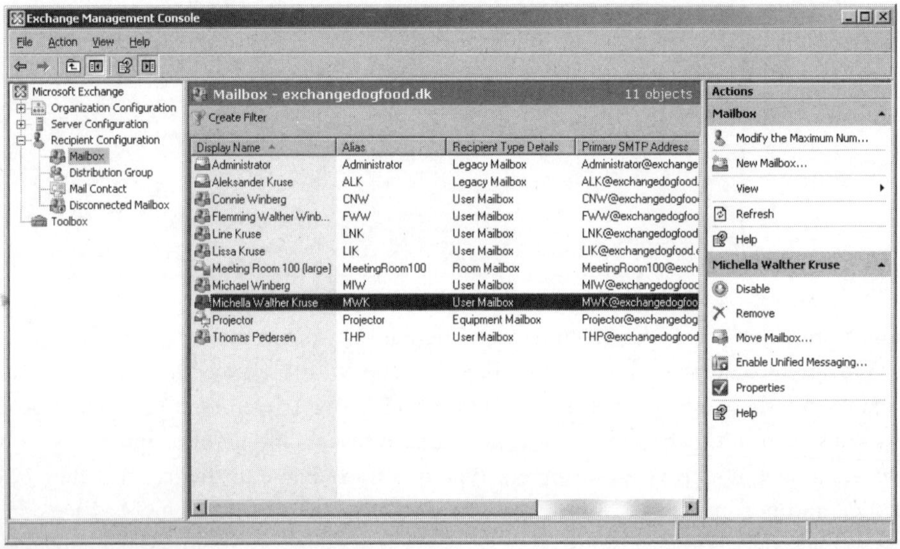

When we look at mailbox user objects, we see that five explicit mailbox recipient types exist in Exchange 2007. Four of these are listed in Figure 3.3, which is a screenshot of the first page you're presented with when you launch the **New Mailbox** Wizard.

Figure 3.3 New Mailbox Wizard Introduction Page

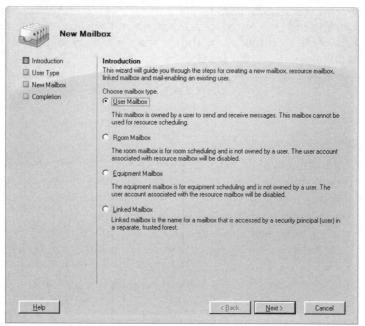

We have *user mailboxes*, which are the type of mailbox you create when mailbox-enabling an ordinary end user. We have *room mailboxes* (a.k.a. resource mailboxes), which are used for room scheduling. Note that this type of mailbox isn't owned by a user and that the associated user account is in a disabled state after creation. We also have *equipment mailboxes*, which are similar to room mailboxes except that they are used for equipment-scheduling purposes, such as booking an overhead projector. Then we have *linked mailboxes*, which are a special type of mailbox that can be used to link to a user account in a separate trusted forest. Finally, we have *shared mailboxes*, which aren't included in the EMC but instead need to be managed via the EMS using the New-Mailbox CMDlet (you need to use the *-Shared* parameter). A shared mailbox is a type of mailbox that multiple users can log onto. It's not associated with a user account that can be used to log onto the Active Directory but is instead associated with a disabled user account, as in the case of room and equipment mailboxes.

SOME INDEPENDENT ADVICE

Because Exchange 2007 uses explicit mailbox recipient types, it's possible to create a search filter that lists all room mailboxes, for example, or perhaps all legacy mailboxes, for that matter. Listing all resource mailboxes in the ADUC snap-in back in Exchange 2000 or 2003 using a search filter was not a trivial process; it required you to use custom attributes because there was no other way to differentiate resource mailboxes from ordinary mailbox-enabled user accounts.

Creating a User Mailbox

Let's go through the steps necessary to create a user mailbox using the EMC. With either the **Recipient Configuration** work center node or the **Mailbox** subnode selected, click **New Mailbox** in the **Action** pane. This will bring up the New Mailbox Wizard, and you will be presented with the page shown back in Figure 3.3. Select **User Mailbox** and click **Next**. On the **User Type** page, you have the option of choosing whether you want to create a new mailbox-enabled user account in Active Directory or whether you want to mailbox-enable an existing Active Directory user account. Choosing the latter will bring up a GUI picker containing a list of all Active Directory user accounts that do not have an associated mailbox. In this example we will select **New User** and click **Next** (see Figure 3.4).

NOTE

To be able to create a new mailbox (also known as creating a new mailbox-enabled user), the account you're logged on with must have the appropriate permissions in Active Directory, in addition to having the Exchange Recipient Administrator permission. Membership in the Account Operators group should be sufficient. If you want to create a new mailbox for an existing user (also known as mailbox-enabling an existing user), you only need Exchange Recipient Administrator permissions.

On the User Information page, select the Organizational unit in which you want the user object to be created by clicking the **Browse** button. Enter the name and account information and click **Next** (see Figure 3.5).

Figure 3.4 Selecting the User Type

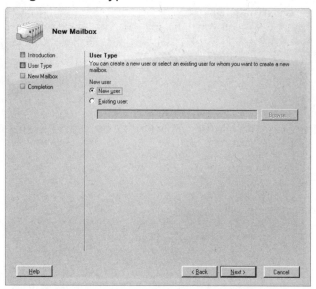

As you can see in Figure 3.5, you can specify that the user must change his password at the next logon, just as you could when provisioning Exchange 2000/2003 users in ADUC.

Figure 3.5 Entering User Name and Account Information

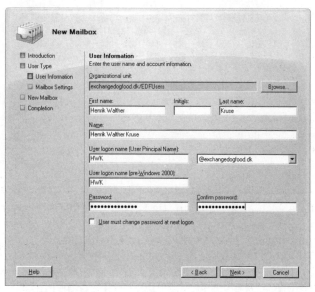

On the Mailbox Settings page, you can specify the Exchange 2007 Mailbox Server Storage group as well as the Mailbox database in which the mailbox for the user should be created (see Figure 3.6). On this page you also have the option of applying any required managed folder mailbox and Exchange ActiveSync mailbox policies. (These are discussed in more detail in Chapter 5.) When you're ready, click **Next** once again.

As you can see in the bottom of the Mail Settings page, you need an Exchange Enterprise Client Access License (CAL) to take advantage of the messaging records management features of Exchange 2007. (Exchange licensing and client CALS were discussed earlier in Chapter 2.)

Figure 3.6 Choosing the Server, Storage Group, and Mailbox Database for the Mailbox

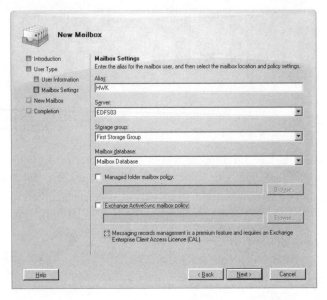

On the New Mailbox page, you can see a configuration summary of the mailbox-enabled user account that will be created. Click **New**, and then click **Finish** on the **Completion** page (see Figure 3.7).

TIP

As is the case with all wizards in the Exchange 2007 Management Console, the Completion page shown in Figure 3.7 will provide you with the CMDlet and any parameters that will be used to create the mailbox-enabled user account. This CMDlet can be copied to the clipboard by pressing **Ctrl + C**, so you can use it for creating mailbox-enabled user accounts directly via the EMS in the future. A good idea is to paste the code into Notepad or another text editor so that you can change parameters, such as the name, alias, and organization unit, to meet your needs.

Figure 3.7 The New Mailbox Completion Page

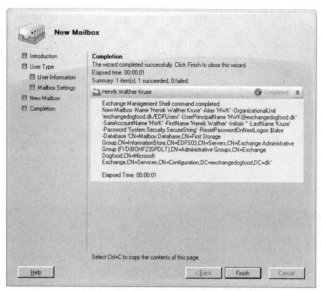

These are all the steps required to create a mailbox-enabled user. This process wasn't harmful at all, was it?

If you want to create a user mailbox using the EMS, you need to use the *New-Mailbox* or *Set-Mailbox* CMDlets, depending on whether you want to create a new mailbox-enabled user or mailbox-enable an existing user account. To get a list of all the available parameters for these two CMDlets, you can open the EMS and type **Get-Help New-Mailbox** and **Get-Help Set-Mailbox**, respectively.

Manipulating Mailboxes in Exchange 2007

Once we have created a user mailbox, we can manipulate it in several ways by highlighting it in the Results pane and then choose the action we want to perform in the Action pane.

As you can see in Figure 3.8, we can disable the mailbox, meaning all of the Exchange attributes are removed from the respective Active Directory user account.

Although the account will no longer be mailbox enabled, the mailbox can still be found under the Disconnected Mailbox subnode. From there, it can be reconnected to the same or any other nonmailbox-enabled user account, until the default 30-day deleted mailbox retention policy for Exchange 2007 databases kicks in and purges the mailbox. (We'll take a closer look at reconnecting mailboxes later in this chapter.) When you try to disable a mailbox, you'll first receive the warning message shown in Figure 3.9.

Figure 3.8 Set of Actions for a User Mailbox in the Actions Pane

Figure 3.9 The Warning Received When You're Disabling a Mailbox

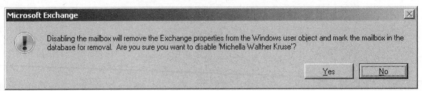

Another option is to remove the mailbox, which not only removes the mailbox but also deletes the associated user account in Active Directory—so think twice before you click Yes to the warning message shown in Figure 3.10. Exchange 2007 beta 2 builds and earlier didn't even include a warning message about this action, which led to a few frustrated Exchange consultants who participated in the Exchange 2007 Rapid Deployment Program (RDP), a program where selected customers deployed Exchange 2007 beta 2 in a production environment.

Figure 3.10 Warning Received When You're Removing a Mailbox

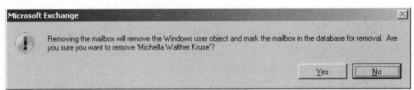

> **NOTE**
>
> Unless you have delivered mail to a mail-enabled user object, selecting either the Disable or the Remove Action pane action will *not* place that mailbox in the Disconnected Mailbox subnode. The reason behind this is simply that the mailbox is created only when it receives its first piece of mail, so there is no mailbox to disconnect.

To disable or remove a user mailbox using the EMS, you need to use the *Disable-Mailbox* and *Remove-Mailbox* CMDlets, respectively. So if, for example, you wanted to disable the mailbox for a user named Michella Kruse Walther with a UPN of MWK, you would need to run the following command:

```
Disable-Mailbox -Identity MWK
```

followed by pressing **Enter**. This will bring you a command-line warning message similar to the one shown in Figure 3.9. Click **Y** for Yes.

Likewise, removing the user mailbox for the same user would be done by running the following command:

```
Remove-Mailbox -Identity MWK
```

followed by pressing **Enter**. This will bring you a command-line warning message similar to the one shown in Figure 3.10. Click **Y** for Yes.

Moving a Mailbox

We can also move a mailbox to another server, storage group, and mailbox database; we do this by clicking the **Move Mailbox** link in the Action pane, bringing up the Move Mailbox Wizard Introduction page, shown in Figure 3.11. Here we specify the server, storage group, and mailbox database the respective mailbox should be moved to. When you have done so, click **Next**.

Figure 3.11 The Move Mailbox Wizard Introduction Page

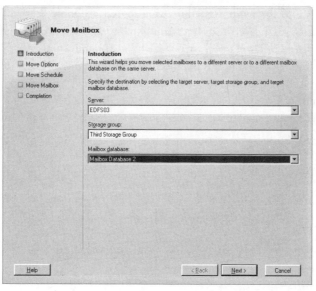

On the Move Options page, we can specify how the mailboxes that contain corrupted messages should be managed. We can configure the Move Mailbox Wizard to skip any

mailboxes containing one or more corrupted messages or simply let it skip corrupted messages (Figure 3.12). If we select the latter, we have even more granular control and can
specify the maximum number of messages to skip before the mailbox move should be cancelled. In this example, we choose **Skip** the mailbox and click **Next**.

Figure 3.12 Move Mailbox Wizard Options

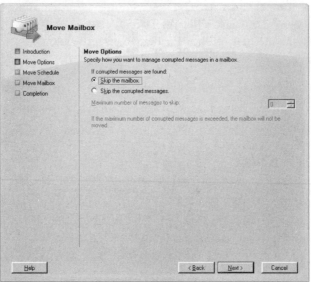

We're now taken to the Move Schedule page shown in Figure 3.13, where we can
specify when the mailbox move should occur as well as the maximum length of time the
move should run before it should be cancelled. The idea behind the Move Mailbox Schedule
option is to allow you to schedule the mailbox moves to occur during nonworking hours. In
this example, we select **Immediately** and click **Next**.

Next we are taken to the Move Mailbox page (see Figure 3.14), where we can verify
that the parameters for the mailbox move are correct before the actual move takes place.
When you're ready, click **Move**.

Figure 3.13 The Move Mailbox Wizard Schedule Page

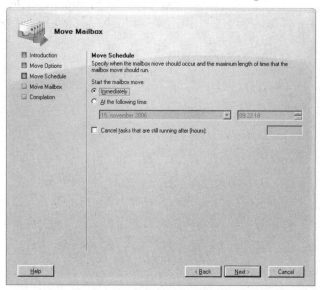

Figure 3.14 The Move Mailbox Wizard Summary Page

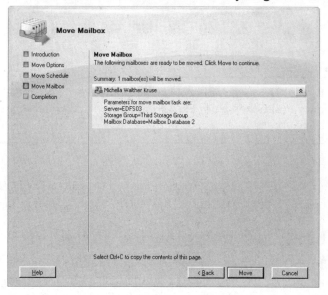

Depending on the size of the mailbox, you will need to have a little patience while the move takes place. The Move Mailbox Wizard needs to first open the source mailbox and then create a destination mailbox on the target database. Only then does it start to move the contents of the mailbox, completing its task by finally deleting the source mailbox and closing its connection. When the mailbox has been moved successfully, you'll be taken to the Completion page, where you can see the CMDlet as well as the parameters used to move the mailbox (see Figure 3.15). Click **Finish** to exit the Move Mailbox Wizard.

Figure 3.15 The Move Mailbox Wizard Completion Page

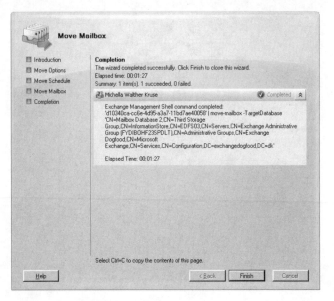

> **NOTE**
>
> The Exchange 2007 Move Mailbox Wizard is the tool you should use for moving legacy mailboxes from Exchange 2000 or 2003 Server to an Exchange 2007 Mailbox Server.

To move a mailbox using the EMS, you can use the *Move-Mailbox* CMDlet. To get a list of available parameters for this CMDlet, type **Get-Help Move-Mailbox** in the EMS.

Enabling Unified Messaging for a Mailbox

If you have installed the Unified Messaging Server role on an Exchange 2007 server in your Exchange organization, you also have the option of enabling Unified Messaging for a user mailbox. When you click the **Enable Unified Messaging** link in the Action pane, you will be faced with the Enable Unified Messaging Wizard shown in Figure 3.16. In addition to enabling Unified Messaging for a user mailbox, this is where you apply any required Unified Messaging Mailbox Policies, a mandatory setting, as well as creating a mailbox extension and personal identification number (PIN), used to access Outlook Voice Access (OVA). When you have enabled Unified Messaging for a user mailbox, an e-mail message will be sent to the respective mailbox, notifying that user that they have been enabled for unified messaging. The e-mail message will include information about the PIN as well as the number and extension the user needs to dial to gain access to the mailbox. When you're ready, click **Enable** and then click **Finish** on the Completion page.

Figure 3.16 Enabling Unified Messaging for a User Mailbox

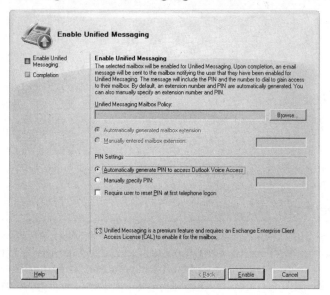

We will talk much more about the Unified Messaging functionality in Chapter 10.

Let's now take a look at the Property page for a mailbox user object, which allows us complete control over all Exchange-related settings from within the EMC. We gain this control by selecting a user mailbox, either beneath the Recipient Configuration work center node or the Mailbox subnode, followed by clicking **Properties** in the Action pane. (Alternatively, you can right-click the user mailbox object and select **Properties** in the context menu.) The tab that will be selected by default is the General tab (see Figure 3.17).

Here we have the option of changing the display name as well as the alias of the user mailbox. In addition, we can see information about which Active Directory OU the user mailbox object is located in, the last user that logged onto the mailbox, the total items and size of the mailbox, and the mailbox server, storage group and mailbox database on which the user mailbox resides. From this tab we also have the option of hiding the user mailbox from any Exchange address list. Finally, we can click the **Custom Attributes** button to specify any custom attributes that should apply to this user mailbox. Like Exchange 2000 and 2003, Exchange 2007 gives you the option of specifying up to 15 different custom attributes.

Figure 3.17 The General Tab on the User Mailbox Property Page

Some Independent Advice

Some of you might be wondering what custom attributes can be used for in the first place. Well, custom attributes can be used for many different purposes. For example, they can be used for personal information about your users that does not easily fit into any existing field. Examples of custom attribute fields include employee numbers, cost center, health insurance data, and Social Security information.

Bear in mind that custom attributes can also be used to create recipient conditions for dynamic distribution groups, e-mail address policies, and address lists. Exchange hosting providers especially can take advantage of custom attributes in segmenting dissimilar customer environments.

Let's move on to the User Information tab. As you will see, this is where you can find and, if required, modify user information such as first name, initials, last name, name (also known as display name), and Web page, in addition to adding special notes about the particular user account (see Figure 3.18). Any changes made here are of course also reflected in Active Directory and visible from the Property page of an Active Directory user account using the ADUC snap-in.

WARNING

Be careful about what you type in the Notes field, since any information entered here can be seen by someone looking at the properties of the respective user mailbox object on the Phone/Notes tab in the Global Address List (GAL) in Outlook.

Figure 3.18 The User Information Tab on the User Mailbox Property Page

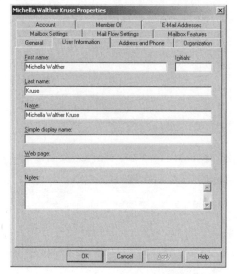

Under the Address and Phone tab, as shown in Figure 3.19, we can find and, if required, modify user information such as street address, city, state/province, ZIP/postal code, country/region, and phone and pager numbers (for the few people who still use a pager).

Under the Organization tab (see Figure 3.20), we have the option of entering user information such as title, company, department, and office as well as specifying the user's manager.

Figure 3.19 The Address and Phone Tab on the User Mailbox Property Page

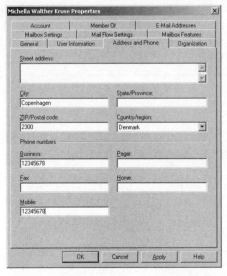

Figure 3.20 The Organization Tab on the User Mailbox Property Page

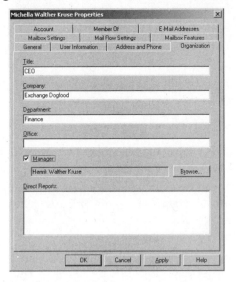

By specifying the manager for each of the recipients in your organization, you can create a virtual organization chart, accessed by looking at the Property page of the user mailbox object in the GAL in Outlook 2007, shown in Figure 3.21.

The Direct Reports field lists mailbox user's accounts and/or contacts that are managed by the respective recipient. Note that the user account Direct Report field is populated automatically when a recipient is designated as a manager for another recipient.

Figure 3.21 A Virtual Organization Chart in Outlook 2007

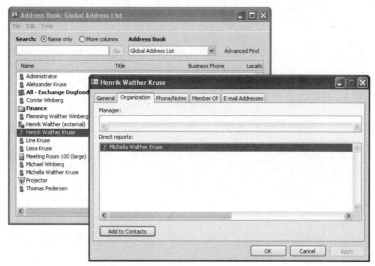

Let's move on to the Mailbox Settings tab shown in Figure 3.22. From here we can apply Managed folder mailbox policies (used for messaging records management purposes) and configure per-user level storage quotas. In addition, we can set deleted items' retention time, which by default uses the mailbox database defaults of 14 days.

We'll cover how you create and apply managed folder mailbox policies in Chapter 4.

Figure 3.22 Storage Quotas for a User Mailbox

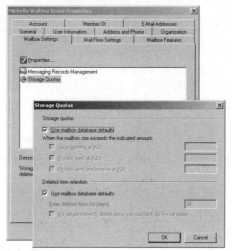

NOTE

The Messaging Records Management feature in Exchange 2007 is considered a premium feature and requires an Exchange Enterprise Client Access License (CAL).

Under the Mail Flow Settings tab, we can choose to manage delivery options, message size restrictions, and message delivery restrictions, as shown in Figure 3.23.

Figure 3.23 The Mail Flow Settings Tab for a User Mailbox

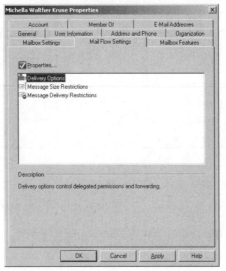

Let's take a look at the Properties for Delivery Options (see Figure 3.24). Highlight **Delivery Options** and then click **Properties**. Here we can grant send-on-behalf permissions to other user mailbox objects in the organization. We can also enable forwarding so that all mail received by the respective mailbox is forwarded to another specified user mailbox. We can even configure the forwarding feature so that the message is delivered to both the originally destined mailbox as well as the configured forwarder user mailbox. Finally, we have the option of setting a recipient limit, used to set the maximum number of recipients the user mailbox is allowed to send in a given e-mail message.

Click **OK** and then click the **Properties** button for **Message Size Restrictions** (see Figure 3.25). Here we can set the maximum receive and send message size (in KB) for the user mailbox.

Figure 3.24 Delivery Options for a User Mailbox

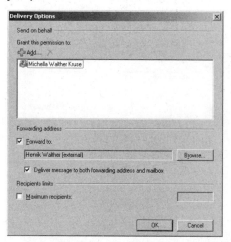

Figure 3.25 Setting Message Size Restrictions for a User Mailbox

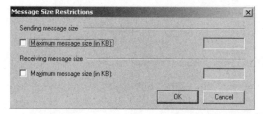

Click **OK** and then click the **Properties** for **Message Delivery Restrictions** (see Figure 3.26). Here we can specify who may send messages to the respective user mailbox, require that all senders are authenticated (preventing anonymous users from sending to the user mailbox), and finally, create a list of senders that should be rejected from sending to this user.

Click **OK** to get back to the property page, and then click the **Mailbox Features** tab, shown in Figure 3.27.

This tab allows you to control client access to Outlook Web Access (OWA), Exchange ActiveSync (EAS), Unified Messaging (UM), and Outlook MAPI. In addition to being able to enable or disable access from all these client access methods, you also have the ability to apply an Exchange ActiveSync policy to the user mailbox account by clicking the **Properties** of **Exchange ActiveSync**.

In Chapter 5 we'll show how you create Exchange ActiveSync policies as well as how to apply them to user mailbox accounts throughout your Exchange organization.

Figure 3.26 Message Delivery Settings for a User Mailbox

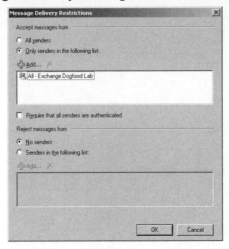

If you have enabled Unified Messaging for the user mailbox object, you can also con-figure UM features by clicking **Properties** of **Unified Messaging**. However, that topic is covered in Chapter 10 and so won't be covered here.

Figure 3.27 The Mailbox Features Tab for a User Mailbox

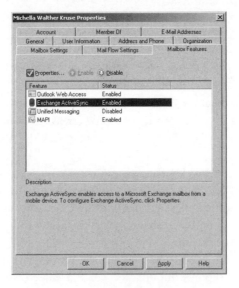

The next tab is the Account tab (see Figure 3.28). There's not much to say about the options available here, since most of you should recognize them from the ADUC snap-in. This is where you can find and modify the user principal name (UPN), the UPN domain, and the user logon name (pre-Windows 2000). Finally, you have the option of specifying that the user must change his or her password at next logon.

Figure 3.28 The Account Tab for a User Mailbox

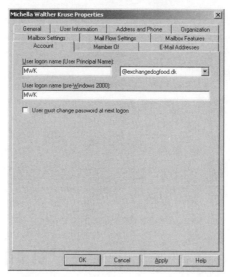

The Member Of tab should not need any explanation, so let's quickly move on to the E-Mail Addresses tab (see Figure 3.29). This is where you can see which e-mail addresses are currently stamped on the user mailbox object. You can change as well as add e-mail addresses from here. Just bear in mind that you'll need to untick **Automatically update e-mail addresses based on e-mail address policy** if you want to manually control which addresses applied as e-mail address policies have the ability to overwrite changes applied here.

We'll talk a lot more about e-mail address policies in Chapter 6.

All right, we have just been through all the tabs available for a user mailbox object. Was it as boring as you had thought it would be?

Figure 3.29 The E-mail Addresses Tab for a User Mailbox

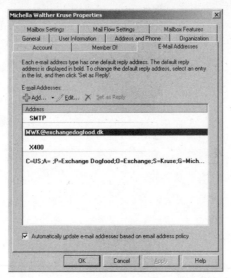

Creating a Room or Equipment Mailbox

Creating a room or equipment mailbox is a very similar process to creating an ordinary user mailbox, so we'll not go through each page in the New Mailbox Wizard again. Instead, let's look at the **User Information** page, where you enter the information about the resource mailbox (see Figure 3.30). As you can see, we have a specific OU called Meeting Rooms set up specifically for housing room mailboxes.

> **NOTE**
>
> You cannot create OUs from within the EMC; instead, you need to do so using the ADUC snap-in.

When the meeting room or equipment mailbox has been created, you can manipulate and modify it the exact same way you can with a user mailbox because it is nothing more than a user mailbox with a disabled account association. Again, there's no reason to take you through all the tabs on the property page again.

Figure 3.30 Creating a New Room Mailbox

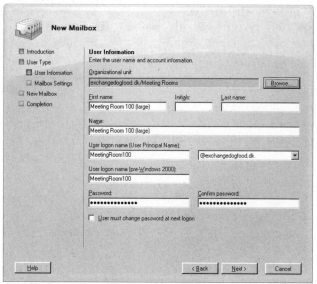

Some of you might be wondering how a room or equipment mailbox is differentiated from an ordinary user mailbox. The only difference (other than the disabled account object association) is that a room mailbox is created with a *–Room* parameter, and an equipment mailbox is created with an *–Equipment* parameter. These mailboxes are also explicit, using their own icon and recipient type details.

> **NOTE**
>
> Room and equipment mailboxes can be included in meeting requests and be configured to automatically process incoming requests.

Creating a Linked Mailbox

A *linked mailbox* is a mailbox that needs to be associated with a user account belonging to another trusted forest. Linked mailboxes are typically used when we choose to use the Exchange resource forest model, where Exchange 2007 is deployed in its own separate Active Directory forest (done to centralize Exchange in a single forest).

Although Figure 3.31 implies that you link the mailbox directly to a user account in another trusted forest, this isn't the case. You still need to create a user account in the Exchange resource forest, because an Exchange 2007 mailbox requires that you have an associated account in the same Active Directory forest in which Exchange 2007 is deployed. This was no different than Associated External Accounts in Exchange 2000 and 2003.

NOTE

The Exchange 2007 resource forest model is considered a complex design and should only be used by large organizations that really need to deploy Exchange 2007 in its own Active Directory forest.

Figure 3.31 Creating a Linked Mailbox

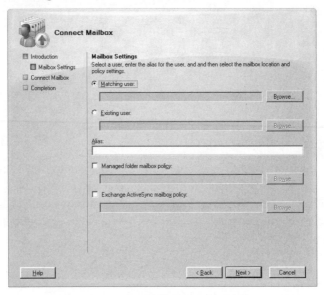

Managing Distribution Groups

As is the case with Exchange 2000 and 2003, Exchange 2007 has two types of distribution groups: *mail-enabled distribution groups*, which are used strictly for distributing messages, and *mail-enabled security groups*, which are used to assign permissions to users as well as to distribute messages. In addition, the query-based distribution group introduced in Exchange 2003 has made its way into Exchange 2007, albeit with a new name and a few changes. These groups are now called *dynamic distribution groups* and, as the name implies, are still dynamic in nature and based on a set of configured criteria. More about them later.

Distribution groups can contain other distribution groups, user mailboxes (mailbox-enabled users), and mail contacts (mail-enabled contacts). You can get a list of the mail-enabled distribution groups in your organization by selecting the **Distribution Group** subnode beneath the Recipient Configuration work center node, as shown in Figure 3.32. This is also the place where you create new groups as well as modify any existing ones.

Just like user mailbox objects, distribution groups are explicit in Exchange 2007, meaning that each type of group is differentiated using an individual icon as well as a *recipient type details* description, as you can see in Figure 3.32. As you can also see in this figure, we have four different explicit group types:

- Mail Universal Distribution groups

- Mail Universal Security groups

- Dynamic Distribution groups

- Mail Non-Universal groups

    - Domain Local groups

    - Global groups

Warning

Although pre-existing Mail Non-Universal groups are shown under the Distribution Group subnode in the figure, you should be aware that the administration of these group types is limited. Actually, it's recommended that you do not use these types of groups for distributing messages in Exchange 2007.

Another word of warning when you are creating groups in ADU&C snap-in console: Any group created as a Distribution Global group will not be available when you're trying to mail-enable that group via the EMC. Groups created in the ADUC MMC snap-in must be Universal Distribution groups if they are later to be mail-enabled using the EMC.

Figure 3.32 Listing Distribution Group Types under the Distribution Group Subnode

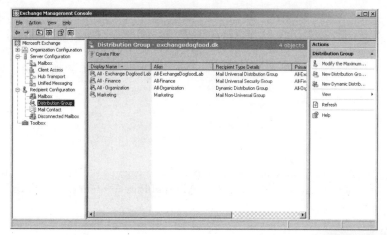

SOME INDEPENDENT ADVISE

You may ask, "What should I use in my organization—mail-enabled security groups or ordinary mail-enabled distribution groups?" That's a really good question, and here is something to consider: Choosing mail-enabled security groups will give you the option of using the group as both a distribution group as well as using it to assign permissions to user account objects in your Active Directory forest. This means that using mail-enabled security groups will lower the number of groups in your organization, thereby lowering the amount of maintenance required. Be careful using mail-enabled security groups; you could accidentally assign too many permissions to the wrong users! Double check the membership of the distribution list before assigning it to a resource's ACL.

When highlighting a group under the Distribution Group subnode, you get a set of actions that can be performed on it in the Action pane. When highlighting a Mail Universal Security group, for example, we get the set of actions shown in Figure 3.33. We can disable the group, removing all Exchange-related properties from the group; remove it (which physically removes the group object from Active Directory!); or access the Properties page for the group by choosing the Properties action.

If we had highlighted a Dynamic Distribution group, we would not have had the option to disable it, but only to remove it.

Figure 3.33 Actions for a Mail Universal Security Group in the Actions Pane

Highlighting a Mail Non-Universal group will also give us the option of converting it to a Universal group, as shown in Figure 3.34. We highly recommend you do this.

Figure 3.34 Actions for a Mail Non-Universal Group in the Actions Pane

Let's access the Properties page for a Mail Universal Distribution group. The first tab we're presented with is the General tab (see Figure 3.35), where we can change the name and alias of the group as well as view or modify any specified custom attributes.

Figure 3.35 The General Tab for a Distribution Group

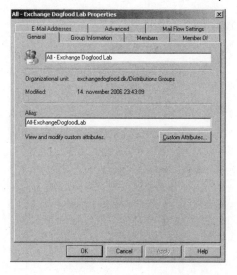

We also have the option of changing the group name under the Group Information tab. We can also specify the person (AD user account) that manages the respective group by selecting the **Managed By** option, clicking **Browse**, and choosing an account in AD. The person specified here will also be shown as the Owner when users user the GAL to open the Properties page of the group from within Outlook. On a side note, this person has the option of receiving delivery reports when messages are sent to the group, which is configurable on the Advanced tab. Finally, we have a Notes field, where we can enter administrative notes about the group. Again, as with user notes, bear in mind that end users will be able to see these notes from their Outlook clients when accessing them in the GAL.

The Members tab should not need any further explanation; it is simply the place where you add and/or remove members from the group. The Member Of tab lists any distribution groups that include this group on its member list. Note that you cannot use this tab to add the selected group to other distribution groups! The E-Mail Addresses tab is the place where you can see all the e-mail addresses for the group as well as modify or add new e-mail addresses. By default, the e-mail addresses are stamped on the distribution group by the e-mail address policy in the Exchange organization; however, you have the option of disabling this behavior and instead administering these lists manually by deselecting the option **Automatically update e-mail addresses based on recipient policy**.

On the Advanced tab, shown in Figure 3.36, we can specify a simple display name, used if the original display name of the group contains Unicode characters and you have third-party applications that don't support Unicode. In addition, you can define an expansion server, used to expand group membership. When a message is sent to a distribution group, Exchange must access the membership list to deliver the message to each member of the group. When dealing with large distribution groups, this can be a very resource-intensive task, thus giving a reason to define a particular hub transport server role as your expansion server.

Figure 3.36 The Advanced Tab

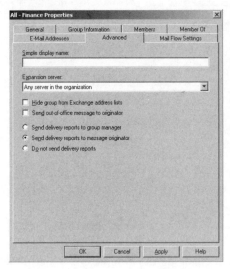

TIP

If you specify an expansion server for a particular distribution group, you should always make sure it's well documented because the group will then depend on this specified server to deliver messages. This means that if you someday find out you want to replace your existing hub transport server with a new one, and that particular hub transport server has been explicitly assigned as an expansion server for one or more distribution groups, those groups will no longer be able to deliver messages to the respective members.

Under the Advanced tab, you also have the option of hiding the group from the Exchange Global Address Lists (GAL) and specify that any out-of-office messages should be sent to the originator (the sender of the message) instead of the group. Lastly, you have the option of specifying whether delivery reports should be sent or not. If you choose to have them sent, you can select whether they should be sent to the message originator or the group manager specified under the Group Information tab. Note that if you decide to send delivery reports to the group manager, a group manager *must* be selected under the Group Information Managed By field or you will receive a warning message telling you to do so.

TIP

Larger "All User" based distribution groups should always have a limited number of allowed senders defined because these groups tend to encompass your entire organization and can get you in trouble if everyday messages can be delivered to everyone in your company.

The last tab is Mail Flow Settings, where you can configure the maximum group receiving size in KB as well as defining who should be allowed to send messages to the group.

NOTE

When accessed via the Exchange Management Console, the property pages are identical for Mail Universal Distribution groups and Mail Universal Security groups, so there's no reason to go through the tabs under the Properties page of a Mail Universal Security group.

Creating a New Distribution Group

To create a new distribution group, click the **New Distribution Group** link in the Action pane, bringing up the New Distribution Group Wizard shown in Figure 3.37. The first page is the Introduction page, where you need to specify whether you want to create a new distribution group or mail-enable an existing security group. If you choose to mail-enable an existing group, click the **Browse** button and you will be presented with a GUI picker, where all security groups that haven't been mail-enabled will be listed. For the purposes of this example, we'll select **New group**, then click **Next**.

Figure 3.37 The Introduction Page in the New Distribution Group Wizard

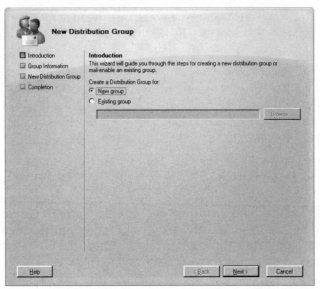

On the Group Information page shown in Figure 3.38, we'll have to specify whether we want to create a new mail-enabled distribution group or a mail-enabled security group. We'll then need to specify the OU in which the group should be created in Active Directory and finally give it an appropriate name and alias. The alias is automatically filled in and duplicated with whatever you used for a name; however, it can still be changed without altering the name.

NOTE

As already mentioned, the only difference between mail-enabled distribution groups and mail-enabled security groups is the ability for security groups to be used to assign permissions to user objects in Active Directory.

Let's click **Next**, which will bring us to the New Distribution Group page, where you should verify the information in the Configuration Summary pane. Once it's verified, click **New** and finally click **Finish**.

Figure 3.38 Selecting the Type of Distribution Group That Should Be Created

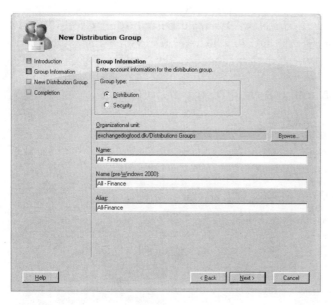

To create or modify existing distribution groups via the EMS, use the *New-DistributionGroup* and *Set-DistributionGroup* CMDlets. An example of creating a distribution group might look like the following:

```
New-DistributionGroup -Name "New Group" -OrganizationalUnit syngress.local/users
-SamAccountName "New-Group" -Type security
```

Creating a New Dynamic Distribution Group

Dynamic distribution groups, which were known as query-based distribution groups in Exchange 2003, provide the same type of functionality as ordinary distribution groups, but instead of manually adding members to the group's membership list, you can use a set of filters and conditions that you predefine when creating the group to derive its membership. When a message is set to a dynamic distribution group, Exchange queries the Active Directory for recipients matching the specified filters and conditions. The primary advantage of using dynamic distribution groups over ordinary distribution groups is that dynamic groups lower the administrative burden, since you don't have to maintain any distribution group membership lists. If we should mention any disadvantage of using dynamic distribution groups, it is that this type of group puts more load on the Global Catalog servers in your Active Directory forest. This is based on the fact that each time a message is sent to a dynamic distribution group, Exchange will have to query them based on the criteria defined in the group.

You create a new dynamic distribution group by clicking **New Dynamic Distribution Group** in the Action pane under the **Distribution Group** subnode of the Recipient Configuration work center node.

This will bring up the **New Dynamic Distribution Group Wizard** shown in Figure 3.39. Here you specify the OU in which the group should be created and give the group a meaningful name. When you have done so, click **Next**.

Figure 3.39 Naming a New Distribution Group

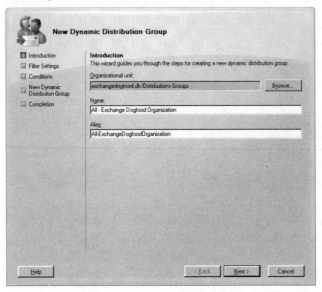

The next page is the Filter Settings page (see Figure 3.40) where you will need to specify the recipient container the filter should be applied to. Clicking the **Browse** button will bring up a GUI picker where you can choose an individual OU or even the whole Active Directory domain, for that matter. On this page you also have the option of specifying the type of recipients that should be included in your filter. For example, this could be **All recipient types** or just **Users with Exchange mailboxes**. When you have made your choices, click **Next**.

We have now reached the most interesting of all pages in the wizard, where we actually select and define the conditions that should be used by the group. As you can see in Figure 3.41, we can select conditions such as **Recipient is in a State or Province**, **Recipient is in a Department**, or **Recipient is in a company** as well as any of the 15 custom attributes that you might have defined on your mailbox-enabled user objects, so there should be plenty of possibilities. For the purposes of our example, we have selected **Recipient is in a Company** and edited the condition so that all recipients in a company called Exchange Dogfood will receive the messages sent to the respective dynamic distribution group. When you have selected the required conditions, you can click the **Preview** button in the lower-right corner to display all recipients who meet your criteria and whether they are the correct recipients you intended for the group. When you're ready, click **Next**, **New**, and finally **Finish**.

Figure 3.40 Selecting Filter Settings for a New Dynamic Distribution Group

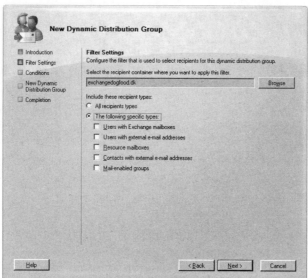

Figure 3.41 Choosing Conditions for a New Dynamic Distribution Group

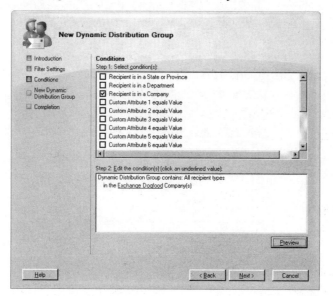

Since most of the Properties pages for a dynamic distribution group are more or less identical to that of an ordinary distribution group, we will not cover them here, with the exception of two tabs, which we want to quickly show you. The Filter and Conditions tabs are where you change the filter and condition behavior for a dynamic distribution group. As you can see in Figure 3.42, the Filter tab is where you can change the recipient container and the recipient types used by the group.

Figure 3.42 The Filter Tab

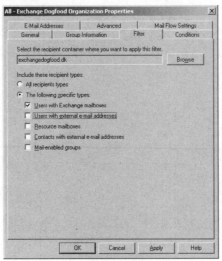

Under the Conditions tab, shown in Figure 3.43, you can change the conditions that should be used to define your group, as well as use the **Preview** button to list all users meeting your conditions.

Figure 3.43 The Conditions Tab

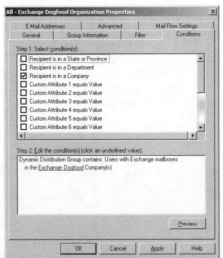

To create or modify existing dynamic distribution groups via the EMS, use the *New-DynamicDistributionGroup* and *Set-DynamicDistributionGroup* CMDlets.

SOME INDEPENDENT ADVISE

So, what do you do if you want to use conditions other than those available in the New Dynamic Distribution Group Wizard? Is this even possible? As a matter of fact, it is, but only by using the *New-DynamicDistributionGroup* CMDlet in the EMS. You should also bear in mind that any conditions and filters other than those provided in the GUI must be *managed* using the EMS. If, for example, you wanted to create a custom recipient filter that included all recipients in an OU called *EDFUsers*, with a mailbox located on a server called EDFS03, you would need to run the following command:

```
New-DynamicDistributionGroup -Name "EDFS03 - Mailbox Users" -
OrganizationalUnit EDFSUsers -RecipientFilter "((RecipientType -eq
'UserMailbox' -and ServerName -eq 'EDFS03') -and -not(Name -like
'SystemMailbox{*'))"
```

When viewing the Filter tab on the Properties page of a dynamic distribution group, created using a custom filter, you will see something similar to the display in Figure 3.44, showing the complete recipient filter.

Figure 3.44 The Filter Tab on the Properties Page When a Filter Has Been Created Through the Exchange Management Shell

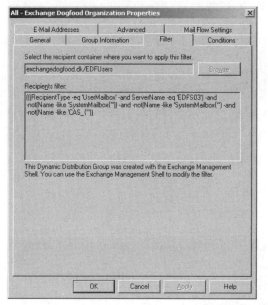

Managing Mail Contacts and Mail Users

We manage mail contacts (mail-enabled contacts) and mail users (mail-enabled users) under the Mailbox Contact subnode beneath the Recipient Configuration work center node. So, what is a mail contact? Most of you should know what it is, since this type of object has existed since Exchange 2000 was released to manufacturing. For those of you who would like a refresher, a mail contact is an AD object without security principals as well as a mailbox. Because this object doesn't have any security principals, it cannot be used to log onto the network and/or be used in an ACL to assign access to a resource. The purpose of this object is simply to represent an external recipient (using a name and an external SMTP address) in the Exchange address lists. This could be customer or a consultant, for example.

A mail user (mail-enabled user) is an object that does have an account in Active Directory as well as an *external* e-mail address associated with it, but this type of recipient does not have an Exchange mailbox in the organization. A mail user is also listed in the Exchange address lists. The only difference between a mail contact and a mail user is that a mail user can log onto the Active Directory and can be used in an ACL to gain access to domain resources. Mail users are typically used for contract employees who are on site for a period of time and require access to the network but want to use their own mailbox (for example, a mailbox in another Exchange organization that they access using OWA or Outlook Anywhere) or simply use a messaging system other than Exchange.

As you can see in Figure 3.45, these recipient types are also explicit and therefore differentiated, using their own icon and recipient type details.

Figure 3.45 Mailbox Contact Subnode in the Exchange Management Console

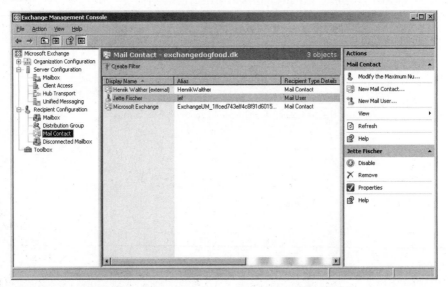

When highlighting an existing mail contact or mail user, we can either disable or remove the Mail object and/or access its Properties page. As is also the case with a user mailbox, disabling a mail contact or a mail user will remove the Exchange properties from the object, whereas removing a mail contact or mail user will instead delete the object entirely in Active Directory, so be careful when using the Remove action.

Creating a Mail Contact

To create mail contacts, you need to click the **New Mail Contact** link in the Action pane under the **Mail Contact** subnode. This will bring up the **New Mail Contact Wizard** shown in Figure 3.46. Here we need to select whether we want to create a new mail contact or want to mail-enable an existing contact. If you select **Existing contact** you can click the **Browse** button, bringing up a GUI picker and listing all contacts that haven't been mail-enabled. In this example, we'll select **New Contact** and click **Next**.

Figure 3.46 Choosing Whether to Create a New Mail-Enabled Contact or to Mail-Enable an Existing Contact

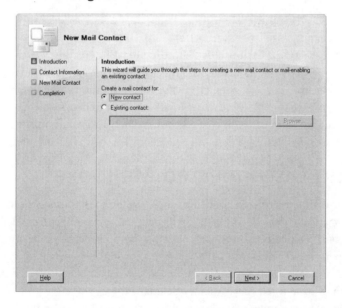

On the Contact Information page shown in Figure 3.47, we'll need to enter the account information that is required to either create a mail contact or mail-enable a contact. We'll need to provide things such as name and alias as well as add the external e-mail address we want to associate with the Mail Contact object. When you have done so, click **Next**, and then click **New** on the **Summary** page, and finally click **Finish**.

Figure 3.47 Creating a New Mail Contact

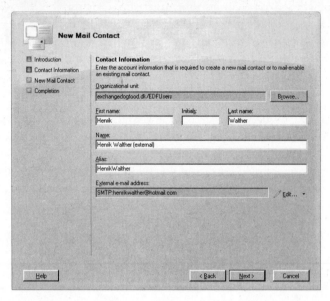

The process of creating a mail user is almost identical to creating a mail contact, the only exception being the need to specify the user account information during creation.

To create a new mail-enabled contact via the EMS, use the *New-MailContact* CMDlet. To modify this type of recipient, use the *Set-MailContact* CMDlet. To create a new mail-enabled user via the EMS, use the *New-MailUser* CMDlet. To modify this type of recipient, use the *Set-MailUser* CMDlet.

Managing Disconnected Mailboxes

When you either disable or remove a mailbox, that mailbox will be *marked* for deletion but will not be automatically deleted. Instead, it will be kept in the respective Mailbox database for the number of days specified on the Mailbox database Properties page (under the Limits tab), called **Keep deleted mailboxes for**, more commonly referred to as *mailbox retention*. Like Exchange 2000 and 2003, Exchange 2007 will, by default, keep deleted mailboxes for 30 days before they are purged (permanently deleted).

After you disable or remove a mailbox, you can then find it under the Disconnected Mailbox subnode, as shown in Figure 3.48. If the mailboxes you have disabled or removed are within the last 30-day retention period and do not show up under this node, chances are that the EMC is connected to another mailbox server other than the one hosting the Mailbox database on which the mailboxes originally resided. As you can see in the top of the Results pane, the EMC informs us which mailbox server the Disconnected Mailbox subnode is connected to. As you also can see in Figure 3.48, you can connect to another mailbox server by clicking the **Connect to Server** link in the Action pane, then clicking the

Browse button to bring up a GUI picker where all mailbox servers in your Exchange 2007 organization will be listed.

Figure 3.48 Connecting to a Specific Mailbox Server

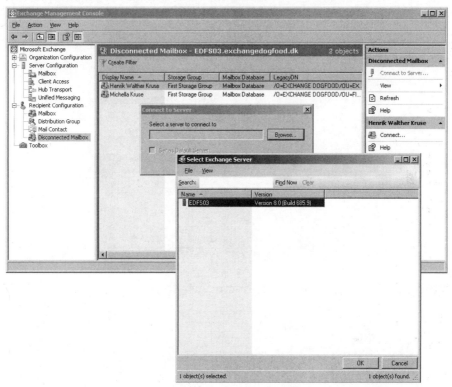

When you're connected to the correct mailbox server, you can reconnect a disconnected mailbox by highlighting the **Mailbox** object and clicking the **Connect** link in the Action pane. This brings up the Connect Mailbox Wizard Introduction page, shown in Figure 3.49. Here you can specify the type of mailbox the disconnected mailbox should be reconnected to. When you have selected a mailbox type, click **Next**.

On the Mailbox Settings page, we select a user, enter the alias for the user, and, if required, select any Managed folder or Exchange ActiveSync mailbox policy settings.

As you can see in Figure 3.50, we can either connect the mailbox to a user using the **Matching user** or **Existing user** option. If we select the **Matching user** option, Exchange will search and try to locate a user matching that of the disconnected mailbox within the Active Directory forest. If you would rather pick an existing user manually, you should select **Existing user**. When you have made your choices, click **Next**, then **Connect**, and finally **Finish**.

Figure 3.49 Selecting the Mailbox Type to Which the Mailbox Will Be Connected

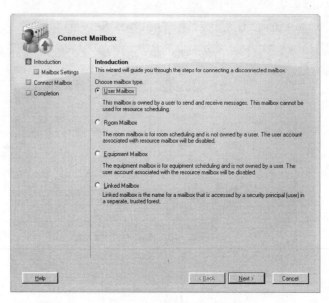

Figure 3.50 Connecting a Disconnected Mailbox

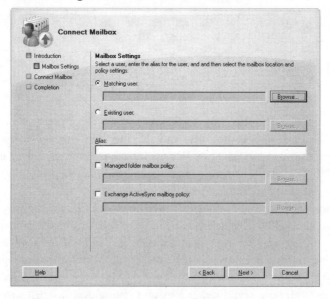

Okay, so what if you don't want the mailbox to be disconnected but would rather permanently delete a user mailbox right away? Well, in this particular scenario, you need to switch to the EMS because there's no way to do so via the GUI. More specifically, you need

to run the *Remove-Mailbox* command with the *Permanent* parameter. So, for example, if you were to delete the AD user account and the mailbox for a user with a UPN named *LIK* in an Active Directory domain called *exchangedogfood.dk*, you would need to run the following command:

```
Remove-Mailbox -Identity exchangedogfood\lik -Permanent $true
```

You will then get the warning message shown in Figure 3.51. Type **Y** to confirm you want to do it, and then press **Enter**.

Figure 3.51 Permanently Removing a User Mailbox

Notice that the warning message says *Will remove the Windows user object and will remove the mailbox from the database,* unlike the warning message back in Figure 3.10, which says *Will remove the Windows user object and mark the mailbox in the database for removal.*

SOME INDEPENDENT ADVICE

So how do you delete a mailbox that has already has been disconnected? This is a little trickier! To do so, you first need to retrieve the mailbox GUID of the disconnected mailbox using the *Get-MailboxStatistics* CMDlet. However, it's not enough to simply run this CMDlet, since it won't list disconnected mailboxes. To delete the disconnected mailbox for a user with a display name of Line Kruse, you instead need to type **$Temp = Get-MailboxStatistics | Where {$_.DisplayName -eq 'Line Kruse'}** followed by pressing **Enter**. Then you need to run a command similar to the following: **Remove-Mailbox –Database "edfs03\mailbox database 2" –StoreMailboxIdentity $Temp.MailboxGuid** followed by pressing **Enter**. You will then get the warning message shown in Figure 3.52. Click **Y** for Yes, and press **Enter**.

The disconnected mailbox has now been deleted from the specified mailbox database.

Figure 3.52 Deleting a Disconnected Mailbox

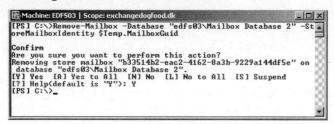

Managing Recipients in an Exchange Coexistence Environment

During a transition from Exchange 2000/2003 to Exchange 2007, deploying Exchange 2007 Server into your existing Exchange organization can take a long time, depending on the size of your existing setup and organizational layout.

Managing Exchange 2000/2003 and 2007 Mailbox–Enabled User Objects in a Coexistence Environment

Which tool (the ADUC snap-in or EMC) should you use to manage mailbox-enabled user objects within a coexistence environment? The choice is actually pretty straightforward; just follow the set of guidelines laid out in Table 3.1.

Table 3.1 Tools to Manage Exchange 2000/2003 and 2007 Mailboxes in a Coexistence Environment

Administrative Task	ADUC Snap-in	EMC/EMS
Create Exchange 2007 Mailbox-enabled users		X
Create Exchange 2000/2003 Mailbox-enabled users	X	
Manage Exchange 2007 Mailbox-enabled users		X
Manage Exchange 2000/2003 Mailbox-enabled users	X	X
Remove Exchange 2007 Mailbox-enabled users		X
Remove Exchange 2000/2003 Mailbox-enabled users	X	X
Move Exchange 2007 Mailbox-enabled users		X
Move Exchange 2000/2003 Mailbox-enabled users	X	X

WARNING

Although you have the option of managing Exchange 2007 Mailbox and Mail-enabled users using the ADUC snap-in, it isn't supported and will result in Exchange 2007 mailboxes that might not be fully functional. In addition, you should opt to use the Exchange 2007 tools to move Exchange 2000/2003 user mailboxes.

Managing Exchange 2000/2003 and 2007 Mail-Enabled Objects in a Coexistence Environment

Unlike mailbox-enabled user objects, you can administer mail-enabled objects (contacts, distribution groups, and the like) using your tool of choice, since these types of objects aren't tied to a specific server version. Best practice, however, is to manage these objects from either the Exchange 2007 EMC or EMS. There's only one mail-enabled object that you *must* manage from the EMC or EMS at all times, and that is dynamic distribution groups. This is based on the fact that this type of object uses the new Exchange 2007 OPATH format for its recipient filter and cannot be managed under the older Exchange tools.

The Recipient Update Service in a Coexistence Environment

The infamous Recipient Update Service (RUS), which most of us know from Exchange 2000 and 2003, is no longer part of the Exchange 2007 product. RUS was responsible for stamping e-mail addresses, in addition to address list membership along with a few other things, but it didn't always work as expected and was very difficult to troubleshoot when it acted up. With Exchange 2007, the RUS (and thereby the asynchronous behavior used to provision objects) has been replaced by a new synchronous process, the *EmailAddressPolicy* CMDlet, used to stamp the e-mail address onto objects immediately! Yes, you no longer have to wait for several minutes to see e-mail addresses on your objects, as was often the case with the antiquated RUS. We'll talk more about this new task in Chapter 6.

There's one important detail to keep in mind about the RUS when you're working in a coexistence environment. You will need to continue using the Exchange 2003 System Manager to provision a RUS for each domain that contains Exchange Recipients; note that this is also the case even when you're provisioning domains with pure Exchange 2007 recipients in them!

Granting Access and/or *SendAs* Permissions to a Mailbox

In some situations, one or more users might need to be granted permissions to access another user's mailbox. This could be a temporary access—for example, during vacations, maternity leave, or for other reasons—where one or more users need to take over the work of the user who will be absent. It could also be a more permanent access, where, for example, a secretary needs to access her boss's mailbox. Another reason could be that all users in a particular department (such as a helpdesk) need a shared mailbox.

You cannot grant permissions to a mailbox using the EMC. Instead, you need to use the EMS for this task—more specifically, the *Add-MailboxPermission* CMDlet, which has been created for granting permissions to a mailbox. To, for example, grant full access permissions to a mailbox, you would need to use the following command:

```
Add-MailboxPermission "respective mailbox" -User "user to have permissions"
-AccessRights: FullAccess
```

To learn more about the *Add-MailboxPermission* CMDlet and any available parameters and syntaxes, you can type **Get-Help Add-MailboxPermission** in the EMS.

There might also be times where you need to grant *SendAs* permission to a mailbox for another user. To do this you can use the *Add-ADPermission* CMDlet or the ADUC MMC snap-in. To do so using the *Add-ADPermission* CMDlet, you should run the following command:

```
Add-ADPermission -Identity "respective mailbox" -User "user to have permissions"
-ExtendedRights: SendAs
```

To grant *SendAs* permissions to a user via the ADUC MMC snap-in, follow these steps:

1. On a domain controller in the Active Directory, click **Start | Run**, type **dsa.msc** and then press **Enter**.

2. In the menu, click **View**, then **Advanced Features**.

3. Drill down to and open the Properties page for the AD user object to which you want to grant another user *SendAs* permissions.

4. Now click the **Security** tab.

5. Click **Add** and select the AD user object that should be granted *SendAs* permission, and then click **OK**.

6. Now select the added user in the **Group or user names** box, and then check **Allow** for the *SendAs* permission in the permissions list, as shown in Figure 3.53.

Figure 3.53 The Security Tab on the AD User Object Properties Page

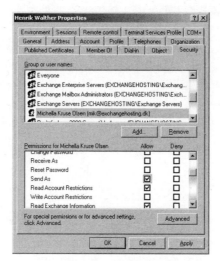

7. Click **OK** and close the ADUC MMC snap-in.

Creating a Custom Recipient Management Console

Depending on the organization, there could be times when you want to create an Exchange 2007 EMC that shows only the Recipient Configuration work center node. This is especially true in situations where you have a helpdesk that is used to having a customized ADUC console snap-in that provided the respective organizational units (OUs) holding the Exchange user objects they were to administer. After the transition to Exchange 2007, it would be a little too drastic to let the helpdesk staff have the full-blown EMC at their disposal, right? To create a custom EMC exposing only the Recipient Configuration work center node, you will first need to click **Start**, then type **MMC.exe**, followed by pressing **Enter**. This will bring up an empty MMC console, as shown in Figure 3.54. Click **File** in the menu, and then click **Add/Remove Snap-in**.

Figure 3.54 An Empty MMC Console

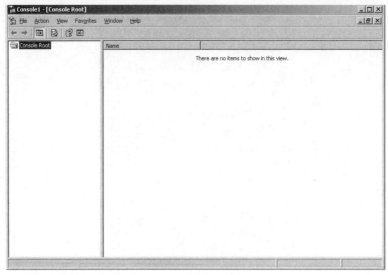

In the **Add/Remove Snap-in** window, click **Add**, then scroll down and select the **Exchange Server 2007** snap-in, as shown in Figure 3.55. Click **Add** again, then click **Close** and finally **OK**.

Figure 3.55 Selecting the Exchange Server 2007 Snap-in

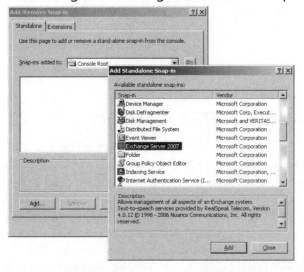

Expand the **Microsoft Exchange** tree and right-click the **Recipient Configuration** work center node, selecting **New Window from Here** in the context menu, as shown in Figure 3.56.

Figure 3.56 Choosing New Window from Here in the Context Menu

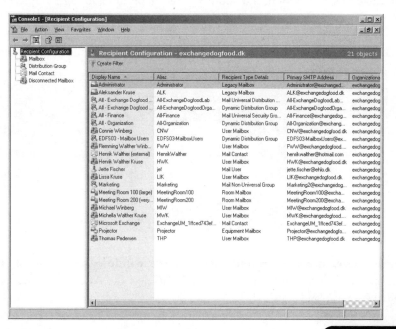

We now have a basic Exchange 2007 Recipient Management snap-in, as you can see in Figure 3.57, but honestly, we can't keep it this simple, right? We need to make it more functional.

Figure 3.57 A Standard Custom Exchange 2007 Recipient Management Console

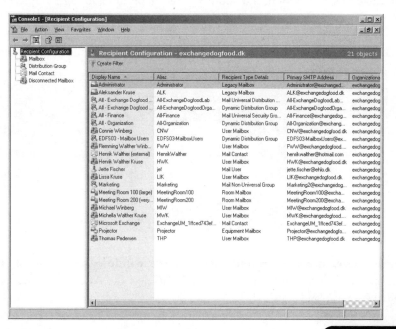

The first thing you want to do is to enable the Action pane in addition to removing the Standard menus and Standard toolbar, since these aren't required by Exchange 2007. To do so, click **View | Customize** and deselect **Standard menus (Action and View)** and **Standard toolbar**. Lastly, select **Action pane**, and click **OK** (see Figure 3.58).

Figure 3.58 Customizing the View for the Exchange 2007 Recipient Management Console

Let's spiff up the console a little more before we save it. To do so, click **File | Options**; in the **Options** window, replace *Console1* with the text **Exchange 2007 Recipient Management**. Now click the **Change Icon** button and navigate to the **Bin** directory under the *C:\Program Files\Microsoft\Exchange Server* folder. Here you can select the **ExSetupUI.exe** file, click **Open**, and you have the option of choosing the Exchange 2007 icon shown in Figure 3.59. Do so and click **Apply**.

Figure 3.59 Choosing the Exchange 2007 Icon for the Console

Now select **User mode – limited access, single window** in the **Console mode** drop-down menu, as shown in Figure 3.60. Finally, deselect the **Allow the user to customize views** option, and click **OK**.

Figure 3.60 Custom Exchange 2007 Recipient Management Console
Options

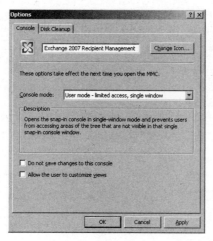

You can now save the console by clicking **File | Save As**. Save the console as
Exchange 2007 Recipient Management Console.msc and answer **Yes** to the message
shown in Figure 3.61.

Figure 3.61 The Single-Window Interface MMC Message

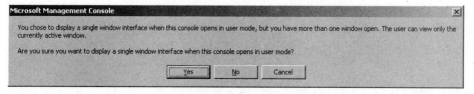

Now close the console and reopen it from where it was saved. It should now look similar to the one shown in Figure 3.62.

Now that looks much better.

You can also create isolated Management Consoles for the Organization Configuration,
Server Configuration, and Toolbox work center nodes. You can do this by following the
same steps but opening a new console window by right-clicking the respective work center
node. If you have both the Exchange 2007 Tools and the Windows AdminPak installed on a
server or workstation, you can even create a single console with access to both the ADUC
snap-in and the Exchange 2007 Management Console, as shown in Figure 3.63.

Figure 3.62 The Custom Recipient Management Console

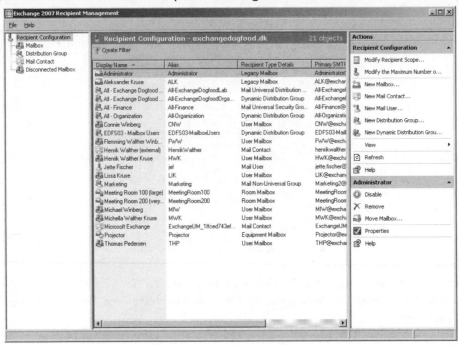

Figure 3.63 A Custom User Management Console

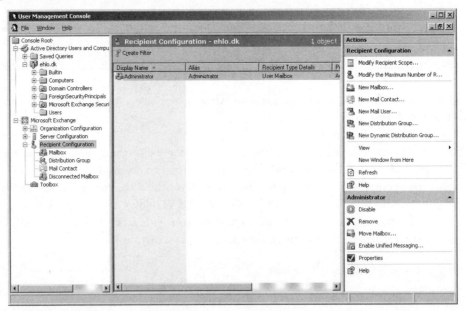

Recipient Filtering in Exchange 2007

If you have already deployed and/or are planning to deploy Exchange 2007 in an organization consisting of several thousand recipients, you can quickly lose the administrative overview. This is where recipient filtering comes into the picture. By creating a filter using either the EMC or the EMS, you will be able to find the recipient or set of recipients you're looking for in a matter of seconds.

Creating a recipient filter is done by selecting the Recipient Configuration work center node or the particular recipient subnode. Let's, for example, select the **Mailbox** subnode. Here we will create a filter by clicking the **Create Filter** button located in the top-left corner of the **Result** pane, as shown in Figure 3.64.

Figure 3.64 The Create Filter Button in the Exchange Management Console

After we have clicked **Create Filter**, we need to specify the type of property we want to filter on, selecting from among 35 available property types such as Alias, Company, Custom Attributes, E-mail Addresses, Recipient Type Details, Server, and Unified Messaging Mailbox Policy. Let's try to create a filter based on the **Recipient Type Details** property, setting it to the **Equals** comparison operator and finally choosing a value it should filter on. In this example we'll choose **Legacy Mailbox** and click **Apply Filter**. We could have also selected User Mailbox, Linked Mailbox, Shared Mailbox, Room Mailbox, or Equipment Mailbox, depending on our preference.

> **NOTE**
>
> A total of six different comparison operators are available: Contains, Does Not Contain, Does Not Equal, Ends With, Equals, and Starts With.

As you can see in Figure 3.65, any legacy mailboxes (mailboxes on an Exchange 2000 or 2003 server) are listed in the Result pane.

Figure 3.65 Displaying Legacy Mailbox Filtered View

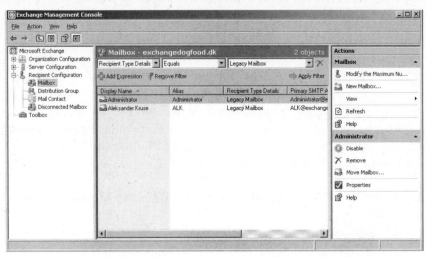

Note that you can add expressions by clicking the **Add Expression** button. You can even remove separate expressions by clicking the red cross icon to the right of the particular filter. You can also remove the complete filter by clicking **Remove Filter**.

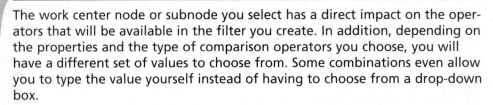

TIP

The work center node or subnode you select has a direct impact on the operators that will be available in the filter you create. In addition, depending on the properties and the type of comparison operators you choose, you will have a different set of values to choose from. Some combinations even allow you to type the value yourself instead of having to choose from a drop-down box.

If you would rather perform recipient filtering using the EMS, you can do so with the *Get-Mailbox –filter* command.

Summary

In this chapter we focused on how recipients are managed in Exchange 2007. First we had a look at how the different recipient type objects are managed using the Exchange Management Console (EMC), then we went through how we should deal with recipients in a coexistence environment. We also examined, step by step, how to create a custom MMC that contains the Exchange 2007 Recipients work center, which can be used, for example, by the helpdesk staff in your organization. Finally, we took a look at the options available when we use the new recipient filtering features in Exchange 2007.

Solutions Fast Track

Managing Recipients Using the Exchange 2007 Management Console

☑ Management of recipients in Exchange Server 2007, as well as their Exchange-related properties, has been moved back into the Exchange Management Console (EMC) in addition to the Exchange Management Shell (EMS), both of which are based on Windows PowerShell. This means that all management of Exchange recipient objects should be modified from within the EMC or EMS, not using the ADUC snap-in.

☑ We have four recipient type subnodes beneath the Recipient Configuration work center. In order, we have a Mailbox, a Distribution Group, a Mail Contact, and a Disconnected Mailbox node.

☑ Each type of recipient object has its own individual icon as well as recipient type description due to the fact that they now are explicit and not implicit, as was the case in Exchange Server 2003. This is a nice addition because it makes it so much easier to differentiate the recipient types in Exchange 2007.

☑ Although legacy mailboxes are exposed via the EMC, not all Exchange 2007-specific features apply to these types of mailboxes.

☑ Because Exchange 2007 uses explicit mailbox recipient types, it's possible to create a search filter that lists all room mailboxes, for example, or perhaps all legacy mailboxes, for that matter. Listing all resource mailboxes in the ADUC snap-in back in Exchange 2000 or 2003 using a search filter was not a trivial process; it required you to use custom attributes because there was no other way to differentiate resource mailboxes from ordinary mailbox-enabled user accounts.

☑ The Exchange 2007 Move Mailbox Wizard is the tool you should use to move legacy mailboxes from Exchange 2000 or 2003 Server to an Exchange 2007 Mailbox Server.

☑ As is the case with Exchange 2000 and 2003, there are two types of Distribution Groups in Exchange 2007: mail-enabled distribution groups, which are used strictly for distributing messages, and mail-enabled security groups, which are used both to assign permissions to users as well as to distribute messages. In addition, the query-based distribution group introduced in Exchange 2003 has also made its way into Exchange 2007, albeit with a new name and a few changes.

☑ Dynamic distribution groups, which were known as query-based distribution groups in Exchange 2003, provide the same type of functionality as ordinary distribution groups, but instead of manually adding members to the group's membership list, you can use a set of filters and conditions that you predefine when creating the group to derive its membership.

☑ We manage mail contacts (mail-enabled contacts) and mail users (mail-enabled users) under the Mailbox Contact subnode beneath the Recipient Configuration work center node.

☑ When you either disable or remove a mailbox, that mailbox will be marked for deletion but will not be automatically deleted. Instead, it will be kept in the respective mailbox database for the number of days specified on the mailbox database Properties page (under the Limits tab), called "Keep deleted mailboxes for," more commonly referred to as *mailbox retention*. Like Exchange 2000 and 2003, Exchange 2007 will, by default, keep deleted mailboxes for 30 days before they are purged (permanently deleted).

Managing Recipients in a Coexistence Environment

☑ During a transition from Exchange 2000/2003 to Exchange 2007, deploying Exchange 2007 server into your existing Exchange organization can take a long time, depending on the size of your existing setup and organizational layout. This means that you might have to manage mail-enabled users from both the EMC and the ADUC MMC snap-in for a period of time.

☑ Although you have the option of managing Exchange 2007 mailbox and mail-enabled users using the ADUC snap-in, it isn't supported and will result in Exchange 2007 mailboxes that might not be fully functional. In addition, you should opt to use the Exchange 2007 tools for moving Exchange 2000/2003 user mailboxes.

☑ The infamous Recipient Update Service (RUS), which most of us know from Exchange 2000 and 2003, is no longer part of the Exchange 2007 product. RUS was responsible for stamping e-mail addresses, in addition to address list membership along with a few other things, but didn't always work as expected and was very difficult to troubleshoot when it acted up. With Exchange 2007, the RUS (and thereby the asynchronous behavior used to provision objects) has been replaced by a new synchronous process, the *EmailAddressPolicy* CMDlet, used to stamp the e-mail address onto objects immediately.

Granting Access and/or *SendAs* Permissions to a Mailbox

☑ In some situations, one or more users might need to be granted permissions to access another user's mailbox. This could be a more temporary access during vacations, maternity leave, or other reasons, where one or more users need to take over the work of the user who will be absent. It could also be a more permanent access, where a secretary needs to access her boss's mailbox, for example. Another reason could be that all users in a particular department (such as a helpdesk) need a shared mailbox.

Creating a Custom Recipient Management Console

☑ Depending on the organization, at times you might want to create an Exchange 2007 Management Console that shows only the Recipient Configuration work center node. This is especially true in situations where you have a helpdesk that is used to having a customized ADUC console snap-in that provides the respective OUs holding the Exchange user objects they were to administer.

☑ You can create isolated Management Consoles for the Organization Configuration, Server Configuration, and Toolbox work center nodes. You can do this by following the same steps but opening a new console window by right-clicking the respective work center node. If you have both the Exchange 2007 Tools and the Windows AdminPak installed on a server or workstation, you can even create a single console with access to both the ADUC snap-in and the Exchange 2007 Management Console.

Recipient Filtering in Exchange 2007

☑ If you have already deployed and/or are planning to deploy Exchange 2007 in an organization consisting of several thousand recipients, you can quickly lose the administrative overview. This is where recipient filtering comes into the picture. By creating a filter using either the EMC or the EMS, you will be able to find the recipient or set of recipients you're looking for in a matter of seconds.

☑   Creating a recipient filter is done by selecting the Recipient Configuration work center node or the particular recipient subnode.

Frequently Asked Questions

The following Frequently Asked Questions, answered by the authors of this book, are designed to both measure your understanding of the concepts presented in this chapter and to assist you with real-life implementation of these concepts. To have your questions about this chapter answered by the author, browse to **www.syngress.com/solutions** and click on the **"Ask the Author"** form.

Q: Can I manage legacy mailboxes (Exchange 2000/2003 mailboxes) using the Exchange Management Console or the Exchange Management Shell?

A: Yes, this is supported, but bear in mind that although legacy mailboxes are exposed via the EMC and the EMS, not all Exchange 2007-specific features apply to these types of mailboxes. However, as soon as a legacy mailbox has been moved to an Exchange 2007 Mailbox Server, the mailbox will have the same feature set as a mailbox created directly on an Exchange 2007 Mailbox Server. Note that managing Exchange 2007 mailboxes using the ADUC MMC snap-in is not supported.

Q: Is it necessary to create the Active Directory user object in the ADUC MMC snap-in before I can create a mailbox using the Exchange 2007 Management Console?

A: No, this is not necessary. When you create a new mailbox in the EMC using the New Mailbox Wizard, you'll have the option of creating an Active Directory user object as well. You can even specify in which OU it should be created.

Q: I've heard that Exchange 2007 has several different recipient type objects. What's that all about?

A: You heard true. Exchange 2007 has a total of 14 different explicit recipient types, all having their own individual icon and recipient type details, which lowers the overall administrative burden. For example, you can create a recipient filter that, say, lists all room mailboxes much more easily than was true back in Exchange 2000/2003 without using a custom attribute field or the like.

Q: Do the new room and equipment mailboxes require an Active Directory User object in the Active Directory, as was the case with a resource/group mailbox in Exchange 2000/2003?

A: Yes. Even though Exchange 2007 includes dedicated room and equipment mailboxes, which aren't logged on to, an Active Directory User object in Active Directory is still required. But keep in mind that the User object that gets created when you create either a room or equipment mailbox will be disabled by default.

Q: What's the difference between disabling and removing a mailbox in Exchange 2007?

A: Disabling a mailbox removes all Exchange attributes from the Active Directory user account, which means that the user account no longer will be mailbox-enabled. The User object will remain in Active Directory, though. Although disabling a mailbox will remove the mailbox from the respective account, the mailbox won't be permanently deleted. By default, it can be found under the Disconnected Mailbox subnode for 30 up to 30 days after the mailbox was disabled. The mailbox can, at any time during this period, be reconnected to another User object from here. Removing a mailbox will not only mark the Exchange data for deletion, but the associated user object will also be deleted from the Active Directory. However, because of the default deleted mailbox retention settings, the mailbox can be reconnected to another user object within 30 days.

Q: Once I've moved a legacy mailbox (Exchange 2000/2003 mailbox) to an Exchange 2007 server, can I then moved it back to an Exchange 2000/2007 server if I need to, for some reason?

A: Yes, this is supported. Mailboxes can be moved both ways. But bear in mind that you'll lose any Exchange 2007-specific features, such as Unified Messaging, once you do so.

Q: How many mailboxes can I move at a time when I'm using the Exchange 2007 Move Mailbox Wizard? I remember that the Exchange 2003 version of the Move Mailbox Wizard could process four mailboxes at the same time.

A: It's correct that the Exchange 2003 Move Mailbox Wizard was limited to processing four mailboxes at the same time, but actually it was possible to run four threads at a time, meaning that you (of course, depending on your hardware) could move 16 mailboxes at the same time. This hasn't changed with Exchange 2007, so the same limitations apply to the Exchange 2007 Move Mailbox Wizard.

Chapter 4

Managing the Exchange 2007 Mailbox Server Role

Solutions in this chapter:

- **Managing the Exchange 2007 Mailbox Server**
- **Exchange 2007 Storage Groups**
- **Exchange 2007 Mailbox Databases**
- **Exchange 2007 Public Folder Databases**
- **Managing Organizationwide Mailbox Server Configuration Settings**

☑ Summary

☑ Solutions Fast Track

☑ Frequently Asked Questions

Introduction

The Exchange 2007 Mailbox Server role is, without surprise, the one hosting mailbox database in which the user's mailboxes are stored. This is also the server role that hosts Public Folder databases, which contain the Public Folders organizations use for sharing documents, calendars, contacts, and tasks as well as for archiving distribution lists. As you saw in Chapter 2, where we went through a typical installation of Exchange Server 2007, a legacy Outlook client (that is, Outlook 2003 and earlier) requires a Public Folder database to connect to Exchange Server 2007.

In addition to being the server that hosts mailbox and Public Folder databases, the mailbox server also provides rich calendaring functionality, resource management, and offline address book downloads. The Mailbox Server role also provides services that calculate e-mail address policies (called *recipient policies* in Exchange Server 2000 and 2003) as well as address lists for recipients. Finally, this server role enforces managed folders.

NOTE

If all end users use Outlook 2007 and you don't use Public Folders for sharing documents, calendars, contacts, and tasks as well as for archiving distribution lists, you don't need to create a Public Folder database on your Exchange 2007 Server(s). The reason is that Outlook 2007, in addition to MAPI, uses Web services for accessing things such as free/busy information, out-of-office (OOF) messages, offline address books (OABs), and the like. Since it's the Exchange 2007 Client Access Server roles that are responsible for these Web services, we won't cover them in this chapter (see Chapter 5 instead).

After reading this chapter, you will have gained a good understanding of how you manage the Mailbox Server roles feature set, both in terms of the Mailbox Server level as well as organizationwide.

Managing the Exchange 2007 Mailbox Server

The mailbox server holds the Exchange Store, which provides a single repository for managing multiple types of unstructured information in one infrastructure. The store hasn't changed much since Exchange Server 2003 but has been further improved and, of course, contains multiple new features. The Exchange Store is still made up of multiple interacting logical components, where the primary three still are storage groups, mailbox databases (formerly known as mailbox stores), and Public Folder databases (formerly known as Public Folder stores).

> **NOTE**
>
> Back in Exchange 2000 and 2003, the databases containing either mailboxes or Public Folders were known as mailbox stores and Public Folder stores, respectively, but with Exchange Server 2007 they are now referred to as *mailbox databases* and *Public Folder databases*.

The Exchange Product Group had several design goals related to mailbox server storage design. One of the goals was to allow an average user to have a considerably larger mailbox (2GB and larger) than was the case in Exchange 2003, where the norm was approximately 100MB to 300MB. Another design goal was to reduce the I/O (to lower the demand from the storage subsystem), done by taking advantage of 64-bit hardware, which gives us the opportunity to use much more memory than was the case in previous Exchange versions. Because Exchange Server 2007 can take advantage of more memory, a larger chunk of each user's mailbox can be stored in the memory, which reduces disk I/O.

In Figure 4.1 you see a screenshot of the Exchange Management Console (EMC) with the Mailbox node selected. As you can see, this particular server holds several storage groups, mailbox databases, and a single Public Folder database.

Figure 4.1 The Mailbox Subnode in the Server Configuration Work Center

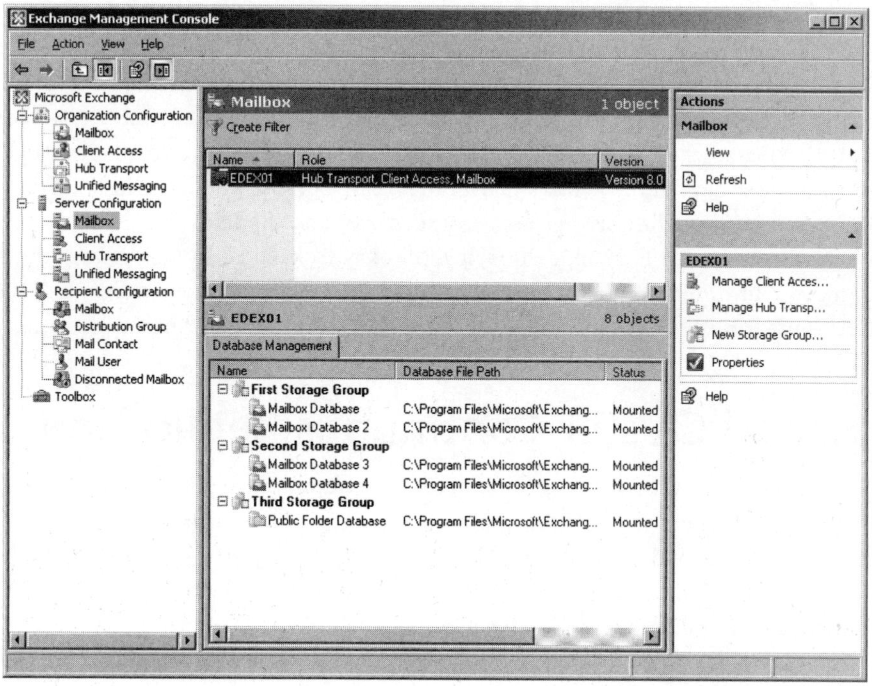

In the following sections, we'll go through how you manage and configure storage groups, mailbox databases, and Public Folder databases.

Exchange 2007 Storage Groups

A *storage group* is a grouping of mailbox and/or Public Folder databases that shares a single backup schedule and a single set of transaction log files. Storage groups are managed using their separate server processes; the idea behind splitting up databases in storage groups is primarily to reduce the overhead that results from multiple sets of transaction log files.

As most of you'll recall, Exchange Server 2003 Standard Edition supported one storage group and two stores—one mailbox and one Public Folder store (when excluding the Recovery Storage Group, of course). Exchange Server 2003 Enterprise Edition supported a total of four storage groups, each containing a maximum of five store databases. The limit of a database in Exchange Server 2003 Standard Edition was 16GB (although raised to 75GB when Exchange 2003 Service Pack 2 was applied). There was no limit on a database in Exchange Server 2003 Enterprise Edition; well, actually, there was a 16 terabyte limit, but this limit was caused by hardware.

As we explained in Chapter 2, Exchange Server 2007 comes in two flavors: a Standard Edition and an Enterprise Edition, just like previous versions of Exchange. The mailbox server in Exchange Server 2007 Standard Edition supports a total of five storage groups and five databases. Unlike Exchange 2003 and previous versions of Exchange, there's no longer a database storage limit in the Standard Edition.

The mailbox server in the Exchange 2007 Enterprise Edition supports up to 50 storage groups and a maximum of 50 databases per server. Exchange 2007 allows you to create up to five databases in each storage group, as is the case with Exchange 2003, but best practice is to create one database per storage group. So, why should you have a one-to-one relationship between storage groups and databases? That's primarily because you'll be up and running a lot faster when dealing with disaster recovery scenarios and the like.

As was the case with Exchange 2003, it's still okay to keep all storage groups on the same spindles, but in terms of performance, it's better to keep them separated—although that would be quite unrealistic for most organizations that were using, for example, 30 storage groups!

Local and Cluster Continuous Replication

Exchange Server 2007 finally has native support for continuous replication, which is a functionality that will make it possible to keep a second copy of a database held in a particular storage group. The second copy of a database will be updated using log file shipping and log file replay. The idea with keeping a second copy of a database is, of course, to get up and running in a couple of minutes by being able to switch to the second database with just a couple of mouse clicks (or CMDlets), should the original database crash or get corrupted. Having a second constantly updated copy of a database also means you don't have to perform a full backup of the database as often as you used to. With local continuous replication or cluster continuous replication deployed, you could, for example, take a weekly backup instead of a daily one, which is the typical backup schedule.

The new continuous replication functionality can be enabled for storage groups on a single Exchange 2007 mailbox server (known as *local continuous replication*), and it can also be used with an Exchange 2007 mailbox cluster (known as a *clustered continuous replication setup*). We won't dive into the details of how you enable, configure, and manage this functionality in this chapter; we cover them in depth in Chapter 8.

Creating a New Storage Group

Let's take a look at how you create a new storage group in Exchange Server 2007:

1. Open the Exchange Management Console and expand the **Server Configuration** work center node, then select the **Mailbox** subnode.

2. Now click **New Storage Group** in the **Action pane**.

3. The **New Storage Group Wizard** shown in Figure 4.2 will appear. Here you'll need to provide a name for the new storage group as well as specify the location for the transaction log files and the system files. Do so by clicking the **Browse** buttons, then click **New**.

NOTE

You also have the option of enabling local continuous replication for the storage group by putting a check mark in the **Enable Continuous Replication for this storage group** box. If you don't do so while creating the storage group, you can easily do so later.

---

4. On the **Completion** page, you can see whether or not the storage group was created successfully, as well as the CMDlet code required to create the storage group using the Exchange Management Shell (EMS). Click **Finish** to exit the wizard (see Figure 4.3).

Figure 4.2 Creating a New Storage Group

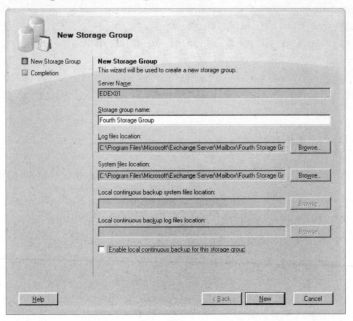

Figure 4.3 Creation of New Storage Group Completed Successfully

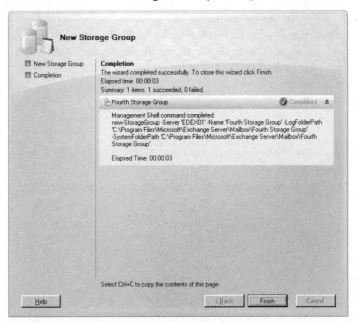

NOTE

As you can see in Figure 4.3, you can also create a new storage group via the EMS using the *New-StorageGroup* CMDlet. For additional information about the *New-StorageGroup* CMDlet, type **Get-Help New-StorageGroup** in the EMS.

Now let's try to open the Properties page for a storage group so that we can see what can be configured here (see Figure 4.4). It looks as though not much can be configured from here; actually, you can only change the name of the respective storage group as well as enable or disable circular logging. Most of us know circular logging, but for the few readers who don't, this is a feature that, when enabled, will allow Exchange to overwrite the transaction log files. This will reduce disk space used by the log files and is a best practice when you, for example, move a large group of mailboxes from one storage group to another. But under normal circumstances, you should keep this feature disabled; enabling it will limit your capability of restoring all data in a database doing a disaster recovery. Here's the reason that this is so: As we already mentioned, enabling the feature will allow Exchange to overwrite the log files every time a new file is generated. This means that you'll only be able to restore data up to the last full backup of a database, and if you do this, say, each night and the database crashes and is corrupted in the afternoon, you'll want be able to restore any data generated in the database between the last full backup and the time of the disaster. So, we repeat: Unless you know what you're doing, keep this feature disabled.

Figure 4.4 The Properties Page of a Storage Group

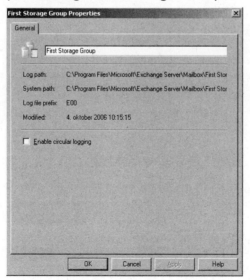

Moving a Storage Group

At times you might need to move a given storage group from one location to another. To do so you need to perform the following steps:

1. In the Exchange Management Console, click the **Server Configuration** work center node, then select the **Mailbox Server** subnode.

2. Now click the **storage group** you want to move and select **Move Storage Group** in the **Action pane**. Alternatively, you can right-click the respective **storage group** and select **Move Storage Group** from the context menu.

3. In the **Move Storage Files Wizard**, click the **Browse** button and specify the new location for the log and system files, then click **Move** (see Figure 4.5).

Figure 4.5 Moving a Storage Group

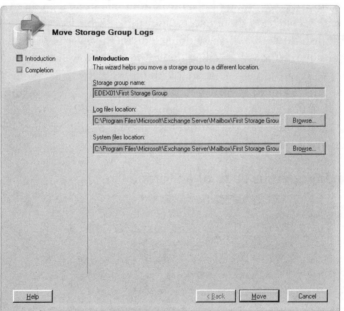

Removing a Storage Group

Removing a storage group is perhaps the simplest task of all, but bear in mind that you'll need to delete any mailbox and/or Public Folder databases contained in the storage group before you do so. When you're ready, perform the following steps:

1. In the Exchange Management Console, click the **Server Configuration** work center node, then select the **Mailbox Server** subnode.

2. Now click the **storage group** you want to delete and select **Remove** in the **Action pane**. Alternatively, you can right-click the respective **storage group** and select **Remove** from the context menu.

3. You'll now be asked whether you're sure that you want to remove the storage group. Click **Yes**.

4. When the storage group has been removed, you will get a warning stating that you need to manually remove the Storage Group folder and any log files beneath it (see Figure 4.6). Click **OK**.

Figure 4.6 Storage Group Removal Warning

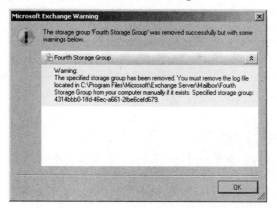

NOTE

If you want to remove a storage group using the EMS, you can do so using the *Remove-StorageGroup* CMDlet. To get a list of the available parameters, type **Get-Help Remove-StorageGroup** in the EMS.

Managing Exchange 2007 Mailbox Databases

As is the case with previous versions of Exchange, databases in Exchange Server 2007 are still based on the Extensible Storage Engine (ESE). The purpose of ESE is to provide an interface to the underlying database structure, which is responsible for managing changes made to the database (more specifically, the .EDB file). To do so, ESE uses transaction log files so that a database is kept in a reliable state. It does so by writing any changes made to a database (for example, via an Outlook MAPI client) first to one or more transaction log files and only thereafter to the database itself.

SOME INDEPENDENT ADVICE

During the early development stages of Exchange Server 2007 (which, back then, was code-named Exchange 12 or simply E12) there were serious plans about moving away from the ESE (which, formerly known as the Joint Engine Technology, or JET, is nothing more than a heavily modified Access database) to a new SQL database. These plans were dropped relatively fast. So, why were the plans about moving to a SQL database dropped in the first place? The decision was based on many factors, but the primary reason was customers. Staying with JET would mean that customers would not be faced with the migration work associated with moving to a new store, which is perhaps a good thing when you look at all the other architectural changes that have been made to the product. Will the next version of Exchange (code-named E14) use a SQL database? We don't know, but there's a good chance ESE won't be replaced with SQL before E15 (yes, that's right, the version *after* E14!).

Saying Goodbye to the Streaming Media File (.STM)

In Exchange Server 2000 and 2003 a database is made up of 2 files: an .EDB file and an .STM file. The purpose of the streaming file (.STM) is, as many of you might be aware, to house raw Internet content message streams as defined in Request for Comment (RFC) 822. Since the .EDB file isn't very suitable for storing raw Internet content message streams, the idea of introducing the .STM file was understandable, but with Exchange Server 2007 the .STM file has been removed, together with the Exchange Installable File System (ExIFS). The reasoning behind this decision was to reduce the overall I/O footprint for Exchange Server 2007.

What about Support for Single-Instance Storage?

As is the case with previous versions of Exchange, Exchange Server 2007 maintains single-instance storage (SIS) of messages. That means that if a message is sent to one recipient and it is copied to 20 other recipients residing in the same mailbox store, Exchange Server 2007 maintains only one copy of the message in its database. Exchange Server 2007 will instead create pointers to the message, and these pointers will link both the original recipient and the 20 additional recipients to the original message. If the original recipient and the 20 additional recipients are moved to another mailbox store, only one copy of the message is maintained in the new mailbox store. Since SIS hasn't changed since Exchange Server 2003, we won't go into this technology in depth but instead refer you to MS KB article 175481 (http://support.microsoft.com/kb/175481) if you want to learn more.

New Size for Transaction Log Files

Another improvement regarding storage changes in Exchange Server 2007 is that the transaction log files now are 1MB instead of 5MB, as was the case in previous version of Exchange. What's the reason behind this decision? In previous versions of Exchange, if a crash destroyed the last few log files that hadn't yet been committed to the database, you would need to restore or repair the database to have it mounted again. Exchange Server 2007 introduces a new feature called *lost log resilience*, or LLR for short, which will hold the last few log files in memory until the database is shut down. This means that you'll never have a case where part of log file 5, for example, has been written to the database, but part of log file 4 hasn't. The benefit of this feature is that if you don't mind losing the last few log files, you can tell Exchange to simply throw away the data and mount the database.

The reason that the log files have been reduced to 1MB is to reduce LLR exposure. Now if you lose the last log, it costs up to 1MB of the most recent data instead of 5MB.

Another improvement worth mentioning in regard to transaction log files in Exchange Server 2007 is that the log file sequence numbers now can go above 1 million. As some of you might be aware, previous versions of Exchange had a limit of 1 million, so if a database had been running long enough to generate a million logs, you had to shut it down and start over from log #1 ("resetting the log sequence"). This would happen every few years, for most databases. With the smaller log sizes and the increasing number of messages passing through most databases, the Exchange Product group decided that 4 billion would be a better maximum log number.

> **NOTE**
>
> It's a best practice to separate database and transaction log files on different disk spindles. This makes it easier to recover your data if there's a disk failure and provides the best overall performance (by optimizing disk I/O).

Creating a New Mailbox Database

Creating a new mailbox database is straightforward; you do so by performing the following steps:

1. In the EMC, click the **Server Configuration** work center node, and then select the **Mailbox Server** subnode.

2. Now select the **storage group** in which you want to create the new mailbox database.

3. Select **New Mailbox Database** in the **Action pane**. Alternatively, you can right-click the respective **mailbox database** and select **New Mailbox Database** from the context menu.

4. Name the new mailbox database, specify the location where you want the .EDB file to be created, and then click **New** (see Figure 4.7).

Figure 4.7 Creating a New Mailbox Database

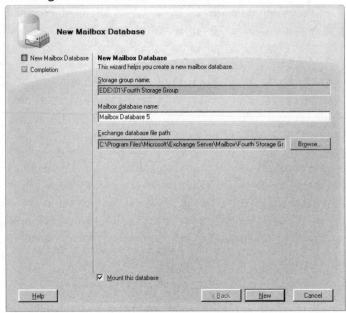

5. On the **Completion** page, click **Finish** to create (and, if selected in the previous screen) mount the new mailbox database (see Figure 4.8).

As shown in Figure 4.8, you can also create a new mailbox database using the *New-MailboxDatabase* CMDlet. To get a list of available parameters, type **Get-Help New-MailboxDatabase**.

Now that we have created a new mailbox database, let's take a look at the Properties page for such a database. We do so by selecting the database and clicking **Properties** in the Action pane.

Figure 4.8 The New Mailbox Database Completion Page

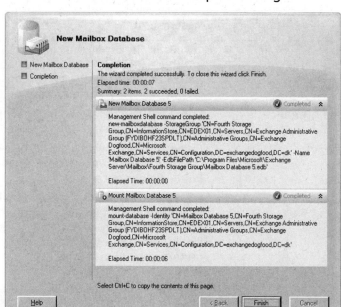

The first tab is General. Here we can rename the mailbox database as well as see information such as database copy path (only available when local continuous replication has been enabled for the storage group containing the particular database), last full backup, and status (mounted or dismounted) as well as the last time a modification was made. In addition, you have the option of enabling Journal Recipient, used to specify the mailbox that should receive a copy of all messages sent to and from mailboxes in a particular mailbox database. We'll talk much more about journaling in Chapter 6.

As is the case with Exchange Server 2003, we also have the option of specifying the maintenance schedule, which is the time where the Exchange maintenance tasks will run. The Exchange maintenance tasks are a series of operations that are performed to ensure logical consistency in a database.

If you're planning to have multiple storage groups with each separate set of databases on a single Exchange 2007 mailbox server, it's recommended that you configure the maintenance schedule for each database so that they don't overlap. In addition, this schedule should be configured so that it doesn't conflict with your backup schedule.

The Exchange database maintenance tasks consist of 10 operations, which are listed in Table 4.1.

Table 4.1 Exchange 2007 Database Maintenance Tasks

Tasks	Description
Purge mailbox and Public Folder database indexes	Purges indices that the client creates in database tables to be used for views; those that have not been used for a specified time are cleaned up when this subtask occurs.
Tombstone maintenance	Compacts the deleted message information that is used for local and Public Folder replication.
Dumpster cleanup	Cleans up any messages that have passed their deleted item retention date on mailbox and Public Folder databases.
Public Folder expiry	Expired messages that are in Public folders and that are older than a specified time value. The setup for message expiration is on the Age Limits tab in the public information store container in the Microsoft Exchange Server Administrator program.
Age folder tombstone	Removes folder tombstone entries that are older than a specified time (the default is 180 days). Folder tombstone information is used by public folder replication. The aging prevents the folder tombstone list from growing without limits.
Folder conflict cleanup	Cleans up any conflicts on messages that have been modified by two different users at the same time and that have resulted in the given message being in conflict.
Update server versions	Updates the version information as necessary for any Public Folder databases that contain a replica of a system configuration folder.
Secure folders cleanup	Checks secure folders to ensure that no message has a reference count of zero, indicating no folder currently has a reference to the particular message.
Site folder check	Used by Public Folder databases to ensure that no duplicate site folders exist.
Deleted mailbox cleanup	Checks Active Directory to determine whether there are any deleted mailboxes. The information store performs an Active Directory lookup for each user in the MDB.

On the General tab (see Figure 4.9), you also have the option of configuring the database not to mount during startup and enable the **This database can be overwritten by a restore** option, which is used when you need to restore a database from backup. Nothing has changed here compared with Exchange Server 2003.

Figure 4.9 The General Tab on the Properties Page for a Mailbox Database

Let's move on to the Limits tab (see Figure 4.10). As is also the case with Exchange Server 2003, we here have the option of configuring the storage limit for the mailboxes in the particular mailbox database. Note that the options "Issue warning at (KB)," "Prohibit send at (KB)," and "Prohibit send and receive at (KB)" in Exchange Server 2007 are by default set drastically higher (around 2GB) than was the case in Exchange Server 2003. Again, this is to take advantage of the Exchange 2007 64-bit architecture.

On this tab you also have the option of changing the warning message interval and the deletion settings. Note that the "Keep deleted items for (days)" and "Keep Deleted mailboxes for (days)" options have other default settings than was the case in Exchange Server 2003. The end user can now retrieve items from the dumpster 14 days back, and any deleted mailboxes will not be purged before approximately a month passes, meaning that the reason for restoring a database to retrieve data in a deleted mailbox will be reduced even further.

Now it's time to take a look at what's hiding under the Client Settings tab. As you can see in Figure 4.11, this is the place where you can specify the public folder database as well as the offline address book (OAB) that should be the default for mailboxes in the particular mailbox database.

Figure 4.10 The Limits Tab on the Properties Page for a Mailbox Database

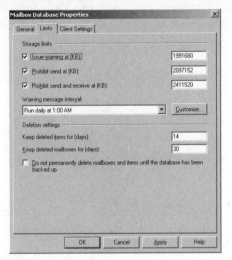

NOTE

The OAB is an address book that Outlook 2003 and 2007 download to the local computer (client). With the OAB file held locally on the client, it doesn't need to have access to Active Directory to browse and look up recipients in the GAL. Outlook 2003 and 2007 also use the OAB when working in cached mode, which means that it can take up to 24 hours before newly created mailbox-enabled recipients can be looked up by clients working in cached mode. OAB files can still be distributed using Public Folders (used by legacy clients such as Outlook 98, 2000, and 2003), but in Exchange 2007, OAB distribution is Web based.

Exchange 2007 Public Folder Databases

Public Folders are still supported in Exchange Server 2007, but bear in mind that they have been deemphasized, which means that there's a good chance they won't be included in the next version of Exchange (currently code-named E14). With this in mind, it's a good idea to start thinking about migrating to another solution, such as SharePoint.

Figure 4.11 The Client Settings Tab on the Properties Page for a Mailbox Database

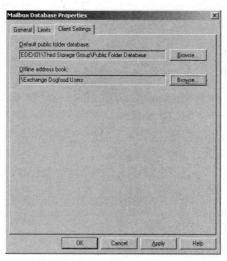

A Public Folder database is a database used to store Public Folders. The data contained in a Public Folder can be accessed by any mailbox-enabled users as long as they have the appropriate permissions. The Public Folders in the Public Folder database can exist as single copies or multiple copies (also referred to as *replicas*). Using replicas, you can configure Public Folders to be synchronized between specified servers so that they always are up to date, no matter which mailbox server a given client is connected to. Since a Public Folder isn't replicated automatically, you must configure which Public Folder database should contain a replica of any given Public Folder.

Because Public Folders are widely used by organizations for sharing documents, calendars, contacts, and tasks and for archiving distribution lists, one would think that you could administer these folders from within the EMC, but unfortunately the administration tasks you can do from within the EMC are extremely limited. So, if you need to do tasks other than create, delete, and move Public Folder databases as well as configure limits and the like, you will, depending on the specific task, need to do so using the EMS, an Outlook client, or System Manager on an Exchange 2003 Server that's still part of the Exchange organization.

The following step-by-step instructions tell you how to perform the most common tasks regarding administration of Public Folders.

Creating a New Public Folder Database

Creating a new Public Folder database is just as straightforward as creating a mailbox database. It is done by performing the following steps:

1. In the Exchange Management Console, click the **Server Configuration** work center node, then select the **Mailbox Server** subnode.

2. Now click the **storage group** in which you want to create the database and select **New Public Folder Database** in the **Action pane**. Alternatively, you can right-click the respective **storage group** and select **New Public Folder Database** from the context menu.

3. In the **New Public Folder Database Wizard**, enter a name for the database, then click the **Browse** button and specify the location for the .EDB file.

4. Finally, click **New** (see Figure 4.12).

Figure 4.12 Creating a New Public Folder Database

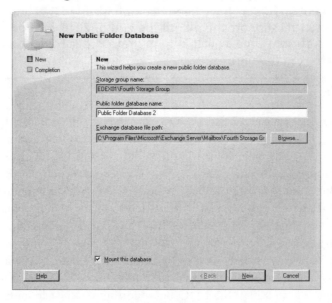

NOTE

You can also create a new Public Folder database via the EMS using the *New-PublicFolderDatabase* CMDlet.

Now that we have created a new Public Folder database, let's take a look at the Properties page for the database.

The General tab is almost identical to that of a mailbox database, so let's move on and click the **Replication** tab. As you can see in Figure 4.13, you can specify the Public Folder database replication interval, the replication interval for "Always Run" (in minutes), and the replication message size limit. The replication intervals used to configure the interval at which replication of Public Folders or content may occur and the Replication interval for "Always Run" (minutes) is used to define what "always run" means (by default, it's 15 minutes).

The "Replication message size limit (KB)" setting is used to specify the size of a replication message. If it's set to a large value, smaller messages can be aggregated into a single replication messages as high as the defined value.

Unless you have a specific reason for changing these settings, we recommend you leave the defaults intact.

Figure 4.13 The Replication Tab on the Properties Page of a Public Folder Database

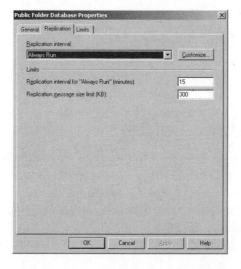

Let's take a look at what's hiding under the Limits tab. As you can see in Figure 4.14, this is the place where we configure the storage limits for a Public Folder database. As is the case with the default storage limits for a mailbox database, the Public Folder database limits are set much higher than was the case in previous Exchange versions. When the database is approximately 2GB in size, a warning will be generated, and when it's over 2GB, end users will be prohibited from posting messages to a Public Folder in the Public Folder database. The maximum item size is approximately 10MB.

Note that the "Keep deleted items for (days)" option is configured to 14 days, just as is the case for a mailbox database—again, a much higher setting than in previous versions of Exchange.

Note that you also have the option of setting an age limit for the Public Folders that exists in the particular Public Folder database.

Figure 4.14 The Public Folder Database Properties Page

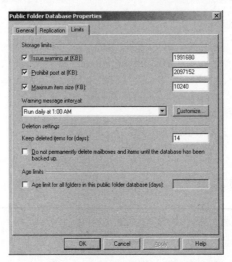

These settings can also be set using either CMDlets or the Exchange 2003 System Manager.

Creating a Public Folder

You can create a Public Folder using the EMS, an Outlook MAPI client, or the System Manager on an Exchange 2003 Server that still exists in the Exchange organization.

Creating a public folder using the EMS is done using the *New-PublicFolder* CMDlet. So, if for example we wanted to create a new Public Folder named *Finance*, we would need to type the following command in the EMS:

```
New-PublicFolder -Name Finance
```

followed by pressing **Enter** (see Figure 4.15).

If you still have an Exchange 2003 Server in your Exchange organization, you can also create new Public Folders using the System Manager by following these steps:

Figure 4.15 Creating a New Public Folder via the Exchange Management Shell

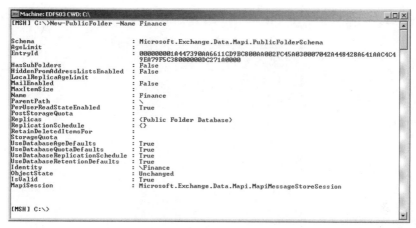

1. On the respective Exchange 2003 server, open the System Manager by clicking **Start | All Programs | Microsoft Exchange | Exchange System Manager**.

2. Drill down to and expand the **Folders** node.

3. Depending on whether you want to create a top-level folder or a child node, right-click the **Public Folders** or the top-level folder in which you want to create the new Public Folder, then choose **New | Public Folder** in the context menu (see Figure 4.16).

Figure 4.16 Selecting a Public Folder Store in the Exchange 2003 System Manager

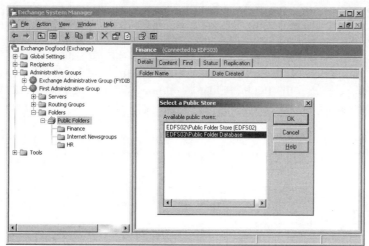

4.   Give the new Public Folder a name and click **OK** (see Figure 4.17).

Figure 4.17 The General Tab on the Properties Page of a Public Folder

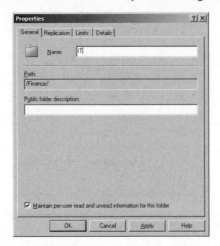

Finally, you create Public Folders using an Outlook MAPI client, although this requires your user account got the appropriate permissions to do so. You do so by using the following steps:

1.   Open an Outlook MAPI client (in this case, Outlook 2007).

2.   If it's not already selected, click the yellow **Folder List** icon in the lower-left corner.

3.   Expand **Public Folders** |**All Public Folders**.

4.   Depending on whether you want to create a top-level or a child-level folder, right-click either **All Public Folders** or the top-level folder in which you want to create the Public Folder.

5.   In the context menu, select **New Folder**.

6.   In the **Create New Folder** window, type a name for the new folder and specify the type of data the Public Folder should be used for, then click **OK** (see Figure 4.18).

If you later want to remove a Public Folder, you can do so using the *Remove-PublicFolder* CMDlet, the Exchange 2003 System Manager, or an Outlook MAPI client.

Figure 4.18 Creating a New Public Folder Using Outlook 2007

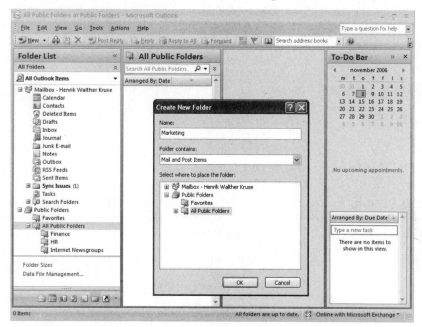

NOTE

To get a list of the Public Folders that exist in the Public Folder hierarchy, use the *Get-PublicfolderStatistics* CMDlet.

Administering Public Folder Permission Settings

As is the case with previous versions of Exchange, Exchange Server 2007 allows you to configure Public Folder client permissions as well as administrative rights. Client permissions are used to grant user accounts access to a Public Folder, and you can do so using a preconfigured set of permissions, or you can set up custom permissions. Administrative rights are used to specify users or groups that should be allowed to use the EMS or Exchange 2003 System Manager or to change the replication limits as well as other settings for a Public Folder.

You can configure client permission settings for a Public Folder using the EMS, the Exchange 2003 System Manager, or an Outlook MAPI client.

To give or remove client permissions using the EMS, you'll need to use the *Add-PublicFolderClientPermission* and/or *Remove-PublicFolderClientPermission* CMDlets. So, to give a user account named *HEW* belonging to a domain named *Exchangedogfood.dk* permissions to create items in a Public Folder called *Finance* on a server called *EDFS03*, we would need to use the following command:

```
Add-PublicFolderClientPermission -Identity \"Finance" -User HEW -AccessRights
CreateItems -Server "EDSF03"
```

To remove this permission again, you would need to type:

```
Remove-PublicFolderClientPermission -Identity \"Finance" -User HEW -AccessRights
CreateItems -Server "EDSF03"
```

The available parameters for the *Add-PublicFolderClientPermission* and *Remove-PublicFolderClientPermission* CMDlets are listed in Table 4.2.

Table 4.2 Public Folder Client Permission Parameters

Parameter	Description
AccessRights	This parameter is used to specify the rights you want to add to the Public Folder (such as *CreateItems* or *DeleteOwnedItems*).
DomainController	This parameter is used to specify the domain controller to use to write this configuration change to Active Directory. You need to use the FQDN of the DC to be used. *Note:* This parameter is optional.
Identity	This parameter is used to specify a unique identifier (name) for the Public Folder.
User	This parameter is used to specify the UPN, domain/user, or alias of the user that should be granted rights to the public folder.
Server	This parameter is used to specify the server on which the selected operations should be performed.

In addition, as is also the case with previous versions of Exchange, you can use the Exchange 2003 System Manager (if you still have an Exchange 2003 server in your Exchange organization) or an Outlook MAPI client to set client permissions on a Public Folder.

To set client permissions on a Public Folder using the Exchange 2003 System Manager, use the following steps:

1. On the respective Exchange 2003 server, open the System Manager by clicking **Start | All Programs | Microsoft Exchange | Exchange System Manager**.

2. Drill down to the **Folders** and expand the **Public Folders** node.

3. Now right-click the **Public Folder** for which you want to add or remove client permissions, then select **Properties**.

4. Click the **Permissions** tab, as shown in Figure 4.19.

5. Click the **Client Permissions** button. Here you can see each user that already has been granted permissions on the Public Folder.

Figure 4.19 The Permissions Tab on the Properties Page of a Public Folder in Exchange 2003 System Manager

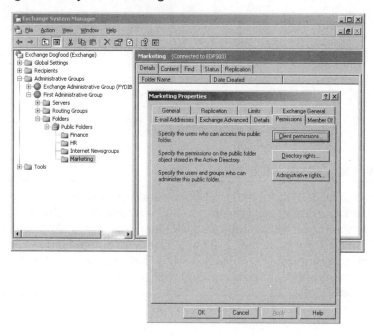

6. Click **Add** and add the respective user(s) to the client permission list, then click **OK**.

7. Now select the user(s) you just added and then grant the type of permission you want the user to have by using the **Roles** drop-down box or by ticking the different permissions individually (see Figure 4.20).

8. Click **OK** twice and close the Exchange 2003 System Manager.

Figure 4.20 Public Folder Client Permissions

SOME INDEPENDENT ADVICE

If you have a large Public Folder hierarchy and on a relatively frequent basis you need to grant user permissions to the Public Folders in the hierarchy, we recommend you use the Manage Public Folder Settings Wizard, which was introduced in Exchange Server 2003 SP2. This wizard (see Figure 4.21) makes it a breeze to grant user permissions to the folders in your Public Folder hierarchy, but it can also be used to modify replica lists and more.

Figure 4.21 The Manage Public Folder Settings Wizard

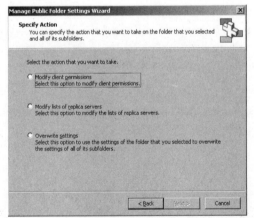

You launch the Manage Public Folder Settings Wizard by right-clicking a top Public Folder, then selecting **Manage Settings** in the context menu. You can read more about this wizard in one of our articles for MSExchange.org at www.msexchange.org/tutorials/Public-Folder-Improvements-Exchange-2003-Service-Pack-2.html.

Adding client permissions using an Outlook MAPI client is done using the following steps:

1. Open the Outlook MAPI client (in this case Outlook 2007).

2. If it's not already selected, click the yellow **Folder List** icon in the lower-left corner.

3. Expand **Public Folders | All Public Folders**.

4. Right-click the respective **Public Folder** and select **Change Sharing Permissions** in the context menu.

> **NOTE**
>
> If you don't have the option of choosing **Change Sharing Permissions** in the context menu, your user account most likely doesn't have administrative permissions for that particular Public Folder.

5. Under the **Permissions** tab, click **Add** and add the respective user(s), then click **OK** (see Figure 4.22).

Figure 4.22 The Permissions Tab on the Properties Page of a Public Folder in Outlook 2007

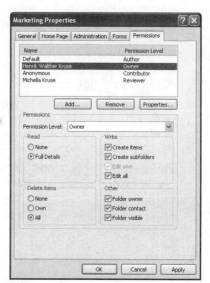

6.   Now grant the user(s) the required permissions, either by using the **Permission Level** drop-down box or by ticking the permissions individually.

7.   Finally, click **OK**.

To add or remove Public Folder Administrative permissions, you can use the *Add-PublicFolderAdministrativePermission* and *Remove-PublicFolderAdministrativePermission* CMDlets.

To give a user account named *HEW* belonging to a domain named *Exchangedogfood.dk* permissions to modify the ACL for a Public Folder called *Finance* on a server called *EDFS03*, we would need to use the following command:

```
Add-PublicFolderAdministrativePermission -Identity \"Finance" -User HEW -
AccessRights ModifyPublicFolderACL -Server "EDSF03"
```

To remove this permission, again you would need to type:

```
Remove-PublicFolderAdministrativePermission -Identity \"Finance" -User HEW -
ModifyPublicFolderACL ModifyPublicFolderACL -Server "EDSF03"
```

Table 4.3 lists the parameters that are relevant to the *PublicFolderAdministrativePermission* and *Remove-PublicFolderAdministrativePermission* CMDlets.

Table 4.3 Public Folder Administrative Permission Parameters

Parameter	Description
AccessRights	This parameter is used to specify the rights to be added. Available values are: *None* *ModifyPublicFolderACL* *ModifyPublicFolderAdminACL* *ModifyPublicFolderDeletedItemRetention* *ModifyPublicFolderExpiry* *ModifyPublicFolderQuotas* *ModifyPublicFolderReplicaList* *AdministerInformationStore* *ViewInformationStore* *AllStoreRights* *AllExtendedRights*
DomainController	This parameter is used to specify the domain controller to use to write this configuration change to Active Directory. You need to use the FQDN of the DC to be used. *Note:* This parameter is optional.
Identity	This parameter is used to specify a unique identifier (name) for the Public Folder.
Instance	This parameter is used to enable passing an entire object to the command to be processed; primarily used in scripts where an entire object must be passed to the command.

Continued

Table 4.3 continued Public Folder Administrative Permission Parameters

Parameter	Description
Owner	This parameter specifies the NT Owner access control list (ACL) on the object. Available values are the user principal name (UPN), domain/user, or alias.
User	This parameter is used to specify the UPN, domain/user, or alias of the user that should be granted rights to the Public Folder.
Deny	This parameter is used to deny permission to the respective Public Folder.
InheritanceType	This parameter is used to specify the type of inheritance. Available values are: None All Descendents SelfAndChildren Children
Server	This parameter is used to specify the server on which the selected operations should be performed.

As is also the case with the user permissions, you can configure administrative permissions using the Exchange 2003 System Manager. You do so by following these steps:

1. On the respective Exchange 2003 Server, open the System Manager by clicking **Start | All Programs | Microsoft Exchange | Exchange System Manager**.

2. Drill down to the **Folders** and expand the **Public Folders** node.

3. Now right-click the Public Folder for which you want to add or remove administrative permissions, then select **Properties**.

4. Click the **Permissions** tab.

5. Click the **Administrative Rights** button. Here you can see each user that has already been granted permissions to administer the Public Folder.

6. Click **Add**, add the respective user(s) to the administrative permission list (see Figure 4.23), and then click **OK**.

7. Now select the **user(s)** you just added, then grant the type of administrative permission you want the user to have. You do so by ticking the respective permission boxes under **Permissions for Administrator**.

Figure 4.23 Administrative Rights on a Public Folder

8. Finally, click **OK** and exit the Exchange 2003 System Manager.

Managing Public Folder Replica Settings

Another feature missing in the Exchange 2007 Management Console is the option of configuring Public Folder replication settings. This also has to be done using either the EMS or an Exchange 2003 server that's still part of your Exchange organization.

To stop or resume Public Folder replication, you can use the *Stop-PublicFolderReplication* and *Resume-PublicFolderReplication* CMDlets, respectively.

To add Public Folder databases to or remove them from a replica list, you'll need to use the Exchange 2003 System Manager.

Mail-Enabling a Public Folder

You might run into situations where you want to mail-enable a Public Folder—perhaps you'll want your users to be able to send messages to the folder in addition to posting messages. Because Public Folders by default are not mail-enabled, you need to mail-enable them using either the *Enable-MailPublicFolder* CMDlet or an Exchange 2003 System Manager. To mail-enable the Finance Public Folder we created earlier using the *Enable-MailPublicFolder* CMDlet, we would need to type:

```
Enable-MailPublicFolder -Identity "\Finance" followed by Enter
```

If you don't want the Public Folder to appear in the GAL, you would need to include the *HiddenFromAddressListsEnabled* parameter, and the command would look like the following:

```
Enable-MailPublicFolder -Identity "\Finance"  -HiddenFromAddressListsEnabled
```

Now press **Enter**.

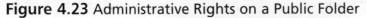

NOTE

You need to create a Public Folder before you can mail-enable it.

To get a list of the mail-enabled Public Folders in your organization, you can use the *Get-MailPublicFolder* CMDlet. To get information for a specific mail-enabled Public Folder, type **Get-MailPublicFolder –Identity <public_folder>**.

If you don't specify an SMTP address when you mail-enable a Public Folder, it will use the name of the Public Folder. So, if the Public Folder is called *Finance* and the domain is *Exchangedogfood.dk*, the address will be *finance@exchangedogfood.dk*. If you want to use another primary SMTP address, you need to set it using the *Set-MailPublicFolder* CMDlet. The command would then be:

```
Set-MailPublicFolder -Identity "\Finance" -PrimarySmtpAddress:
economy@exchangedogfood.dk
```

Now press **Enter**.

Many other *Set-MailPublicFolder* CMDlet parameters are available. We won't go into details on each of them, but instead we list each of them with a short description in Table 4.4.

Table 4.4 Parameters Available for a Mail-Enabled Public Folder

Parameter	Description
AcceptMessagesOnlyFrom	Accept messages only if sent by the specified recipients.
AcceptMessagesOnlyFromDLMembers	Accepts messages sent to the DL only if sent by DL members.
Alias	Used to specify the alias (mail nickname) of the Public Folder. If not specified, it is stamped as the Public Folder Name. The string must comply with RFC 2821 requirements for valid "local part" SMTP addresses.
Contacts	Specifies the contacts for the Public Folder.
CustomAttribute (1-15)	Used to specify a custom attribute.
DeliverToMailboxAndForward	Specifies whether or not e-mail will be sent to a forwarding address.
DisplayName	Specifies the display name of the Public Folder Proxy Object.
DomainController	Specifies which DC to connect to.
EmailAddresses	Proxy addresses. Example: user@exchangedogfood.dk.

Continued

Table 4.4 continued Parameters Available for a Mail-Enabled Public Folder

Parameter	Description
EmailAddressPolicyEnabled	Used to have a recipient policy applied to the Public Folder.
ForwardingAddress	Delivery options: Sets the forwarding address for the folder.
GrantSendOnBehalfTo	Distinguished name of other mailboxes that can send on behalf of this folder.
HiddenFromAddressListsEnabled	Specifies whether or not the mailbox is viewable from address lists.
Instance	This is an actual ADObject instance that is piped to and consumed by the task.
MaxReceiveSize	This parameter specifies the maximum size of e-mail messages that can be received, from 1KB to 2,097,151KB. If not specified, there is no limit.
MaxSendSize	This parameter specifies the maximum size of e-mail messages that can be sent, from 1KB to 2,097,151KB. If not specified, there is no limit.
Name	Used to specify the name of the Public Folder.
PrimarySmtpAddress	Used to specify the primary SMTP address to be used by the Public Folder.
PublicFolderType	Used to specify the type of Public Folder.
RejectMessagesFrom	Used to specify SMTP addresses that should not be allowed to send messages to the Public Folder.
RejectMessagesFromDLMembers	Used to specify distribution lists that should not be allowed to send to this Public Folder.
RequireSenderAuthenticationEnabled	Specifies whether or not senders must be authenticated.
SimpleDisplayName	Used to specify a simple (a.k.a. friendly) display name.
WindowsEmailAddress	An e-mail address in the format E-mailAddress@exchangedogfood.dk.

NOTE

If you want to remove the mail attributes from a mail-enabled public folder, use the *Disable-MailPublicFolder* CMDlet.

To mail-enable a Public Folder using an Exchange 2003 System Manager, perform the following steps:

1. On the respective Exchange 2003 Server open the System Manager by clicking **Start | All Programs | Microsoft Exchange | Exchange System Manager**.

2. Drill down to the **Folders** and expand the **Public Folders** node.

3. Now right-click the **Public Folder** you want to mail-enable, then select **Properties**.

4. Select the **E-mail Addresses** tab (see Figure 4.24).

Figure 4.24 The E-mail Addresses Tab on the Properties Page for a Public Folder

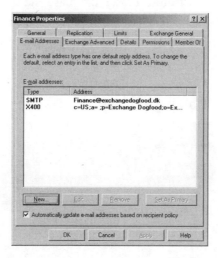

5. Click the **New** button, then click **SMTP Address**.

6. Type the SMTP address you want to assign to the Public Folder, then click **OK** twice and exit the **Exchange 2003 System Manager**.

> **NOTE**
>
> Features such as delivery restriction, Send on behalf, etc., can of course also
> be configured via the Exchange 2003 System Manager. You do so under the
> **Exchange General** tab.

Moving a Mailbox
or Public Folder Database

Moving either a mailbox or Public Folder database is very similar to moving a storage group.
You do so by performing the following steps:

1. In the Exchange Management Console, click the **Server Configuration** work
   center node, then select the **Mailbox Server** subnode.

2. Now click the **mailbox** or **Public Folder database** you want to move and select
   Move Database Files in the **Action pane**. Alternatively, you can right-click the
   respective **mailbox** or **Public folder database** and select **Move Database Files**
   from the context menu.

3. In the **Move Database Files Wizard**, click the **Browse** button and specify the
   new location of the .EDB file, then click **OK** and click **Move** (see Figure 4.25).

Figure 4.25 Moving a Database

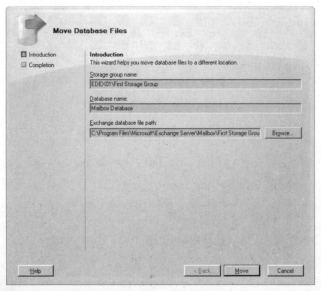

Removing a Mailbox or Public Folder Database

You might come across situations where you need to remove either a mailbox or Public folder database. You do so by performing the following steps:

1. In the Exchange Management Console, click the **Server Configuration** work center node, then select the **Mailbox Server** subnode.

2. Now click the **mailbox** or **Public Folder database** you want to remove and select **Remove** in the **Action pane**. Alternatively, you can right-click the respective **mailbox** or **Public Folder database** and select **Remove** from the context menu.

3. You will now be warned that the database file (.EDB file) needs to be removed manually. Click **OK** (see Figure 4.26).

Figure 4.26 Database Removal Warning

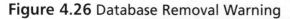

NOTE

To remove a mailbox or Public Folder database via the EMS, you can use the *Remove-MailboxDatabase* and *Remove-PublicFolderDatabase* CMDlets, respectively.

Managing Organizationwide Mailbox Server Configuration Settings

In addition to the features and functionality available at the mailbox server level, Exchange Server 2007 also has a feature set that is organizationwide. In this section we'll take a look at the feature set that can be applied to the entire Exchange Server 2007 organization.

If it's not already open, open the EMC and click the **Mailbox** node under the **Organization Configuration** work center in the navigation tree in the left side of the MMC console. This will bring us to a screen similar to the one shown in Figure 4.27.

Figure 4.27 The Address Lists Tab on the Organization Configuration Mailbox Node

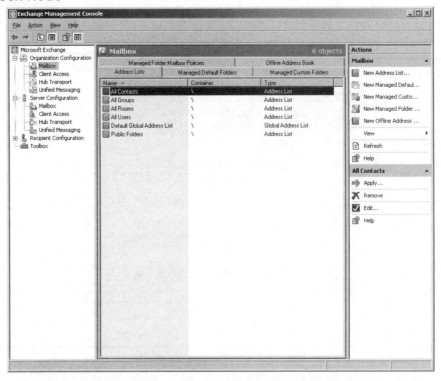

As you can see, a total of six tabs are available under the Mailbox node. We will go through each of them in the following sections.

Address Lists

The first tab is the Address Lists tab, on which all the default created address lists are listed. The purpose of address lists is to help you organize the different types of recipients within your Exchange organization so that they are listed in a meaningful way when your end users look up recipients in their mail clients. As you can see, we have an All Contacts list, which contains all mail contact objects within Active Directory. We have an All Groups list, which contains all distribution group objects. Then we have an All Rooms list, which is a type of list that didn't exist in Exchange Server 2000 or 2003, and there's a simple explanation why it is so. As you saw in Chapter 3 Exchange Server 2007 introduces a new type of mailbox, a so-called room mailbox, which basically is a mailbox that is used for room scheduling and not owned by a user. The All Rooms list contains all room mailboxes.

> **NOTE**
>
> There are two types of resource mailbox in Exchange Server 2007. One of them is the room mailbox; the other is the equipment mailbox (which is used to schedule equipment such as projectors and the like). Only the room mailboxes are listed in the All Rooms address list.

We also have an All Users list, which, as its name indicates, lists all mailbox user objects (including room and equipment mailboxes as well as linked, shared, and legacy mailboxes) within Active Directory. As in previous versions of Exchange, there is also a Default Global Address List (also known as the GAL), which lists all recipients within the Exchange organization. Finally, we have a Public Folders list, which surprisingly enough lists all Public Folders in the organization, if you have any.

Although the default address lists might be sufficient for some, they are far from enough for large organizations that have an Active Directory forest with multiple Active Directory domains. If this is the case, you might want to create additional address lists, which is done by following these steps:

1. Select the **Mailbox** subnode under the **Organization Configuration** work center node in the navigation tree to the left, then click **New Address List** in the **Action pane**. Alternatively, right-click the **Mailbox** subnode or somewhere in the white space in the **Work pane**.

2. Type a name for the new address list, then choose the container in which you want to create the address list (a backslash [\ ] creates it as a top address list), but you can also create it as a subaddress list to an existing one. Now specify the type of recipients that should be included in the address list. In this example, we choose **All recipient types**. When you have decided which one should be included, click **Next** (see Figure 4.28).

Figure 4.28 Creating a New Address List

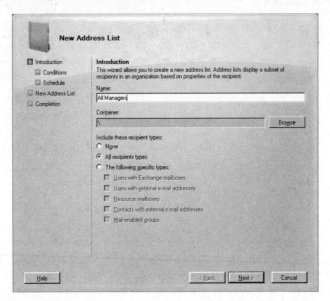

3.   We now have the option of selecting the conditions we want to associate with the new address list (see Figure 4.29). For the purposes of this example, we chose **Recipient is in a Department**. In **Step 2**, click the blue **specified** link.

Figure 4.29 Specifying the Conditions for the New Address List

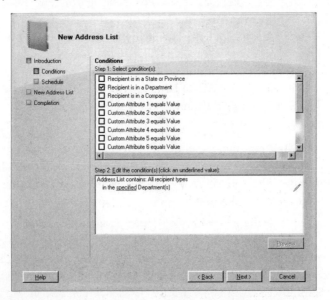

4. Type the name the **Department** field of the recipients you want to have listed in the address list. In this example, we want to list all recipients belonging to the management department. Click **Add** to add department(s) to the list (see Figure 4.30), then click **OK**.

Figure 4.30 Specifying the Department

5. Now click the **Preview** button to verify that the respective recipients are listed as in Figure 4.31, and then click **OK** again.

NOTE

You can also create an address list based on a custom recipient filter (also called an *OPath filter*), but doing so is only possible using the EMS. Once you've created an address list using a custom recipient filter, you can also only manage it via the EMS. To create an address list using a custom recipient filter, you need to use the following command: New-AddressList –Name <String> -RecipientFilter <String>.

For examples as well as a further explanation, see the Exchange 2007 Help File or type **Get-Help New-AddressList** in the EMS.

Figure 4.31 Address List Preview

6. We now have the option of specifying when the address list should be applied and the maximum length of time it is permitted to run. In this example, we will apply it immediately, but you could also schedule it to be applied sometime in the future. Click **Next** when you have decided when to apply the address list (see Figure 4.32).

Figure 4.32 Specifying When the Address List Should Be Applied

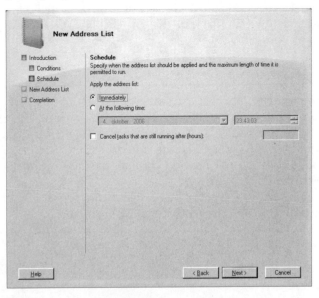

7. You now will see a **Configuration Summary**. Here you can see the type of recipients that will be included in the address list, and you can also see the recip-

ient filter. If everything looks good, click **New** to create and apply the list see (Figure 4.33).

Figure 4.33 The New Address List Summary Page

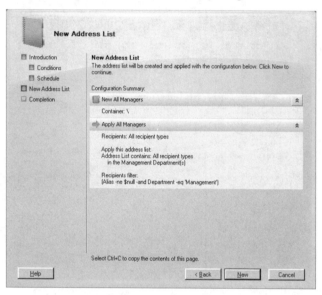

8. After a few seconds, the **New Address List Wizard** will have completed successfully, and you can then click **Finish** (see Figure 4.34).

Figure 4.34 The New Address List Completion Page

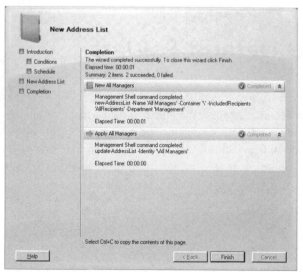

The address list has now been created as well as applied (unless you chose to schedule it), and you should be able to see it immediately in any mail client that is connected to the Exchange 2007 server. In Figure 4.35, we can see the list address list we just created via the OWA 2007 client.

Figure 4.35 Viewing the Address List Using OWA 2007

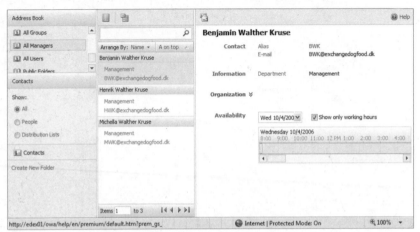

Any address list you create can also be edited later. You do this by selecting the respective **address list**, then clicking **Edit** in the **Action pane**. Alternatively, you can right-click the **address list** and select **Edit** in the context menu. You can also reapply or remove an address list using this method.

To create an address list using the EMS, you need to use the *New-AddressList* CMDlet. For a description of this CMDlet as well the available parameters, type **Get-Help New-AddressList** in the EMS.

Managed Default Folders

Under the Managed Default Folders tab (see Figure 4.36), we can manage the default mailbox folders (such as Inbox, Calendar, and Sent Items) by applying managed content settings to a specific folder or, if needed, the entire mailbox. For example, we would be able to apply a managed content setting to a default folder such as the Inbox so that particular types of items in this folder (and any subfolders) are either deleted or moved to another folder after, say, 15 days. If the items are deleted, we can even enable journaling (also called *archiving*) for the items, if required.

Figure 4.36 The Managed Default Folders Tab

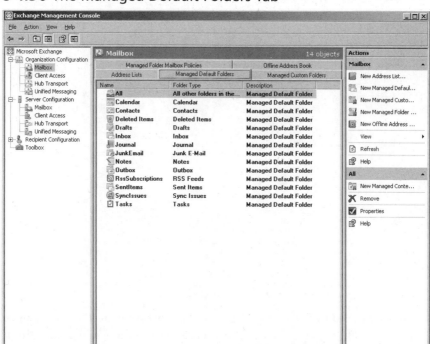

Since this is a new feature in Exchange that can be a bit difficult to understand, let's look at an example:

1. To apply managed content settings to a specific default folder, select the appropriate **default folder**, then click **New Managed Content Settings** in the **Action pane**. Alternatively, you can right-click **default folder**, then click **New Managed Content Settings** in the context menu.

2. In the **New Managed Content Settings Wizard**, type a name for the managed content settings (see Figure 4.37). This is merely the name that will be displayed in the EMC.

3. Select the type of messages these settings should apply to, then tick **Messages expire after (days)** and specify the number of days after which the messages will expire.

Figure 4.37 The New Managed Content Settings Introduction Page

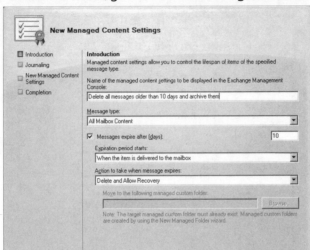

4. Now you need to select when the expiration period starts. Here you can choose between **When the item is delivered to the mailbox** and **When the item is moved to the folder**.

5. Finally, you need to decide what action should be taken when the message or item expires. Here you can choose among **Delete and Allow Recovery**, **Mark as Past Retention Limit**, **Move to a Managed Custom Folder**, **Move to the Deleted Items Folder**, and **Permanently Delete**. If you choose the action **Move to a Managed Custom Folder**, you also need to specify the managed custom folder by clicking the **Browse** button. (Note that the managed custom folder must already exist!)

6. Now click **Next**.

7. We now have the option of enabling journaling by putting a check mark in **Forward copies to:** and selecting a mailbox that should be used for journaling. In addition, we can assign a label to the copy of the respective message or item as well as select the appropriate message format (**Exchange MAPI Message FORMAT – TNEF** or **Outlook Message Format *.MSG**).

8. When you're done, click **Next** (see Figure 4.38).

Figure 4.38 Configuring Journaling Settings

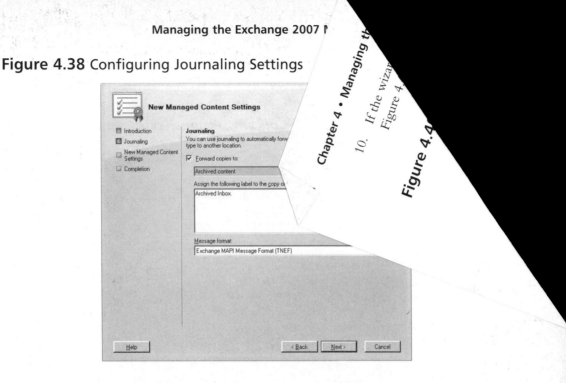

9. We're now taken to the Configuration Summary page, where you can verify that everything has been configured as required. If this is the case, you can click **New** (see Figure 4.39) so that the Managed Content Settings are created.

Figure 4.39 The New Managed Content Settings Summary Page

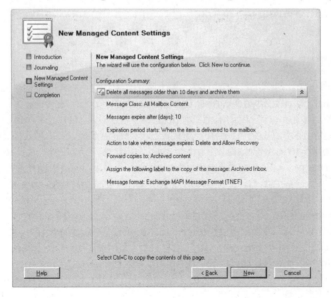

d completes successfully, we'll get a screen like the one shown in
0, and we can click **Finish** to exit the wizard.

0 The New Managed Content Settings Completion Page

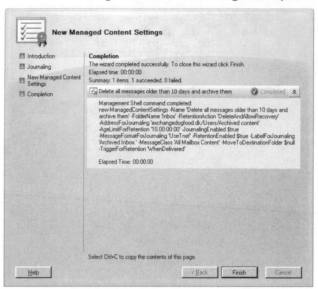

The Managed Content Settings have now been applied to a managed default folder.
Should you for some reason want to change it later, you can do so by clicking the respective
Managed Content Settings, then selecting **Properties** in the **Action pane**.

SOME INDEPENDENT ADVICE

By taking Properties of a managed default folder, you can type a comment
that should be displayed when the respective folder is viewed in Outlook.

Although it's not required, in addition to the default managed folders
that are created automatically when Exchange Server 2007 is installed, you
can create additional default managed folders. Typically you would want to
create managed custom folders (which we cover next), but in some situations
it would make sense to create an additional instance of one or more default
managed folders. Let's say, for example, that some users should have items in
their inboxes deleted after 30 days, but others require items to be left in
their mailboxes for one year. In this case you would need to created two
managed content settings, with different names for the inbox, and then
apply them to the users, depending on their message retention needs, using
managed folder mailbox policies (which we will cover later in this chapter).

If you want to apply managed content settings to default folders using the EMS, you will need to use the *New-ManagedContentSettings* CMDlet with the respective parameters. For details on how to do this, open the EMS and type **Get-Help New-ManagedContentSettings**.

Managed Custom Folders

Under the Managed Customer Folders tab, we can create custom folders that are used for messaging records management. Custom folders differ from default folders in that they do not show up in a mailbox by default.

As you can see in Figure 4.41, no custom folders exist after an installation of Exchange Server 2007. Instead, you must add them manually as required.

Figure 4.41 The Managed Custom Folders Tab

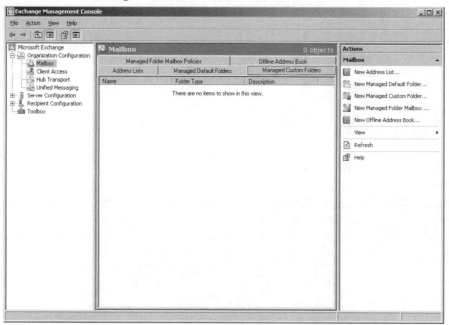

Let's try to create a custom folder. To do so, perform the following steps:

1.   If you haven't already done so, click the **Managed Custom Folders** tab.

2.   Click **New Managed Custom Folder** in the **Action pane**.

3.   In the **New Managed Custom Folder Wizard**, type a name for the new custom folder.

4. Type the name you want the folder to have when viewed in an Outlook client.

5. Specify the storage limit in KB for the custom folder and any subfolders.

6. If you want to display a comment when the custom folder is viewed in Outlook, you can type one as well.

7. Now click **New** (see Figure 4.42).

Figure 4.42 The New Managed Custom Folder Wizard

8. On the **Completion** page, click **Finish** (see Figure 4.43).

Figure 4.43 The New Managed Custom Folder Wizard Completion Page

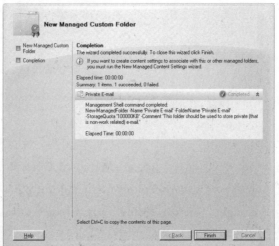

When the managed custom folder has been created, you can always modify it by selecting it in the **Work pane**, then clicking **Properties** in the **Action pane**. This way you can change one or more of the specified settings (see Figure 4.44), if you should require to do so.

Figure 4.44 The Properties Page of a Managed Custom Folder

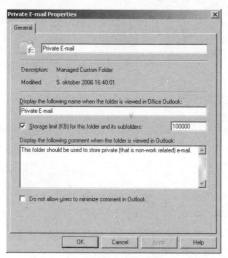

When the managed custom folder has been created, it would also make sense to apply managed content settings to the folder. This procedure is identical to applying managed content settings to a managed default folder: You select the respective managed custom folder, then click the **New Managed Content Settings** link in the **Action pane**.

Managed Folder Mailbox Policies

When we have created a set of Managed Default Folders and Managed Custom Folders, they would need to be linked with one or more Managed Folder Mailbox Policies, so that they the managed folders can be applied to the recipients within the organization. In the following we will go through how you create a Managed Folder Mailbox Policy.

1. Click the **Managed Folder Mailbox Policies** tab.
2. Click **New Managed Folder Mailbox Policy** in the **Action pane**.
3. In the **New Managed Folder Mailbox Policy Wizard** (see Figure 4.45), type a name for the new managed folder mailbox policy.
4. Click **Add** to specify the managed folders that you want to link to this policy.

Figure 4.45 The New Managed Folder Mailbox Policy Wizard

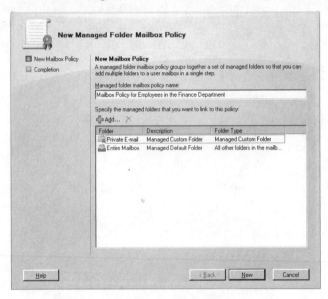

5. Now select the managed folders you want to link to the new managed folder mailbox policy, then click **OK** (see Figure 4.46).

Figure 4.46 Selecting the Managed Folder That Should Be Linked with the Policy

6. Click **New**, then click **Finish** (see Figure 4.47).

Figure 4.47 The New Managed Folder Mailbox Policy Wizard Completion Page

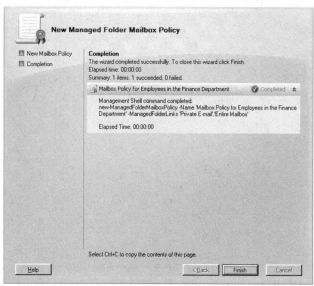

When you have created a managed folder mailbox policy, you can always add and remove managed folders from it by select the respective policy under the **Managed Folder Mailbox Policy** tab, then clicking **Properties** in the **Action pane**. This will bring you to the screen shown in Figure 4.48.

> **NOTE**
>
> If you want to create a new managed folder mailbox policy using the EMC, you can do so with the *New-ManagedFolderMailboxPolicy* CMDlet. For details about the necessary parameters, type **Get-Help New-ManagedFolderMailboxPolicy**.

Now we have created a couple of managed folders and linked them to a policy, but we're not quite finished yet. For a managed folder to show up in a recipient mailbox, we need to do two more things. First, we need to apply the policy to a recipient mailbox. To do so, follow these steps:

Figure 4.48 The Properties Page for the Mailbox Policy

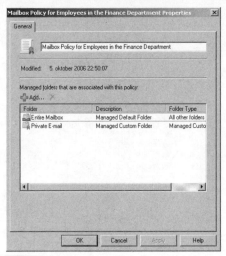

1. In the Exchange Management Console, click the **Mailbox** subnode under the **Recipient Configuration** work center node.

2. Take **Properties** for the mailbox for which you want to apply the policy.

3. Now click the **Mailbox Settings** tab (see Figure 4.49).

Figure 4.49 The Mailbox Settings Tab

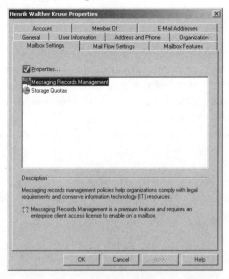

4. Select **Messaging Records Management,** then click the **Properties** button.

5.   Tick **Managed folder mailbox policy**, then click **Browse** (see Figure 4.50).

Figure 4.50 Messaging Records Management

NOTE

As shown in Figure 4.50, it's possible to suspend expiration of items from a mailbox for a specified period. This could be a good idea.

6.   Select the respective **managed folder mailbox policy**, then click **OK** three times (see Figure 4.51).

Figure 4.51 Selecting the Managed Folder Mailbox Policy

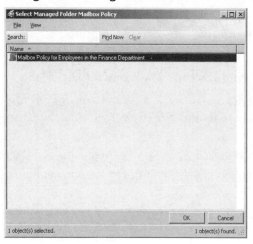

The final thing we need to do is to schedule the messaging records management enforcement process to run at a specified time.

SOME INDEPENDENT ADVICE

The messaging records management enforcement process is disabled by default. This means that although you have applied a managed folder mailbox policy to one or more recipients, the respective managed folders will not show up in the user's client (Outlook 2007 or OWA 2007) until the process has run at least one time.

Depending on your organization's legal needs with regard to messaging records resource management, this could be every 24th hour, or if your legal needs are more relaxed, perhaps once a week.

The messaging records management enforcement process is actually a managed folder assistant, or more precisely, an Exchange mailbox assistant, that's responsible for creating the managed folders in your user mailboxes as well as applying the configured managed content settings to them throughout your organization. One managed folder assistant exists for each mailbox server deployed in your organization. When the managed folder assistant begins, it will process all mailboxes on the given mailbox server. If it doesn't finish processing all the mailboxes in the scheduled time, it will start where it left off the next time it's scheduled to run.

To enable the managed folder assistant, you need to follow these steps:

1. In the Exchange Management Console, click the **Mailbox** subnode under the **Server Configuration** work center node.

2. Select the respective **Mailbox server** in the **Result pane**.

3. Now click the **Properties** link under the mailbox server name in the **Action pane**.

4. Click the **Messaging Records Management** tab.

5. The Messaging Records Management Enforcement Process is set to **Never Run**. Change that to **Use Custom Schedule**, then click the **Customize** button (see Figure 4.52).

6. In the schedule, specify the times and days when the managed folder assistant should run. In Figure 4.53, we set it to run for one hour at midnight every day.

Figure 4.52 Starting the Messaging Records Management Enforcement Process

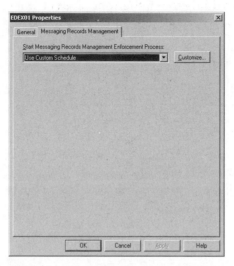

Figure 4.53 Specifying the Schedule

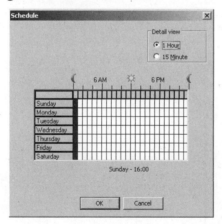

7. Click **OK** twice to return to the EMC.

NOTE

To configure the schedule using the EMS, you need to run the *Set-MailboxServer* CMDlet with the *ManagedFolderAssistantSchedule* parameter. For detailed syntax and parameter information, type **Get-Help Set-MailboxServer** in the EMS.

> Bear in mind that even though the managed mailbox assistant has been scheduled to run for one hour, it doesn't mean it will do so. If the assistant has processed all mailboxes in under one hour, it will stop.

Now that you have scheduled the mailbox folder assistant, the managed folders you have linked to a policy that has been applied to a set of mailboxes will appear after the managed folder assistant has run. But what if you want to force a newly created managed folder to appear in the mailboxes, before the schedule runs? Don't worry; you can use the *Start-ManagedFolderAssistant* CMDlet in the EMS to process all mailboxes immediately. But think twice before doing so, because the managed folder assistant can be a resource-intensive process for the mailbox server and the network in general.

When the managed folder assistant has run, the managed folders will appear in the mail client (Outlook 2007 and Outlook 2007), as shown in Figure 4.54.

Figure 4.54 Managed Folders in Outlook 2007

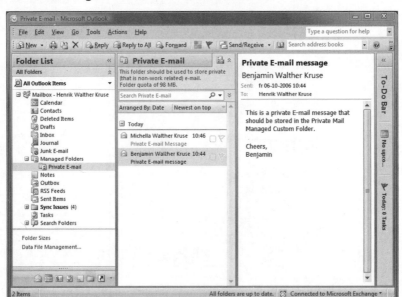

Here we see the Private e-mail folder we created earlier in this chapter. Notice the comment we specified as well as the configured quota for this managed folder.

Offline Address Books

We have reached the last tab under the Mailbox subnode, which is the Offline Address Book tab (see Figure 4.55). As you might have guessed, this is where we can view a list of the offline address books in the Exchange organization.

Figure 4.55 The Offline Address Book Tab

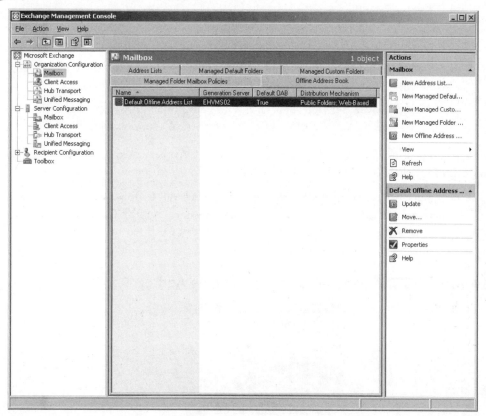

The OAB functionality has change radically in Exchange Server 2007, so before we dive into the configuration settings for OABs, a little introduction to the new behavior of this type of address book is in order. Exchange Server 2007 introduces a completely new distribution mechanism for OABs, a mechanism that isn't based on Public Folders, as was the case with Exchange Server 2000 and 2003. OABs in Exchange Server 2007 use HTTP(S) and the Background Intelligent Transfer Service (BITS), which provides us with several benefits, such as support for more concurrent clients, even more reduced bandwidth usage, and finally, much better control over the distribution points. (We'll bet that many of you have had your issues with OABs!) To use the new distribution mechanism, it's required that the clients run Outlook 2007, but there's still support for legacy clients (Outlook 2003 and earlier), since you can choose to have both a Public Folder and a Web-based distribution point. (In Exchange Server 2007, OABs are located on the Client Access Server in the site.) The OAB mechanism depends on the following components:

- **OABGen Service** This is the service that is running on the OAB Generation server (Exchange 2007 Server with the Mailbox server role installed) in order for the OABs to be created.

- **Exchange File Distribution Service** This runs on a CAS server and is the service responsible for getting the OAB content from the Exchange 2007 Mailbox server (OABGen server).

- **OAB Virtual Directory** This is an IIS virtual directory on the Client Access Server (CAS). This is where the clients download the OABs from.

- **Autodiscover Service** This service also runs on a CAS server and is the one that makes sure the correct OAB URL is returned to Outlook clients.

When you install an Exchange Server 2007, one OAB is created by default. Let's take a look at the settings configured for the default OAB. To do so, follow these steps:

1. Select the OAB in the **Work pane**, then click the **Properties** link in the **Action pane**. Alternatively, right-click the **OAB** to bring up its context menu, and select **Properties**. As you can see in Figure 4.56, this OAB has been scheduled for updates at 5:00 A.M. each day.

Figure 4.56 The General Tab on the Offline Address Book Properties Page

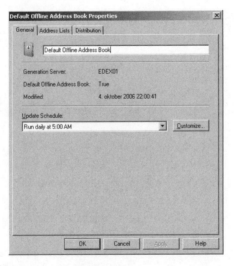

2. Click the **Address Lists** tab. As we can see in Figure 4.57, the default OAB includes the default GAL, which contains all mail-enabled objects.

Figure 4.57 The Address Lists Tab on the Offline Address Book Properties Page

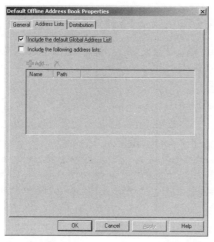

3. Now click the **Distribution** tab. As you can see in Figure 4.58, this is the place where you specify the type of Outlook clients OAB should support. By default, only Outlook 2003 SP2 and later are supported. This is also the place where you enable the type of distribution point you want to provide to the clients. When you're installing Exchange Server 2007 into an Active Directory forest that doesn't contain an Exchange 2000 or 2003 organization and you select **No** when the Exchange Server 2007 Installation Wizard asks whether you've got any Outlook 2003 or earlier clients in your organization, only the Web-based distribution point will be enabled. If you answer **Yes** to this question, the Installation Wizard will create and mount a Public Folder database on the Exchange 2007 server as well as enable the Public Folder distribution mechanism.

Figure 4.58 The Distribution Tab on the Offline Address Book Properties Page

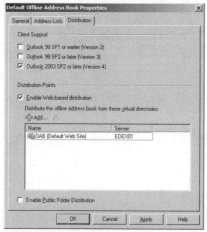

4. Click **OK** to exit the Properties for the Default OAB.

Creating a New Offline Address Book

Now that you have seen the default settings configured for the default OAB, let's try to create a new OAB. We do this the following way:

> **NOTE**
>
> The default OAB should be sufficient for most organizations, but using multiple OABs is common practice in environments where there's a need to isolate users from each other based on country, organization, or the like. Multiple OABs are especially commonly used by Exchange hosting providers that host multiple customers (domains) in their Exchange environments.

1. Click **New Offline Address Book** in the **Action pane**.
2. In the **New Offline Address Book Wizard** that appears, type a name for the OAB (see Figure 4.59).

Figure 4.59 Creating a New Offline Address Book

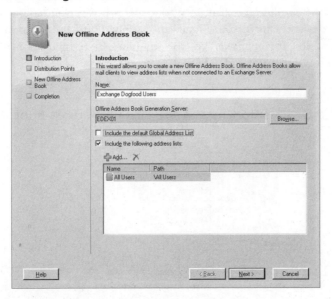

3. Click the **Browse** button to specify the mailbox server that should be the OAB generation server for this OAB, select the respective **server**, and click **OK** (see Figure 4.60).

Figure 4.60 Selecting the Mailbox Server

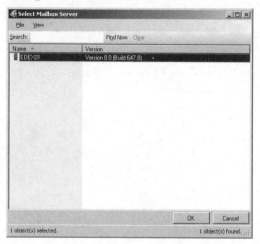

4. Now click the **Add** button, select the server address lists that should be included in the OAB, and click **Next**.

5. Choose whether you want to enable Web-based distribution or Public Folder distribution or both. If you enable Web-based distribution, you also need to select the OAB virtual directory in which this OAB should be stored (see Figure 4.61).

Figure 4.61 Specifying the Type of Distribution Point to Use

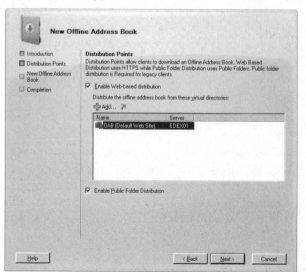

6. Click **Next**, then click **New** on the Configuration Summary page (see Figure 4.62).

Figure 4.62 The New Offline Address Book Wizard Summary Page

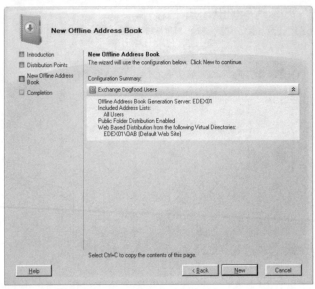

7. On the completion page click **Finish**.

When you have multiple OABs on a mailbox server, you can select the one that should be the default (via the Action pane or associated context menu).

Since OABs relating to Outlook 2007 are downloaded using a Web-based distribution method, you also have the option of specifying the internal URL (which refers to the URL from which Outlook clients inside the corporate network can access the virtual directory) as well as the external URL (which refers to the URL from which Outlook clients outside the corporate network can access the directory) to the OAB Web site. This is not configured under the Mailbox node but by taking the Properties page of OAB (the default Web site), which can be found under the Server Configuration work center, where you select the Client Access Server node (see Figure 4.63).

TIP

When it comes to detailed information about OABs, one of the best resources on the Internet is a blog run by Dave Goldman. Dave works as an Exchange Escalation Engineer (EE) for Microsoft in North Carolina and is, among other things, the guy behind the OABInteg tool, which is used to troubleshoot OAB issues. You can visit Dave's blog at http://blogs.msdn.com/dgoldman.

If you want to create a new OAB using the EMS, you can do so with the *New-OfflineAddressBook* CMDlet. For details about the necessary parameters, type **Get-Help New-OfflineAddressBook**.

Figure 4.63 The URLs Tab of the Properties Page for OAB (Default Web Site)

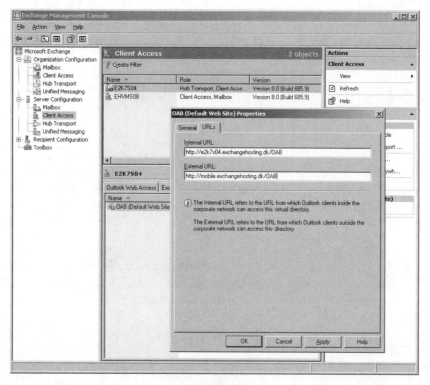

Summary

In this chapter, we had a look at the feature set that can be configured on an Exchange 2007 server with the Mailbox Server role installed. As you have seen throughout the chapter, many tasks can be performed on this server role. We didn't cover every single task, but we primarily concentrated on how you deal with storage groups, mail and Public Folder databases, and administering Public Folders in Exchange 2007. In addition, we had a quick look at each of the organizationwide settings available on this server, but most of them were relatively superficial.

Solutions Fast Track

Managing the Exchange 2007 Mailbox Server

☑ The Exchange Store hasn't changed much since Exchange Server 2003 but has been further improved and of course contains multiple new features.

☑ Back in Exchange 2000 and 2003, the databases containing either mailboxes or Public Folders were known as *mailbox stores* and *Public Folder stores*, respectively, but with Exchange Server 2007 they are now referred to as *mailbox databases* and *Public Folder databases*.

☑ 64-bit hardware gives us the opportunity to use much more memory than was the case in previous Exchange versions. Because Exchange Server 2007 can take advantage of more memory, it means that a larger chunk of each user's mailbox can be stored in memory, which reduces disk I/O.

Exchange 2007 Storage Groups

☑ The Mailbox server in the Exchange 2007 Enterprise Edition supports up to 50 storage groups and a maximum of 50 databases per server. Exchange 2007 allows you to create up to five databases in each storage group, as was the case with Exchange 2003, but best practice is to create one database per storage group. The Standard Edition supports up to five databases in a single storage group.

☑ As is the case with Exchange 2003, it's still okay to keep all storage groups on the same spindles, but in terms of performance, it's better to keep them separated, although this would be quite unrealistic for most organizations that were using, for example, 30 storage groups!

☑ Exchange Server 2007 finally has native support for continuous replication, which is a functionality that will make it possible to keep a second copy of a database held in a particular storage group. The second copy of a database will be updated using log file shipping and log file replay. The idea of keeping a second copy of a database is, of course, to get up and running in a couple of minutes by being able to switch to the second database using a few mouse clicks (or CMDlets), should the original database crash or become corrupted.

Exchange 2007 Mailbox Databases

☑ As is the case with previous versions of Exchange, databases in Exchange Server 2007 are still based on the Extensible Storage Engine (ESE). The purpose of ESE is to provide an interface to the underlying database structure, which is responsible for managing changes made to the database (more specifically the .EDB file).

☑ With Exchange Server 2007, there's no longer a database limit for the Standard Edition.

☑ In Exchange Server 2000 and 2003, a database was made up of two files: an .EDB file and an .STM file. The purpose of the streaming file (.STM) is, as many of you might be aware, to house raw Internet content message streams as defined in Request for Comment (RFC) 822. The .STM has been removed from Exchange Server 2007.

☑ The default limit for mailboxes in Exchange Server 2007 is 2GB.

☑ As was the case with previous versions of Exchange, Exchange Server 2007 maintains single-instance storage of messages.

Exchange 2007 Public Folder Databases

☑ The default limit for Public Folders in Exchange Server 2007 is 2GB.

☑ Public Folders are still supported in Exchange Server 2007, but they have been deemphasized. This means that there's a chance Public Folders won't be included in the next version of Exchange (currently code-named E14), but Microsoft will support Public Folders until the end of 2016.

☑ The Public Folders tasks you can perform through the EMC are extremely limited, which means that you need to do most of these tasks via either the EMS or the System Manager on an Exchange 2003 server that still is part of the Exchange organization.

Managing Organizationwide Mailbox Server Configuration Settings

☑ The purpose of address lists is to help you organize the different types of recipients within your Exchange organization so that they are listed in a meaningful way when your end users look up recipients in their mail clients.

☑ Using the Managed Default Folders feature, we can manage the default mailbox folders (such as Inbox, Calendar, and Sent Items) by applying managed content settings to a specific folder or, if needed, the entire mailbox. For example, we would be able to apply managed content settings to a default folder such as the Inbox so that particular types of items in this folder (and any subfolders) are either deleted or moved to another folder after, say, 15 days.

☑ Messaging records management is a premium feature that requires an Exchange 2007 Enterprise CAL to enable on a mailbox.

☑ Exchange Server 2007 introduces a completely new distribution mechanism for OABs, a mechanism that isn't based on Public Folders, as was the case with Exchange Server 2000 and 2003. OABs in Exchange Server 2007 use HTTP(S) and the Background Intelligent Transfer Service (BITS), which provides us with several benefits, such as support for more concurrent clients, even more reduced bandwidth usage, and finally, much better control over the distribution points.

Frequently Asked Questions

The following Frequently Asked Questions, answered by the authors of this book, are designed to both measure your understanding of the concepts presented in this chapter and to assist you with real-life implementation of these concepts. To have your questions about this chapter answered by the author, browse to www.syngress.com/solutions and click on the "Ask the Author" form.

Q: Wasn't Exchange Server 2007 supposed to use SQL instead of ESE as the database repository?

A: During the early development phases of Exchange Server 2007, this was the plan, but it was changed rather quickly. We'll not see SQL as the database repository until E15 (the Exchange version after E14!).

Q: You mentioned that 2GB is the default limit for mailboxes in Exchange Server 2007. Won't that put quite an I/O load on the disk spindles holding the mailbox databases?

A: No, actually, this isn't the case, since Exchange Server 2007 is 64-bit, which means that much more address space can be allocated in memory and will result in reduced I/O load on the disk spindles holding the mailbox databases.

Q: I really miss being able to manage Public Folders using the Exchange 2007 Management Console (EMC). Is there a chance that Public Folder management will be implemented in the EMC GUI sometime in the future?

A: Yes, if the Exchange Product Group receives sufficient customer feedback on this issue, this will be implemented in a post-RTM version. If we're lucky, it's already in Exchange 2007 Service Pack 1.

Q: After reading this chapter, I can see that Public Folders still are supported in Exchange Server 2007, but what will happen to Public Folders in future versions of the Exchange product?

A: Although Public Folders are supported in Exchange Server 2007, bear in mind that they have been deemphasized and will be dropped in a future version of Exchange (most likely E15, which is the version after E14), but since Microsoft has committed to support Public Folders until the end of 2016, there should be plenty of time for migrating your Public Folder data to a SharePoint-based or similar solution.

Q: Is it possible to get logon statistics for the users connecting to the mailbox and Public Folder databases on my Exchange 2007 Mailbox Servers?

A: Yes, you can use the *Get-LogonStatistics* CMDlet for this purpose. Running this CMDlet in the EMS will give you information about things such as the number of open attachments, folders, and messages as well as number of messaging operations, progress operations, table operations, transfer operations, total operations, and successful RPC calls. Finally, you can retrieve information such as latency, client version, client IP address, and access and logon times. To get the full list of information, type **Get-LogonStatistics | FL**.

Chapter 5

Managing the Client Access Server

Solutions in this chapter:

- **Managing the Exchange 2007 Client Access Server**
- **The AutoDiscover Service**
- **The Availability Service**
- **Client Access Servers and the SSL Certificate Dilemma**
- **Managing Outlook Anywhere**
- **Managing Outlook Web Access 2007**
- **Managing Exchange ActiveSync**
- **Managing POP3/IMAP4**

- ☑ **Summary**
- ☑ **Solutions Fast Track**
- ☑ **Frequently Asked Questions**

Introduction

The Client Access Server (CAS) replaces the front-end server we all know from Exchange 2000 and 2003 and adds some additional functionality. The CAS provides mailbox access for all types of Exchange clients except Outlook MAPI clients, which, as most of you are aware, connect directly to the Mailbox Server on which the respective mailbox is stored. This means the CAS manages access for any user who opens their mailbox using Outlook Anywhere (formerly known as RPC over HTTP), Outlook Web Access (OWA), Exchange ActiveSync (EAS), POP3, and last but not least, IMAP4.

In addition to providing client access, the CAS is responsible for supplying access to things such as automatic profile configuration, free/busy information, Out of Office (OOF) messages, the Offline Address Book (OAB), as well as Unified Messaging (UM), but only for Outlook 2007 and Outlook Web Access 2007. Only these two client versions can take advantage of the new Web-based Exchange services known as the AutoDiscover and Availability services. Legacy clients such as Outlook 2003 and earlier cannot use these two new Exchange Web services.

After reading this chapter, you should have a good understanding of how you can manage the feature set on the CAS, at both the server level and organizationwide.

Managing the Exchange 2007 Client Access Server

The Client Access Server should always be deployed on a domain-member server on the internal network, and not in the DMZ, which many thought was a security best practice for front-end servers in Exchange 2000 and 2003. This is true for several reasons: one is the fact that CAS servers communicate with mailbox servers using RPC traffic, and to make this work, it required several open ports into your network via your intranet firewall. This is not a best practice since it makes it easier for an intruder to gain access to your Active Directory (especially since it is RPC-specific ports that must be opened!). In addition, a member server has too many access rights to domain-member servers on the internal network, and thus does not justify deployment in your DMZ.

Alternatively, it is highly recommended to publish the CAS using an Internet Security and Acceleration (ISA) Server (ISA Server 2006 is preferred) in your perimeter network. This makes it possible to have your users pre-authenticated on the ISA Server before actually reaching the internal network.

A typical CAS scenario following security best practices is shown in Figure 5.1.

Figure 5.1 A Typical Client Access Server Scenario

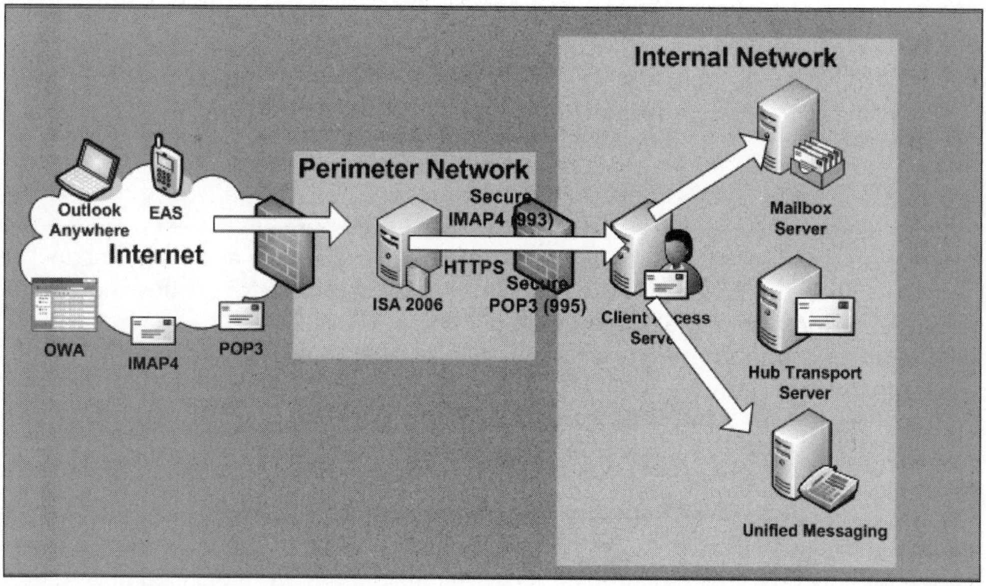

If you plan to split your Exchange 2007 Server roles onto different servers, bear in mind that the CAS is the first server role you should deploy. In addition, at least one CAS is required in each site a Mailbox Server has been deployed.

The AutoDiscover Service

Several features in Exchange Server 2007 are based on Exchange Web services. One of these services is known as the AutoDiscover service. As most of you are aware, few end-users know how to configure an Outlook profile; this is where the AutoDiscover service shines by simplifying Outlook client deployment through creation of an automatic connection between the Exchange Server and Outlook 2007 clients. No longer are special scripts, complex user intervention, or tools such as the Custom Installation Wizard from the Office Resource Kit needed. Before Outlook 2007 and Exchange Server 2007, information such as the name of the Exchange server and the user account and password were all required when configuring an Outlook profile. With the advent of the AutoDiscover service, all you need to enter is the e-mail address and password and the AutoDiscover service will do the rest, automatically discovering and configuring the client's home mailbox server information. Entering a username and password, however, is only required when you are configuring clients not logged on to the Active Directory domain. If you're configuring an Outlook 2007 profile on a machine logged on to the Active Directory domain, AutoDiscover will fetch the domain information from the account you are logged on with, meaning you only have to click Next a few times to configure your Outlook 2007 profile.

Other features provided via the AutoDiscover service are the Offline Address Books (OABs), Unified Messaging (UM) information, and Outlook Anywhere settings.

As similar services did in previous versions of Outlook and Exchange, the AutoDiscover service will automatically update an Outlook profile should a user's respective mailbox be moved to another server in the organization.

NOTE

You can read more about the new AutoDiscover Service, and how to configure Outlook 2007 using this Exchange Web service in the following article, which is located at MSExchange.org:
http://www.msexchange.org/tutorials/Uncovering-New-Outlook-2007-Discover-Service.html.

It's not only Outlook 2007 that can take advantage of the new Web-based AutoDiscover services, but Windows mobile devices running the next versions of Windows Mobile (code-named Crossbow [5.2] and Photon [6.0], and at the time of this writing, still in beta) can also be provisioned automatically using this service.

When the Client Access Server role is installed on an Exchange 2007 Server, a virtual IIS directory named AutoDiscover is created under the Default Web Site, as shown in Figure 5.2.

Figure 5.2 AutoDiscover Virtual Directory in IIS Manager

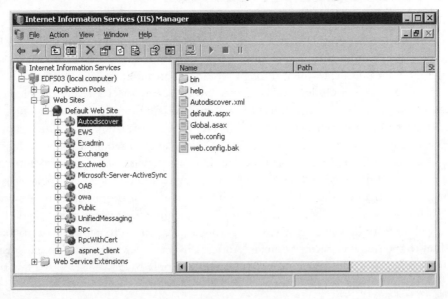

When you open an Outlook 2007 client, this is the virtual directory it connects to in order to download any necessary information.

In addition to this virtual directory, a new object named the service connection point (SCP) is also created in Active Directory. The SCP object contains the authoritative list of AutoDiscover service URLs in the forest, and can be updated using the *Set-ClientAccessServer* cmdlet.

Figure 5.3 illustrates what happens when Outlook 2007 connects to an Exchange 2007 server.

Figure 5.3 The AutoDiscover Service Process from an Internal Outlook Client

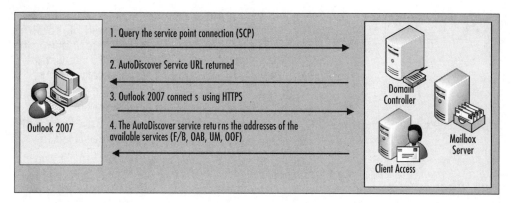

To see the URLs to each of these services in Outlook, hold down the **Ctrl** key and right-click your Outlook icon in the Systray. Choose **Test E-mail AutoConfiguration** in the context menu. In the **Test E-mail AutoConfiguration** window, enter your e-mail address and password and make sure you only have **Use AutoDiscover** ticked. Then, click **Test**. Outlook will now test each of the services provided by the AutoDiscover service and list the URLs it finds, as well as list any issues or errors for each.

The Availability Service

Just like the AutoDiscover service, the Availability service is an Exchange Web service, which is installed by default when deploying the Client Access Server role on an Exchange 2007 server. The purpose of the Availability service is to provide secure, consistent, and up-to-date (that is, data in real time!) free/busy data to clients using this service. Since only Outlook 2007 and OWA 2007 can take advantage of this new service, legacy clients, (Outlook 2003 and earlier, as well as OWA 2003), still depend on a Public Folder database, containing the SCHEDULE+ FREE/BUSY system folder. Since only Outlook 2007 and OWA 2007 can use the Availability service to obtain free/busy information, it's important that Exchange 2007 be able to interact with legacy systems, too. Table 5.1 shows how free/busy data is

obtained based on which front-end client version is used compared to the version of
Exchange Server the back-end source and target mailboxes resides.

Table 5.1 Free/Busy Retrieval Methods

Client	Source Mailbox	Target Mailbox	Free/Busy Retrieval
Outlook 2007	Exchange 2007	Exchange 2007	The Availability service will read the free/busy info directly from the calendar in the target mailbox.
Outlook 2007	Exchange 2007	Exchange 2003	The Availability service will make an HTTP connection to the /Public virtual directory of the Exchange 2003 mailbox.
Outlook 2003	Exchange 2007	Exchange 2007	Free/busy info will be published in source Public Folders.
Outlook 2003	Exchange 2007	Exchange 2003	Free/busy info will be published in source Public Folders.
Outlook Web Access 2007	Exchange 2007	Exchange 2007	OWA 2007 will call the Availability service API, which reads the free/busy info from the target mailbox.
Outlook Web Access 2007	Exchange 2007	Exchange 2003	OWA 2007 will call the Availability service API, and then make an HTTP connection to the /Public virtual directory of the Exchange 2003 mailbox.
Any	Exchange 2003	Exchange 2007	Free/busy info is published in source Public Folders.

Outlook 2007 discovers the Availability Service URL using the AutoDiscover service. Actually, the AutoDiscover service is to Outlook what DNS is to a Web browser, acting like a DNS Web Service for Outlook. It is used to find various services like the Availability service, and the UM and OAB services. It simply tells Outlook 2007 where to go to locate the various Web services required: UM, OAB, and Availability.

You should be aware of many aspects when configuring the Availability service. So many, in fact, that covering all of them is outside the scope of this book. Instead, I recommend you check out the Availability Service FAQ over at the Exchange 2007 Wiki, found at www.exchangeninjas.com/AvailabilityServiceFAQ.

Client Access Servers and the SSL Certificate Dilemma

In previous versions of Exchange, you simply issued a request for an SSL certificate, and when received, assigned this certificate to the Default Web Site in the IIS Manager. That was basically it. Exchange 2007, however, is a different beast, especially when it comes to securing client connectivity to the CAS using SSL certificates.

You may have noticed that a default self-signed SSL certificate is assigned to the Default Web Site during the installation of the Exchange 2007 CAS role. If you take a closer look at this certificate, you'll notice it contains multiple *subject alternative names* (Figure 5.4).

Figure 5.4 SSL Certificate with Subject Alternative DNS Names

I hear some of you grumbling, "So, what is that all about?" Well, instead of having to require multiple certificates, maintain the configuration of multiple IP addresses, IIS Web sites for each IP port, and a certificate combination, you can create a single certificate that enables clients to successfully connect to each host name using SSL and subject alternative names. You see, in order to support Outlook Anywhere, OWA, Exchange ActiveSync (EAS) and especially the new Web-based AutoDiscover service, which requires a common name of *autodiscover.domain.com*, you must use an SSL certificate containing subject alternative names.

Since the default SSL certificate is self-signed and, therefore by default, untrusted by clients, and because Outlook Anywhere and Exchange ActiveSync require a trusted SSL certificate, we have to replace this certificate with an SSL certificate issued by a trusted third-party provider. Unfortunately, only a few SSL certificate providers can issue an SSL certificate containing one or more subject alternative names. To make matters worse, these providers charge something like $600 per year for such a certificate.

NOTE

At the time of this writing, only Entrust.com, GeoTrust.com, and VeriSign offered these types of SSL certificates. Hopefully this will change as more and more organizations begin to deploy Exchange 2007.

If you don't assign an SSL certificate with additional subject alternative names, where one of these matches the hostname of the Exchange 2007 CAS, internal Outlook 2007 clients will generate certificate security warnings since the SSL certificate won't match the name used to configure these clients. Notice, however, that Outlook 2007 won't generate a warning if the self-signed untrusted default SSL certificate assigned to the Default Web Site. This is by design. When the Exchange 2007 CAS role is installed, the setup wizard creates an Active Directory service discovery record, and if the Outlook 2007 client can see that record (meaning they are on the internal network), it ignores the trust warning. It uses the service discovery record as the trust (assuming someone that can write that to the Active Directory can be trusted regarding the URL for the CAS), rather than checking that it trusts the issuer of the cert. The idea behind this is that while you are on the intranet, Exchange is secure out of the box, using SSL and ignoring any prompts.

So why not just leave the self-signed SSL certificate on the Default Web Site? Well, because then Outlook Anywhere and Exchange ActiveSync wouldn't work, since these two features require the common name on the SSL certificate to match the external URL used to access the CAS, so the certificate will be trusted by the client. In addition, OWA 2007 would generate a security warning when a user connects to his mailbox using OWA 2007.

"Okay," you say, "fair enough, but what do I do if my organization can't afford to throw $600 towards an SSL certificate each year?" Well, in that case, the solution would be to use multiple Web sites. Besides the Default Web Site (which you should leave in its default state with the self-signed untrusted SSL certificate assigned), we would need two additional Web sites.

- One for Exchange ActiveSync (EAS), OWA, and Outlook Anywhere
- One for the AutoDiscover service

In order to configure this type of setup, you must do the following:

First, add two additional virtual IP addresses to the NIC on your Exchange 2007 CAS, as shown in Figure 5.5.

Figure 5.5 Additional Virtual IP Addresses

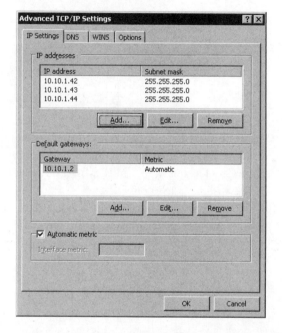

Now assign a specific IP address to the Default Web Site, as shown in Figure 5.6.

Figure 5.6 Assigning a Specific IP Address to the Default Web Site

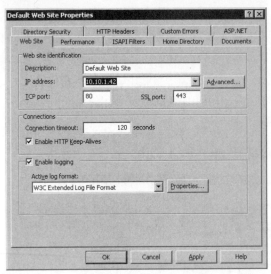

Create two new Web sites using IIS Manager, and call them something like **Clients** and **AutoDiscover**. When creating the Web sites, use the default settings and specify the same path as the one configured in the Default Web Site (C:\InetPub\wwwroot). Make sure to also select *Read* and *Run Scripts (such as ASP)* only.

When the Web sites have been properly created, we can create the required virtual directories using the Exchange Management Shell. To create the OWA and Exchange ActiveSync directories, enter the following commands, bearing in mind that the −*WebSiteName* value is case sensitive:

```
New-OWAVirtualDirectory -OwaVersion: Exchange2007 -Name "owa" -WebSiteName
"Clients"
```

```
New-ActiveSyncVirtualDirectory -WebSiteName "Clients"
```
```
New-AutodiscoverVirtualDirectory -WebSiteName AutoDiscover -
BasicAuthentication:$true -WindowsAuthentication:$true
```

If you still have Exchange 2000 or 2003 back-end servers in your organization and these are accessed via the CAS, you also need to create the legacy OWA virtual directories. You do so using the following commands:

```
New-OwaVirtualDirectory -OwaVersion: "Exchange2003or2000" -Name "Exchange"
-WebSite "Clients" -VirtualDirectoryType: Mailboxes
New-OwaVirtualDirectory -OwaVersion: "Exchange2003or2000" -Name "Public" -WebSite
"Clients" -VirtualDirectoryType: PublicFolders
New-OwaVirtualDirectory -OwaVersion: "Exchange2003or2000" -Name "Exadmin"
-WebSite "Clients" -VirtualDirectoryType: Exadmin
```

```
New-OwaVirtualDirectory -OwaVersion: "Exchange2003or2000" -Name "ExchWeb"
-WebSite "Clients" -VirtualDirectoryType: ExchWeb
```

The last virtual directory we must create is the /Rpc and /RpcWithCerts virtual directories used by Outlook Anywhere. These directories cannot be created using the Exchange
Management Shell, thus we must create them from a file. To do so, we first save both of the
directories to a file. This is done by right-clicking the directory name and choosing **All
Tasks | Save Configuration to a File** in the context menu. Type a name for the file and
click **OK** to save it as an XML file. Now, right-click the new Clients Web site, select **New |
Virtual Directory (from file)**. Next, specify the location to the XML file storing the virtual directory configuration settings, open it, click **Read File**, highlight the location name,
and click **OK** to create the new virtual directory as shown in Figure 5.7.

NOTE

The Rpc and RpcWithCerts virtual directories are created under the Default
Web Site when you add the RPC over HTTP Proxy component. Instructions on
how this is done are included in the next section.

Figure 5.7 Importing the Virtual Directory from the XML File

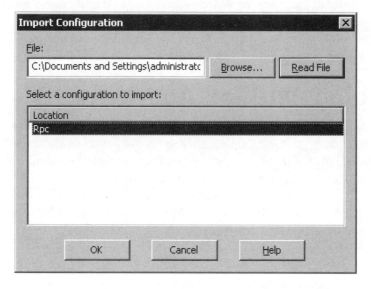

When all Web sites and virtual directories have been created, your IIS Manager should
look similar to Figure 5.8.

Figure 5.8 Web Sites in IIS Manager

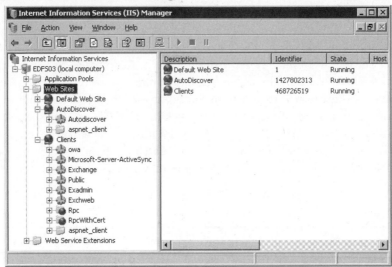

Now you just need to assign an SSL certificate to each Web site. You should leave the self-signed SSL certificate assigned to the Default Web Site and assign a traditional third-party SSL certificate to the Clients and AutoDiscover Web sites, respectively. The name specified in the common name field of the SSL certificate, which will be assigned to the AutoDiscover Web site, should be autodiscover.domain.com. The common name for the Clients Web site can be anything you like (such as mobile.domain.com).

Instructions on how you request and then assign an SSL certificate to a Web site is covered in the following section.

Managing Outlook Anywhere

Outlook Anywhere makes it possible for your end users to remotely access their mailbox from the Internet using their full Outlook client. Those of you with Exchange 2003 experience most likely know the technology behind the Outlook Anywhere feature already since Outlook Anywhere is just an improved version of RPC over HTTP.

The technology behind Outlook Anywhere is basically the same as in Exchange 2003. It still works by encapsulating the RPC-based MAPI traffic inside an HTTPS session, which is then ultimately directed toward the server running the RPC over HTTP proxy component on your internal network, giving you the same functionality when using the Outlook client from a machine on your internal network. When the HTTPS packets reach the RPC over HTTP proxy server, all of the RPC MAPI traffic protocols are removed from the HTTPS packets and forwarded to the respective Mailbox server. This means that by using RPC over HTTP, your end-users no longer have to use a virtual private network (VPN) connection to connect to their respective Exchange mailboxes using their favorite, *fatter*, Outlook client.

The first necessary step when deploying Outlook Anywhere is the valid installation of a Secure Sockets Layer (SSL) certificate from a trusted Certificate Authority (CA), one your clients trust by default.

SOME INDEPENDENT ADVICE

Security best practice is to publish Outlook Anywhere using a reverse proxy such as an ISA 2006 Server in your perimeter network (aka DMZ or screened subnet). By using ISA Server 2006 in the perimeter network to route RPC over HTTP requests and positioning the Client Access Server on the internal network, you only need to open port 443 on the intranet firewall in order for you Outlook clients to communicate with the Mailbox server.

Installing a Third-Party SSL Certificate

To issue a request for an SSL certificate, you can use the IIS Manager, a method most of us are already familiar with. I have included the required steps for those who need a refresher.

1. Log on to the Exchange 2007 Server on which the Client Access Server role is installed.

2. Click **Start | All Programs | Administrative Tools** and select **Internet Information Services (IIS) Manager**.

3. Expand **<Server name>** (*local computer*) | **Web Sites**, and then open the **Property** page for the **Default Web Site**.

4. Click the **Directory Security** tab, as shown in Figure 5.9.

5. Click **Server Certificate**, and then click **Next**.

6. Select **Create a new certificate**, as shown in Figure 5.10, and then click **Next**.

Figure 5.9 The Directory Security Tab of the Default Web Site in the IIS Manager

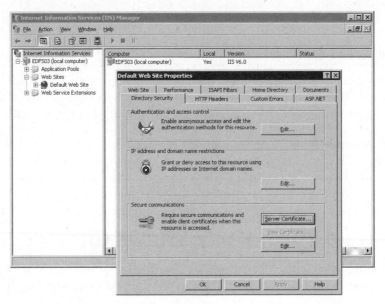

As mentioned earlier in this chapter, during setup Exchange 2007 installs an SSL certificate on the default Web site by default. If you haven't removed this certificate yet, do so now before you proceed with the next steps.

Figure 5.10 Selecting to Create a New Certificate

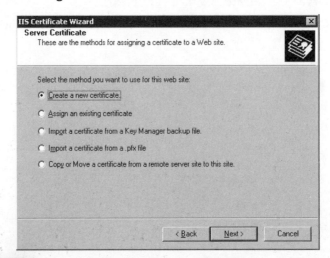

7. Since we're preparing a certificate request for a third-party SSL certificate, select **Prepare the request now, but send it later** and click **Next**.

8. Type a name (such as **SSL Client Access to Exchange**) for the new certificate, one that's easy to refer to and remember. Leave the bit length at 1024 and click **Next**.

9. Enter the **organization** and **organizational unit name**, and then click **Next**.

10. We have now reached the most important step in the IIS Certificate Wizard, where we have to enter the common name for the Default Web Site. This common name *must* match the name of the URL through which we access the Client Access Server from a client on the Internet. The common name is usually *mail.domain.com*, *mobile.domain.com*, or *owa.domain.com*. When you have entered the common name, click **Next** (Figure 5.11).

NOTE

It is very important you enter the correct common name since it cannot be changed once you have received your SSL certificate from your third-party provider.

Figure 5.11 Typing the Common Name for the SSL Certificate

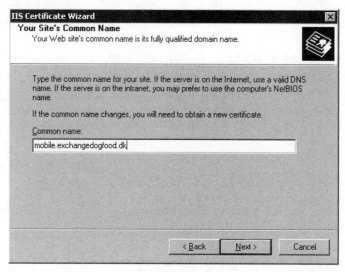

11. Now enter the respective geographical information and click **Next**.

12.   Specify the path and file name to save the certificate request, and then click **Next**.

13.   Verify that the information in the request is correct (especially the Issued To information), then click **Next** and finally **Finish**, exiting the IIS Certificate Wizard.

SOME INDEPENDENT ADVICE

You can also issue a request for an SSL certificate using the *New-ExchangeCertificate* cmdlet in the Exchange Management Shell. In order to request a certificate using this cmdlet, type:

```
New-ExchangeCertificate -GenerateRequest -FriendlyName
"SSL Client Access to Exchange" -DomainName mobile.exchange-
dogfood.dk -path c:\certreq.txt
```

If you're going to issue a request for an SSL certificate with additional DNS names in the Subject Alternative Name property, you actually need to use the *New-ExchangeCertificate* cmdlet. For more information, see the Exchange 2007 Documentation at http://technet.microsoft.com/en-us/library/aa995942.aspx.

Okay, now that I have a pending certificate request, what certificate authority provider should I use? Well, if you want a good and extremely cheap SSL certificate, trusted by 99 percent of all browsers as well as all Windows Mobile 5.0 devices on the market, I can highly recommend GoDaddy (www.godaddy.com). Unfortunately, they don't support adding additional DNS names in the Subject Alternative Name property, however. Here you can get an SSL certificate for a mere $20 per year. I don't think you'll find it much cheaper anywhere else.

When you have decided on which certificate authority provider you want to use, you'll need to send the certreq.txt file to them. I won't go into detail on how this is accomplished since this process is different from provider to provider, and because each provider typically has very detailed information about how you do this.

When you have received the SSL certificate from the certificate provider, you need to perform the following steps:

1.   Log on to the Exchange 2007 Server on which the Client Access Server role is installed.

2.   Click **Start | All Programs | Administrative Tools** and select **Internet Information Services (IIS) Manager**.

3.   Expand *<Server name> (local computer)* | **Web Sites**, and then open the **Property** page for the Default Web Site.

4.   Click the **Directory Security** tab and select the **Server Certificate** button.

5. Select **Process the pending request and install the certificate**, as shown in Figure 5.12, and then click **Next**.

Figure 5.12 Processing the Pending Request

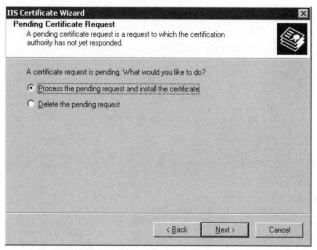

6. Specify the path to the certificate file or the file containing the Certificate Authority response, and then click **Next**.

7. Specify the SSL port that should be used (443), click **Next** and then **Finish** to exit the IIS Certificate Wizard.

8. Now that we have installed the SSL certificate we can enable SSL on the Default Web Site. This is done by clicking the **Edit** button shown back in Figure 5.9, and then checking the option button **Require secure channel (SSL)**, as shown in Figure 5.13.

Figure 5.13 Enabling SSL on the Default Web Site

9. Click **OK** twice and exit the IIS Manager.

Adding the RPC over HTTP Proxy Component

Next, we need to install the RPC over HTTP Proxy component on the Exchange 2007 Server on which the Client Access Server role has been installed. Since this is a standard Windows 2003 Server component, you install it using the following steps:

1. Log on to the respective Client Access Server.

2. Click **Start | Control Panel**, and then open **Add or Remove Programs**.

3. Click **Add/Remove Windows Components**.

4. Select **Network Services** and then click the **Details** button.

5. Check **RPC over HTTP Proxy**, as shown in Figure 5.14.

Figure 5.14 Installing the RPC over HTTP Proxy Component

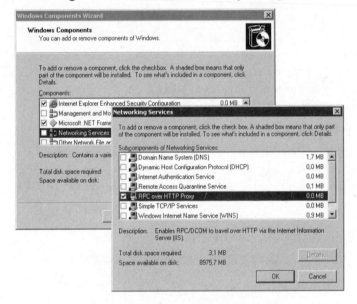

6. Click **Ok | Next** and let the installation complete.

Enabling Outlook Anywhere

With the SSL certificate in place and the RPC over HTTP Proxy component installed, we can move on and enable Outlook Anywhere. In order to do so, perform the following steps:

1. Open the **Exchange Management Console**, then expand the **Server Configuration** work center and select **Client Access**.

2. Click the **Enable Outlook Anywhere** link in the Action pane.

3. In the Outlook Anywhere wizard that appears, type the *external host name* for your Exchange organization, as shown in Figure 5.15.

Figure 5.15 Enabling Outlook Anywhere

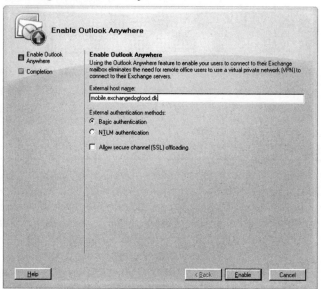

> **NOTE**
>
> The external host name you specify should match the common name entered in the SSL certificate that has been used to secure your Default Web Site. Typically, this name is something like *mobile.domain.com*, *mail.domain.com*, or *owa.domain.com*.

4. Select the type of external authentication method you want to use for Outlook clients accessing their mailbox over the Internet. You can select Basic or NTLM authentication, but it is recommended you select NTLM authentication, especially if you have a firewall such as an ISA 2006 Server, which supports this authentication method.

SOME INDEPENDENT ADVICE

So, why is it I should choose NTLM over Basic authentication when enabling Outlook Anywhere? Well, because if you choose Basic authentication, you will need to enter your password each time Outlook is opened, even when you're located on your internal network.

5. You have the option of allowing secure channel (SSL) offloading, which should be selected if you have a device that can handle this capability.

6. When you have made your selections, click the **Enable** button and then select **Finish** to exit the wizard.

SOME INDEPENDENT ADVICE

If for some reason you would rather enable Outlook Anywhere using the Exchange Management Shell, you can do so with the *Enable-OutlookAnywhere* cmdlet. In order to enable Outlook Anywhere with the same settings as those configured in Figure 5.15, you would need to type:

```
Enable-OutlookAnywhere –Server <servername> –
ExternalHostname "mobile.exchangedogfood.dk"
–ExternalAuthenticationMethod "NTLM" –SSLOffloading $False
```

Configuring the Outlook Client

In this section, we'll go through the needed steps required to configure an Outlook 2007 client to be able to take advantage of Outlook Anywhere.

To configure an Outlook 2007 client for Outlook Anywhere access, perform the following steps:

1. Open the respective Outlook client (Outlook 2003 or 2007), and then click **Tools | Account Settings**.

2. Double-click the **E-mail** profile, and then select **More Settings**.

3. Choose the **Connection** tab and check **Connect to Microsoft Exchange using HTTP** (as shown in Figure 5.16), and then click **Exchange Proxy Settings…**

Figure 5.16 Enabling Outlook Anywhere in Outlook 2007

4.   Enable and fill out each field as shown in Figure 5.17. Make sure you select NTLM Authentication if that's the method you use in the publishing rule on your ISA server. Click **OK** twice, then select **Next**, **Finish**, and **Close** to exit Outlook Account Settings.

Figure 5.17 Configuring the Exchange Proxy Settings

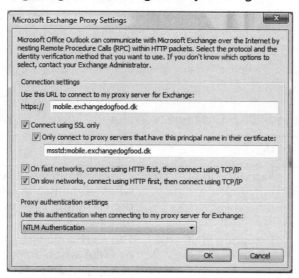

The next time the respective end user is away from the office, they will be able to connect to the Exchange Server using their Outlook client.

Managing Outlook Web Access 2007

During the development of Exchange Server 2007, one of the goals for the Exchange Product group was to make the best Web mail client in the world even better. This task resulted in Outlook Web Access (OWA) 2007 having to be completely rewritten in managed code in order to make it scale even better, and to make it easier to add new features to the UI in the future. Speaking of the UI, one thing you'll notice immediately is that it has been completely redesigned. The number of clicks required to get tasks done has been drastically reduced. Actions and responses are now in place, meaning they are opened in the same browser window instead of in separate multiple dialogs or property sheets. All pop-up notifications have been removed so there are no concerns of being blocked by pop-up blockers. In addition, the drag-and-drop functionality and right-click context menus have been vastly improved. Additionally, OWA 2007 supports 47 different languages!

Finally, unlike OWA 2003, which did all the UI rendering on the back-end server, OWA 2007 now does all the UI rendering on the CAS, thereby significantly reducing the load on the Mailbox server.

Configuring Outlook Web Access Server-Side

After having installed the CAS role on a server, you can manage most of the OWA-related features directly from within the Exchange Management Console, more specifically under the Client Access node located beneath the Server Configuration work center.

As you can see in the Work pane, when selecting one of the CAS servers in the Result pane, Outlook Web Access 2007 displays all of the virtual directories listed in Table 5.2. Notice all of them but one (owa) are legacy OWA virtual directories, only used when accessing mailboxes and/or Public Folders stored on a legacy Exchange Server (Exchange 2000 or 2003).

Table 5.2 Exchange 2007 and Legacy Exchange Virtual OWA Directories

Virtual Directory	Version	Description
Exadmin	Exchange 2000, 2003	The /Exadmin virtual directory is used when administering Public Folders via the Exchange 2000 or 2003 System Manager.
Exchange	Exchange 2000, 2003	The /Exchange virtual directory is used by OWA when accessing mailboxes on legacy Exchange Servers (Exchange 2000 or Exchange 2003).

Continued

Table 5.2 continued Exchange 2007 and Legacy Exchange Virtual OWA
Directories

Virtual Directory	Version	Description
ExchWeb	Exchange 2000, 2003	The /ExchWeb virtual directory is used by the /Exchange virtual directory for accessing mailboxes on legacy Exchange Servers (Exchange 2000 or Exchange 2003).
owa	Exchange 2007	The /owa virtual directory is used by Outlook Web Access when accessing mailboxes on Exchange 2007 mailbox servers.
Public	Exchange 2000, 2003	This virtual directory is used to access public folders by using the Outlook Web Access application for mailboxes located on computers running Exchange 2007, Exchange Server 2003, or Exchange 2000 Server. Only public folders on servers that are running Exchange 2003 or Exchange 2000 will be available through Outlook Web Access.

NOTE

With Exchange Server 2007, you can longer access Public Folders using the
OWA 2007 interface.

Because the /owa virtual directory (vdir) is the only vdir used when accessing a user
mailbox stored on an Exchange 2007 Mailbox Server, this is also the vdir under which you
configure most of the OWA-related functionally (I say most since some settings must still be
configured using the IIS Manager).

Let's take a closer look at the configuration options available on the Property page of
the owa virtual directory.

The first tab, which is the General tab shown in Figure 5.18, shows us information such
as the name of the CAS, the Web site to which the owa vdir belongs, as well as the
Exchange version and the last time the vdir was modified. In addition, this is where we can
specify the Internal and External URL used to access OWA (the internal URL will always
be pre-entered).

Figure 5.18 The General Tab on the OWA Property Page

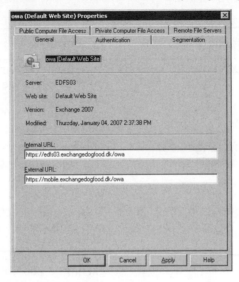

Moving on to the **Authentication** tab (Figure 5.19), here we have the option of specifying the authentication method used to authenticate OWA users. Notice forms-based authentication is enabled by default, unlike OWA 2003 where you had to enable this feature manually. If for some reason you don't want to have forms-based authentication enabled, you can choose to switch to basic by clicking **Use one or more standard authentication methods**. One reason you might want to do this is because you have an ISA Server 2006 deployed in your perimeter network and you are using it to pre-authenticate user logons, thus enabling **Basic authentication** instead.

Figure 5.19 The Authentication Tab on the OWA Property Page

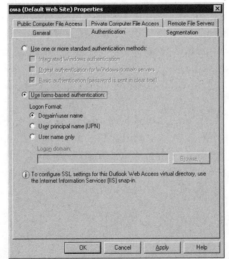

Before we move on, I want to bring your attention to the sentence in the bottom on the Authentication window pane, which says that in order to configure SSL settings for the Outlook Web Access virtual directory, you should use the IIS Manager. Since the SSL certificate that is installed on the Default Web Site is a self-signed untrusted SSL certificate, there will come a day where you want to replace it with an SSL certificate from a third-party certificate provider (I showed you how this was done in the previous section in this chapter).

Now click the **Segmentation** tab shown in Figure 5.20. In previous versions of Exchange, segmentation was very complex to configure, because you had to do so directly in the Registry (at least until the Exchange 2003 Outlook Web Administration tool was released). With Exchange Server 2007 it couldn't be easier. You simply select the feature you want to disable, click the **Disable** button and that's it. You don't even have to do an *IIS-RESET /noforce* afterwards. Most impressively, there is no need to log off and back on since the change is applied immediately!

Figure 5.20 The Segmentation Tab on the OWA Property Page

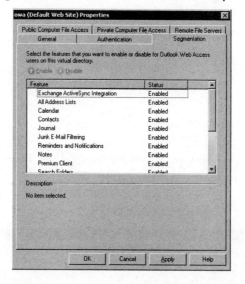

> **TIP**
>
> If you want to turn off an OWA feature for one or more users, you can do so using the *Set-CASMailbox* cmdlet. For example, we can turn off the calendar for a user with the following command:
>
> **Set-CASMailbox <user> -OWACalendarEnabled: $False**

The next tab is the Public Computer File Access tab, shown in Figure 5.21. Here we can enable and disable direct file access. Direct file access is a feature that makes it possible for your users to open any file that is available through OWA. This is not only file attachments, but also files located in Windows SharePoint Services document libraries and/or on Windows file server shares.

Figure 5.21 The Public Computer File Access Tab on the OWA Property Page

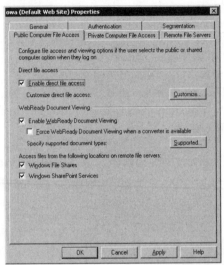

When you have enabled the direct file access feature, click the **Customize** button. Here you can specify which types of files users can access without having to save them first. You can do this by clicking the **Allow** button under *Always Allow* (Figure 5.22) and then adding or removing file types from the list as necessary.

Figure 5.22 Direct File Access Settings

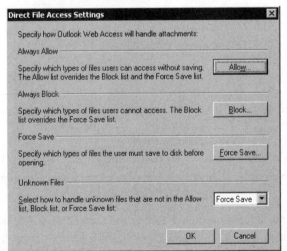

TIP

For more comprehensive coverage of the configuration options of the Direct file access feature, you might want to read the following article of mine at the MSExchange.org site: http://www.msexchange.org/tutorials/Drilldown-OWA-Direct-File-Access-Exchange-Server-2007-Part1.html.

Under the Block list button, you can specify any file types your users should not be allowed to access via OWA. The Force Save list is used to specify file types your users must save to disk before they can be opened. The last option, called Unknown Files, is used to specify how unknown file types that haven't been specified in the Allow list, Block list, or Force Save list should be handled. Here you can select between Force Save, Allow, and Block.

NOTE

The Allow list overrides the Block list and the Force Save list, so choose wisely when adding/removing file types from the Allow list.

Let's click OK in order to get back to the main Public Computer File Access tab. The next option here is called **WebReady Document Viewing**. When this option is enabled (the default setting), the file types specified can be viewed simply by using Internet Explorer (Exchange renders the specified file types into HTML), instead of opening the actual file type's locally associated application, such as Word, Excel, PowerPoint, and so on. This is a great feature when using a public Internet kiosk, for example, which may not have the required application installed.

Note that you can configure to mandate this feature, such that WebReady Document Viewing is forced, even when a converter is available.

Lastly, we can specify whether our OWA users should be able to access files from internal Windows File Shares or Windows SharePoint Services. OWA 2007 has a document access feature built into the UI, making it possible for users to access documents on any of these types of servers. Coverage of this feature as seen from the client-side is outside the scope of this book. Instead, I suggest you read the following article of mine at MSExchange.org: http://www.msexchange.org/tutorials/Drilldown-OWA-Direct-File-Access-Exchange-Server-2007-Part2.html.

Let's skip the next tab, the Private Computer File Access tab, since the configurable options are identical to the ones we just went through. The reason why there's a private and public computer file access tab is because you have the option of further locking down access from a public computer, such as an Internet kiosk. These are directly related to the OWA forms–based logon options: "This is a public or shared computer" and "This is a private computer."

This brings us to the last Remote File Servers tab. As you can see in Figure 5.23, this tab is used to specify remote file server access. OWA accesses only internal Windows file share and Windows SharePoint Services document libraries. In addition, a file name can be specified by using a fully qualified domain name (FQDN) that is internal, or that is included in the list of sites to be treated as internal.

Figure 5.23 The Remote File Servers Tab on the OWA Property Page

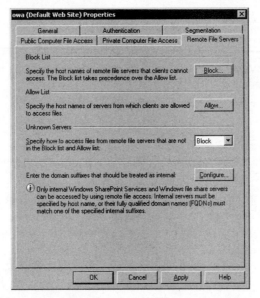

You can also specify how to access files from unknown remote file servers, not in the **Block** or **Allow** lists. Here, you can choose either Allow or Block.

The very last configuration option to cover is related to which domain suffixes should be treated as internal Web sites. This is done by clicking the **Configure** button and then entering the domain suffix for sites whose FQDN names should be treated as internal.

Outlook Web Access Client-Side Features

The first thing you'll notice when you log on to your mailbox using OWA 2007 is the new and improved logon page shown in Figure 5.24. Here you can specify whether you're logging on from a public/shared computer or a private computer, as was also the case in OWA 2003. You should select public or shared computer if you're logging on to your mailbox from an Internet kiosk or a shared computer at a customer site, and so on. If this is the case, also make sure you log off correctly, closing all browser windows when you have finished checking your e-mail.

Figure 5.24 The New OWA 2007 Logon Page

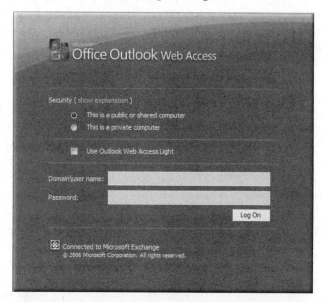

If you are logging on from one of your own private computers, you can safely select This is a private computer. Doing so will allow you a longer period of inactivity before the session expires, as well as grant you access to features that have been configured for private computer logons only.

> **NOTE**
>
> The OWA 2007 logon page will remember your "private" selection and the username you entered on trusted machines, meaning you only have to enter your password the next time you log on from a trusted machine.

Finally, you have the option of checking Use Outlook Web Access Light. OWA Light is the solution for all browsers and operating systems other than IE6 or IE7 on a Windows platform. So if you're a Firefox, Mac, or even a Linux user, this Web mail client is for you. Simply put, if you like to use off-brand browsers, something else other than IE6+, use OWA light. Although OWA 2007 Light should be considered a light version of the rich OWA 2007 Web mail client, I can assure you it's better than most of the other Web mail clients on the market. Actually, it's very impressive!

> **NOTE**
>
> Covering the OWA 2007 Light Web mail client is outside the scope of this book, but if you want to know more about the features in this version, I recommend you check out the following post on the MS Exchange team blog: http://msexchangeteam.com/archive/2006/09/13/428901.aspx.

If this is your first time accessing your mailbox using OWA 2007, after you have entered your username (by default you need to use domain\username) and password, and clicked the **Log On** button, you'll be presented with the screen shown in Figure 5.25. On this screen, you can check **Use the blind and low vision experience** if required, as well as choose the primary language for your OWA 2007 GUI. Lastly, you can change your time zone if desired. When ready, click **OK**.

Figure 5.25 The OWA 2007 Logon Settings Page

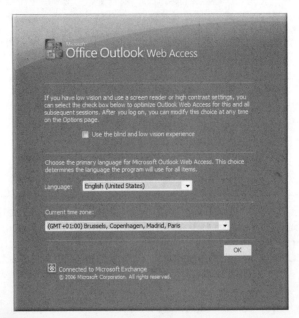

Your mailbox will now be opened. As you can see in Figure 5.26, the OWA 2007 UI is totally different from OWA 2000 and 2003; it's much crisper.

Figure 5.26 The New OWA 2007 UI

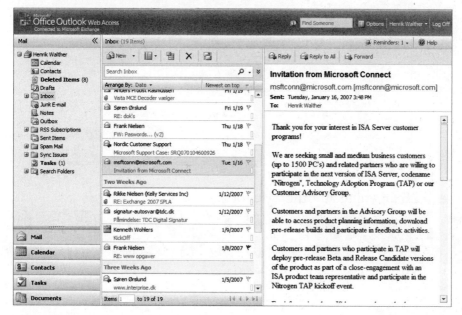

Going through all of the OWA 2007 features is outside the scope of this book, so instead I suggest you explore the OWA 2007 client for yourself. In the following, however, you will find some of my personal favorite features in OWA 2007. To be honest, some of these would have been quite hard to find, no matter how intensively you explored the OWA UI.

Mailbox Limit Notification

When you're nearing the quota of your mailbox, you'll get a notification. In addition, you'll always be able to see your mailbox limit, as well as the current size of your mailbox, by simply holding the cursor over the mailbox in the top left corner, as shown in Figure 5.27.

Open Other Mailbox

A feature that was requested by many in OWA 2003 was the option of opening an additional mailbox using OWA. Although OWA 2007 includes this feature, making it possible to enter the name of a user's mailbox and then open it as shown in Figure 5.28, the mailbox will be opened in a separate browser window. Although many would like the option of being able to open an additional mailbox in the same OWA session, this is definitely a step in the right direction.

Figure 5.27 Mailbox Limit Notification

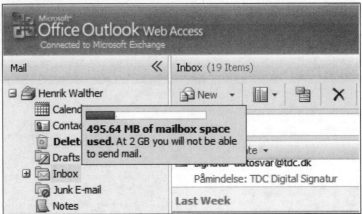

Figure 5.28 Opening Another Mailbox

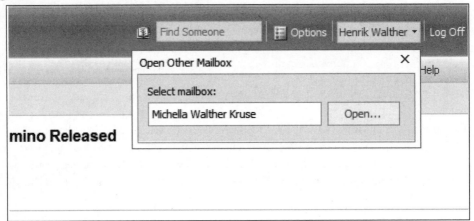

View Message Header

Finally, it's possible to see the message header for an e-mail message using OWA 2007! In order to do so, open the respective message and click the envelope icon to the left of the printer icon in the toolbar, shown in Figure 5.29.

Figure 5.29 Message Header in OWA 2007

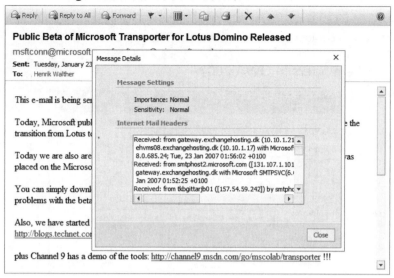

Creating Multiple Calendars

With OWA 2007, you can now create multiple calendars in your mailbox. For example, you can create both a work and a private calendar, as shown in Figure 5.30.

Figure 5.30 Multiple Calendars in OWA 2007

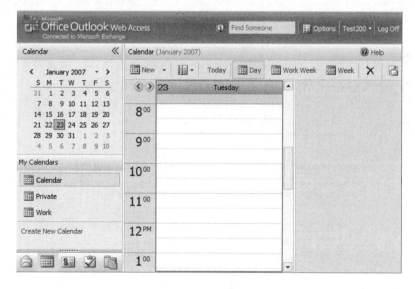

Meeting and Appointment Reminders

Reminders are now integrated into OWA 2007 and are viewable by clicking the reminders drop-down box in the folder title area, as shown in Figure 5.31.

Figure 5.31 Reminders in OWA 2007

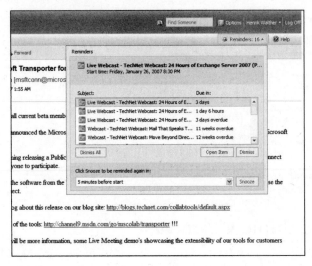

Change Password Option

The change password option is now integrated directly in the OWA 2007 UI (Figure 5.32), meaning you no longer need to mess with configuring this feature in IIS Manager. It simply just works. As in previous versions of Exchange, this feature can be found on the OWA options page.

Figure 5.32 The Change Password Option in OWA 2007

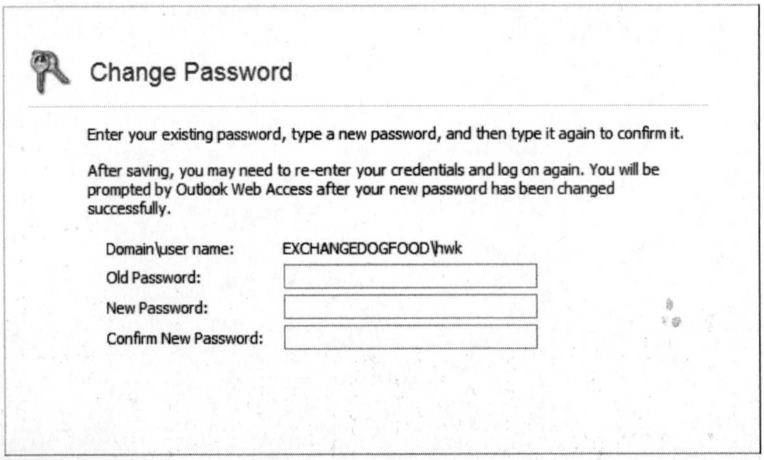

Change Password

Enter your existing password, type a new password, and then type it again to confirm it.

After saving, you may need to re-enter your credentials and log on again. You will be prompted by Outlook Web Access after your new password has been changed successfully.

Domain\user name: EXCHANGEDOGFOOD\hwk

Old Password:

New Password:

Confirm New Password:

Direct Link Access

Another new feature in OWA 2007 is the new direct link access feature (Figure 5.33), which allows OWA users to access documents located in a share on a file server or documents on a SharePoint Server.

Figure 5.33 Direct Link Access

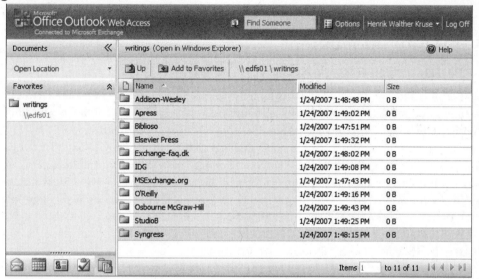

In-depth coverage of this feature is outside the scope of this book, but you can instead refer to one of my previous articles on MSExchange.org: http://www.msexchange.org/tutorials/Drilldown-OWA-Direct-File-Access-Exchange-Server-2007-Part2.html.

Compose Messages in HTML

OWA 2007 now supports HTML as a message formatting tool, which means you're no longer bound to those boring plain text messages. You can now create great looking messages from directly within OWA 2007.

Junk E-mail Lists

You can now add senders to your Safe Senders, Blocked Senders, and Safe Recipients lists by right-clicking on the respective message and selecting Junk E-mail. These lists can be viewed via the OWA options page. Note that the Junk Mail feature is not turned on by default and must be enabled.

Improved Signature Editor

The signature editor in OWA 2007 is also light years better than the one included in OWA 2003. Now you can actually create great looking signatures just like in Outlook. The signature shown in Figure 5.34 is my signature at work.

Figure 5.34 The Rich Signature Editor in OWA 2007

WebReady Document Viewing Feature (Open as Webpage)

Another nice addition to OWA 2007 is the new WebReady Document Viewing feature, which lets you tell Exchange to render certain types of file types into HTML if you don't have the right application installed locally. Exchange 2007 will ship with support for transcoding the following file types by default: DOC, DOT, RTF, WBK, WIZ, XLS, XLK, PPT, PPS, POT, PWS, and PDF. The transcoding engine has a pluggable architecture so the Exchange Product group can add support for new file types in future service packs if necessary. To use the WebReady Document Viewing feature, click the **Open as Web Page** link to the right of the respective attachment shown in Figure 5.35.

Figure 5.35 WebReady Document Viewing

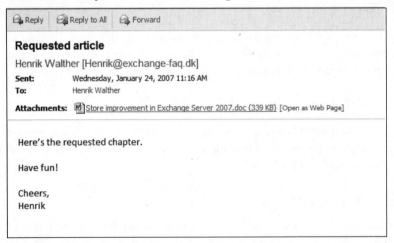

This will render the document file into HTML, and after a few seconds you'll be able to read it directly in the browser window, as shown in Figure 5.36. Now that is pretty impressive, right?

Figure 5.36 An HTML Rendered Word Document

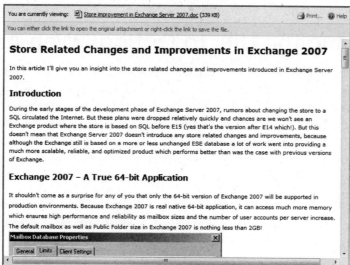

Mark All as Read

A small, and personally very useful feature not in OWA 2003, was the option to mark all items in a specific folder as read when using the Outlook client. With OWA 2007, this feature has finally made its way into the UI, as shown in Figure 5.37.

Figure 5.37 Mark All Messages in a Folder as Read

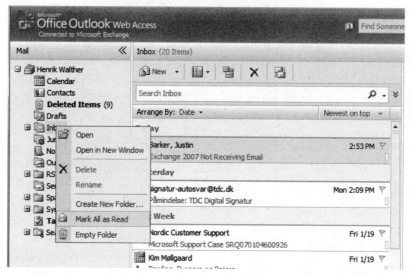

All right, I better stop here! Be sure to explore the new OWA 2007 UI intensely since there are lots of great features buried within.

Simplifying the URL to Outlook Web Access

As was possible with previous versions of Exchange, you can simplify the URL to OWA in order to provide an even easier experience for your end users. As mentioned earlier in this section, the default URL to OWA 2007 is https://server.domain.com/owa. Although your users have to type fewer characters compared to previous versions of OWA, why not skip the /owa part and just use https://server.domain.com? Possibly because it may be more complicated to configure than it is a benefit to end users, I hear some of you grumbling. Actually, however, this is extremely easy to configure. Simply perform the following steps:

1. Log on to the server upon which the Client Access Server role has been installed.

2. Open the IIS Manager by clicking **Start | All Programs | Administrative Tools | Internet Information Services (IIS) Manager**.

3. In the IIS Manager, expand **Server (local computer) | Web Sites**, and then right-click the **Default Web Site** and select **Properties**.

4. Click the **Home Directory** tab, as shown in Figure 5.38.

5. Select **A redirection to a URL**, and then type **/owa** in the **Redirect to:** field.

6. Check **A directory below URL entered**.

Figure 5.38 Specifying Redirection URL

7. Click **OK** and exit the IIS Manager.

You can now tell your end users they can access the Web mail client using https://mail.domain.com, or whatever URL you use to access OWA from the Internet.

Although the preceding solution should be sufficient for most end users, several of you may have end users who don't understand they must type https instead of http before the actual URL. Most of them probably don't know the difference between a secure and a non-secure site. In order to eliminate frustrations for the end user, you can configure OWA in such a way that they simply need to type http://mail.domain.com to be redirected to the proper OWA URL. In order to both simplify the OWA URL as well as redirect from HTTP to HTTPS, you must create a custom HTML page. In order to do so, perform the following steps:

1. Create the HTML page. You can do so in a Notepad document. Enter the HTML code shown in Figure 5.39.

Figure 5.39 Code Snippet Used for Redirection

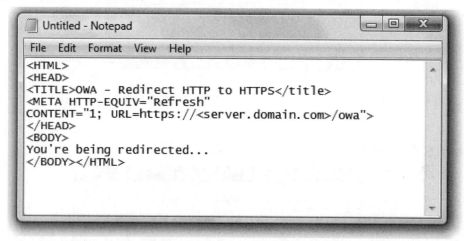

2. Save it as **SSL_OWA.HTM** (remember to select **All Files** in **Save As type**: drop-down box).

3. Open the IIS Manager by clicking **Start | All Programs | Administrative Tools | Internet Information Services (IIS) Manager**.

4. In the IIS Manager, expand **Server (local computer) | Web Sites**, and then right-click the **Default Web Site** and select **Properties**.

5. Click the **Home Directory** tab and select **A redirection to a URL**.

6. In the **Redirect to:** field, type **/owa** and then check **A directory below URL entered**.

7. Click the **Custom Errors** tab.

8. In the HTTP Error table, select **403;4**, as shown in Figure 5.40.

Figure 5.40 Modifying the 403-4 Custom Error Message File

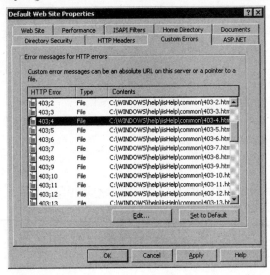

9. Click **Edit** and then point to the **SSL_OWA.HTM** file you saved earlier, as shown in Figure 5.41.

Figure 5.41 Specifying the New HTM File

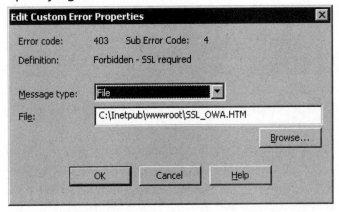

10. Click **OK** twice and exit the IIS Manager.

11. Open a **Command Prompt** windows and type **IISRESET /noforce** in order to apply the changes.

Your end users should now be able to access OWA using http://mail.domain.com or whatever the URL is to OWA in your environment.

Managing Exchange ActiveSync

One of the features that have really been improved upon in Exchange Server 2007 is, without doubt, the Exchange ActiveSync communication protocol. Exchange Server ActiveSync is still based on the DirectPush technology, (sometimes also referred to as AUTD v2) introduced first in Exchange Server 2003 SP2, improving the mobile messaging experience for your users by providing close to real-time over-the-air access to your e-mail messages, schedules, contacts, tasks lists, and other Exchange server mailbox data. Actually, DirectPush is the only method available when synchronizing your mailbox using Exchange ActiveSync (EAS) in Exchange Server 2007, and is thus enabled by default. That means AUTD v1, based on text messaging (SMS), has officially been dropped. But who would miss it? I seriously doubt anyone, as AUTD wasn't very widely used, especially since very few mobile carriers (especially in Europe) supported this method.

To refresh your memory, I thought it would be a good idea to include Figure 5.42, showing you how DirectPush works behind the scenes.

Figure 5.42 DirectPush behind the Scenes

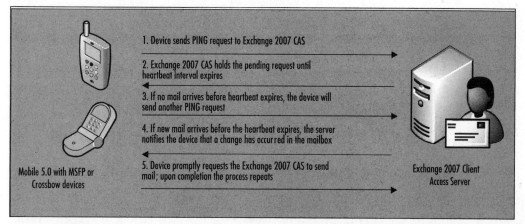

DirectPush works by keeping an HTTPS connection alive between a mobile device and the Exchange 2007 CAS server. Because DirectPush uses long-standing HTTPS requests, it's important that both your mobile carrier and your firewall are configured with a time-out value from the default to 15 to 30 minutes. If a short time-out value is configured, it will cause the device to initiate a new HTTPS request much more frequently, which not only shortens battery life on your device, but is also more costly since more data will be transferred.

TIP

If you use an ISA 2004 or 2006 firewall in your organization, Microsoft KB article 905013 (http://support.microsoft.com/kb/905013) describes the steps necessary in order to configure the firewall to support long-standing HTTPS requests.

So what about the current Windows mobile devices on the market today? Are they supported by Exchange Server 2007? Yes, all devices with Exchange ActiveSync will be able to synchronize with an Exchange 2007 mailbox. If you don't have a Windows mobile 5.0 device with the Messaging and Security Feature Pack (MSFP) installed, a part of the Adaptation Kit Update V2 (AKU2) ROM, you can use a third-party solution such as RoadSync from DataViz (http://www.dataviz.com) to sync with Exchange 2007. Currently, the Exchange ActiveSync protocol is licensed by the following companies:

- Nokia
- Sony Ericsson
- Motorola
- Symbian
- Palm
- DataViz

For more information about mobile device support in Exchange Server 2007, see www.microsoft.com/exchange/evaluation/features/owa_mobile.mspx.

Okay, enough talk about DirectPush. Let's take a look at the other new or enhanced mobile features included with Exchange Server 2007:

- **Support for HTML messages** Messages can now be viewed in HTML format, which means you now can read messages containing HTML code, tables, and so on (just as with most newsletters). Replies to an HTML-formatted e-mail message will not disrupt formatting either, keeping HTML e-mail threads intact. In the past, the mobile device converted the message to plain text. This was also true when you replied to or forwarded the HTML formatted message.

- **Support for follow-up flags** Exchange Server 2007 supports using quick flags from a mobile device running Crossbow, the codename for the next release of Windows mobile (in beta at the time of this writing). This means that quick flags set from a Crossbow device will be synchronized to the mailbox, and be visible in both Outlook and OWA, too. The same is true the other way.

- **Support for fast message retrieval** Fetching the body of an e-mail message has been improved further. You no longer need to select **Mark for download** or click **Get the rest of this message** since this will happen automatically in the background. Note also that this feature requires the new Crossbow version of Windows Mobile.

- **Meeting attendee information** You can now synchronize information about attendee availability to your mobile device; pretty much the same as you do in Outlook now. You can forward or reply to a meeting request, as well as see the acceptance status of attendees. In addition, you can even see GAL information for each attendee.

- **Enhanced Exchange Search** With the enhanced Exchange search feature, you can now search your whole mailbox, instead of just the messages cached locally on the mobile device. The search feature supports rich/query filters, meaning you can search for messages using the *test, data, from, to, flags, categories, attachments, importance,* and *restricted to* specific fields. The number of items returned can be constrained and/or paged through. Lastly, the search is lightning fast since it's only initiated from the device and is physically executed on the server. Note that this feature requires Crossbow on the mobile device.

- **Windows SharePoint Services and Universal Naming Convention (UNC) document access** Just as with OWA 2007, you can access documents stored on either a file server (UNC shares) or a SharePoint server. You can even forward a large document without downloading it to the mobile device first! Note that this feature requires Crossbow on the mobile device.

- **Reset PIN/Password** With Exchange Server 2007, you can require that a device password be entered on a mobile device after a period of inactivity. If this device password should be forgotten at a later time, it's possible to unlock the device by using a device recovery password. Note that this feature requires Crossbow on the mobile device.

- **Enhanced device security through password policies** With Exchange Server 2007, you can enhance the security of a Windows mobile device by configuring additional password requirement settings, such as password history tracking, password expiration, and by prohibiting the use of passwords that are too simple (password complexity). We take a closer look at these features later in this section. Note that this feature requires Crossbow on the mobile device.

- **AutoDiscover for over the air (OTA) provisioning** Exchange 2007 ActiveSync supports the new Web-based AutoDiscover service, which we talked about earlier in this section. Support for AutoDiscover simplifies provisioning since you only need to specify your e-mail address and password when configuring the mobile device for Exchange ActiveSync. Note that this feature requires Crossbow on the mobile device.

■ **Support for Out of Office configuration** Like with Outlook 2007 and OWA 2007, you can set Out of Office (OOF) messages directly from your mobile device. The OOF messages are saved directly to the Exchange 2007 server so an OOF message set on a mobile device can be seen in Outlook and OWA as well. Note that this feature requires Crossbow on the mobile device.

I bet you agree this is a pretty comprehensive list of new features and improvements. Unfortunately, there are also a few features that didn't make it into the RTM version of Exchange Server 2007. The following is a list of those features:

■ **Information Rights Management (IRM)** Originally, the plan was to include IRM support for mobile devices in the RTM version of Exchange Server 2007, but because of some stability issues in rare situations this feature was removed just before its release.

■ **Outlook Mobile Access (OMA)** OMA has been dropped completely and will therefore not be included in an Exchange 2007 SP. I'm certain only a very few of us will miss this, shall I say, slightly clumsy Web-based mobile device Web mail client.

■ **Support for S/ MIME** As with OWA 2007, unfortunately the RTM version of Exchange Server 2007 doesn't support S/MIME. This is not because the feature has been dropped, but due to the fact that the Exchange Product group simply didn't have the time to finish it before its release. I am sure many of us would not have had any issues waiting a few more months for the RTM version if S/MIME for OWA 2007 and Windows mobile devices were included.

Configuring the Exchange ActiveSync Virtual Directory

As with Exchange Server 2003, Exchange ActiveSync is still accessed using the Microsoft-Server-ActiveSync virtual directory, which by default is located under the Default Web Site in IIS Manager, as can be seen in Figure 5.43.

The IIS Manager is still the tool used to configure settings such as authentication methods, IP addresses, and domain name restrictions, as well as secure channel (SSL). However, with the EAS virtual directory related settings, you can control many directly from within the Exchange Management Console.

Figure 5.43 Microsoft Server ActiveSync Virtual Directory in IIS Manager

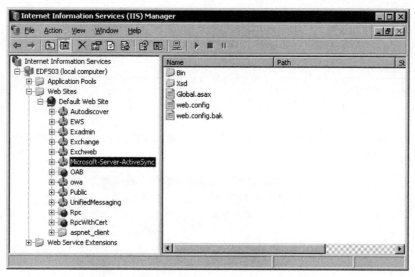

TIP

All Microsoft-Server-ActiveSync virtual directory–related settings, with the exception of SSL which must be configured using the IIS Manager, can also be configured using the Exchange Management Shell. You do so using the *Set-ActiveSyncVirtualDirectory* cmdlet. You can view the properties of the virtual directory using the *Get-ActiveSyncVirtualDirectory* cmdlet.

If we expand the Server Configuration work center node and click the Client Access subnode, we'll get a list of the CAS servers in our Exchange 2007 organization. Select a CAS, and then click the Exchange ActiveSync tab in the Work pane. Open the Property page for the Microsoft-Server-ActiveSync virtual directory. On the General tab, you can find information such as the name of the CAS, the Web site to which the virtual directory belongs, whether SSL is enabled or not, and when the virtual directory was last modified (see Figure 5.44). In addition, we have the option of specifying the internal and external URL used to access the CAS using Exchange ActiveSync. The internal URL is configured by default, but the external URL must be entered manually. The external URL is used by the AutoDiscover service when a mobile device supporting AutoDiscover tries to connect to the CAS using only the e-mail address and password.

NOTE

Windows Mobile 5.0 and earlier don't support the AutoDiscover service, only the next version of Windows mobile, codenamed Crossbow and currently in beta, supports this feature.

Figure 5.44 The Properties Page of the Microsoft Server ActiveSync Virtual Directory in EMC

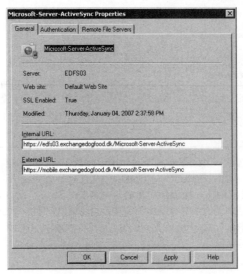

Let's move on to the **Authentication** tab (Figure 5.45). Here we have the option of enabling **Basic authentication (password sent in clear text)**, typically the authentication method used by Exchange ActiveSync clients. In addition, we can specify how the CAS should handle client certificates.

Finally, we have a **Remote File Servers** tab. We won't go through the available options here since they are identical to those covered in the Outlook Web Access section in this chapter and simply allow the access of files on remote file shares or SharePoint servers.

Figure 5.45 The Authentication Tab on the Microsoft Server ActiveSync
Properties Page

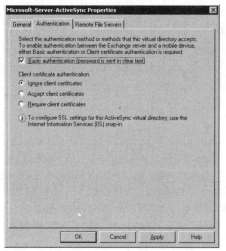

> **TIP**
>
> Windows mobile 5.0 and earlier devices cannot take advantage of the direct
> link access feature, which allows you to access documents in a share on a file
> server, or documents located on a SharePoint Server. Only the next version of
> Windows mobile, codenamed Crossbow and currently in beta at the time of
> this writing, supports the direct link access feature.

Configuring ActiveSync Policies

As many of us remember, Exchange Server 2003 SP2 introduced a set of device security settings that allowed us to push out a policy to mobile devices accessing the Exchange 2003
Server using Exchange ActiveSync. We had the option of *enforcing passwords on the devices, setting the minimum password length, setting the inactivity timeout, setting a device to be remotely wiped
after x number of failed logon attempts, setting how often the device security settings should be pushed
out to the devices,* and more. One problem with the device security settings feature in
Exchange Server 2003 SP2 was its limitation to one global policy, which applied to all users,
unless they were explicitly added to an exception list, excluding them from all security
policy. With Exchange Server 2007, it is now possible to create multiple Exchange
ActiveSync policies, giving you much more control of your mobile deployment.

In the following example, I'll show you step by step how an Exchange ActiveSync
policy is created.

1. Open the **Exchange Management Console**, and then expand the **Organization Configuration** work center node.

2. Click the **Client Access** subnode, and then select **New Exchange ActiveSync Mailbox Policy** in the Action pane.

3. In the **New Exchange ActiveSync Mailbox Policy**, enter a name for your policy and then check and configure the options that should be applied to the user mailboxes to which this policy is assigned, as shown in Figure 5.46.

NOTE

If you have experience with configuring the device security settings in Exchange 2003 SP2, the options listed in Figure 5.46 should be familiar, with the exception of four. The four new options are **Enable password recovery**, **Require encryption on device, Password expiration (days)**, and **Enforce password history**. The first option, **Enable password recovery**, will store a user's password on the Exchange Server so it's possible to retrieve a lost device password should the user forget it. A lost password can be retrieved by the IT staff using the Exchange Management Console or the Exchange Management Shell, but a user can also retrieve it himself via the Mobile Device page in OWA 2007. The second option, **Require encryption on device**, will encrypt the data on the storage card in a device, but keep in mind this option is only supported with devices running the next version of Windows mobile, codenamed "Crossbow." The third option, **Password expiration (days)**, allows us to specify after how many days a device password should stay active before expiring. The fourth option, **Enforce password history**, makes it possible to enforce password history so users must use a completely new password when it has expired.

4. When ready, click **New**, and then **Finish** on the following page.

Figure 5.46 Creating a New Exchange ActiveSync Mailbox Policy

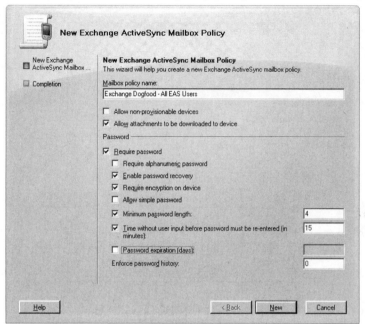

If you would rather create an Exchange ActiveSync policy using the Exchange Management Shell, you can do so using the *New-ActiveSyncMailboxPolicy* cmdlet. For example, the policy configured in Figure 5.46 could be created using the Exchange Management Shell by typing:

New-ActiveSyncMailboxPolicy –Name "Exchange Dogfood – All EAS Users" –AllowNonProvisionableDevices $false –DevicePasswordEnabled $true –AlphanumericDevicePasswordRequired $false –MaxInactivityTimeDeviceLock "00:15:00" –MinDevicePasswordLengh "4" –PasswordRecoveryEnabled $true –DeviceEncryptionEnabled $true –AttachmentsEnabled $true –AllowSimpleDevicePassword $false –DevicePasswordExpiration "unlimited" –DevicePasswordHistory "0"

After you have configured an Exchange ActiveSync Mailbox Policy, you can always change it later if required. You can do this by selecting the respective policy in the Result pane, and then clicking the Properties link in the Action pane. This will bring you to a screen similar to the one shown in Figures 5.47 and 5.48.

Figure 5.47 The General Tab on the Properties Page of an Exchange ActiveSync Mailbox Policy

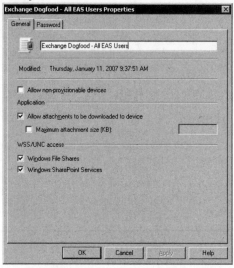

Figure 5.48 The Password Tab on the Properties Page of an Exchange ActiveSync Mailbox Policy

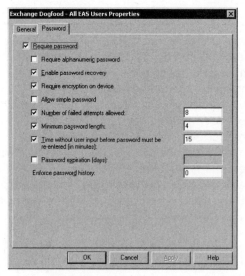

NOTE

Notice that mobile device users, by default, are allowed access to any Windows File Shares and Windows SharePoint Service Servers you may have configured. Again, this feature is only supported from a Crossbow device.

Assigning an Exchange ActiveSync Policy to a User

So how do we assign an Exchange ActiveSync (EAS) policy to one or more users once it's created? This can be done using either the Exchange Management Console or the Exchange Management Shell. To assign an EAS policy to a user, perform the following steps:

1. Open the **Exchange Management Console**, and then expand the **Recipient Configuration** work center node.

2. Select the **Mailbox** subnode and highlight the *user mailbox* to which you want to assign the EAS policy.

3. Click **Properties** in the **Action pane**.

4. Click the **Mailbox Features** tab, as shown in Figure 5.49.

Figure 5.49 Enabling/Disabling Exchange ActiveSync on a Per User Basis

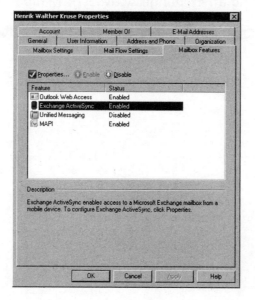

5. Select **Exchange ActiveSync**, and then click the **Properties** button.

6. Check **Apply an Exchange ActiveSync mailbox policy**, and then click **Browse**, as shown in Figure 5.50.

Figure 5.50 Assigning an Exchange ActiveSync Mailbox Policy to a User Mailbox

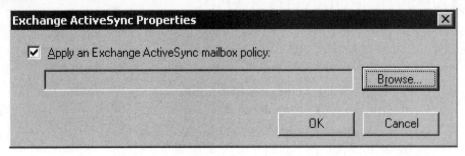

7. In the **Select ActiveSync Mailbox Policy** window (Figure 5.51), choose the respective EAS mailbox policy and then click **OK** three times.

Figure 5.51 Selecting an Exchange ActiveSync Mailbox Policy

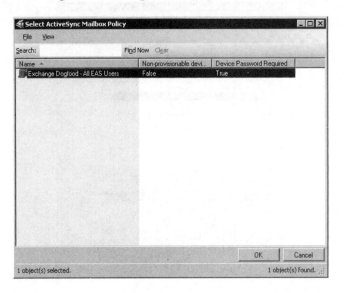

TIP

To assign an EAS mailbox policy to a mailbox using the Exchange Management Shell, use the *Set-CASMailbox* cmdlet. For example, if you want to assign an EAS mailbox policy named *Exchange Dogfood – All EAS users* to a user alias called HWK, type the following command:

    Set-CASMailbox HWK –ActiveSyncMailboxPolicy "Exchangedogfood – All EAS Users"

Managing Mobile Devices

Now that we have finished our mobile deployment, how do we go about managing the mobile devices in our organization? Well, unlike Exchange Server 2003 SP2, which required you to download a separate Web administration tool (called the Mobile Administration Web tool) that among other things allowed you to delete device partnerships and remote wipe stolen or lost devices from a central location, these features and more are an integral part of the Exchange Management Console.

To manage the mobile device(s) for a specific user, you must perform the following steps:

1. Open the **Exchange Management Console**.

2. Expand the **Recipient Configuration** work center and click **Mailbox**.

3. Select the *user mailbox* for which you want to manage a mobile device.

4. Click **Manage Mobile Device**.

5. The Manage Mobile Device wizard now appears (Figure 5.52).

Figure 5.52 Managing Mobile Devices

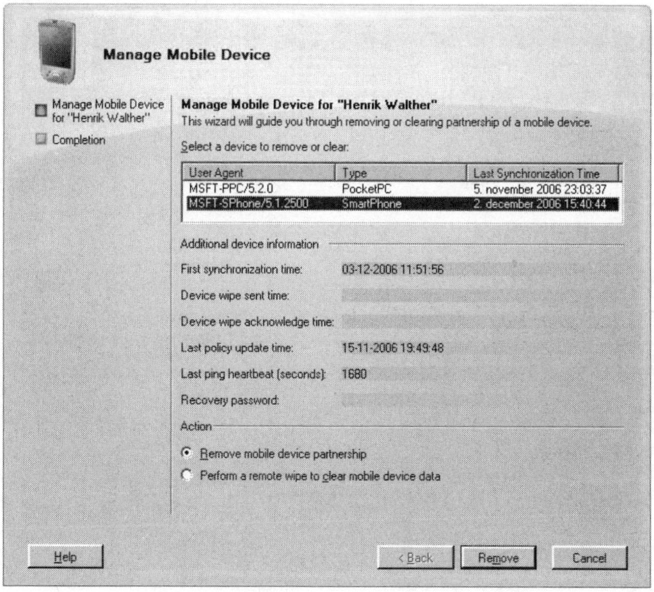

Here you can see the mobile devices that have an established partnership with the respective user mailbox. Under **Additional device information**, you can see when the first synchronization occurred, when the last device wipe command was issued, the acknowledge time for the device wipe, when the device was last updated with a policy, as well as the last ping heartbeat in seconds (this should be between 15 and 30 minutes, depending on how keep alive sessions have been configured with your mobile service provider and on your firewall). Finally, you can see the recovery password here (if enabled by policy).

Under Action, you have the option of either removing (a.k.a., deleting) a mobile device partnership, as well as performing a remote wipe of a mobile device. Performing a remote wipe of a mobile device will delete any data held in memory as well as on the storage card. In other words, the device will be reset to its factory defaults.

NOTE

Removing a mobile device partnership will not delete any data on the mobile device.

In order to reduce the load on IT staff (primarily the Helpdesk), the Exchange Product group also implemented these mobile device management features into OWA 2007. This means users can manage their own devices, as shown in Figure 5.53.

Figure 5.53 Managing Mobile Devices in OWA 2007

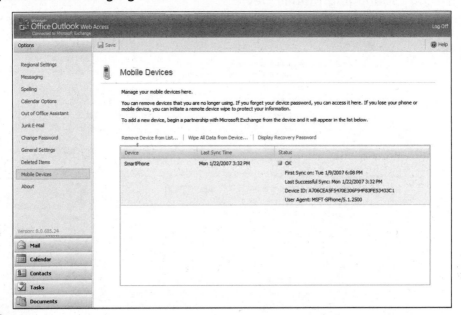

TIP

To remove a mobile device partnership or remote wipe a mobile device using the Exchange Management Shell, you must use the *Remove-ActiveSyncDevice* and *ClearActiveSyncDevice* cmdlets, respectively. For further details on how to do this, type **Get-Help Remove-ActiveSyncDevice** and/or **Get-Help ClearActiveSyncDevice** in the Exchange Management Shell.

Managing POP3/IMAP4

Like its predecessors, Exchange Server 2007 also supports the Post Office Protocol version 3 (POP3) and Internet Message Access Protocol version 4 (IMAP4) clients; however, since these client protocols aren't that popular anymore (especially now that we have Outlook Anywhere, a superb Web mail client and EAS), the POP3 and IMAP4 protocols are disabled by default.

Both the POP3 and IMAP4 protocols have been rewritten from the ground up in managed code, and are no longer dependent on the IIS component. Instead, they run as a separate Windows Service.

Because the Exchange Product group focused on rewriting the POP3 and IMAP4 protocols in managed code, and because of the general time pressure that lay over their heads during the development of the Exchange Server 2007 product, they unfortunately didn't have time to build a GUI to administer these protocols. This means that you cannot use the Exchange Management Console to configure or manage the POP3 and IMAP4 protocols. Instead, this must be done using the respective cmdlets in the Exchange Management Shell.

> **NOTE**
>
> If the Exchange Product group receives sufficient feedback from customers requiring a GUI for managing the POP3 and IMAP4 protocols, we can expect one to be included in Exchange Server 2007 Service Pack 1.

Other things worth noting about the POP3 and IMAP4 services in Exchange Server 2007 is that we are limited to only one POP3 or IMAP4 service per server, and the same SSL certificate must be used for all POP3 and IMAP4 connections to the respective Client Access Server. In addition, Public Folder access through an IMAP4 client is no longer supported. Also, bear in mind that IPSec isn't supported when you have an ISA Server deployed between clients and the Exchange server.

Okay, enough focus on what's missing with the POP3 and IMAP4 protocols. After all, there are a few new improvements. Support for TLS encryptions has been added, Kerberos authentication is now supported, and, finally, the search feature for both POP3 and IMAP4 clients has been heavily improved.

Enabling the POP3 and IMAP4 Services

As mentioned earlier, both the POP3 and IMAP4 services are disabled by default. If you decide to use one or both of these services, the first thing you must do is enable them and set them to an Automatic service startup type using the Services MMC snap-in. You can do this by clicking **Start | Run** and typing **Services.msc**, which brings up the Services snap-in (shown in Figure 5.54).

Figure 5.54 Starting the POP3 and IMAP4 Services in the Services Snap-in

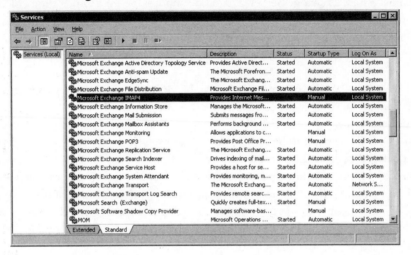

Then drill down and open the property page for **Microsoft Exchange POP3**, as shown in Figure 5.55. Select **Automatic** in the **Startup type** drop-down menu, and then click **Start**.

Figure 5.55 Setting the Service to Automatic Startup

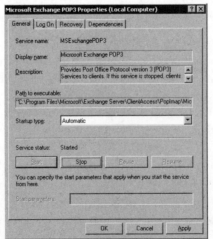

Repeat these steps for the **Microsoft Exchange IMAP4** service, if needed.

> **NOTE**
>
> You can also enable the POP3 and IMAP4 services using the *Set-Service* and *Start-Service* cmdlets in the Exchange Management Shell. To set the services to start automatically, use the ***Set-Service MSExchangePOP3*** and ***Set-Service MSExchangeIMAP4*** cmdlet options, respectively. Next, you can start the services by typing ***Start-Service MSExchangePOP3*** and ***Start-Service MSExchangeIMAP4***.

When you have enabled the POP3 or IMAP4 service, you can verify functionality by making a telnet call to the Client Access Server on port 110 or 143, respectively. To do so, open a Command Prompt window and type: Telnet <server> 110 or Telnet <server> 143, and press Enter. You will then get the POP3 or IMAP4 banner, as shown in Figure 5.56.

Figure 5.56 Verifying the Service Is Running

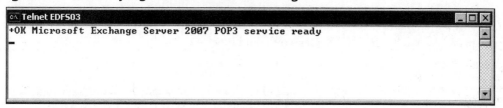

Configuring the POP3 or IMAP4 Services

In order to configure more specific settings for the POP3 or IMAP4 services, you must use the *Set-PopSettings* and *Set-ImapSettings* cmdlets. We won't dive further into the parameters available with these commands, but instead will briefly mention that you can configure features such as *maximum connections*, *connection timeouts*, *banner to displayed*, *login method*, and so on.

To see a full list of each parameter available, as well as their descriptions, type either Get-Help Set-PopSettings or Get-Help Set-ImapSettings, depending on which service you want to configure further.

Limiting Access to the POP3 and IMAP4 Service

When the POP3 and IMAP4 services have been started, all mailbox-enabled users can access their mailbox using one of these two services. Since there might be situations where you want to lock down access to these two services to a specific set of users (for example, in a shared hosting environment), I thought it would be a good idea to show you how to set access these services on a per-user basis.

To enable or disable access to POP3, use the following cmdlets:

```
Set-CASMailbox <user mailbox> -ImapEnabled $true
```

```
Set-CASMailbox <user mailbox> -ImapEnabled $false
```

To enable or disable access to IMAP4, use the following cmdlets:

```
Set-CASMailbox <user mailbox> -PopEnabled $true
```

```
Set-CASMailbox <user mailbox> -PopEnabled $false
```

If you need to enable or disable one of these services for thousands of users, you could make use of piping. Let's say you wanted to enable IMAP4 access to all users with a mailbox on a particular Exchange 2007 Server, you could type:

```
Get-Mailbox <servername> | Set-CASMailbox -ImapEnabled $true
```

Of course this is just a simple command to show you how powerful the Exchange Management Shell is when it comes to bulk-enabling a feature for a set of users.

Summary

In this chapter, we had a look inside the services that are provided by, and can be configured for, an Exchange 2007 Server with the Client Access Server role installed. As you have seen throughout the chapter, many tasks can be performed on this server role. The CAS role is the one responsible for providing access to the AutoDiscover and Availability Services, used by features such as free/busy information, Unified Messaging, Out of Office messages, and Offline Address Books, as well as providing auto-profile settings to Outlook 2007 clients. Since the CAS replaces the earlier front-end server we know from Exchange 2000 and 2003, this server role is also responsible for proxying Internet clients such as Outlook Anywhere (formerly known as RPC over HTTP), Exchange ActiveSync devices, Outlook Web Access (OWA), and, finally, POP3 and IMAP4 to the Mailbox servers in the organization.

Solutions Fast Track

Managing the Exchange 2007 Client Access Server

- ☑ The Client Access Server role replaces the front-end server we know from Exchange 2000 and 2003, and adds some additional functionality.

- ☑ The Client Access Server is also responsible for providing access to the Offline Address Book (OAB), but only for Outlook 2007 clients—Outlook 2007 being the only client version that can take advantage of the new Web-based distribution method.

- ☑ The AutoDiscover service and the Availability service are two new Web-based services that provide functionalities such as automated profile configuration, free/busy time, meeting suggestions, and Out of Office (OOF) messages.http://blogs.msdn.com/mca/rss.xml. Another Web-based service on the CAS is the Unified Messaging (UM) service, which provides automatic UM settings in Outlook 2007.

- ☑ The Client Access Server should always be deployed on a domain-member server, on the internal network, and not in the DMZ (which many thought was a security best practice for Exchange 2000 or 2003 front-end servers).

The AutoDiscover Service

- ☑ The AutoDiscover service simplifies Outlook client deployment by creating an automatic connection between Exchange Server and Outlook 2007 clients without the need for using special scripts, complex user intervention, or tools such as the Custom Installation Wizard from the Office Resource Kit.

☑ If you're configuring an Outlook 2007 profile on a machine logged on to the Active Directory, AutoDiscover will fetch the domain account information from the logged-on user credentials, meaning you only have to click Next a few times and that's it.

☑ When the Client Access Server role is installed on an Exchange 2007 Server, a virtual IIS directory named AutoDiscover is created under the Default Web Site

☑ When installing the CAS, a new object named the *service connection point (SCP)* is also created in Active Directory. The SCP object contains the authoritative list of AutoDiscover service URLs in the forest, and can be updated using the *Set-ClientAccessServer* cmdlet.

The Availability Service

☑ The purpose of the Availability service is to provide secure, consistent, and up-to-date (that is, data in real time!) free/busy data to clients using this service. Since only Outlook 2007 and OWA 2007 can take advantage of this new service, legacy clients such as Outlook 2003 and earlier, as well as OWA 2003, still depend on a Public Folder database containing the SCHEDULE+ FREE/BUSY system folder.

☑ Since only Outlook 2007 and OWA 2007 can use the Availability service to obtain free/busy information, it's important that Exchange 2007 can interact with legacy systems, too.

☑ Outlook 2007 discovers the Availability Service URL using the AutoDiscover service. Actually, the AutoDiscover service is like a DNS Web Service for Outlook, since it's used to find various services like Availability Service, UM, and OAB. It simply tells Outlook 2007 where to go when searching for these Web services.

Client Access Servers and the SSL Certificate Dilemma

☑ In previous versions of Exchange, you simply issued a request for an SSL certificate, and when received, assigned this certificate to the Default Web Site in the IIS Manager. But in Exchange 2007, it is a different beast when it comes to securing client connectivity to the CAS using SSL certificates.

☑ A default self-signed SSL certificate is assigned to the Default Web Site during the installation of the Exchange 2007 CAS role. If you take a closer look at this certificate, you'll notice that it contains multiple *subject alternative names*.

☑ An SSL certificate that supports additional *subject alternative names* typically costs in the range of $600 per year.

Managing Outlook Anywhere

☑ Outlook Anywhere makes it possible for your end users to remotely access their mailbox from the Internet using their full Outlook client. Those of you with Exchange 2003 experience most likely know the technology behind the Outlook Anywhere feature already since Outlook Anywhere is just an improved version of RPC over HTTP.

☑ The technology behind Outlook Anywhere is basically the same as in Exchange 2003 since it still works by encapsulating the RPC-based MAPI traffic inside an HTTPS session, which then is directed toward the server running the RPC over HTTP proxy component on your internal network. This gives you the same functionality as you get by using the Outlook client from a machine on your internal network. When the HTTPS packets reach the RPC over HTTP proxy server, all the RPC MAPI traffic is removed from the HTTPS packets and forwarded to the respective Mailbox server.

☑ In order to use Outlook Anywhere, you must install a valid Secure Sockets Layer (SSL) certificate from a trusted Certificate Authority (CA) that the clients trust by default.

Managing Outlook Web Access 2007

☑ During the development of Exchange Server 2007, one of the goals for the Exchange Product group was to make the best Web mail client in the world even better. In order to do this, Outlook Web Access (OWA) 2007 was completely rewritten in managed code to make it scale even better and make it easier to add new features to the GUI in the future. Speaking about the GUI, one thing you'll notice immediately is that the interface has been completely redesigned.

☑ OWA 2007 supports 47 different languages in total!

☑ Forms-based authentication is enabled by default, unlike OWA 2003 where you had to enable this feature manually.

☑ We can specify whether our OWA users should be able to access files from internal Windows File Shares or Windows SharePoint Services. OWA 2007 has a document access feature built right into the UI, which makes it possible for the users to access documents on any of these types of servers.

☑ OWA Light is the solution for all browsers and operating systems other than IE6 or IE7 on a Windows platform. So if you're a Firefox, Mac, or even a Linux user, or simply just a user of something other than IE6+, this Web mail client is for you.

☑ The new URL for OWA 2007 is https://mobile.domain.com/owa.

☑ Just as with previous versions of Exchange, you can simplify the URL to OWA in order to provide an even better experience for your end users.

Managing Exchange ActiveSync

☑ One of the features that have really been improved in Exchange Server 2007 is, without a doubt, the Exchange ActiveSync communication protocol. Exchange Server ActiveSync is still based on the DirectPush technology (sometimes also referred to as AUTD v2) that was introduced in Exchange Server 2003 SP2. This improves the mobile messaging experience for your users by providing close to real-time over-the-air access to your e-mail messages, schedules, contacts, tasks lists, and other Exchange server mailbox data.

☑ DirectPush is the only method you can use when synchronizing your mailbox using Exchange ActiveSync (EAS) in Exchange Server 2007, and is therefore enabled by default. That means AUTD v1, which was based on text messaging (SMS), has been dropped.

☑ DirectPush works by keeping an HTTPS connection alive between a mobile device and the Exchange 2007 CAS server. Because DirectPush uses long-standing HTTPS requests, it's important that both your mobile carrier and your firewall are configured with a time-out value from the default to between 15 and 30 minutes. If a short time-out value is configured, it will cause the device to initiate a new HTTPS request much more frequently, which not only shortens battery life on your device, but becomes more expensive since more data will be transferred.

☑ With Exchange Server 2007, it's possible to create multiple Exchange ActiveSync policies, giving you much more control of your mobile deployment.

Managing POP3/IMAP4

☑ Like its predecessors, Exchange Server 2007 also supports the Post Office Protocol version 3 (POP3) and Internet Message Access Protocol version 4 (IMAP4) clients, but since these client types aren't that popular anymore (especially with the evolution of Outlook Anywhere, a superb Web mail client and EAS), they are disabled by default.

☑ Both the POP3 and IMAP4 protocols have been rewritten from the ground up in managed code, and are no longer dependant on the IIS component. Instead, they run as a separate Windows Service.

☑ Other things worth noting about POP3 and IMAP4 services in Exchange Server 2007, is the fact that we are limited to one POP3 or IMAP4 service per server, and the same SSL certificate must be used for all POP3 and IMAP4 connections to the respective Client Access Server.

☑ When the POP3 and IMAP4 services have been started, all mailbox-enabled users can access their mailbox using one of these two services. Since there might be situations where you want to lock down access to these two services to a specific set of users (for example, in a shared hosting environment), you can use the Exchange Management Shell cmdlets *Set-PopSettings* and *Set-ImapSettings* to enable or disable specific users individually.

Frequently Asked Questions

The following Frequently Asked Questions, answered by the authors of this book, are designed to both measure your understanding of the concepts presented in this chapter and to assist you with real-life implementation of these concepts. To have your questions about this chapter answered by the author, browse to **www.syngress.com/solutions** and click on the **"Ask the Author"** form.

Q: Can the CAS be used to proxy requests to Exchange 2000 or 2003 back-end servers?

A: Yes, the CAS is capable of proxying requests to both Exchange 2000 and 2003 back-end servers.

Q: If I deploy a CAS in my legacy Exchange organization, will I get the OWA 2007 UI when logging on to OWA?

A: No. As is also the case with previous versions of Exchange, you will always get the UI of the back-end server. So, in this case you'll get the OWA 2003 UI.

Q: How can I configure the /owa virtual directory using the Exchange Management Shell?

A: You can use the *Set-OwaVirtualDirectory* cmdlet to configure OWA-related settings via the Exchange Management Shell. For example, in order to enable forms-based authentication for the /owa virtual directory, you would need to run the following command: *Set-OwaVirtualDirectory -Identity "owa (default Web site)" -FormsAuthentication:$true*. For more information about available parameters, type **Get-Help Set-OwaVirtualDirectory** in the Exchange Management Shell.

Q: I've noticed an SSL certificate is installed on the Default Web Site, by default. Would you recommend I replace it?

A: Yes, if you plan on using all of the Mobile Exchange 2007 features, OWA, ActiveSync, and Outlook Anywhere since they require the *subject alternative name* in the SSL cert to match what is configured on the client for accessibility from the Internet.

Q: Can I assign an Exchange 2007 ActiveSync Mailbox Policy to a legacy (Exchange 2000 or 2003) Exchange mailbox?

A: No. You can only assign Exchange 2007 ActiveSync Mailbox policies to mailboxes stored on Exchange 2007 Mailbox Servers.

Q: Does CAS support clustering?

A: No, only Exchange 2007 Mailbox servers can be clustered (using Single Copy Cluster or Cluster Continuous Replication), but you can use NLB to load balance CAS roles— either using Windows NLB or some sort of hardware solution.

Q: Where does the UI rendering for OWA 2007 take place?

A: Unlike OWA 2003, which did all the UI rendering on the back-end server, OWA 2007 now does all the UI rendering on the CAS and thereby significantly reduces the load on the Mailbox server.

Q: I can't seem to find the place where you manage the POP3 and IMAP4 services in the Exchange Management Console?

A: That is because there is no UI for these services. You must configure these two services using the Exchange Management Shell since the Exchange Product group didn't add management tasks for the services to the EMC. Expect these services to be added to the UI in Exchange 2007 Service Pack 1.

Chapter 6

Managing the Hub Transport Server Role

Solutions in this chapter:

- Message Transport and Routing Architecture in Exchange 2007

- Managing the Hub Transport Server

- Managing Message Size and Recipient Limits

- Message Tracking with Exchange Server 2007

- Using the Exchange 2007 Queue Viewer

- Introduction to the Exchange Mail Flow Troubleshooter Tool

- Configuring the Hub Transport Server as an Internet-facing Transport Server

☑ Summary

☑ Solutions Fast Track

☑ Frequently Asked Questions

Introduction

The Exchange 2007 Hub Transport server role should be installed on a domain-member server, and should always be deployed on your internal network, not in the perimeter network as some might. The Hub Transport server replaces the bridgehead server we know from Exchange 2000 and 2003, and therefore takes care of all the internal mail flow in the organization. All internal messages will pass through the Hub Transport server, even if the sender and recipient mailbox are located in the same AD site—heck, even if they're on the same Mailbox server!

In addition to being responsible for all mail flow inside the organization, the Hub Transport server has a set of transport agents that lets us configure rules and settings that can then be applied as messages pass through the server. The Hub Transport server also allows us to create messaging policies and rule settings that match the specific regulations and compliance requirements in the organization.

Since the Hub Transport server typically sends and receives Internet messages through an Edge Transport server in the perimeter network, it doesn't have any anti-spam agents installed, and doesn't allow inbound messages from unauthenticated (untrusted) e-mail servers on the Internet—at least not in its default state. Since not all organizations can, nor will, deploy an Edge Transport server in their perimeter network, I'll show you how you can configure the Hub Transport server to be the Internet-facing transport server in your organization.

Message Transport and Routing Architecture in Exchange 2007

A lot has changed in regards to transport and routing architecture in Exchange Server 2007. First, Exchange no longer uses the SMTP protocol stack included with Internet Information Services (IIS), as was the case with previous versions of the product. Instead, the Exchange Product group has rewritten the SMTP transport stack in managed code, resulting in a much more stable and secure protocol stack. For example, the new transport stack runs as the Network Service account and uses several new mechanisms that reduce the risks associated with Denial-of-Service attacks and other security issues. The new SMTP transport stack is now known as the Microsoft Exchange Transport service (MSExchangeTransport.exe), and because it's no longer dependent on IIS, it is not located within the IIS Manager anymore. As a matter of fact, you don't even install IIS on the Hub Transport server unless it's combined with the Mailbox or Client Access server role on the same hardware.

You no longer need to set up routing group connectors between routing groups in the Exchange organization when you design your Exchange topology, as there is no such functionality built into the Exchange 2007 product. "Why has this flexible way of routing messages throughout an Exchange organization been removed?" I hear some of you grumble. Well, routing groups actually have several drawbacks, including long stretches of time where two servers disagree about a connection state, possibly causing routing loops. Another drawback is that when tracking a message, it can be quite confusing when trying to determine why a message took a given route at a given point in time, because the link state table for the Exchange topology was never persistent or logged. Lastly, the routing groups and routing group connector concept forced Exchange administrators to re-create and mimic the underlying network, which can be quite a time-consuming and even redundant task.

So how do you set up your routing topology in Exchange Server 2007? Well, you don't! Exchange Server 2007 is a site-aware application, which means it can determine its own Active Directory site membership and the Active Directory site membership of other servers by querying Active Directory. So, instead of using its own routing group topology, Exchange makes use of the AD directory service site topology to determine how messages are transported in the organization. This means that the Hub Transport servers in your Exchange organization retrieve information from Active Directory in order to determine how messages should be routed between servers. You need to deploy a Hub Transport server in each site that contains a Mailbox server, such that when user A in one site sends a message to user B in another site, the Mailbox server contacts the Hub Transport server in its own site, and then routes the message to the Hub Transport server in user B's site, ultimately delivering the message to the mailbox server hosting user B's mailbox.

NOTE

All Hub Transport servers use secure SMTP when exchanging messages internally in the organization. They use the industry standard SMTP Transport Layer Security (TLS) so that all traffic between the Hub Transport servers are authenticated and encrypted. This removes the capability for internal snooping. In addition, all RPC communication between Hub Transport and Mailbox servers is encrypted.

I've tried to illustrate how messages are routed in a basic Exchange 2007 organization in Figure 6.1. Notice that the Mailbox and Hub Transport servers use RPC as the basis of communication, but that two Hub Transport servers speak SMTP when exchanging messages.

Figure 6.1 Path for Message Sent from a User in One AD Site to a User in Another AD Site

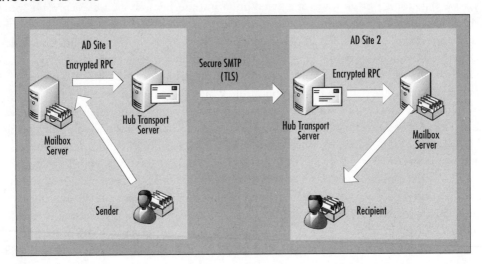

NOTE

When multiple paths exist to a specific AD site, a Hub Transport server will use deterministic algorithms to choose one of the available paths. Since one of the paths will always be chosen, the algorithms are deterministic. To read more about AD site and connector selection algorithms used by routing, see the following blog post on the MS Exchange Team blog: http://msexchangeteam.com/archive/2006/09/15/428920.aspx

When a Hub Transport server in an AD site establishes an SMTP connection to a Hub Transport server in another AD site, in order to deliver a message, it makes use of round-robin load balancing mechanisms. This means that if the first Hub Transport server contacted doesn't respond to a connection, it will try to establish an SMTP connection to the next Hub Transport server in the AD site. This makes Hub Transport servers are fault-tolerant out of the box.

Since routing is determined from Active Directory sites, the Exchange link state update functionality, used in previous versions of Exchange, has been discontinued. The link state functionality of old was used by each routing group master to update and keep their link state tables current, propagating this information back to the other Exchange Servers in the organization. The use of Active Directory sites in Exchange 2007 creates a more deterministic routing topology.

Managing the Hub Transport Server

All organizationwide Hub Transport settings are stored in Active Directory. This means that any modifications or configuration settings, except receive connector specific settings, are reflected on all Hub Transport servers in the organization. In the following, we'll go through each of the tabs available under the Hub Transport subnode shown in Figure 6.2. Since it would be silly to cover the receive connectors in a section of their own, they will be included in this section as well.

Figure 6.2 Available Tabs under the Hub Transport Node

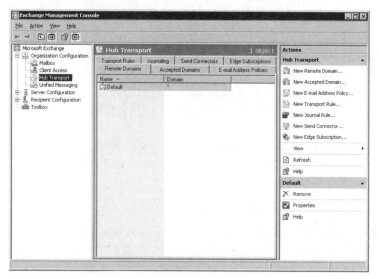

Remote Domains

The first tab is the Remote Domains tab. Here, you can configure message transfer settings between Exchange 2007 and external SMTP domains. When you set up a remote domain, you can control mail flow with more precision, designate message formatting and policy, and specify acceptable character sets for messages that are sent to, and received from, the remote domain. As you can see in Figure 6.2, there's a default remote domain entry configured after installation of the Hub Transport server role. The domain address space is configured as *, which represents all external domains. This means the settings configured in the remote domain entry are applied to all outbound messages. If you have specific requirements for one or more external SMTP domain names, you can configure additional remote domain entries as necessary. I'll show you how a new remote domain entry is created later on, but first let's take a look at the settings configured for the default remote domain entry. When looking at the Properties of the Default Remote Domains entry, you are presented with the General tab, as shown in Figure 6.3.

Figure 6.3 Out-of-Office Message Options

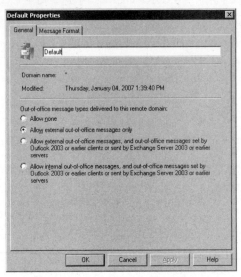

Here, we can specify how the Hub Transport server should handle out of office (OOF) messages to the specified SMTP domains in the remote domains entry. We have four options to choose from:

- **Allow none** No out-of-office messages will be delivered to the remote domain.

- **Allow external out-of-office messages only** Only out-of-office messages configured as external using an Outlook 2007 or OWA 2007 client, and where the respective mailbox is stored on an Exchange 2007 Mailbox server, will be delivered to the remote domain.

- **Allow external out-of-office messages, and out-of-office messages set by Outlook 2003 or earlier clients or sent by Exchange Server 2003 or earlier servers** Out-of-office messages that are configured as external with an Outlook 2007 or OWA 2007 client, and where the respective mailbox is stored on an Exchange 2007 Mailbox server, will be delivered to the remote domain. In addition, out-of-office messages set by Outlook 2003 and earlier, regardless of the server version of their mailbox store, will be delivered to the remote domain. In other words, out-of-office messages that are sent by Exchange 2003 or earlier servers, no matter what client version was used to set the out-of-office message, will be delivered to the remote domain.

- **Allow internal out-of-office messages, and out-of-office messages set by Outlook 2003 or earlier clients or sent by Exchange Server 2003 or earlier servers** Only out-of-office messages that are configured as external with an Outlook 2007 or OWA 2007 client, and where the respective mailbox is stored on an Exchange 2007 Mailbox server, will be delivered to the remote domain. In addition out-of-office messages that are set by Outlook 2003 and earlier, regardless of the server version of their mailbox store, will be delivered to the remote domain. Out-of-office messages that are sent by Exchange 2003 or earlier servers, no matter what client version was used to set the out-of-office message, will be delivered to the remote domain.

The *Allow external out-of-office messages only* option is selected by default.

Let's continue on to the next tab, the Message Format tab, shown in Figure 6.4. I bet this tab looks familiar to many of you, as it's very similar to the one we all know from Exchange 2003, although Exchange 2007 offers a few new options.

Figure 6.4 Message Format Options

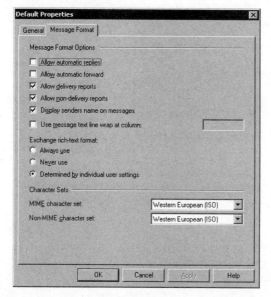

The following is a short description of each option under the Message Format tab:

- **Allow automatic replies** This option allows automatic replies to be sent to the remote domain.

- **Allow automatic forward** This option will allow automatic forwards to be sent to the remote domain.

- **Allow delivery reports** This option allows delivery reports to be sent to all recipients in any remote domain.

- **Allow non-delivery reports** This option allows NDRs to be sent to all recipients in any remote domain.

- **Display sender's name on messages** This option allows a user's display name to be visible to the recipient of the message.

- **Use message text line wrap at column** If you want to use line-wrap in message text for outgoing messages, this option should be enabled. When enabled, you must specify the line-wrap size (between 0 and 132 characters). To set the value to unlimited, leave the field blank.

Creating a New Remote Domains Entry

To create a new Remote Domains entry, click **New Remote Domain** in the Action pane. This will launch the New Remote Domain wizard shown in Figure 6.5. Here, you simply need to enter a name for the new entry, as well as specify the external SMTP domain to which you want to apply the settings. If the domain contains subdomains, you may also want to check **Include all subdomains**. When you have entered the necessary information, click **New** and then **Finish** on the completion page.

Figure 6.5 The New Remote Domain Page

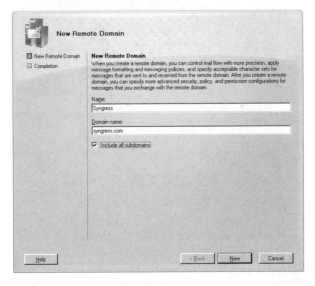

Notice that you don't specify the different settings during the creation of the Remote Domains entry. Instead, this is done by opening the Property page of the remote domain entry after the fact.

TIP

To create a Remote Domains entry via the Exchange Management Shell, you need to use the *New-RemoteDomain* cmdlet. For example, to create a remote domain entry similar to the one we created in Figure 6.5, you would need to run the following command:

New-RemoteDomain –Name "Syngress" –DomainName "*.syngress.com"

Accepted Domains

Under the **Accepted Domains** tab, we specify the SMTP domains for which our Exchange 2007 organization should either be authoritative, relay to an e-mail server in another Active Directory Forest within the organization, or relay to an e-mail server outside the respective Exchange organization. The difference between internal and external relayed domains is that internal relaying simply sends the e-mail messages directly to the e-mail server in the organization. Messages sent to an external relayed domain will first be delivered to the Edge Transport server in the perimeter network, and from there will be routed to the respective external e-mail server on the Internet.

When the first Hub Transport server is deployed in the Exchange 2007 organization, the domain name of the Active Directory Forest root domain is configured as an authoritative domain by default. Since the Hub Transport server used as an example throughout this book has been installed into an Active Directory Forest named exchangedogfood.dk, this domain name is the authoritative domain for this Exchange 2007 organization by default (Figure 6.6). Since we use a split-DNS setup, where the internal and external domain names match, we don't need to do any configuration changes after the Hub Transport server has been deployed. Many organizations use an internal domain name that differs from the external domain name, which among other things is used for inbound mail. For example, it's common to use a domain.local domain internally. If this is the case in your organization, you must manually create an accepted domain matching your external domain name.

Figure 6.6 The Properties Page for an Accepted Domain

Creating a New Accepted Domain

Creating a new accepted domain is a straightforward task. You simply click **New Accepted Domain** in the Action pane. In the New Accepted Domain wizard, enter a name for the accepted domain entry and the domain for which you want to receive e-mail.

> **NOTE**
>
> Any accepted domain that is added under the Accepted Domains tab can be linked to an E-mail Address Policy (EAP), such that it will generate recipient e-mail addresses for the accepted domain. As a matter of fact, every EAP must link to an accepted domain, such that e-mail messages sent to e-mail addresses specified in an EAP are allowed to be routed by the Hub Transport servers in the organization. You'll see what I mean when we cover e-mail address policies next.

As we already talked about, the Hub Transport server can handle messages for a particular domain in several different ways, as shown in Figure 6.7. Choose the desired option and click New and then Finish on the next page.

Figure 6.7 The New Accepted Domain Wizard

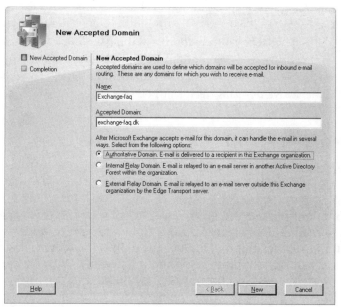

TIP

To create an accepted domain entry via the Exchange Management Shell, you need to use the *New-AcceptedDomain* cmdlet. For example, to create an accepted domain entry similar to the one we created in Figure 6.7, you would need to run the following command:

New-AcceptedDomain –Name "Exchange-faq" –DomainName "exchange-faq.dk" –DomainType "Authoritative"

E-mail Address Policies

E-mail address policies were known as recipient policies back in Exchange 2000 and 2003. Exchange address policies define the proxy addresses stamped onto recipient objects in the Exchange organization. With Exchange 2007, the recipient policies have been separated into two types: accepted domains (which we just covered) and e-mail address policies. Those of you with Exchange 2000 and/or 2003 experience know that recipient policies also controlled which SMTP namespaces were accepted by the Exchange organization. Some of you probably are wondering why these two features were separated in Exchange 2007. The Exchange Product group made this separation for three chief reasons. First, if a domain was specified for an e-mail address recipient policy but wasn't configured as the authoritative domain, the e-mail sent to the recipients with e-mail addresses defined by the policy would not be routed within the Exchange organization for this domain. Even though this is an invalid scenario, the Exchange 2000 and 2003 System Manager allowed this type of configuration. Secondly, the authoritative domain concept was hidden under the e-mail address recipient policy GUI, which wasn't very intuitive for administrators. Lastly, relay domains were controlled via the SMTP connectors GUI, allocated in a completely different location from where the authoritative domains (recipient policies) were controlled.

Some Independent Advice

This separation of accepted domain and e-mail address policies is not the only change in regards to e-mail address policies. The infamous Recipient Update Service (RUS), which most of us know from Exchange 2000 and 2003, is also no longer part of the Exchange 2007 product. RUS was responsible for stamping e-mail addresses on AD objects, in addition to address list membership, and a few other things. However, it didn't always work as expected and was very difficult to troubleshoot when it acted up. With Exchange 2007, the RUS (and thereby the asynchronous behavior used to provision objects) has been replaced by a new synchronous process (the *EmailAddressPolicy* cmdlet), which is used to stamp e-mail address onto objects immediately! Yes, you no longer have to wait for several minutes to see e-mail addresses on your objects, as was often the case with the antiquated RUS.

For a detailed explanation about the removal of RUS, see the following blog on the MS Exchange Team blog: http://msexchangeteam.com/archive/2006/10/02/429053.aspx.

Okay, so to carve it in stone, before you begin creating a new e-mail address policy, you must first add the respective domain name under the Accepted Domains tab.

As you can see in Figure 6.8, we have several e-mail address policies in our Exchange 2007 organization, listed in prioritized order (the lower the number, the higher the priority), as was also the case in Exchange 2000 and 2003. If you want to move a particular policy up the list, highlight the policy and click Change Priority in the Action pane. You must have at least two EAPs aside from the default in order to see the Change Priority Action pane option.

Figure 6.8 A Prioritized List of the E-mail Address Policies in the Organization

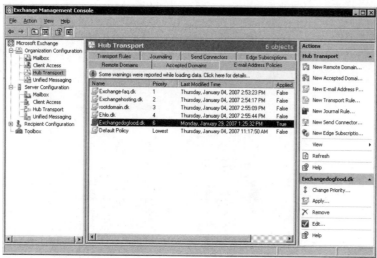

Creating a New E-mail Address Policy

Creating a new e-mail address policy is a straightforward task, although much different from Exchange 2000 and 2003. In order to do so, perform the following steps:

1. Click **New E-mail Address Policy** in the Action pane.

2. On the Introduction page of the New E-Mail Address Policy wizard, enter a *name* for the new policy, and then specify what type of recipients should be included (Figure 6.9). Afterward, click **Next**.

Figure 6.9 The New E-Mail Address Policy Window

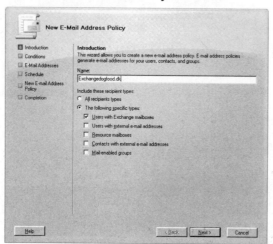

3. You can now be a bit more selective when defining your target group by using the filter and selecting one or more conditions, as shown in Figure 6.10. When you have configured any conditions you want applied to the policy, click **Next**.

Figure 6.10 The New E-Mail Address Wizard Conditions Page

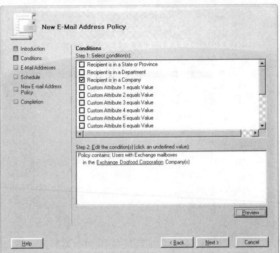

4. Click **Add** and select the **E-mail address local part** to be used to create the username portion of the e-mail address. Then, choose an e-mail domain from the **E-mail address domain** in the drop-down box, as shown in Figure 6.11. When ready, click **OK** and **Next**.

Figure 6.11 Specifying the Local Part of the E-mail Addresses and the E-mail Address Domain

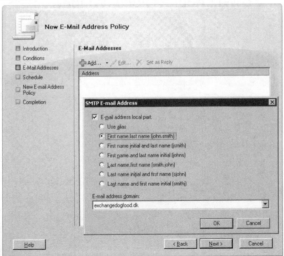

As you can see in Figure 6.11, you can choose between seven local e-mail address parts. The local part of an e-mail address is the name format appearing before the *at sign* (@). If none of the default seven local parts fit what you need to use for your e-mail address policy, you can use the variables listed in Table 6.1.

Table 6.1 Available E-Mail Address Parameters

Variable	Description
%g	Used for given name (first name)
%i	Used for middle initial
%s	Used for surname (last name)
%d	Used for display name
%m	Used for Exchange alias
%xs	Uses the x number of letters of the surname. For example, if x = 2, then the first two letters of the surname are used.
%xg	Uses the x number of letters of the given name. For example, if x = 2, then the first two letters of the given name are used.

5. On the **Schedule** page, specify when the e-mail address policy should be applied and the maximum length of time it is permitted to run (Figure 6.12). Then, click **Next**.

Figure 6.12 The New E-mail Address Wizard Schedule Page

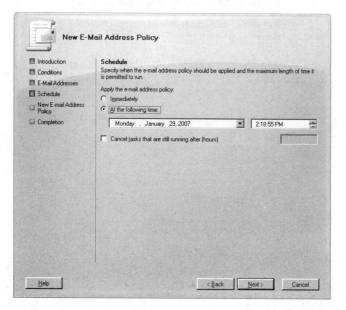

6. On the **Configuration Summary** page, click **New**. If you selected to apply the policy immediately, the proxy address will now be applied to all recipients matching the filter. When this task has completed, click **Finish** on the Completion page.

TIP

To create a new e-mail address policy via the Exchange Management Shell, you need to use the *New-EmailAddressPolicy* cmdlet. For example, to create a policy similar to the one we created using the GUI wizard, you would need to run the following command:

New-EmailAddressPolicy -Name "Exchangedogfood.dk" -IncludedRecipients "MailboxUsers" -ConditionalCompany "Exchange Dogfood Corporation" -Priority "Lowest" -EnabledEmailAddressTemplates "SMTP:%g.%s@exchangedogfood.dk"

When a new E-mail address policy has been created and applied to the recipients, you can verify that the proxy address has been stamped on the respective user objects under the **E-Mail Addresses** tab on the Properties page of a recipient object, as shown in Figure 6.13.

Figure 6.13 The E-mail Addresses Tab on the User Mailbox Property Page

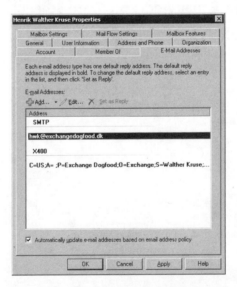

When a recipient has Automatically Update E-mail Addresses Based On Email Address Policy option enabled, all primary e-mail addresses (default reply addresses) of e-mail address

types will always be set from the e-mail address policy. This means that if you edit the primary address to be a different e-mail address, it will always revert back to the one specified in the e-mail address policy.

Transport Rules

With the increasing complexity of government and industry regulations, there's a greater need for efficient management of internal message routing. Exchange 2007, or more specifically the Hub Transport Server role, now includes a new transport rules agent, providing an easy and flexible way to set rules for internal message routing and content restriction throughout the Exchange organization. We can now, for example, append disclaimers to all messages sent within the organization, or create an ethical wall between two departments or groups that exchange confidential data every day. An ethical wall can help isolate an individual or group from information to which they should not have access.

Transport rules consist of three components: conditions, exceptions, and actions. These rules can be created under the **Transport Rules** tab. In-depth coverage of Transport Rules are outside the scope of this book, however. I'll demonstrate to you how easy it is, for example, to append a disclaimer to all messages sent within the organization. To do so, perform the following steps:

1. Click the **Transport Rules** tab shown back in Figure 6.2.
2. Click **New Transport Rule** in the Action pane.
3. On the **Introduction** page of the New Transport Rule wizard, type **Corporate Disclaimer**, and enter a relevant *comment*, as shown in Figure 6.14.

Figure 6.14 The New Transport Rule Wizard Introduction Page

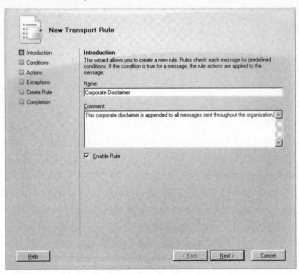

4. Click **Next**.

5. On the **Conditions** page, check **from users inside or outside the organization** (Figure 6.15), and then click **Next**.

Figure 6.15 The New Transport Rule Wizard Conditions Page

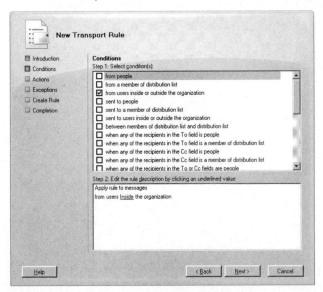

6. Now, check **append disclaimer text using font, size, color, with separator and fallback to action if unable to apply**. In Step 2, click the *disclaimer text* link shown in Figure 6.16.

Figure 6.16 The New Transport Rule Wizard Actions Page

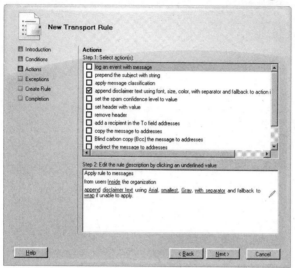

7. In the **Disclaimer text** box, type the disclaimer you want to be appended to messages inside your organization. When finished, click **OK**, as shown in Figure 6.17.

Figure 6.17 The Specify Disclaimer Text Box

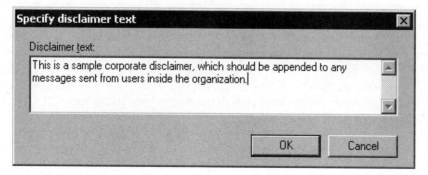

8. Click **Next**.

9. On the **Exceptions** page, click **Next**.

10. Click **New** on the **Create Rule (Configuration Summary)** page.

11. On the **Completion** page, click **Finish**.

Now, any message sent from a user within the organization will have a disclaimer appended to each outgoing message, like the one shown in Figure 6.18.

Figure 6.18 A Test Message with Disclaimer Appended

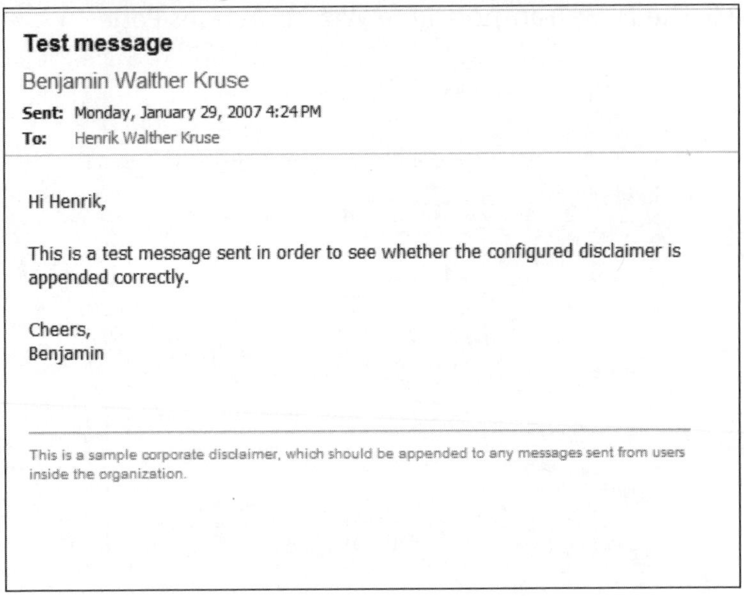

Test message

Benjamin Walther Kruse

Sent: Monday, January 29, 2007 4:24 PM
To: Henrik Walther Kruse

Hi Henrik,

This is a test message sent in order to see whether the configured disclaimer is appended correctly.

Cheers,
Benjamin

This is a sample corporate disclaimer, which should be appended to any messages sent from users inside the organization.

Any time after a transport rule has been created, you can modify it as required. You do this by selecting the rule and clicking **Edit Rule** in the Action pane.

TIP

To create a transport rule via the Exchange Management Shell, you need to use the *New-TransportRule* cmdlet. For example, to create a rule similar to the one we generated using the GUI wizard, you would need to run the following command:

New-TransportRule –Name "Corporate Disclaimer" –Comments "This corporate disclaimer is appended to all messages sent throughout the organization." –Conditions "Microsoft.Exchange.MessagingPolicies.Rules.Tasks. FromScopePredicate" –Actions "Microsoft.Exchange.MessagingPolicies. Rules.Tasks.ApplyDisclaimerAction" –Exceptions –Enabled $true –Priority "0"

Journaling

Exchange Server 2003 natively supported journaling on a per *mailbox store* level. This functionality is also included in Exchange Server 2007, and is known as *standard journaling*. Standard journaling allows you as an Exchange administrator to enable journaling on a *per mailbox database* level. There's not much to say about standard journaling, other than that it is enabled on the property page of a Mailbox database. It then simply works.

Although standard journaling is sufficient for some, it's too basic for most organizations today. Keeping up with increasing regulatory and compliance regulations requires a much richer archival solution. Therefore, Exchange 2007 also includes premium journaling, a Hub Transport server feature based on a new journaling agent that can be configured to match the specific needs of an organization. Premium journaling lets you create journal rules for single mailbox recipients or for entire groups within the organization.

> **NOTE**
>
> Premium journaling, also known as per-recipient journaling, requires an Exchange Enterprise Client Access License (CAL).

Rules can apply to inbound or outbound messages, or both. In addition, the scope can apply to global, internal or external messages. The messages can be archived to any SMTP address, meaning you are not forced to archive to an Exchange mailbox anymore, but can archive to an Exchange-hosted archive solution. You can even archive to a third-party archive solution.

In order to create a journal rule, perform the following steps:

1. With the **Journaling** tab selected, click **New Journal Rule**.
2. In the New Journal Rule wizard (Figure 6.19), enter a *descriptive name*.
3. Click **Browse** and select the *recipient* who should receive the *journal reports*.
4. Choose the **scope** you want the journal rule to apply to.
5. If the rule should apply to a single mailbox, check **Journal message for recipient**, then click **Browse** and select the *recipient*.

> **NOTE**
>
> If you don't tick **Journal messages for recipient**, the Journal rule will archive all messages sent by all users throughout the Exchange organization.

6. Click **New** to create the rule. On the **Completion** page, click **Finish**.

Figure 6.19 The New Journal Rule Wizard

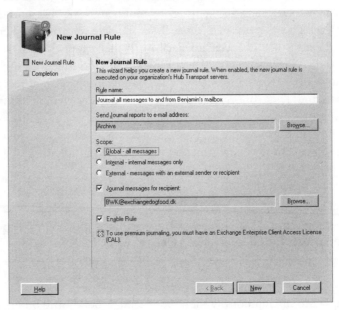

TIP

To create a Journal rule via the Exchange Management Shell, you need to use the *New-JournalRule* cmdlet. For example, to create a rule similar to the one we generated using the GUI wizard, you would need to run the following command:

    New-JournalRule –Name "Journal all messages to and from Benjamin's mailbox" –JournalEmailAddress "exchangedogfood.dk/users/Archive" –Scope "Global" –Enabled $True –Recipient "BWK@exchangedogfood.dk"

When the user Benjamin sends an e-mail message, a journal report will be sent to the specific Journal report e-mail address, as shown in Figure 6.20. As you can see, the journal report includes the message sent by Benjamin as an attachment, as well as information such as sender, subject, and message-ID.

Figure 6.20 A Test Journal Report Message

Send Connectors

Send connectors are used to control how Hub Transport servers send messages using SMTP. That is, how it handles connections to other e-mail servers. This means that a Hub Transport server requires a Send connector in order to successfully deliver messages to their destination. It's important to note that an *explicit* Send connector isn't created during the installation of a Hub Transport server. However, internal Hub Transport servers use SMTP when delivering messages to each other, and although an explicit Send connector is not created by default, this doesn't mean that internal Hub Transport servers cannot deliver a message to another internal Hub Transport server. The reason behind this is that *implicit*, and invisible, Send connectors are automatically computed based on the Active Directory site topology, and based on the topology internal messages they are then routed between the Hub Transport servers in the organization.

Send connectors are stored in Active Directory, and when such a connector is created, their scope is global, not local like receive connectors.

If you don't have an Edge Transport server deployed in your organization's perimeter network, or if no Edge Subscription has been configured (which creates a Send connector automatically), you cannot send mail to other e-mail servers outside your organization. In this case, you must create a Send connector manually. To do so, perform the following steps:

1. Click the **Send Connectors** tab shown back in Figure 6.2.

2. Select **New Send Connector** in the Action pane.

3. The **New SMTP Send Connector** page will appear. On this **Introduction** page, enter a descriptive name (such as *To ISP* or *To Internet*) for the connector, and then select the type of Send connector you want to create, as in the drop-down box shown in Figure 6.21. As you can see, you can choose between four different types of Send connectors:

- **Custom** Select Custom in order to create a customized connector used to connect with other systems that are not Exchange servers.

- **Internal** Internal Send connectors are used to send e-mail to servers in your Exchange organization. When selected, the connector will be configured to route e-mail to your internal Exchange servers as smart hosts.

- **Internet** Internet Send connectors are used to send e-mail to the Internet. When selected, the connector will be configured to use Domain Name System (DNS) MX records to route e-mail.

- **Partner** Partner Send connectors are used to send e-mail to partner domains. When selected, this connector will be configured to only allow connections to servers that authenticate with Transport Layer Security (TLS) certificates for Simple Mail Transfer Protocol (SMTP) domains that are included in the list of domain-secured domains. You can add domains to this list by using the -*TLSSendDomainSecureList* parameter in the *Set-TransportConfig* command.

Figure 6.21 Selecting the Required Send Connector Type

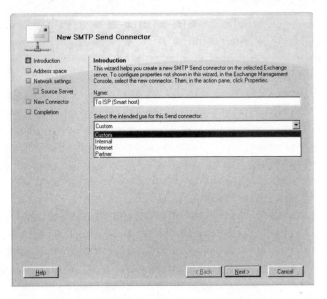

4. On the **Address space** page shown in Figure 6.22, enter the domain or domains to which the Send connector should route mail. If the connector should be used to route outbound mail to the Internet simply add an asterisk (*). When ready click **Next**.

Figure 6.22 Specifying the Address Space

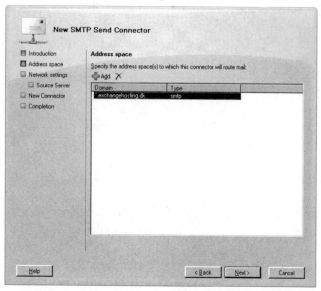

5. On the **Network Settings** page shown in Figure 6.23, specify how you want to send mail with the connector. Here, you can choose to use Domain Name System (DNS) "MX" records to route the mail automatically, or you can choose to have all mail routed to a specified smart host.

Figure 6.23 Configuring Network Settings

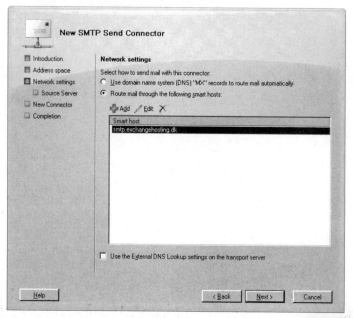

IMPORTANT

If you're a small shop using a cheap ISP that doesn't allow outbound traffic on port 25 from your DSL, you typically need to route outbound mail through a smart host located at your ISP.

6. If you elected to use a smart host in the previous step, you now need to configure the authentication method used to properly authenticate with the specified smart host. If this is a smart host located at your ISP, you typically don't need to authenticate, and can safely select **None**, as shown in Figure 6.24. Click **Next**.

Figure 6.24 Configuring the Smart Host Authentication Settings

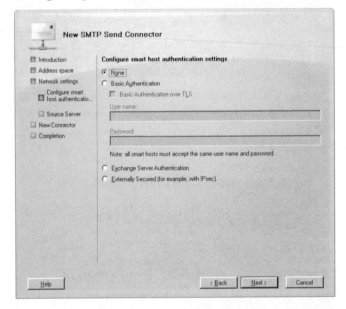

7. Now it's time to associate the connector with a Hub Transport server in the organization (Figure 6.25). The wizard will try to do this for you, but you can change the selection if required. Click **Next**.

Figure 6.25 Specifying the Source Server

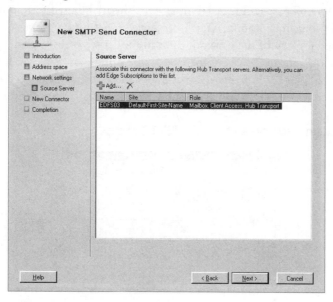

8. On the **Configuration Summary** page, make sure you configured the connector as required, and then click **Next**.

9. On the **Completion** page, click **Finish**.

TIP

To create a Send connector via the Exchange Management Shell, you must use the *New-SendConnector* cmdlet. For example, to create a Send Connector similar to the one we generated in the previous steps, run the following command:

New-SendConnector -Name 'To ISP (Smart host)' -Usage 'Internet' -AddressSpaces 'smtp:*.exchangehosting.dk;1' -DNSRoutingEnabled $true -UseExternalDNSServersEnabled $false -SourceTransportServers 'EDFS03'

When you have created a Send connector, you can disable, enable, modify, and remove it by selecting the respective Send connector, and then choosing the required tasks in the Action pane.

Configuring DNS Lookups

You can configure a Hub Transport server to use different settings for external and internal DNS lookups. Click the **Properties** of your Hub Transport server under the **Server Configuration | Hub Transport** work center node. On the **External DNS Lookups** tab shown in Figure 6.26, specify that DNS server(s) should be used to resolve IP addresses of servers outside your organization. As you can see, you have the option of using the DNS settings configured for one of the network cards in the server, or by specifying the IP address of the DNS server(s) directly. You have the exact same options available under the Internal DNS Lookups tab. The only difference is that under this tab you specify the DNS server(s) that should be used to resolve IP addresses of servers inside your organization.

Figure 6.26 Configuring External DNS Lookups

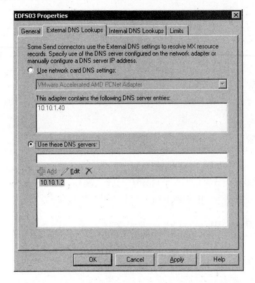

Configuring Outbound Message Limits

You can configure how the Hub Transport server should process outbound messages. This is done by opening the Property page of the respective Hub Transport server object in the Result pane. Here, you click the **Limits** tab. As you can see in Figure 6.27, you have the option of setting the retry interval—in other words, how often the Hub Transport server should try to resend an outbound message to a destination server, which for some SMTP servers don't accept the message the first time it's sent.

Under Message expiration, we can specify the amount of days a message held locally in a message queue as undeliverable should expire. As you can see, the default setting is 2 days, wherein the message will be removed from the message queue and a non-delivery report (NDR) will be sent to the sender of the message.

Figure 6.27 Configuring Outbound Message Limits

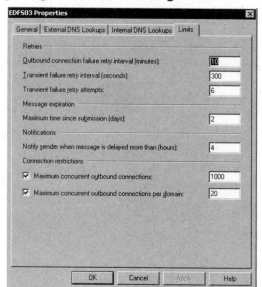

In addition, we can specify after how many hours a non–deliver report (NDR) should be generated and delivered to the sender of the message. By default, the sender will be notified every fourth hour.

Finally, we can configure connection restrictions for concurrent outbound connections and concurrent outbound connections per domain. Unless you're dealing with a very large organization, you should leave the connection restrictions at their defaults.

Typically, the default settings should be sufficient for most organizations, but if you're in a situation where you need to adjust them a little, this is the place to do it.

Receive Connectors

A *Receive connector* represents an inbound connection point for SMTP, and controls how a Hub Transport server receives messages over SMTP. No Receive connector, no inbound mail. This means that in order for a Hub Transport server to receive messages from the Internet (from e-mail clients as well as other e-mail servers), at least one Receive connector is required.

When you install the Hub Transport server role on a server, two Receive connectors are created by default. A Client <servername> and a Default <servername> receive connector, as shown in Figure 6.28. These two connectors are required in order for internal mail flow to work.

Figure 6.28 Default Receive Connectors

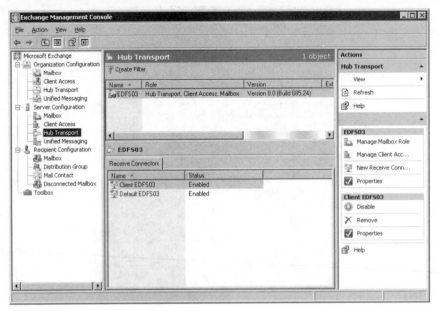

NOTE

By default, a Hub Transport server only accepts inbound messages from other Transport servers (that is, Hub Transport and Edge Transport servers) that are part of the Exchange organization, authenticated Exchange users, and internal legacy Exchange servers (Exchange 2000 and 2003). This means that e-mail servers that are external to the organization by default cannot deliver messages to a Hub Transport server. The reason behind this decision is to make Hub Transport servers secure out of the box by default. "But isn't it a little too aggressive to not allow inbound messages from the Internet?" I hear some of you grumble. Well, perhaps it is, but since the Exchange Product group is convinced that all organizations around the globe will deploy an Edge Transport server in their perimeter networks, the Exchange Product Group doesn't see this as an issue at all. Luckily, it's a rather painless process to allow untrusted e-mail servers (that is, e-mail servers not part of the Exchange organization except the Edge Transport server) to deliver messages directly to a Hub Transport server. I'll show you how in the section titled "Configuring the Hub Transport Server as an Internet-Facing SMTP Server" later in this chapter.

A Receive connector only listens for connections that match the settings configured on the respective connector. That is, connections that are received through a specific local IP address and port, and from a particular IP address range. Receive connectors are local to the Hub Transport server on which they're created. This means that a receive connector created on one Hub Transport server cannot be used by another Hub Transport server in the organization. So, by creating Receive connectors, you can control which server should receive messages from a particular IP address or IP address range. In addition, you can create custom connector properties for messages arriving from a particular IP address or IP address range. You could, for example, allow larger message sizes, more recipients per message (both of these will be covered later in this chapter) or perhaps more inbound connections.

Creating a Receive Connector

To create a Receive connector, you must perform the following steps:

1. Open the **Exchange Management Console** and select **Hub Transport** under the **Server Configuration work center node** (shown back in Figure 6.28).

2. In the Result pane, select the Hub Transport server on which you want to create the Receive connector.

3. Now click **New Receive Connector** in the Action pane.

4. The **New SMTP Receive Connector** wizard will appear. Type a *descriptive name* for the connector, and select the type of connector you want to create. As can be seen in Figure 6.29, you can select between five different Receive connector types:

   - **Custom** This option is used to create customized Receive connectors, which are used to connect with systems that are not Exchange servers.

   - **Internet** This option is used to create a Receive connector that will receive e-mail from servers on the Internet. This connector will be configured to accept connections from anonymous users.

   - **Internal** Internal Receive connectors are used to receive e-mail from servers within your Exchange organization. Note that this connector type will be configured to only accept connections from internal Exchange servers.

   - **Client** Client Receive connectors are used to receive e-mail from authenticated Exchange users. This means that this connector will be configured to only accept client submissions from authenticated Exchange users.

   - **Partner** Partner Receive connectors are used to receive e-mail from partner domains. This connector will be configured to only accept connections from servers that authenticate with Transport Layer Security (TLS) certificates for SMTP domains included in the list of domain-secured domains. You can add domains to this list by using the *-TLSReceiveDomainSecureList* parameter in the *Set-TransportConfig* command.

Figure 6.29 Selecting the Receive Connector Type

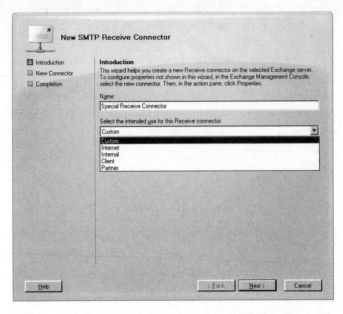

5. When you have selected the type of connector you want to create, click **Next**.

6. As shown in Figure 6.30, you now have the option of modifying the IP address and port that should be used to receive mail. With Custom, Internet, and Partner Receive connectors, you also have the option of entering a FQDN that should be provided in response to *HELO* and *EHLO* commands. When ready, click **Next**.

Figure 6.30 Entering the Local IP Addresses that Should Be Used to Receive Mail

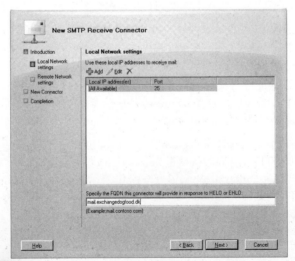

7. On the **Configuration Summary** page, click **New**. On the **Completion** page, click **Finish**.

> ### TIP
>
> To create a Receive connector via the Exchange Management Shell, you must use the *New-ReceiveConnector* cmdlet. For example, to create a Receive Connector similar to the one we generated in the previous steps, run the following command:
>
> New-ReceiveConnector -Name 'Special Receive Connector' -Usage 'Custom' -Bindings '0.0.0.0:25' -Fqdn 'mail.exchangedogfood.dk' - RemoteIPRanges '0.0.0.0-255.255.255.255' -Server 'EDFS03'

At any time, you can modify an existing Receive connector as required. You do this by selecting the respective Receive connector and clicking **Properties** in the **Action** pane. In addition, any existing Receive connectors can be disabled, enabled, and removed as necessary. You do this by selecting the particular Receive connector and clicking the required task in the **Action** pane.

Managing Message Size and Recipient Limits

Like previous versions of Exchange, Exchange 2007 allows you to restrict the size of messages users can send and receive. The message size limits can be set globally in the organization on a per-server, per-connector level, and/or a per-user basis. Message size and recipient limits can only be configured using the Exchange Management Shell. In the following, I'll show you how to configure these limits.

Configuring Global Limits

By default, the global limits are set to unlimited, as can be seen in Figure 6.31.

Figure 6.31 Listing Global Limits

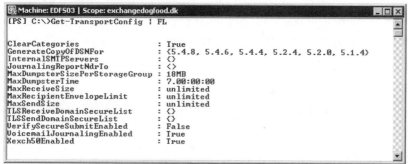

To configure new limits that apply to all Exchange 2007 Servers in the organization, you must use the following command:

```
Set-TransportConfig -MaxReceiveSize:<value> -MaxSendSize:<value> -
MaxRecipientEnvelopeLimit:<value>
```

> **NOTE**
>
> When you set the MaxReceiveSize or MaxSendSize, it's important to note that if you only specify a number such as 100, it defaults to kilobytes (KBs). This means that it is generally a good idea to specify the number followed by either KB or MB.

Configuring Server Limits

Since message size limits are controlled via Send and Receive connectors, you cannot configure message size limits per server. You can, however, configure the maximum number of recipients allowed per message. That is, the maximum number of recipients that can be included on a single e-mail message and submitted to the Pickup directory. By default, the maximum number of recipients is 100, which can be verified by running **Get-TransportServer | FL** in the Exchange Management Shell. To change this setting, you must use the following command:

```
Set-TransportServer -PickupDirectoryMaxRecipientsPerMessage:<value>
```

Configuring Connector Limits

By default, the default maximum message size for both Send and Receive connectors is 10MB. You can verify this by running *Get-SendConnector | FL* and *Get-ReceiveConnector | FL*, respectively.

Send Connectors

To change the maximum message size limit on a Send connector, use the following command:

```
Set-SendConnector <name of connector> -MaxMessageSize:<value>
```

Receive Connectors

To change the maximum message size limit on a Receive connector, use the following command:

```
Set-ReceiveConnector <name of connector> -MaxMessageSize:<value>
```

NOTE

When you set the MaxMessageSize, it's important to note that if you only specify a number such as 100, it defaults to kilobytes (KBs). This means that it is generally a good idea to specify the number followed by either KB or MB.

Configuring Per-User Limits

You can also configure message size limits on a per-user level, if required. Message size limits set on a user override global limits and connector limits. The default message size limit for both sent and received messages on a user mailbox is unlimited, as can be seen by running **Get-Mailbox | FL**. In order to change this setting, run the following command:

```
Set-Mailbox -MaxReceiveSize:<value> -MaxSendSize:<value>
```

NOTE

When you set the MaxReceiveSize and MaxSendSize, it's important to note that if you only specify a number such as 100, it defaults to kilobytes (KBs). This means it's generally a good idea to specify the number followed by either KB or MB.

Message Tracking with Exchange Server 2007

When message tracking is enabled, all Simple Mail Transfer Protocol (SMTP) transport activity on all messages that transfer to and from an Exchange 2007 computer with a Hub Transport, Mailbox, or Edge Transport server role installed are recorded into a log, located by default in the C:\Program Files\Microsoft\Exchange Server\TransportRoles\Logs\MessageTracking directory. Message tracking logs can be used for message forensics, mail flow analysis, reporting, and troubleshooting.

When message tracking is enabled (which is the case by default), the maximum age for message tracking log files is 30 days. After 30 days, the oldest message tracking log files are deleted using circular logging. This is only true if the message tracking log reaches its specified maximum size (which, by default, is 10MB), or a message tracking log file reaches its specified maximum age.

NOTE

The Message Tracking directory, which is responsible for holding the message tracking log files, has a default size limit of 250MB.

In order to launch the Message Tracking tool, perform the following steps:

1. Open the **Exchange Management Console**.

2. Select the **Toolbox** work center node.

3. Click the **Message Tracking** icon and select **Open Tool** in the **Action** pane.

The tool will launch after a few seconds and look for any available updates. If updated, click **Go to Welcome screen** and you will be brought to the Message Tracking Parameters screen shown in Figure 6.32. Here you can check the different parameters you want to include in your search criteria. In this example, I have specified to get a list of all messages sent to me between January 1 and January 30, 2007 from a specific e-mail address. When the relevant parameters have been checked and specified, click **Next**.

Figure 6.32 The Message Tracking Parameters Page

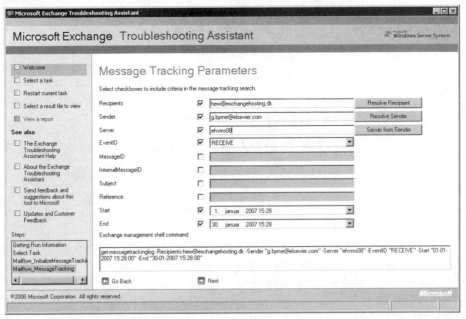

The Message Tracking tool will now search for all messages matching the search criteria specified on the previous screen, as shown in Figure 6.33. Here we get all sorts of information about the messages, and if we want to further filter our search, we can click **Next** and check or change any relevant parameters.

Figure 6.33 List of Messages Included Based on Search Criteria

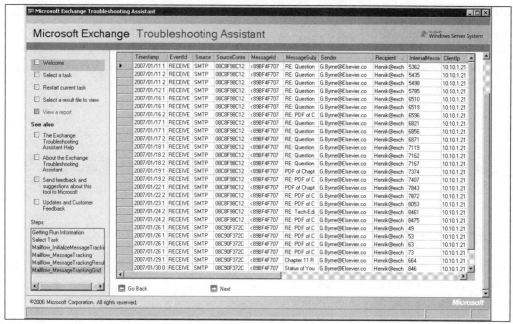

TIP

In order to use the message tracking feature to search for particular messages via the Exchange Management Shell, you can use the *Get-MessageTrackingLog* cmdlet.

Using the Exchange 2007 Queue Viewer

Typically, mail flow within the organization just simply works; however, as an Exchange administrator, one of your jobs is to regularly keep an eye on the message queues within the Exchange organization. This is where the Queue Viewer comes in. With the Queue Viewer, now an Exchange *tool*, and therefore located under the Toolbox work center node in the Exchange Management Console, you can view information about queues and examine the messages held within them.

Exchange Server 2007 uses five different types of queues, and the routing of a message determines the type of queue where a particular message is stored. In the following, I list the five different queues types:

Submission Queue

The submission queue is a persistent queue used by the categorizer in order to gather the messages that need to be resolved, routed, and processed by Transport agents. Each message received by the categorizer is a component of Exchange transport and therefore processes all inbound messages as well as determines what to do with the messages based on information about the intended recipients. All messages received by a transport server enter processing in the Submission queue. Messages are submitted through SMTP-receive, the Pickup directory, or the store driver. The categorizer retrieves messages from this queue and, among other things, determines the location of the recipient and the route to that location. After categorization, the message is moved to a delivery queue or to the unreachable queue. Each Exchange 2007 transport server has only one Submission queue. Messages that are in the Submission queue cannot be in any other queues at the same time.

Mailbox Delivery Queue

The Mailbox Delivery queues hold messages that are being delivered to a mailbox server by using encrypted Exchange RPC. Mailbox Delivery queues exist on Hub Transport servers only. The Mailbox Delivery queue holds messages that are being delivered to mailbox recipients whose mailbox data is stored on a Mailbox server not located in the same site as the Hub Transport server. More than one mailbox delivery queue can exist on a Hub Transport server. The next hop for a Mailbox Delivery queue is the distinguished name of the mailbox store.

Remote Delivery Queue

Remote Delivery queues hold messages that are being delivered to a remote server using SMTP. Remote Delivery queues can exist on both Hub Transport servers and Edge Transport servers, and more than one Remote Delivery queue can exist on each server. Each Remote Delivery queue contains messages that are being routed to recipients that have the same delivery destination. On a Hub Transport server, these destinations are outside the Active Directory site in which the Hub Transport server is located. Remote Delivery queues are dynamically created when they are required and are automatically deleted from the server when they no longer hold messages and the configurable expiration time has passed. By default, the queue is deleted three minutes after the last message has left the queue. The next hop for a Remote Delivery queue is an SMTP domain name, a smart host name or IP address, or an Active Directory site name.

Poison Message Queue

The Poison Message queue is a special queue used to isolate messages that are detected to be potentially harmful to the Exchange 2007 system after a server failure. Messages that contain errors potentially fatal to the Exchange Server system are delivered to the Poison Message queue. This queue is typically empty, and if no poison messages exist, the queue does not appear in the queue viewing interfaces. The Poison Message queue is always in a ready state. By default, all messages in this queue are suspended. The messages can be deleted if they are considered to be harmful to the system. In the event a message in the Poison Message queue is determined to be unrelated to the message itself, delivery of the message can be resumed. When delivery is resumed, the message enters the Submission queue.

Unreachable Queue

The Unreachable queue contains messages that cannot be routed to their destinations. Typically, an unreachable destination is caused by configuration changes that have modified the routing path for delivery. Regardless of the destination, all messages that have unreachable recipients reside in this queue. Each transport server can have only one Unreachable queue.

When a message is received by transport, the mail item will be created and then saved into the queue database.

TIP

With Exchange Server 2007, message queues are stored in the ESE database unlike previous versions of Exchange, where the messages (.EML files) were stored in a queue folder in NTFS.

As mail items are saved in the queue database, they are assigned a unique identifier. If a particular mail item is routed or being sent to more than one recipient, the item can have more than one destination. Each destination represents a separate routing solution for the mail item, and each routing solution causes a routed mail item to be created. A message that is being sent to recipients in two different domains appears as two distinct messages in the delivery queues, even if only one transport mail item is in the database.

To launch the Queue Viewer, perform the following steps:

1. Open the **Exchange Management Console**.
2. Click the **Toolbox** work center node.
3. Click the **Queue Viewer** icon, and then select **Open Tool** in the **Action** pane.

If you have launched the Queue Viewer from a Hub Transport server, it will connect to the local queue by default. If you want to connect to a queue stored on another Hub Transport server, click **Connect to Server** in the **Action** pane (Figure 6.34).

Figure 6.34 The Queue Viewer Tool

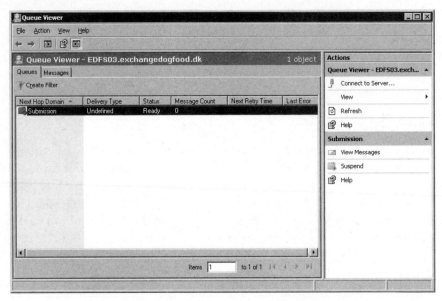

From within the Queue Viewer, you can view queues and messages, as well as suspend and resume them. In addition, you can retry a queue or message, remove a queue or message completely, or export either of them so they can be transferred to another Hub Transport server for further delivery.

TIP

To view or manipulate message queues or individual messages via the Exchange Management Shell, use the *Get-Queue* and *Get-Message* cmdlets.

Introduction to the Exchange Mail Flow Troubleshooter Tool

If you're experiencing mail flow issues in your organization, you can also give the new Exchange Mail Flow Troubleshooter a try. This diagnostic tool helps perform the following functions:

- Starting with the mail flow symptoms, it moves customers through the correct troubleshooting path.

- Provides easy access to various data sources that are required to troubleshoot problems with mail flow.

- Automatically diagnoses the retrieved data and presents an analysis of the possible root causes.

- Suggests corrective actions.

- Provide guidance to help users manually diagnose the data where and when automation is not possible.

In order to launch the Exchange Mail Flow Troubleshooter, perform the following steps:

1. Open the **Exchange Management Console**.

2. Select the **Toolbox** work center node.

3. Click the **Exchange Mail Flow Troubleshooter** icon, and then select **Open Tool** in the **Action** pane.

When the tool has been launched, it will check to see whether any updates are available on Microsoft.com, and then bring you to the welcome screen. You then need to enter an identifying label for the analysis you're about to perform, and then specify what symptoms you're seeing. As you can see in Figure 6.35, you can choose between six different symptoms, and depending on which one you select, the tool will programmatically execute a set of troubleshooting steps to identify the root cause of the mail flow issue you're experiencing. The tool automatically determines what set of data is required to troubleshoot the identified symptoms and collects configuration data, performance counters, event logs, and live tracing information from an Exchange server and other appropriate sources. The tool analyzes each subsystem to determine individual bottlenecks and component failures, and then aggregates the information to provide root cause analysis.

Figure 6.35 The Exchange Mail Flow Troubleshooter Tool

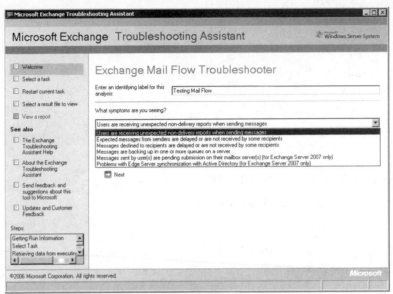

Configuring the Hub Transport Server as an Internet-Facing Transport Server

One of the design goals for Exchange 2007 was to be as secure as possible, by default, in the same way that the Hub Transport server is configured to only accept messages from internal Exchange users, Exchange servers, and legacy Exchange servers. This means that the Hub Transport server doesn't accept inbound messages sent from unauthenticated (untrusted) e-mail servers, which typically define external e-mail servers on the Internet. Instead, it expects to receive inbound messages from the Internet via an Edge Transport server in the perimeter network.

If you're an Exchange administrator in a small organization, or if you're primarily doing Exchange consulting for small shops, chances are IT budgets hinder you from deploying an Edge Transport server in the perimeter network, when transitioning to Exchange Server 2007 (especially if the environment will only consist of a single Exchange 2007 server). Luckily, it's a pretty simple process to change this behavior since you just need to allow untrusted servers to deliver messages to the Hub Transport server. This is accomplished by enabling **Anonymous users** under the **Permission Groups** tab of the **Default Receive connector**.

To get to this property page, you must do the following:

1.   Open the **Exchange Management Console**.

2.   Expand the **Server Configuration** work center node, and then select **Hub Transport**.

3. Highlight the respective Hub Transport server in the Result pane, as shown in Figure 6.36.

Figure 6.36 The Default Receive Connector in the Exchange Management Console

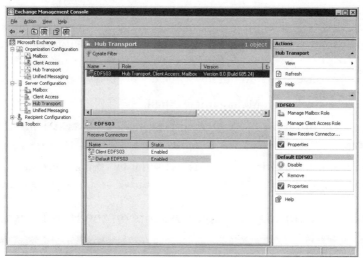

4. Open the **Properties** page of the **Default** *<servername>* **Receive Connector** in the **Work** pane.

5. Click the **Permissions Groups** tab, check **Anonymous users** and click **OK**, as shown in Figure 6.37

Figure 6.37 The Permission Groups Tab on the Default Receive Connector Properties Page

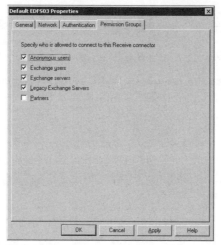

Although we haven't covered the Edge Transport server yet, this server role is also the one that holds all the message hygiene features available in Exchange Server 2007. If you decide not to deploy an Edge Transport server in your perimeter network, you might wonder whether it's possible to let the Internet-facing Hub Transport server take care of filtering out spam and other unwanted e-mail before it reaches your mailbox servers. The answer is yes it is; however, because there are not any anti-spam filtering agents installed on a Hub Transport server by default (since the Exchange Product group expects you to deploy an Edge Transport server in the perimeter network), you must do so manually by running the *install-AntispamAgents.ps1* script located in the Exchange 2007 scripts folder. This can be found under C:\Program Files\Microsoft\Exchange Server. To run this script, do the following:

1. Open the **Exchange Management Shell**.

2. Type **CD "program files\microsoft\exchange server\scripts"** and press **Enter**.

3. Run the **install-AntispamAgents.ps1** script by typing **.\install-AntispamAgents.ps1**, and then pressing **Enter**, as shown in Figure 6.38.

Figure 6.38 Installing the Anti-Spam Agents on the Hub Transport Server

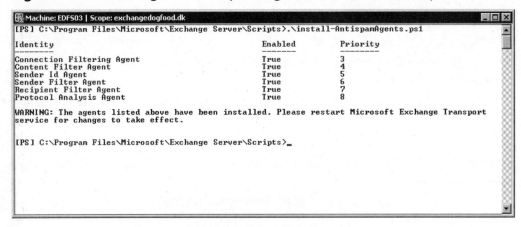

4. Restart the **Microsoft Exchange Transport** service.

5. Close and re-open the **Exchange Management Console** in order for the change to be reflected in the UI.

We now have a new Anti-spam tab under the Hub Transport node beneath the Organization Configuration work center, as shown in Figure 6.39. As you can see, all the anti-spam filtering agents normally found on an Edge Transport server are now listed here. For an explanation of each, see Chapter 7.

Figure 6.39 List of Available Anti-Spam Agents

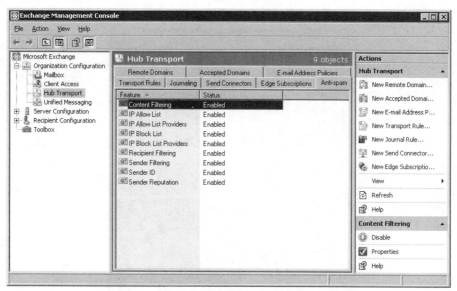

Of course, this solution allows all spam messages and other unwanted e-mail to enter your internal network before it's filtered, but most small shops should be able to live with that. If not, you might want to consider using a hygiene service such as **Exchange Hosted Services (EHS)**, which not only provides efficient anti-spam filtering, but also virus protection and other interesting services. You can read more about EHS at http://www.microsoft.com/exchange/services.

Changing the SMTP Banner

Something else you might want to do in a scenario where inbound messages are directly routed to a Hub Transport server is to change the advertised FQDN sent in *HELO/EHLO* commands in SMTP. This is done under the General tab of the Default Receive connector property page, as shown in Figure 6.40.

Figure 6.40 The General Tab on the Default Receive Connector Properties Page

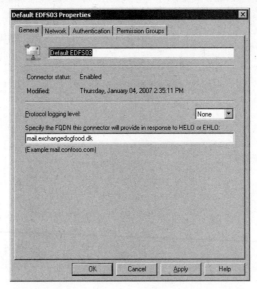

Disabling the EdgeSync Service

Since the EdgeSync service on the Hub Transport server isn't used, when you don't have an Edge Transport server deployed in your perimeter network, it's also a good idea to disable this service (Figure 6.41) in order to save a few system resources. Just by simply running and not replicating with an Edge Transport server, this service actually uses a little under 30MB.

Figure 6.41 Disabling the EdgeSync Service

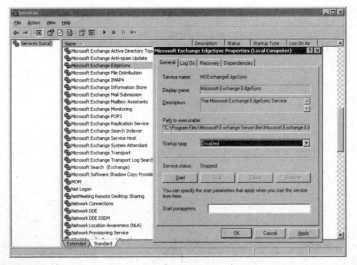

Pointing the MX Record to the Hub Transport Server

The final thing you must do is point your domain's MX record to the Hub Transport server. This is done differently depending on your specific scenario, but typically you just need to redirect port 25 to the IP address of the Hub Transport server in your firewall. If you're publishing your messaging environment using an ISA 2006 Server, this is done under the **To** tab on the **Inbound SMTP** properties page, as shown in Figure 6.42.

Figure 6.42 Redirect Inbound Mail on an ISA 2006 Server

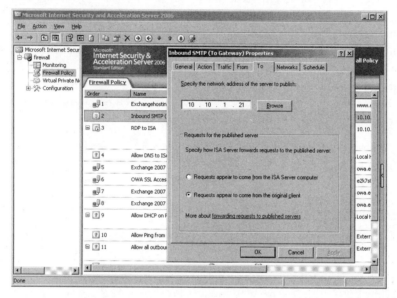

Missed Features

There are a few drawbacks in choosing to have inbound messages go directly to a Hub Transport server instead of via an Edge Transport server in your perimeter network, as best practices tell us.

Attachment Filter

Although the Hub Transport server does contain some attachment options, you won't be able to scan the incoming MIME stream for malicious attachment types, and thereby reject them at the protocol layer. However, you could get this functionality on a Hub Transport Server by installing an anti-virus product such as **Microsoft Forefront for Exchange Server**.

Address Rewrite Agent

You also won't be able to take advantage of the address rewrite functionality since the Address Rewrite agent can only be installed on an Edge Transport server. An explanation of this feature is outside the scope of this chapter. Instead, refer to Chapter 7.

Summary

In this chapter, we started out taking a brief look at the changes made in regards to message routing and architecture in Exchange Server 2007. We then went through the configuration settings available on the Hub Transport server. Next, we discussed how you can create journaling and transport rules so your organization can navigate the ever-increasing complexity of government and industry regulations and compliance demands. We also covered the purpose of Send and Receive connectors, and how to control message size limits in your organization. In addition, we took a look at the different transport server–related tools such as Message Tracking, the Queue Viewer, and the Exchange Mail Flow Troubleshooter tools. Finally, we went through the steps necessary to configure a Hub Transport server as the Internet-facing transport server in your organization.

Solutions Fast Track

Message Transport and Routing Architecture in Exchange 2007

☑ A lot has changed in regards to transport and routing architecture in Exchange Server 2007. First, Exchange no longer uses the SMTP protocol stack included with Internet Information Services (IIS), as was the case with previous versions of the product. Instead, the Exchange Product group has rewritten the SMTP transport stack in managed code, resulting in a much more stable and secure protocol stack.

☑ The new SMTP transport stack is now known as the Microsoft Exchange Transport service (MSExchangeTransport.exe), and because it's no longer dependent on IIS, it is not located within IIS Manager.

☑ With Exchange Server 2007, the Exchange routing topology is no longer based on separate Exchange routing groups. Instead Exchange 2007 takes advantage of the existing site topology in Active Directory. Because Exchange 2007 is now dependent on Active Directory sites—that is, Hub Transport servers use Active Directory sites as well as the cost assigned to the Active Directory IP site link to determine the least-cost routing path to other Hub Transport servers within the organization—all sites containing one or more Mailbox servers must also have at least one Hub Transport server.

☑ Bear in mind that Mailbox and Hub Transport servers use RPC as the basis of communication, but that two Hub Transport servers use SMTP/TLS when exchanging messages.

☑ Exchange Server 2007 is no longer dependent on Link State updates.

Managing the Hub Transport Server

☑ All organizationwide Hub Transport settings are stored in Active Directory. This means that any modifications or configuration settings, except Receive connector specific settings, are reflected on all Hub Transport servers in the organization.

☑ When you set a remote domain, you can control mail flow with more precision, specify message formatting and policy, and designate acceptable character sets for messages that are sent to, and received from, the remote domain.

☑ Under the Accepted Domains tab, we specify the SMTP domains for which our Exchange 2007 organization should either be authoritative, relay to an e-mail server in another Active Directory Forest within the organization, or relay to an e-mail server outside the respective Exchange organization.

☑ E-mail address policies were known as recipient policies back in Exchange 2000 and 2003. Exchange address policies define the proxy addresses stamped onto recipient objects in the Exchange organization.

☑ With the increasing complexity of government and industry regulations, there's a greater need for the efficient management of internal message routing. Exchange 2007, or more specifically the Hub Transport Server role, includes a new transport rules agent that provides easy and flexible ways to set rules for internal message routing and content restriction throughout the Exchange organization.

☑ Exchange Server 2007 supports both Standard and Premium journaling (the latter requires Exchange 2007 Enterprise CALs). Standard journaling is similar to the journaling functionality we had in Exchange 2003 since it's journaling per Mailbox database. Premium journaling is a Hub Transport server feature based on a new journaling agent that can be configured to match the specific needs of an organization. Premium journaling lets you create journal rules for single mailbox recipients or for entire groups within the organization.

☑ Send connectors are used to control how Hub Transport servers send messages using SMTP, and how connections are handled with other e-mail servers. This means that a Hub Transport server requires a Send connector in order to deliver messages to the next hop on the way to their destination.

☑ A Receive connector only listens for connections that match the settings configured on the respective connector—that is, connections that are received through a specific local IP address and port, and/or from a particular IP address range. Receive connectors are local to the Hub Transport server on which they're created. This means a receive connector created on one Hub Transport server cannot be used by another Hub Transport server in the organization.

Managing Message Size and Recipient Limits

☑ Like previous versions of Exchange, Exchange 2007 allows you to restrict the size of messages a user can send and receive. The message size limits can be set globally in the organization, or on a per-server, per-connector, or per-user basis. Message size and recipient limits can *only* be configured using the Exchange Management Shell.

Message Tracking with Exchange Server 2007

☑ When message tracking is enabled, the Simple Mail Transfer Protocol (SMTP) transport activity of all messages transferred to and from an Exchange 2007 computer that has the Hub Transport, Mailbox, or Edge Transport server role installed are recorded into a log that, by default, is located in the C:\Program Files\Microsoft\Exchange Server\TransportRoles\Logs\MessageTracking directory. Message tracking logs can be used for message forensics, mail flow analysis, reporting, and troubleshooting.

☑ When message tracking is enabled (which is the case, by default), the maximum age for message tracking log files is 30 days. After 30 days, the oldest message tracking log files are deleted using circular logging.

☑ The Message Tracking directory, responsible for holding the message tracking log files, has a default size limit of 250MB.

☑ The Message Tracking tool can be found in the Toolbox Work Center.

Using the Exchange 2007 Queue Viewer

☑ With the Queue Viewer now an Exchange *tool*, and thus located under the Toolbox work center in the Exchange Management Console, you can view information about queues and examine the messages held within them.

☑ Exchange Server 2007 uses five different types of queues, and the routing of a message determines which type of queue a particular message is stored in.

☑ With Exchange Server 2007, message queues are stored in the ESE database, unlike previous versions of Exchange where the messages (.EML files) were stored in a queue folder in NTFS.

Introduction to the Exchange Mail Flow Troubleshooter Tool

☑ If you're experiencing mail flow issues in your organization, you can also give the new Exchange Mail Flow Troubleshooter a try. It's used by starting with mail flow symptoms and slowly moving customers through the correct troubleshooting path, providing easy access to various data sources required to troubleshoot problems with mail flow. Based on the collected data, it will present an analysis of the possible root causes and then suggest corrective actions as necessary.

Configuring the Hub Transport Server as an Internet-facing Transport Server

☑ If you're an Exchange administrator in a small organization, or if you're primarily doing Exchange consulting for small shops, chances are the IT budget may hinder you from deploying an Edge Transport server in the perimeter network when transitioning to Exchange Server 2007 (especially if the environment will only consist of a single Exchange 2007 server). In this case, you can configure a Hub Transport server as the Internet-facing transport server in your organization.

☑ By default, no anti-spam filtering agents are installed on a Hub Transport server (since the Exchange Product group expects you to deploy an Edge Transport server in the perimeter network as a best practice). If you want to use the anti-spam agents on a Hub Transport server, you can install them by running the *install-AntispamAgents.ps1* script located in the Exchange 2007 \scripts folder, which can be found, by default, under C:\Program Files\Microsoft\Exchange Server.

Frequently Asked Questions

The following Frequently Asked Questions, answered by the authors of this book, are designed to both measure your understanding of the concepts presented in his chapter and to assist you with real-life implementation of these concepts. To have your questions about this chapter answered by the author, browse to **www.syngress.com/solutions** and click on the **"Ask the Author"** form.

Q: What protocol is used when two internal Hub Transport servers exchange messages?

A: Hub Transport servers use secure SMTP when exchanging messages internally. They use the industry standard SMTP Transport Layer Security (TLS), so that all traffic between the Hub Transport servers are authenticated and encrypted. This will remove the capability for internal snooping.

Q: What protocol is used when a Hub Transport server delivers a message to a mailbox on a Mailbox server?

A: When a Hub Transport server communicates with a Mailbox server, it's done using encrypted RPC. Again, this will remove the capability for internal snooping.

Q: Is there no way to make use of the Exchange 2007 anti-spam agents if I don't deploy an Edge Transport server in my organization's perimeter network?

A: Yes, you can install the anti-spam agents on a Hub Transport server by running the *install-AntispamAgents.ps1* script located in the Exchange 2007 \scripts folder, found by default under C:\Program Files\Microsoft\Exchange Server.

Q: I've deployed Exchange 2007 in my organization, but I cannot receive inbound messages from the Internet. Why?

A: One of the design goals for Exchange 2007 was to be as secure as possible, by default—for example, the Hub Transport server has been configured in such a way that it only accepts messages from internal Exchange users, Exchange servers, and legacy Exchange servers. This means that the Hub Transport server doesn't accept inbound messages sent from unauthenticated (untrusted) e-mail servers, which typically are external e-mail servers on the Internet. Instead it expects to receive inbound messages from the Internet via an Edge Transport server in the perimeter network. In order to be able to receive inbound messages from e-mail servers on the Internet, you must check to allow Anonymous users, located under the Permission Groups tab on the Default <server-name> Receive connector property page.

Q: I don't see any Routing Groups in the Exchange Server 2007 Management Console?

A: Routing groups have been discontinued in Exchange 2007. Instead, Exchange 2007 takes advantage of the existing site topology in Active Directory.

Q: Since a Hub Transport server uses the SMTP protocol to exchange messages with internal transport servers and other e-mail servers on the Internet, I don't understand why I shouldn't install the Windows IIS SMTP component prior to installing the Exchange 2007 Hub Transport server role?

A: Exchange 2007 no longer uses the SMTP protocol stack included with Internet Information Services (IIS), as was the case with previous versions of the product. Instead, the Exchange Product group has rewritten the SMTP transport stack in managed code, resulting in a much more stable and secure protocol stack.

Chapter 7

Managing the Edge Transport Server

Solutions in this chapter:

- Deploying the Edge Transport Server Role

- Enabling Name Resolution Lookups between the Edge Transport and Hub Transport Servers Suffix

- Installing the ADAM Component

- Verifying That the EdgeSync Service Works as Expected

- Manually Configuring the Required Connectors

- Pointing Your MX Records to the Edge Transport Server

- Deploying Multiple Edge Transport Servers in the Organization

☑ Summary

☑ Solutions Fast Track

☑ Frequently Asked Questions

Introduction

The Exchange Product Group developed the Edge Transport server to give enterprises powerful out-of-the-box protection against spam without needing to go out and invest in a third-party solution. The messaging hygiene features in the Edge Transport server role are agent based and consists of multiple filters that are frequently updated.

Although the primary role of the Edge Transport server is to route mail and do message hygiene, it also includes features that will let you do other things, such as rewriting SMTP addresses, configuring transport rules, and enabling journaling and associated disclaimers.

After reading this chapter you will have learned what the Edge Transport server is all about; you will be aware of how an Edge Transport server is properly deployed as well as know how to configure most of the features available with this server role.

NOTE

Exchange 2007 also includes a new feature called *Domain Security*, which provides a set of functionality that offers a low-cost alternative to S/MIME or other message-level security solutions. The purpose of the Domain Security feature set is to provide administrators a way to manage secured message paths over the Internet with business partners. Although without doubt this is an interesting topic for some readers, it's unfortunately beyond the scope of this book.

Deploying the Edge Transport Server Role

The Edge Transport server role in Exchange Server 2007 is meant to be installed in your organization's perimeter network (also called a *demilitarized zone [DMZ]* or *screened subnet*). This server role supports Simple Mail Transfer Protocol (SMTP) routing (more specifically, SMTP-relay and Smart Host functionality) and provides several antispam filtering agents and support for antivirus extensibility. The Edge Transport server is the only server role that shouldn't be part of your Active Directory directory service forest; it should instead be installed on a stand-alone server in a workgroup as shown in Figure 7.1.

Figure 7.1 A Typical Edge Transport Server Scenario

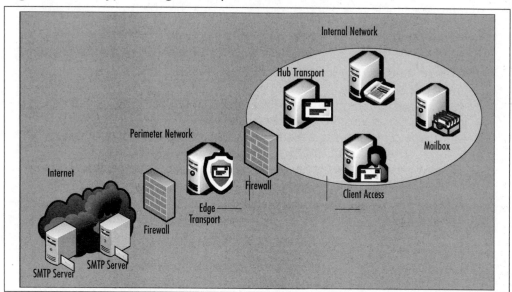

Although the Edge Transport server role is isolated from Active Directory, it's still able to communicate with the Active Directory using a collection of processes known as EdgeSync, which runs on the Hub Transport server. Since it is part of the Active Directory, the Hub Transport server has access to the necessary Active Directory data. The Edge Transport server uses Active Directory Application Mode (ADAM) to store the required Active Directory data, which is data such as accepted domains, recipients, safe senders, send connectors, and a Hub Transport server list (used to generate dynamic connectors so that you don't need to create them manually).

It's important to understand that the EdgeSync replication is encrypted by default and that the replication is a one-way process from Active Directory to ADAM. This means that no data is replicated from ADAM to AD.

The first time that EdgeSync replication occurs, the ADAM store is populated, and after that, data from Active Directory is replicated at fixed intervals. You can specify the intervals or use the default settings, which, for configuration data, is every hour and every fourth hour for recipient data.

SOME INDEPENDENT ADVICE

Although the Edge Transport server role has been designed to provide improved antispam and antivirus protection for an Exchange 2007 environment, you can deploy this server role in an existing Exchange 2003 organization as well. Since you install the Edge Transport server role on a stand-alone machine in the perimeter network (the DMZ or screened subnet), this is even a relatively simple task. Even though you would be able to use the Edge Transport server role as a smart host or an SMTP relay server in an Exchange 2003 environment, you will not be able to replicate configuration and recipient data from Active Directory to ADAM, because this requires an Exchange 2007 Hub Transport server. This doesn't hinder you from using the filtering agent that doesn't rely on the EdgeSync service. If you use the Intelligent Message Filter (IMF) only in your Exchange 2003 environment, deploying an Edge Transport server in the perimeter network (the DMZ or screened subnet) would make sense because it would provide an additional layer of antispam protection. You could also install ForeFront for Exchange Server 2007 on the Edge Transport server so that you could filter out antivirus messages as well.

The Edge Transport server has its own Jet database to process the delivery of inbound as well as outbound e-mail messages. When inbound e-mail messages are stored in the Jet database and are ready for delivery, the Edge Transport server looks up the respective recipient(s) in the ADAM store, which, as mentioned, among other things contains recipient data replicated from the Active Directory using the EdgeSync service.

In a scenario in which you have deployed multiple Edge Transport servers in your organization, the Edge Transport servers use DNS round robin (which is supported by most DNS servers today) to network and load-balance network traffic between the servers.

Prerequisites

The Exchange 2007 Edge Transport server role can be installed on either a Windows 2003 Server R2 Standard Edition or Windows 2003 Server SP1 Standard Edition. As already mentioned, it's important that you install the Edge Transport server role on a standalone machine outside the Active Directory forest, since installing this server role on a server that is member of Active Directory isn't supported, nor it would be a good idea, since doing so would introduce a major security risk.

Since the Edge Transport server should be deployed in the perimeter network (the DMZ or screened subnet), it's recommended that you use a multihomed setup, meaning that the server has two network adapters: one connected to the perimeter network and one to the internal network. This will give you the option of specifying the ports and/or services that should be allowed on each adapter. For example, we want to allow LDAP replication from only the internal network when we show you how to configure the Security Configuration Wizard (SCW) later in this chapter. But the choice is yours, really, since an Edge Transport server will work just fine using a single network adapter as well, albeit in a less secure way.

Creating a DNS Suffix

Before you can install the Exchange 2007 Edge Transport server role on the server, you should make sure that you have created a DNS suffix, because you cannot change the server name once the server role has been installed. In addition, the readiness check will fail if a DNS suffix cannot be located. Creating the DNS suffix is a very simple process, performed via the following steps:

1. Log onto the Edge Transport server with the Administrator account or another account with administrator permissions.

2. Click **Start,** right-click **My Computer,** and select **Properties** in the context menu.

3. Now click the **Computer Name** tab and then click the **Change** button (see Figure 7.2).

Figure 7.2 The Computer Name Tab

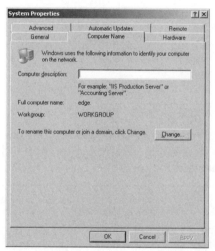

4. Click the **More** button.

5. Now enter the respective **DNS suffix** (see Figure 7.3) and then click **OK** four times.

6. Click **Yes** to reboot the server so that the changes take effect.

Figure 7.3 The DNS Suffix and NetBIOS Computer Name

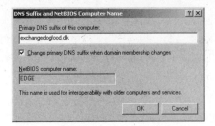

Enabling Name Resolution Lookups between the Edge Transport and Hub Transport Servers Suffix

It's important that the Edge Transport server and any Hub Transport servers in your Exchange 2007 organization are able to see each other using name resolution. To accomplish this goal, you can create the necessary host record in a forward lookup zone on the internal DNS server used by the edge transport and Hub Transport servers.

> **NOTE**
>
> Since any Exchange 2007 Hub Transport server in your Exchange organization needs to be added to the Active Directory, before you can install this role only the host name of the Edge Transport server needs to be manually added to the respective forward lookup zone.

You do so by performing the following steps:

1. Log onto the internal DNS server used by the edge transport and Hub Transport servers.

2. Click **Start | Administrative Tools** and then click **DNS**.

3. In the **DNS Management snap-in**, expand the **Server** node and then **Forward Lookup Zones** (see Figure 7.4).

4. Now right-click the respective **Forward Lookup Zone** and select **New Host (A)** in the context menu.

Figure 7.4 DNS Management MMC Snap-in

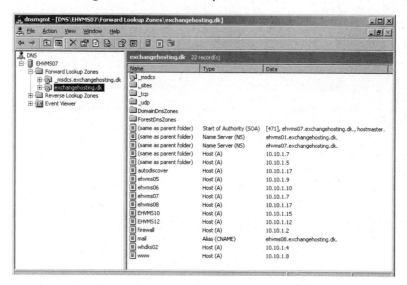

5. Enter the **hostname** and **IP address** of the Edge Transport server and click **Add Host** (see Figure 7.5).

Figure 7.5 Creating a New Host (A) Record

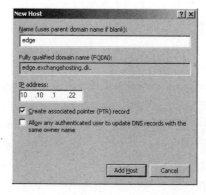

6. Close the **DNS Management snap-in** and log off the internal DNS server.

You may also choose to simply add the hostname and IP address of the Edge Transport server to the local hosts file on each Hub Transport server, and the hostname and IP address of any Hub Transport server to the local hosts file on the Edge Transport server in your Exchange organization. Although this is a perfectly supported solution, we don't recommend you use it unless you're dealing with a small shop that has maybe one Edge Transport server and one or perhaps two Hub Transport servers. If you're a messaging administrator/consultant in a large Exchange organization that contains multiple Edge Transport servers as well as several Hub Transport servers, it's far better to keep the name resolution centralized on an internal DNS server.

You add the hostname and IP address to the local hosts file on the server by performing the following steps:

1. Log onto the edge transport or Hub Transport server.

2. Click **Start | Run** and type **C:\windows\system32\drivers\etc** and press **Enter**.

3. Now open the **hosts** file in **Notepad**.

4. Type the **IP address** and **hostname** of the server (see Figure 7.6).

Figure 7.6 Entering the IP Address in the Hosts File

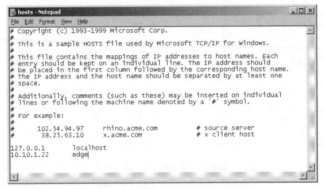

5. Save the changes and close **Notepad**.

6. Now open a **Command Prompt Window** by clicking **Start | Run** and then typing **CMD.EXE**.

7. You now need to purge and reload the remote cache name table, which is done by typing **NBTSTAT –R** followed by pressing **Enter** (see Figure 7.7).

8. Verify that you can ping the respective servers using the fully qualified domain name, and make sure it's the correct IP address that's resolved (see Figure 7.8).

NOTE

You need to perform Steps 1 through 8 on each edge transport and Hub Transport server in your Exchange organization.

Figure 7.7 Purging and Preloading NBT Remote Cache Name Table

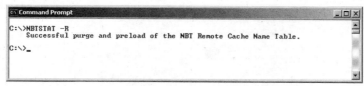

```
C:\>NBTSTAT -R
        Successful purge and preload of the NBT Remote Cache Name Table.
C:\>_
```

Figure 7.8 Pinging the Edge Transport Server

```
C:\>ping edge.exchangehosting.dk

Pinging edge.exchangehosting.dk [10.10.1.22] with 32 bytes of data:

Reply from 10.10.1.22: bytes=32 time<1ms TTL=128
Reply from 10.10.1.22: bytes=32 time<1ms TTL=128
Reply from 10.10.1.22: bytes=32 time<1ms TTL=128
Reply from 10.10.1.22: bytes=32 time<1ms TTL=128

Ping statistics for 10.10.1.22:
    Packets: Sent = 4, Received = 4, Lost = 0 (0% loss),
Approximate round trip times in milli-seconds:
    Minimum = 0ms, Maximum = 0ms, Average = 0ms

C:\>_
```

Configuring DNS Settings

If you choose to run the Edge Transport server in a multihomed setup where you have a
network adapter connected to the internal network and one to the external network
(perimeter network), you need to pay special attention in configuring DNS. Since the
external network adapter doesn't have access to the DNS server in your Active Directory on
the internal network, you should configure this network adapter to use a public DNS server
(or a DNS server located in your perimeter network), so that the Edge Transport server can
perform name resolutions, required to resolve SMTP domain names to MX or Mail
Exchange records as well as route mail to the respective SMTP servers on the Internet.

The internal network adapter should be configured to use a DNS server located in the
perimeter network or, alternatively, to use a hosts file. As you saw in the section of this
chapter titled "Enabling Name Resolution Lookups between the Edge Transport and Hub
Transport Servers," the edge transport and Hub Transport servers must be able to locate each
other using name resolution.

As was also the case with Exchange Server 2000 and 2003, you can configure the Edge
Transport server to use a DNS server (typically an external DNS server) for routing mail
other than the DNS server specified on the external network adapter. In Exchange 2000 and
2003, this was done by taking the Properties of the default SMTP virtual server in the
System Manager and then clicking the Delivery tab and finally the Advanced button. On an
Edge Transport server, you configure the DNS servers by taking Properties for the **Edge
Transport** server object in the **Result pane**. On the **Properties** page, click the **External
DNS Lookups** tab and specify the DNS server that should be used for routing mail to
other SMTP servers on the Internet (see Figure 7.9).

Figure 7.9 External DNS Lookups

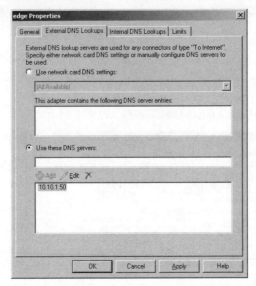

Installing the ADAM Component

Since the Edge Transport server role uses ADAM directory service as the repository for the replicated configuration and recipient data, it should come as no surprise that you'll need to install ADAM before you can install the Edge Transport server role. If you plan to install the Edge Transport server role on a Windows 2003 R2 server, you can install the component via **Add or Remove Programs | Add/Remove Windows Components | Active Directory Services**, where you need to tick **Active Directory Application Mode (ADAM)**, as shown in Figure 7.10. Next, click **OK** twice.

To install ADAM on a Windows 2003 server with SP1 or later will require downloading the ADAM installation package by clicking **Active Directory Application Mode** in the **Downloads** section under the following link: **www.microsoft.com/windowsserver2003/adam**.

Figure 7.10 Adding the ADAM Component

Installing .NET Framework 2.0 and Windows PowerShell

As is the case with any other Exchange 2007 Server role, you also need to install both the .NET Framework 2.0 component as well as Windows PowerShell, which we showed you how to do in Chapter 3.

Saying Goodbye to the Windows SMTP and NNTP Protocol Stacks

As most of you might recall, Exchange Server 2000 and 2003 extended and made use of the Windows Server 2000 or 2003 SMTP and NNTP services and thus required you to install both the Windows NNTP and the SMTP components (which both are part of IIS) prior to installing the Exchange Server product itself. Since NNTP is one of the features that aren't supported in Exchange Server 2007, you need to make sure that this component isn't installed on the server. If it is, the Exchange Server 2007 readiness check will fail. In addition, because Exchange Server 2007 no longer uses the Windows Server SMTP service but instead has its own, which has been written from the ground up in managed code, you also need to make sure that the Windows Server SMTP component isn't installed on the server. As with NNTP, the Exchange Server 2007 readiness check will fail if this component is found on the server. You might ask why the Exchange Product Group replaced the Windows SMTP component with its own. Well, by doing so, the Exchange Product Group has reduced the risks that are associated with DoS attacks, eliminated the dependency on IIS, and reduced the work required to properly secure the server for deployment in the perimeter network (the DMZ or screened subnet).

Installing the Edge Transport Server Role

Now you can begin the actual installation of the Exchange 2007 Edge Transport server role. As is the case with all the other Exchange Server 2007 roles, you install this role by performing the following steps:

1. Navigate to the **Exchange Server 2007 source directory** (DVD media or the network share containing the Exchange Server 2007 binaries).

2. Double-click **Setup.exe**.

3. When the Exchange Server 2007 setup splash screen appears, click **Step 4: Install Microsoft Exchange**.

SOME INDEPENDENT ADVICE

Although we're using the Exchange Server 2007 Installation Wizard to install the Edge Transport server role, you can, as we stated in Chapter 3, also install this server role in unattended mode. To do so, you need to execute a command similar to the following: **Setup.exe /mode:Install /role: ET**.

The MMC 3.0 component will only appear as installed if you're installing Exchange Server 2007 on a Windows Server 2003 R2 edition. If you're installing the Edge Transport server role on a Windows 2003 server with SP1 or later applied, you need to download and install MMC 3.0 manually.

4. When the Exchange Server 2007 Installation Wizard has initialized, click **Next**.

5. Accept the End User License Agreement (EULA) and click **Next**.

6. You now have the option of enabling **Error Reporting** (which is recommended so that the Exchange Product Group receives information about any issues you encounter; in the end this information will give us a better product). When you have decided whether you want to enable error reporting or not, you can click **Next**.

7. Since you're going to install the Edge Transport server role, you now need to choose **Custom Exchange Server** Installation and then click **Next** (see Figure 7.11). This is also the screen where you have the option of changing the path for the Exchange Server installation (in the bottom of the screen).

Figure 7.11 The Exchange Server 2007 Setup Wizard

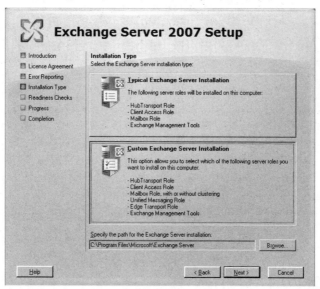

8.   Tick **Edge Transport Role** (see Figure 7.12) and click **Next**.

Figure 7.12 Selecting the Edge Transport Role

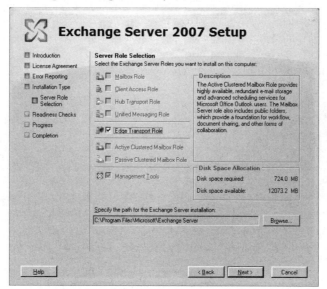

> **NOTE**
>
> Selecting the Edge Transport role automatically checks and installs the Exchange Management Tools and grays out any other server role.

9.   When you have selected the **Edge Transport server role** as well as the installation path, click **Next**. If the readiness check completes without any issues, you can begin the installation by clicking the **Install** button. The Installation Wizard will now copy the required files and then begin the installation. Since the server on which the Edge Transport role exists is a standalone machine that doesn't belong to an Active Directory forest, and since this type of installation is pretty small, the installation process will complete relatively fast.

10.   When the installation has completed, click **Finish**.

Verifying Deployment

Now that the Exchange 2007 Edge Transport server role has been properly installed, you're faced with several tasks that need to be completed before you're done. The first task on the list is to verify the installation and review the server setup logs. If the installation process fails or errors occur during the installation, it's a very good idea to follow the suggestions to track down the source of the problem (reviewing the setup logs, confirming that events 1003 and 1004 appear in the Application log, and checking that all required services are installed as well as operating in the correct startup mode and so on), but if the installation process completes without any issues, you can move right on to the next task on the list.

Creating and Importing an Edge Subscription File

This task is perhaps the most interesting one of them all; it's the task where you subscribe the Edge Transport server by establishing a one-way replication of recipient and configuration information from the Active Directory service to ADAM using the EdgeSync service (see Figure 7.13).

The EdgeSync service makes it a rather painless process to configure the Edge Transport server so that you can take advantage of its full feature set.

Figure 7.13 One-Way Replication with the EdgeSync Service

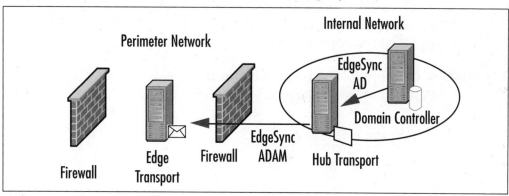

SOME INDEPENDENT ADVICE

Although the recommended method for establishing end-to-end mail flow between the Edge Transport server(s) and the Hub Transport servers within the Exchange organization is to create an edge subscription for the Edge Transport server, you can also do so by manually creating and configuring the Send connectors (that the EdgeSync service creates automatically). Although this will establish working end-to-end mail flow between the Edge Transport server(s) and the Hub transport server(s), you should bear in mind that you cannot use the recipient lookup feature or safe list aggregation, because these features require that the Edge Transport server has a subscription to the organization.

To configure an Edge Transport server subscription, you need to perform the following steps:

1. Export the Edge Transport server to an XML file using the *New-EdgeSubscription* CMDlet. To do so, open the Exchange Management Shell (EMS), type **New-EdgeSubscription –file "C:\EdgeSubscriptionFile.xml"** (or whatever you want to name the file; the name of the file doesn't have any impact on anything), and press **Enter**, as shown in Figure 7.14.

NOTE

When you run the *New-EdgeSubscription* CMDlet, an ADAM account is created as well. This account is used to secure Lightweight Directory Access Protocol (LDAP) communications during data transfer. The credentials for the account are also retrieved when you run the CMDlet.

2.   You now need to confirm that you really want to create an edge subscription, since this process makes certain configurations of the Edge Transport server so that it's ready to be managed via EdgeSync. Because this is exactly what you want to do, type **Y** and then press **Enter**.

Figure 7.14 Creating a New Edge Subscription File

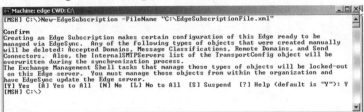

!**W**ARNING

Any accepted domains, message classifications, remote domains, and send connectors will be overwritten when you make a new edge subscription file. Also bear in mind that the Internal SMTP Servers list (a list of all internal SMTP server IP addresses or IP address ranges that should be ignored by the Sender ID and Connection filtering agents) of the *TransportConfig* object will be overwritten during the synchronization process. In addition, the Management Shell tasks that manage these types of objects will be locked out on the Edge Transport server, which means that you need to manage those objects from within the organization and then have the EdgeSync service update the Edge Transport server. When you run the *New-EdgeSubscription* CMDlet on a newly installed Edge Transport server, this information can be ignored, since you haven't configured anything manually on the server yet.

---

3.   Since the XML file, which you can see in Figure 7.15, saved in the root of the C: drive needs to be imported on a Hub Transport server, you need to transfer the file to a Hub Transport server in the Exchange 2007 organization. You could do so by copying the file to a diskette or, perhaps even smarter, by using the Disk Drives feature in a Remote Desktop Connection client (if you have enabled Remote Desktop on the Edge Transport server and have TCP port 3389 open in the firewall between the parameter network and the internal network).

Figure 7.15 The Edge Subscription XML File

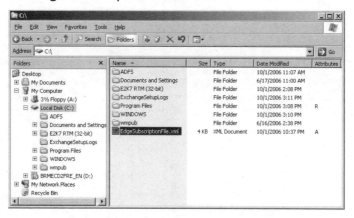

4. When the file has been transferred to a Hub Transport server, you need to import it by opening the **Exchange Management Console (EMC)**, expanding the **Organization Configuration** node, and selecting **Hub Transport**.

> **NOTE**
>
> To import the Edge Subscription file on a Hub Transport server, you must log on with an account that is local Administrator on the respective Hub Transport server as well as belonging to the Exchange Organization Administrators group.

5. Now click the **Edge Subscriptions** tab (see Figure 7.16).

6. Since you have to create a new edge subscription, click **New Edge Subscription** in the **Action pane** (or if you prefer, right-click somewhere in the **Work pane** and select **New Edge Subscription** in the context menu).

Figure 7.16 The Edge Subscriptions Tab on the Hub Transport Server

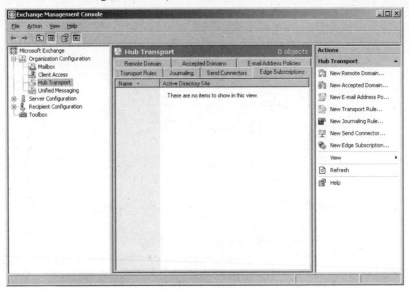

NOTE

Importing the Edge Subscription file will establish an authenticated communication channel as well as completing the edge subscription process by beginning an initial replication. The Send connector, which is used when messages are sent to the Internet via the Edge Transport server, is created by default. In addition, the EdgeSync service will replicate the Send Connector configuration, accepted domains, remote domains, and safe sender lists as well as recipient data (SMTP address including contacts, distribution lists, and proxy addresses) from Active Directory to the ADAM store.

7. You will now be taken to the **New Edge Subscription Wizard**, where you have to specify the Active Directory site in which the Edge Transport server will become a member. If you have only one site, select **Default-First-Site-Name**. If your Exchange organization is deployed across multiple sites, click the drop-down list and choose the respective site.

NOTE

If your Active Directory topology consists of multiple Active Directory sites, it's recommended that you import the Edge Subscription file on a Hub Transport server that is located in the site that has the best network connectivity to the perimeter network (the DMZ or screened subnet) in which the Edge Transport server is deployed.

8. Now specify the location of the **Edge Subscription** file by clicking **Browse** and then **New** (see Figure 7.17).

Figure 7.17 Creating a New Edge Subscription

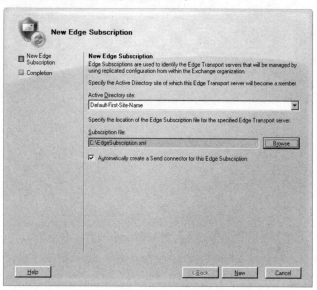

9. Wait for the **New Edge Subscription Wizard** to complete and then click **Finish**.

SOME INDEPENDENT ADVICE

If you instead wanted to import the Edge Subscription file using Exchange Management Shell (EMS), you could do so using the *New-EdgeSubscription –FileName:"C:\EdgeSubscriptionFile.xml" –Site:"Default-First-Site-Name"* CMDlet, as shown in Figure 7.17.

When the Edge Subscription file has been imported, it's a good security practice to delete the XML file.

Now that you have created an edge subscription, the EdgeSync service on the Hub transport server will synchronize configuration data such as each hour and recipient data every fourth hour to the Edge Transport server.

If you don't want to wait for four hours before the replication occurs, you can force the EdgeSync synchronization manually. To do so, open the EMS on a Hub Transport server and type **Start-EdgeSynchronization**, as shown in **Figure 7.18**.

Figure 7.18 Manually Starting the Edge Synchronization

Forcing a synchronization using *Start-EdgeSynchronization* is also a very good idea if you have made bulk changes in Active Directory (perhaps added 50 new mail–enabled or mailbox–enabled users) so that these changes are replicated immediately.

NOTE

When the EdgeSync service synchronizes data from Active Directory to the ADAM store on the Edge Transport server, it is sent hashed to protect the synchronized data. In addition, the LDAP connection is secured by the ADAM credentials, which are stored in the Edge Subscription file.

Verifying That the EdgeSync Service Works As Expected

To see whether the Hub Transport server configuration data has propagated properly to the Edge Transport server, you should verify that a send connector has been created on the server. You do so by performing the following steps:

1. Log onto the Edge Transport server.

2. Open the **EMC**.

3. Click the **Edge Transport** node in the navigation tree in the **left pane**.

4. Now click the **Send Connectors** tab in the **Work pane** (see Figure 7.19).

Figure 7.19 The Send Connector on the Edge Transport Server

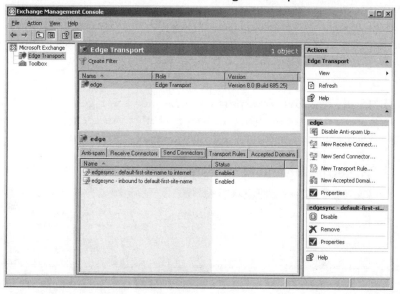

5. Verify that a **Send connector** has been created. Also make sure that each domain listed under the **Accepted Domains** tab on the **Hub Transport server** is listed when you type **Get-AcceptedDomain** in the **EMS** on the **Edge Transport server**. You should get a list similar to the one shown in Figure 7.20.

Figure 7.20 Listing the Accepted Domain

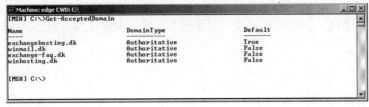

If everything is as expected, you now have a working Edge Transport server in your parameter network (your DMZ or screened subnet). Congratulations!

Creating a Postmaster Mailbox

No matter whether you plan to deploy an Edge Transport server in your organization or you simply will configure the Hub Transport server as the Internet-facing server, it's recommended that you create a postmaster mailbox. Since by now you most likely have installed a Hub Transport server in your organization, chances are you already have created a postmaster mailbox. But if you haven't, you need to perform the following steps:

1. On the edge transport or the Hub Transport server in your organization, open the **EMS** and type **Get-TransportServer**, as shown in Figure 7.21. This CMDlet will tell us the name of the transport server, whether message tracking has been enabled, and the external SMTP address used for the postmaster.

Figure 7.21 Retrieving the Postmaster Address

2. If no postmaster address is specified, you can do so by typing **Set-TransportServer –ExternalPostmasterAddress postmaster@*exchange-hosting.dk*** (replace the domain name with the SMTP domain used in your organization) and pressing **Enter**.

To associate the configured external postmaster SMTP address with a specific mailbox, perform the following steps:

1. On an Exchange 2007 server in your organization, open the **EMC**, expand the **Recipient Configuration** work center node, and select the **Mailbox** subnode.

2. Now choose **Properties** for the mailbox you wa[...] master SMTP address and click the **E-mail addresse**[...]

3. Click **Add**; type **postmaster@*exchangehosting.dk*** (replaci[...] with the SMTP domain used in your organization), as shown i[...] click **OK** twice.

Figure 7.22 The E-mail Addresses Tab

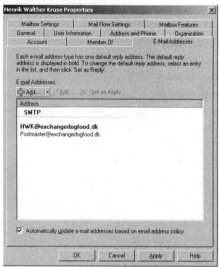

If you originally did a transition from Exchange Server 2000 or 2003, the postmaster SMTP address will most likely already be associated with the Administrator mailbox. If this is the case, you need to remove the SMTP address from this mailbox before you can associate it with another mailbox.

SOME INDEPENDENT ADVICE

The EdgeSync service supports edge subscription with only one Active Directory forest, so if your organization consists of multiple forests and you want to replicate each with your Edge Transport server(s), you will first need to synchronize the recipient addresses to one forest, which you then replicate with the Edge Transport server using the EdgeSync service.

~~ng~~
~~~~ctors

ate an edge subscription for the Edge Transport
meter network (DMZ or screened subnet). Since
reate the connector necessary to get a mail flow
to and from the Hub Transport server in the
st-tasks are necessary regarding connectors; they will
rver to the Edge Transport server. But if for some
ync subscription, you'll need to create these connec-
er will need four connectors: two receive connectors
of the Edge Transport server) and two send connectors.

Since ~~~~ is located in the perimeter network (the DMZ or
screened subnet), we a~~~~ ou have installed two network adapters in the server so
that you can bind one receive connector and one send connector to the internally configured network adapter and one receive connector and one send connector to the externally
configured network adapter.

To create and configure the required connectors, follow these steps:

1. Create a **Send connector** that is configured to send messages to the Internet. To
   do so, log on to the **Edge Transport server,** open the **EMC,** and click **Edge
   Transport** in the navigation tree.

2. Now select the **Edge Transport** server in the **Result pane** and then click the
   Send Connectors tab.

3. Click **New Send Connector** in the **Action pane** to launch the **New Send
   Connector Wizard**.

4. Give the new Send connector a name, such as **Send Connector (To Internet)**,
   choose **Custom** in the Intended Usage drop-down menu, and click **Next** (see
   Figure 7.23).

5. Now set the address space to *, which means *all domains*, and click **Next**.

6. You now need to decide whether you want to route mail using domain name
   system (DNS) MX records or using a smart host. If you're required to route mail
   through an SMTP gateway located at your ISP or perhaps in your perimeter network (the DMZ or screened subnet), select **Smart Host** and enter the IP address
   of the respective SMTP server. (If you choose to use a smart host, select **None** on
   the **Smart host security settings** page, which will appear when you click
   Next.) Otherwise, select to route it using **DNS MX records**. On this page you
   also have the option of using external DNS lookup settings on the server. If you
   have or will create external DNS servers, enable this option and click **Next** (see
   Figure 7.24).

Figure 7.23 The New SMTP Send Connector Wizard

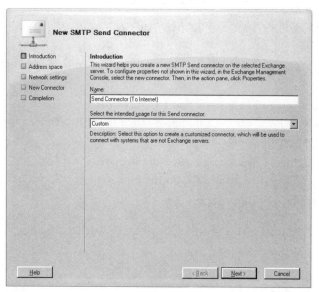

TIP

If you're using a smart host, you can, of course, also enter the FQDN of the SMTP server, but we recommend that you enter the IP address to reduce the performance load on the Edge Transport server.

Figure 7.24 The New SMTP Send Connector Network Settings

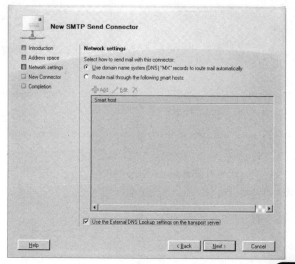

7. On the **Configuration Summary** page, click **New** and then click **Finish** on the Completion page.

   Okay, you have created the first Send connectors; now let's move quickly on to the second.

8. Once again, click **New Send Connector** in the **Action pane** to launch the New Send Connector Wizard.

9. Call the new Send connector **Send Connector** (to internal Hub Transport server) or something similarly meaningful and then select **Internal** in the intended usage drop-down menu. Click **Next**.

10. On the **Address Space** page, enter the **domains** that you already have added under the accepted domains tab on the Hub Transport server and click **Next** (see Figure 7.25).

Figure 7.25 The New SMTP Send Connector Address Space

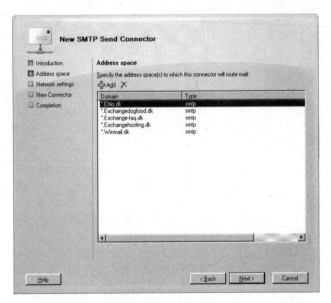

12. Now select to route mail using a smart host. Enter the **IP address** of your Hub Transport server and click **Next**.

13. On the **Smart host security settings** page, select **None** and click **Next** (see Figure 7.26).

14. Click **New** on the **Configuration Summary** page and click **Finish** on the **Completion** page.

Figure 7.26 The Smart Host Security Settings

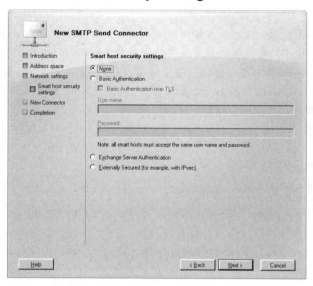

The next thing to do is to change the settings for the Receive connector, which are created automatically when you install an Edge Transport server. You'll need to perform these steps:

1. To change the settings for this connector, click the **Receive Connectors** tab, open **Properties** for the **Default internal receive connector** *<server name>*, and click the **Network** tab.

2. Change the local IP address(es) from **(All available)** to the **IP address** configured on the Internet-facing network adapter (see Figure 7.27). Then click **OK**.

Figure 7.27 The Properties Page of the Default Internal Receive Connector

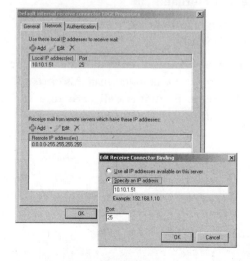

That's all you need to modify on the default receive connector. Now you can move on and create an additional Receive connector:

1. With the **Receive Connectors** tab selected, click **New Receive Connector** in the **Action pane** to launch the New Receive Connector Wizard.

2. Give the new Receive connector a name, such as **Receive Connector (from internal Hub Transport server)**; select **Internal** in the intended usage drop-down menu; and click **Next**.

3. On the **Remote Network Settings** page, enter the **IP address** of the Hub Transport server on the internal network. (Make sure you removed the default address range!) Then click **Next**.

4. On the **Configuration Summary** page, click **Finish** on the **Completion** page.

5. Now bring up the **Properties** page for the new Receive connector and then click the **Network** tab.

6. Change the **local IP address(es)** from **(All available)** to the IP address configured on the internally facing network adapter and then click **OK**.

Manually Configuring Accepted Domains

If you choose not to use an edge subscription, you also have to manually add the domains accepted by your organization. If you have configured an edge subscription, this step isn't necessary, since the accepted domains configured on the Hub Transport server automatically will be replicated to the Edge Transport server.

To manually add accepted domains to an Edge Transport server, perform the following steps:

1. On the Edge Transport server, open the **EMC** and click **Edge Transport** in the **Navigation tree**. Next, select the **Edge Transport server** in the **Result pane**.

2. Click the **Accepted Domains** tab.

3. Click **New Accepted Domain** in the **Action pane** to launch the New Accepted Domain Wizard.

4. Give the **new accepted domain entry** a name and type in the **domain name** for which you want to accept inbound mail. Also make sure that you select **Authoritative Domain. E-mail is delivered to a recipient in this Exchange organization** and then click **New** (see Figure 7.28).

Figure 7.28 The New Accepted Domain Wizard

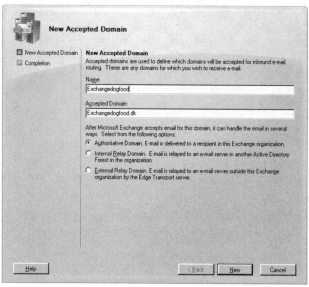

5. On the **Completion** page, click **Finish**.

Repeat Steps 1 through 5 for each domain for which you want to accept inbound mail.

NOTE

We'll talk much more about configuring accepted domains on a Hub Transport server in Chapter 6.

Configuring and Managing the Antispam Filtering Agents

It's very likely that you have deployed an Exchange 2007 Edge Transport server to filter out most of the spam and other unsolicited e-mail messages sent to your organization so that they never reach the Exchange servers on your internal network. The Edge Transport server includes several antispam features that have been created to do just that. Most are features that we already know from Exchange Server 2003 and Exchange Server 2003 SP2; they have simply changed names and of course been improved further. In Table 7.1 you can see a comparison of antispam features from Exchange Server 2003 RTM, Exchange 2003 SP1, Exchange 2003 SP2, and Exchange Server 2007. It's not difficult to see that the Exchange

Product Group invested significantly in improving the antispam features in the Exchange product.

Table 7.1 A Comparison of Antispam Features in Exchange Versions

Antispam Feature	E2K3 RTM	E2K3 SP1	E2K3 SP2	E2K7 RTM
IP Allow and Deny List	Yes			Yes
IP DNS Black Lists	Yes			Yes
IP Safe List (Bonded Senders)				Yes
Sender Filtering	Yes			Yes
Sender ID		No	Yes	Yes
Recipient Filtering	Yes			Yes
Content Filtering (IMF)		Yes		Yes
Content Filter Updates			Bi-weekly	Intra
Computational Puzzle Validation				Yes
Protocol Analysis Data Gathering				Yes
Protocol Analysis Sender Reputation				Yes
Open Proxy Validation				Yes
Dynamic Spam Data Update Service				Yes
Per User/OU spam Settings				Yes
Admin Quarantine Mailbox				Yes
Automatic DNS Block Lists				Yes

In addition to antispam features, the Edge Transport server also has full support for antivirus scanning. Surprisingly enough, the company's own ForeFront Security for Exchange server is a perfect match for the Edge Transport server. But the server also got full support for third-party products.

The antispam features on the Edge Transport server are known as *filtering agents*. You can see a list of these agents in Figure 7.29.

SOME INDEPENDENT ADVICE

Did you know you can install the Exchange 2007 antispam agents on the Hub Transport server in case you don't want to deploy an Edge Transport server in your organization? Yes, that's right! It's done by opening the EMS and then typing **CD C:\Program Files\Microsoft\Exchange Server\Scripts**. Now type **.\Install-AntispamAgents.msh**. When the script has finished, you can control the antispam agent settings under the **Organization Configuration | Hub Transport | Anti-spam** tab in the EMC, as shown in Figure 7.30.

Figure 7.29 Filtering Agents on the Edge Transport Server

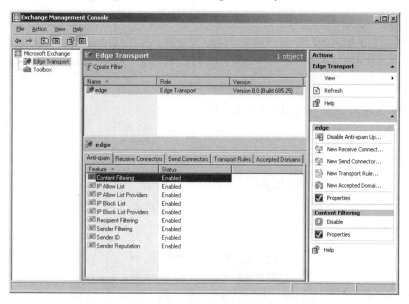

Figure 7.30 Installing the Filtering Agents on the Hub Transport Server

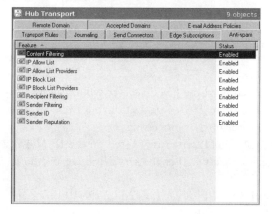

When an SMTP session is established between an external SMTP server and the Edge Transport server, the filters listed in Figure 7.29 are applied in a specific order. In the next section, we'll look at the order in which the various filters are applied.

Connection Filtering

When an SMTP session is established to the Edge Transport server, the first filter applied is the Connection Filter. The Connection Filtering agent will first check whether the IP address of the external SMTP server is listed on the **IP Allow list**, which is shown in Figure 7.31.

NOTE

You can specify individual IP addresses as well as a range of IP addresses under the **Allowed Addresses** tab on the **IP Allow List** Properties page (see Figure 7.31).

Figure 7.31 The IP Allow List

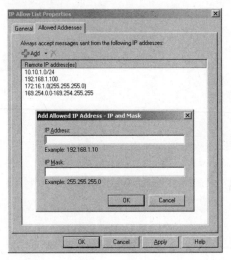

If the IP address is listed here, the SMTP server will be allowed to connect and transmit e-mail messages to the Exchange 2007 organization, but the e-mail messages will be sent to the Sender Filtering agent for further processing.

If the IP address of the SMTP server isn't listed on the IP Allow list, the Connection Filtering agent will check to see whether the server is listed on the IP Block list shown in Figure 7.32.

If the IP address of the SMTP server is listed on the IP Block list, connections from the server will be refused.

Figure 7.32 The IP Block List

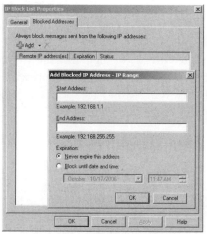

A neat little improvement to the IP Address Block list is that you now can set an expiration date and time for an individual IP address or a range of IP addresses. This was not possible with Exchange Server 2003 SP2.

If the IP address of the SMTP server isn't listed on either the IP Allow list or the IP Block list, the Connection Filtering agent will check to see whether the IP address is allowed by any IP Allow list provider you have specified (see Figure 7.33).

Figure 7.33 IP Allow List Providers

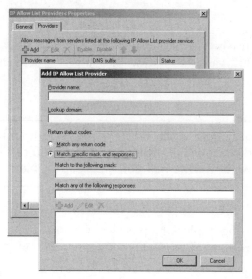

An IP Allow list provider is a provider that maintains a list of sender domains/IP addresses that you can rely on for sending legitimate e-mail messages and not spam. You can specify multiple IP Allow list providers and even specify how the providers' features should interpret the returned status.

If the SMTP server isn't listed on any of these lists, the Connection Filtering agent will do one last check before it allows the SMTP connection. It will check whether the server is listed on any real-time block lists (RBLs) you have specified under the Providers tab on the IP Block List Providers Properties page (see Figure 7.34).

Figure 7.34 Adding an IP Block List Provider

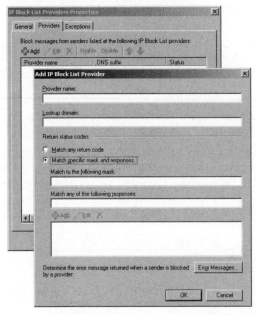

An RBL is an Internet-based service that tracks systems (and then adds those systems' IP addresses to a public list) that are known to send or suspected of sending out spam.

> **NOTE**
>
> You can read more about what RBLs are as well as how they work at http://en.wikipedia.org/wiki/DNSBL. In addition, you can find a list of the most popular RBLs at www.email-policy.com/Spam-black-lists.htm.

In addition to specifying IP Block list providers, you can also enter a custom error message that should be returned to the blocked SMTP server. Last but not least, there's an

Exceptions tab where you can specify IP addresses to which e-mail messages shouldn't be blocked, regardless of the feedback from the RBL.

Sender Filtering

When the Connection Filtering agent has processed the SMTP connection, the next filtering agent involved is Sender Filtering, which will check the e-mail address of the sender against the list of e-mail addresses or domains you have specified under the **Sender Filtering Properties** page (see Figure 7.35).

Figure 7.35 Blocked Sender List on the Sender Filtering Properties Page

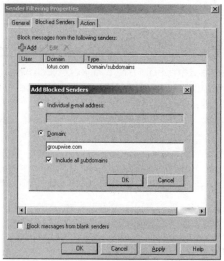

The Sender Filtering agent lets you reject individual e-mail addresses, single domains, or whole blocks of domains (that is, a domain and any subdomains). When the Sender Filtering agent rejects an e-mail message, a "554 5.1.0 Sender Denied" message is returned to the sending server. The agent also lets you reject any e-mail messages that don't contain a sender.

In addition to rejecting e-mail address and/or domains specified on the Blocked Senders list on the Sender Filtering Properties page, you can also choose to stamp messages instead of rejecting them (done under the **Action** tab). When you choose this action, the metadata of the message will be updated to indicate that the message was sent by a blocked sender. The stamp will then be used when the Content Filtering agent calculates the spam confidence level (SCL) of the message.

Bear in mind that the Sender Filtering agent overrides the Outlook Safe Senders list (which we will talk about later in this section), which means that senders specified on the Block Senders list will be rejected even though they are included on a Outlook Safe Senders list.

Recipient Filtering

When a message has been processed by the Sender Filtering agent and hasn't been rejected, it will be handed over to the Recipient Filtering agent. (Well, this isn't exactly true; the Connection Filtering agent will run once more, before doing so.) This will check the recipient of a given e-mail message against the Recipient Block list. As you can see in Figure 7.36, you can block recipients based on their e-mail addresses (that is, the SMTP address in the RCPT TO: field) as well as messages sent to recipients not listed in the Global Address List (GAL). The Edge Transport server can only check whether a recipient is in the GAL if you use EdgeSync subscription; otherwise, recipient data will not be replicated from Active Directory to ADAM.

> **NOTE**
>
> Any SMTP addresses entered on the Blocked Recipients list will only be blocked for senders located on the Internet. Internal users will still be able to send messages to these recipients.

Figure 7.36 The Blocked Recipients List on the Recipient Filtering Properties Page

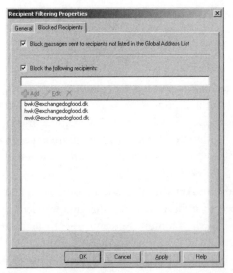

If an external sender sends an e-mail message to a recipient that is either listed on the Blocked Recipient list or not present in the GAL, a "550 5.1.1 User unknown SMTP" session error will be returned to the sending server.

It worth noting that the Recipient Filtering agent works for only domains for which the Edge Transport server is authoritative. This means that any domains for which the Edge Transport server is configured as a relay server won't be able to take advantage of Recipient Filtering. Diagrams of the Edge Transport Server with the Recipient Filtering Agent disabled and enabled are shown in Figures 7.37 and 7.38, respectively.

SOME INDEPENDENT ADVICE

As mentioned earlier in this chapter, the EdgeSync service will replicate recipient data from Active Directory to ADAM every fourth hour. With this in mind, be aware that any new recipients created on your mailbox server on the internal network won't be able to receive e-mail messages from external senders before the EdgeSync service has taken place hereafter.

The Recipient Lookup feature also includes a SMTP Tarpitting feature that helps combat *directory harvest attacks (DHAs)*. A DHA is a technique spammers use in an attempt to find valid SMTP addresses within an organization. This is typically done with the help of a special program that is capable of generating random SMTP addresses for one or more domains. For each generated SMTP address, the program also sends out a spam message to the specific address. Because the program will try to deliver a message to each generated SMTP address, an SMTP session is, of course, also established to the respective Edge Transport server (or whatever SMTP gateway is used in the organization). The program can therefore collect a list of valid SMTP addresses, since the SMTP session will either respond with "250 2.1.5 Recipient OK" or "550 5.1.1 User unknown," depending on whether the SMTP address is valid or not.

This is where the SMTP Tarpitting feature comes into the picture. This feature basically delays the "250 2.1.5 Recipient OK" or "550 5.1.1 User unknown" SMTP response codes during an SMTP session. By default, the SMTP Tarpitting feature on an Edge Transport server is configured to a delay of 5 seconds (but the value can be changed for each Receive connector), which should help make it more difficult for a spammer to harvest valid SMTP addresses from your domain.

SOME INDEPENDENT ADVICE

The SMTP Tarpitting feature was originally introduced in Exchange Server 2003. In Exchange 2003 the administrator had the option of specifying a tarpit value in which he or she could define the number of seconds to delay a response to the *RCPT TO* command during an SMTP session. The problem in Exchange 2003 was that this value was fixed, which enabled spammers to detect this behavior so they could work around it. A common practice was to have the spam application establish a new SMTP session, if it detected it was being tarpitted. To solve this problem, the Edge Transport server uses a random number of seconds, making predictions much harder. Even if the spam application reconnects, it won't be in better shape; the Edge Transport server will know it's the same sending server, so it will retain the tarpit state.

Figure 7.37 The Edge Transport Server with the Recipient Filtering Agent Disabled

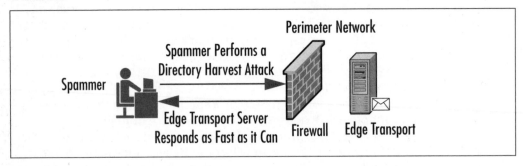

Figure 7.38 The Edge Transport Server with the Recipient Filtering Agent Enabled

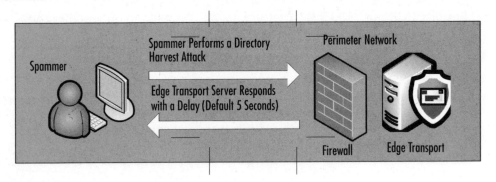

Sender ID Filtering

When an e-mail message has been processed by the Recipient Filtering agent and still hasn't been rejected, it will be handed over to the Sender ID Filtering agent.

The Sender ID is an e-mail industry initiative invented by Microsoft and a few other industry leaders. The purpose of Sender ID is to help counter spoofing (at least to make it more difficult to spoof messages), which is the number-one deceptive practice used by spammers. Sender ID works by verifying that every e-mail message indeed originates from the

Internet domain from which it was sent. This is accomplished by checking the address of the server sending the mail against a registered list of servers that the domain owner has authorized to send e-mail.

If you don't have any experience with Sender ID, it can be a bit difficult to understand, so let's take a closer look at how it works.

An organization can publish a Sender Policy Framework (SPF) record on the public DNS server(s) hosting their domain. The published SPF record contains a list of the IP addresses that should be or are allowed to send out messages for a particular domain. If a particular organization has published a SPF record and someone at that organization sends a message to a recipient behind an Edge Transport server in another organization, the Edge Transport server will examine the SPF record to see whether the SMTP server that sent the message is listed there (see Figure 7.39).

Figure 7.39 How Sender ID Works Behind the Scenes

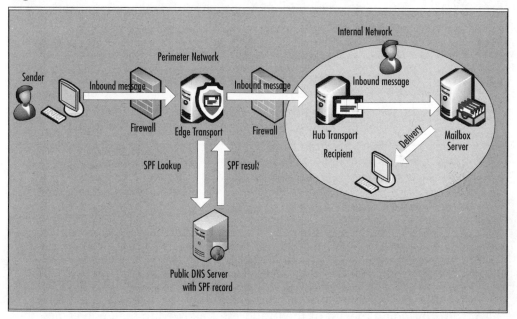

Sender ID can provide several different results and stamp them appropriately. Table 7.2 lists each of the results as well a short description and the action taken.

Table 7.2 Sender ID Results

Sender ID Result	Description	Action Taken
Neutral	Domain is neutral (makes no decision about IP address)	Stamp and Accept
Pass (+)	IP address for PRA permitted set	Stamp and Accept
Fail (-) - Domain doesn't exist - Sender isn't permitted - Malformed domain - No Purported Responsible Address (PRA) in header	IP address for PRA not permitted set	Stamp and Accept then either Delete or Reject
Soft Fail (~)	IP address for PRA not permitted set	Stamp and Accept
None	No SPF record published for the domain	Stamp and Accept
Temp Error	Transient error (could be unreachable DNS server)	Stamp and Accept
Perm Error	Possible error in record so couldn't be read correctly	Stamp and Accept

No matter what the result of the SPF check, the result will be used in the calculation process when an SCL rating is generated for a message.

TIP

In you want to check which IP addresses are allowed to send e-mail messages for a given domain, you can use a wizard such as the one at www.dnsstuff.com/pages/spf.htm, or open a command prompt and type **nslookup –q=TXT domain.com**. You should then be able to see the SPF record, including the list of the IP addresses allowed to send e-mail messages for this domain.

For additional information about Sender ID, visit http://en.wikipedia.org/wiki/Sender_id.

When the Sender ID Filtering agent checks whether a sending SMTP server has an appropriate purported responsible address (PRA), you can specify what action it should take for a given e-mail message that doesn't have an appropriate PRA.

You can configure it to **Reject message**, **Delete message** or **Stamp message with Sender ID result and continue processing**; the last one is the option selected by default (see Figure 7.40).

Figure 7.40 The Action Tab on the Sender ID Properties Page

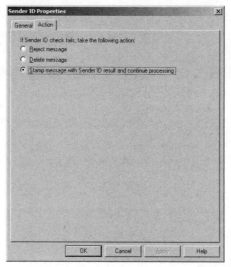

If you set Sender ID to reject the message, the message will be rejected by the Edge Transport server and an SMTP error response will be returned to the sender.

If you configure Sender ID to delete message, the message will be deleted without sending an SMTP error response to the sender. Since the message is deleted without informing the sending SMTP server, you would think that the sending SMTP server would retry sending the message, but this is not the case. The Sender ID filter has been made so cleverly that the Edge Transport server will send a fake *OK* SMTP command before deleting the message.

When you configure Sender ID to stamp messages with the Sender ID result and continue processing, the e-mail message will be stamped with information that will be used when the message is evaluated by the Content Filtering agent (which we will look at in a moment) to calculate the SCL.

SOME INDEPENDENT ADVICE

If you haven't already done so, we highly recommend that you create an SPF record for your domain. This will make it much more difficult for spammers to forge your domain so that they can spam domains in other organizations. Creating your own SPF record is a relatively simple process; Microsoft even provides a Web-based GUI wizard that will help you do it (see Figure 7.41).

You can find the wizard by visiting www.microsoft.com/mscorp/safety/content/technologies/senderid/wizard.

Figure 7.41 The Sender ID Framework SPF Record Wizard

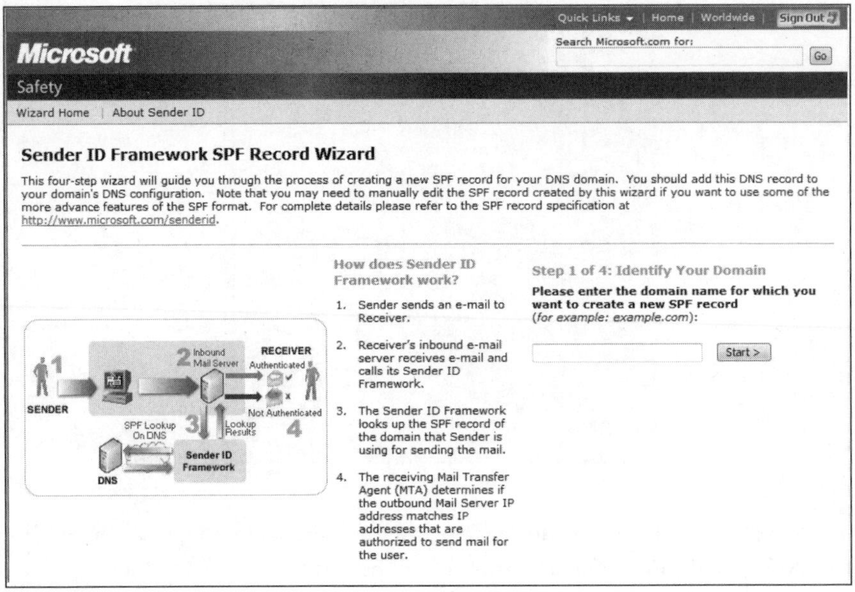

Content Filtering

The Content Filtering agent can be considered the next generation of the Intelligent Message Filter (or IMF version 3), which most of us know from Exchange Server 2003 (version 2 came with Exchange 2003 SP2). This means that the Content Filter is based on the SmartScreen technology, originally developed by Microsoft Research. When an e-mail message is received by an Edge Transport server with the Content Filtering agent enabled, it will evaluate the textual content of the messages and then assign the message an SCL rating based on the probability that the message is spam. This rating is stored as a message property called an *SCL rating*. The Content Filter is regularly updated using the Antispam Update Service (Windows Update) to ensure that it always contains the most up-to-date information when it's running. Since the Content Filter is based on the characteristics of many millions of messages (Hotmail, among others, is used to collect the necessary information about both legitimate as well as spam messages), it recognizes both legitimate messages and spam messages. The Content Filter can very precisely determine whether an inbound e-mail message is a legitimate message or spam.

The Content Filter can also, via spam signatures, analyze messages for phishing characteristics. If the message is a phishing attempt, the Content Filtering agent will stamp it with a property before delivering it to the recipient's inbox. When the message is delivered, Outlook 2007 will render it differently and warn the user that this most likely is a phishing attempt. When the message is viewed in Outlook 2007, all content will be flattened, any links will be disabled, and no images will be loaded.

Just as was the case with IMF in Exchange Server 2003, you can, with the help of the Content Filter, assign an SCL rating to the messages flowing into your organization. The Content Filter stamps the messages that it inspects with an SCL property (actually a MAPI property) with a value between 0 and 9. As you can see in Figure 7.42, depending on how a message is rated, you can delete, reject, or quarantine it to a specified mailbox.

Figure 7.42 The Action Tab on the Content Filtering Properties Page

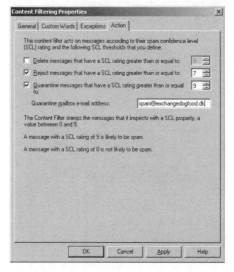

If a message equals the SCL delete threshold, the message will be deleted without notifying the sending server. If the message equals the SCL reject threshold, the message will also be deleted, but a rejection response will be returned to the sending server. If a message equals the SCL quarantine threshold, the message will be sent to the e-mail address specified in the **Quarantine mailbox e-mail address:** field. Bear in mind, though, that before a message can be quarantined, you need to create and configure a mailbox that should be used for this purpose. To do so, perform the following steps:

1. Create a new mailbox called **Quarantined Messages** or similar.

2. Depending on how many recipients as well as how many messages are received by your Exchange organization, configure a reasonable **quota** for this mailbox.

3. Set up delegation if you're going to open the mailbox as an additional mailbox under your primary mailbox account.

4. On the Edge Transport server, open the **EMS**, type **Set–ContentFilterConfig – QuarantineMailbox <*SmtpAddress*>**, and press **Enter**.

All quarantined messages will now be sent to the specified e-mail address, so be sure to check it for any false positives on a regular basis. When you find a false positive, you can resend it to the original recipient by opening the message and clicking **Resend**.

In addition, you can create a list of words and/or phrases that won't be blocked no matter the SCL rating of the particular message (the Content Filter will assign an SCL rating of 0 to messages including these words and/or phrases). You can also create a list of words and/or phrases that should be blocked no matter the SCL rating (see Figure 7.43).

Figure 7.43 The Custom Word List on the Content-Filtering Properties Page

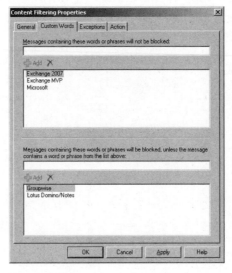

If for some reason you don't want to block any messages destined for a particular SMTP address, you can add the address to an exceptions list (see Figure 7.44).

Safelist Aggregation

The content-filtering agent includes another antispam feature that isn't visible in the EMC GUI. Called *safelist aggregation*, it is a feature that basically collects data from the Safe Senders and Safe Recipients lists, which can be found under the Junk E-Mail Options in Outlook 2007 (see Figure 7.45).

Figure 7.44 The Exceptions List on the Content-Filtering Properties Page

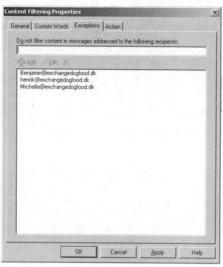

Figure 7.45 The Safe Senders List in Outlook 2007

The e-mail addresses and/or domains that the end users in your Exchange organization have added to the Safe Senders and/or Safe Recipients list are stored on the respective mailbox servers on which a mailbox is located and can from here be pushed to Active Directory service, where the lists can be stored on each user object. If you use the EdgeSync service, these lists will, as part of the recipient data, be replicated from Active Directory to the ADAM store on the Edge Transport server.

To reduce the number of false positives on the Edge Transport server, the Content Filtering agent can, using safelist aggregation, let the e-mail addresses and domains configured on the Safe Sender list be allowed to pass through to end users' mailboxes without additional processing by the rest of the filtering agents. If you enable **Also trust e-mail from my Contacts** on the **Safe Senders** tab in Outlook 2007, shown in Figure 7.45, all Outlook contacts in user mailboxes will be allowed to pass through the filtering agents as well. Pretty neat, right?

Even though you have enabled the Content Filtering agent, you still need to enable and configure the safelist aggregation feature before you can use it. To do so, perform the following steps:

1. Log on to the Exchange 2007 server that has the Mailbox server role installed and open the **EMS**.

2. To read the Safelist collection from each user's mailbox and then hash and write it to the respective user objects in Active Directory, you will need to run the *Update-Safelist* CMDlet. When using the *Update-Safelist* CMDlet, you are expected to provide the identity for the mailbox you want to run the CMDlet on. Since you want to run the *Update-Safelist* CMDlet on all mailbox users on the mailbox server, you will need to use piping. To run *Update-Safelist* for all mailbox users, type **"get-mailbox | where {$_.RecipientType -eq [Microsoft.Exchange.Data.Directory.Recipient.RecipientType]::Mailb oxUser } | update-safelist"** and then press **Enter**.

3. Since the *Update-Safelist* CMDlet is a onetime-only command, you need to use the Windows Scheduler to schedule the CMDlet to run, let's say, once every 24 hours. To do so, create a batch file with the following code:

```
"C:\Program Files\Windows Powershell\v1.0\Powershell.exe" -psconsolefile
"C:\Program Files\Microsoft\Exchange Server\bin\exshell.psc1" -command
"Get-Mailbox | where {$_.RecipientType -eq
[Microsoft.Exchange.Data.Directory.Recipient.RecipientType]::MailboxUser } |
Update-Safelist"
```

4. Save the batch file as **Update-Safelist.bat** or something similar. (Remember to change Notepad to all files instead of .txt files.)

5. Now schedule this batch file to be run every 24th hour (for example, at 00.00). To do this, open a command prompt window (or use the Windows Scheduler, which can be found in the Control Panel), type **AT 00.00 /every:M,T,W,Th,F,S,SU cmd /c "C:\Update-Safelist.bat"**, and press **Enter**.

6. To see whether *Update-Safelist* has updated the respective Active Directory user objects, you can check the *msExchSafeRecipientsHash* and *msExchSafeSendersHash* attributes for a couple of user objects using ADSI Edit or a similar tool. If these attributes have a value of *<Not Set>*, they haven't been updated, but if they instead have a value similar to *0xac 0xbd 0x03 0xca*, the user objects have been updated.

NOTE

To use ADSI Edit, you need to install the Windows Server 2003 Support Tools on the respective Exchange 2007 server.

To see whether safelist aggregation works as expected on the Edge Transport server, try to add a custom word or phrase to the Custom Words block list, which is found on the Properties page of the Content Filter. Now add the e-mail address of the private e-mail account (such as a Hotmail) to the Safe Senders list of your mailbox in Outlook 2007. Finally, send an e-mail message containing the word or phrase you added to the block list to your Exchange 2007 Mailbox user account. If the message appears in your mailbox, the safelist aggregation feature works as expected.

Outlook E-mail Postmark Validation

In addition to the safelist aggregation feature, the Content Filtering agent includes one more feature that will help reduce the number of false positives in your Exchange organization. The feature, called Outlook E-Mail Postmark Validation, is a computational proof that Outlook applies to all outbound messages to help recipient messaging systems distinguish legitimate e-mail messages from junk. With Outlook E-Mail Postmark Validation enabled, the Content Filtering agent will parse all inbound messages for a computational postmark header. If a valid as well as solved computational postmark header is present in a message, it means that the client computer that generated the message solved the computational postmark. The result of a postmark validation will be used when the overall SCL rating for an inbound message is calculated.

NOTE

If no computational postmark header exists or if the header is invalid, the SCL rating will not be changed.

On a default installation of the Edge Transport server role, the Outlook E-Mail Postmark Validation feature is enabled by default, but to verify that the feature indeed is enabled on your system, you can open the **EMC** and type **Get-ContentFilterConfig** (see Figure 7.46).

Figure 7.46 The Content Filter Configuration Settings

If the feature is set to **False** for some reason, you can enable it by typing **Set-
ContenFilterConfig –OutlookEmailPostmarkValidationEnabled $True** and pressing
Enter.

Attachment Filtering

As most of you are aware, Exchange Server 2003 didn't include a function that let you filter
out specific attachments. Instead you had to create your own SMTP OnArrival Event Sink,
use a third-party product, or strictly rely on the OWA 2003 and Outlook 2003 attachment
control feature. However, since you really should filter out unwanted attachment types on an
SMTP gateway in your perimeter network (the DMZ or screened subnet) before they arrive
at your internal network, the last two options aren't recommend. An attachment filtering
mechanism should have been a native feature in Exchange a long time ago, but finally the
wait is over with the Edge Transport server in Exchange Server 2007. Let's do attachment
filtering at the server level (hooray!). You now have the possibility of filtering out messages
based on attachment filename, filename extension, or file MIME content type. You even have
the choice of filtering out both the message and the attachment or just stripping the attachment. You can even choose to delete both the message and the attachment "silently,"
meaning that both will be deleted without notifying the sender of the message.

SOME INDEPENDENT ADVICE

In recent years more and more focus has been placed on deploying messaging environments, where each individual e-mail message is ether digitally signed or encrypted, or even protected using Information Rights Management (IRM). Here in Denmark where I live, the governmental institutions have an especially strong desire for protecting messages while they're in transit. If you're doing the same in your organization or are planning to do so, you should bear in mind that stripping an attachment from a digitally signed, encrypted, or IRM-protected e-mail message will invalidate the message so that it becomes unreadable. One way to solve this problem in dealing with digitally signed or encrypted messages is to put up some kind of black box that takes care of signing and encrypting the messages after the attachment filter processes them. The company I work for got such a product, which is becoming more and more popular here in Denmark.

The Attachment Filtering agent applies right after the Content Filtering agent and can be configured using the *Add-AttachmentFilterEntry* CMDlet. Unfortunately, there's no way to configure Attachment Filtering via the EMC GUI; you will have to do so using the EMS. We don't really know why this feature hasn't been included in the GUI, but our guess is that the Exchange Product team didn't have the time to integrate the feature in the GUI. If this is the case, we expect it to be included in Exchange Server 2007 Service Pack 1, but only time will tell.

Before you start to configure the Attachment Filter agent, you first need to make sure that the agent is enabled. To do so, you will need to open the EMS and type **Get-TransportAgent**. On a default installation of an Edge Transport server, this agent should be enabled by default, but if it for some reason is disabled, you can enable it by typing **Enable-TransportAgent –Identity "Attachment Filtering Agent"** and then pressing **Enter**.

Now that the agent is enabled, type **Get-AttachmentFilterEntry | FL** and press **Enter**. This will give you a list of all filename extensions and content types on which the Attachment Filtering agent can filter (see Table 7.3).

Table 7.3 Filename Extensions and Content Types

Type	Name	Identity
ContentType	Application/x-msdownload	ContentType:application/x-msdownload
ContentType	Message/partial	ContentType:message/partial
ContentType	Text/scriptlet	ContentType:text/scriptlet
ContentType	Application/prg	ContentType:application/prg

Continued

Table 7.3 continued Filename Extensions and Content Types

Type	Name	Identity
ContentType	Application/msaccess	ContentType:application/msaccess
ContentType	Text/javascript	ContentType:text/javascript
ContentType	Application/x-javascript	ContentType:application/x-javascript
ContentType	Application/javascript	ContentType:application/javascript
ContentType	x-internet-signup	ContentType:x-internet-signup
ContentType	Application/hta	ContentType:application/hta
FileName	*.wsh	FileName:*.wsh
FileName	*.wsf	FileName:*.wsf
FileName	*.wsc	FileName:*.wsc
FileName	*.vbs	FileName:*.vbs
FileName	*.vbe	FileName:*.vbe
FileName	*.vb	FileName:*.vb
FileName	*.url	FileName:*.url
FileName	*.shs	FileName:*.shs
FileName	*.shs	FileName:*.shb
FileName	*.sct	FileName:*.sct
FileName	*.scr	FileName:*.scr
FileName	*.scf	FileName:*.scf
FileName	*.reg	FileName:*.reg
FileName	*.prg	FileName:*.prg
FileName	*.prf	FileName:*.prf
FileName	*.pcd	FileName:*.pcd
FileName	*.ops	FileName:*.ops
FileName	*.mst	FileName:*.mst
FileName	*.msp	FileName:*.msp
FileName	*.msi	FileName:*.msi
FileName	*.ps11xml	FileName:*.ps11xml
FileName	*.ps11	FileName:*.ps11
FileName	*.ps1xml	FileName:*.ps1xml
FileName	*.ps1	FileName:*.ps1
FileName	*.msc	FileName:*.msc
FileName	*.mdz	FileName:*.mdz

Continued

Table 7.3 continued Filename Extensions and Content Types

Type	Name	Identity
FileName	*.mdw	FileName:*.mdw
FileName	*.mdt	FileName:*.mdt
FileName	*.mde	FileName:*.mde
FileName	*.mdb	FileName:*.mdb
FileName	*.mda	FileName:*.mda
FileName	*.lnk	FileName:*.lnk
FileName	*.ksh	FileName:*.ksh
FileName	*.jse	FileName:*.jse
FileName	*.js	FileName:*.js
FileName	*.isp	FileName:*.isp
FileName	*.ins	FileName:*.ins
FileName	*.inf	FileName:*.inf
FileName	*.hta	FileName:*.hta
FileName	*.hlp	FileName:*.hlp
FileName	*.fxp	FileName:*.fxp
FileName	*.exe	FileName:*.exe
FileName	*.csh	FileName:*.csh
FileName	*crt	FileName:*.crt
FileName	*.cpl	FileName:*.cpl
FileName	*.com	FileName:*.com
FileName	*.cmd	FileName:*.cmd
FileName	*.chm	FileName:*.chm
FileName	*.bat	FileName:*.bat
FileName	*.bas	FileName:*.bas
FileName	*.asx	FileName:*.asx
FileName	*.app	FileName:*.app
FileName	*.adp	FileName:*.adp
FileName	*.ade	FileName:*.ade

You can add file extensions or filenames to this list using the *Add-AttachmentFilterEntry* CMDlet. For example, if you wanted to filter out zip files, you would need to run the following command: *Add-AttachmentFilterEntry -Name *.zip -Type FileName*. If you wanted to filter out messages with a specific MIME type, such GIF files, you would need to use the command *Add-AttachmentFilterEntry -Name image/gif -Type ContentType*. If you wanted to filter out messages that contain an attachment with a specific filename, say one called *dangerous_file*, you would use the command *Add-AttachmentFilterEntry -Name dangerous_file -Type FileName*.

If you want to remove an attachment filter entry later, you do so using the *Remove-AttachmentFilterEntry* CMDlet. For example, if you wanted to remove the ZIP attachment filter entry, you would need to type *Remove-AttachmentFilterEntry —Identity filename: * .zip*.

That's pretty simple, right?

To be able to use more advanced features such as scanning files in a ZIP file, you would need to install Forefront Security for Exchange Server (which we will talk a bit about later in this chapter) or a supported third-party product.

As mentioned, you can choose to block a whole message, including the attachment (will return a delivery status notification to the sender); strip the attachment but allow the message through (will replace the attachment with a text file explaining why the attachment was stripped); or silently delete both the message as well as the attachment (will delete both without notifying the sender).

You can also configure a custom response message that will be included in the delivery status notification, which is returned to the sender when a message and an attached file are blocked. This is done using the *Set-AttachmentFilterListConfig* CMDlet. An example could be *Set-AttachmentFilterListConfig —Action Reject -RejectResponse "This message has been rejected since the attached file type isn't allowed in this organization"*.

NOTE

All attachment filter entries on an Edge Transport server use the same attachment filtering behavior—that means the same custom response message as well as action (reject, strip, or silent delete).

If you only want to strip the attachment but allow the message through, you would need to use the command *AttachmentFilterConfigList —Action Strip.* If you want to include a custom admin message in the text file that replaces the stripped attachments, you would need to use the command *AttachmentFilterConfigList —Action Strip —AdminMessage "The attachment in this message has been filtered as it's not allowed in this organization."* Finally, to silently delete both the message and the attachment, use the command *AttachmentFilterConfigList —Action SilentDelete.*

The last thing we'll mention regarding the Attachment Filtering agent is that you can exclude a list of connectors from attachment filtering, which means that attachment filtering won't be applied to messages flowing through the specified connectors. You can exclude one or more connectors using *Set-AttachmentFilterListConfig —Action Reject —ExceptionConnectors*

<Connector_GUID>. To get the GUID for a receive connector, type **Get-ReceiveConnector | FL**.

If you want to see a list of the current settings for *AttachmentFilterListConfig*, type **Get-AttachmentFilterListConfig** and press **Enter** (see Figure 7.47).

Figure 7.47 The Attachment Filter List Configuration Settings

For any additional information on how to configure the attachment filtering behavior using the *Set-AttachmentFilterListConfig* CMDlet, see the Exchange Server 2007 Help file or type **Get-Help Set-AttachmentFilterListConfig** in the EMS.

Sender Reputation

The Edge Transport server also includes a brand-new antispam feature called *Sender Reputation*. The Sender Reputation agent, which is enabled by default (although only for externally received messages), is an antispam feature that blocks inbound messages according to characteristics of the sender. The agent actually relies on persistent data about the sender so that it can determine which action to take on inbound messages.

The Sender Reputation agent analyses whether a sender forges the *HELO/EHLO* statement when establishing an SMTP session to the Edge Transport server. This is done on a per-sender basis, which makes it easier to see whether it's a spammer or a legitimate sender. A spammer typically provides many different unique *HELO/EHLO* statements in a specific time period, and they often also provide an IP address in the *HELO/EHLO* statement that doesn't match their original IP address (that is, the IP address from which the connection originated). In addition, they often try to provide a local domain name, which is the name of the organization to which the Edge Transport server belongs. In most cases the behavior of a legitimate sender is to use a different but more constant set of domains in the *HELO/EHLO* statement.

The Sender Reputation agent also performs a reverse DNS lookup when an external SMTP server establishes an SMTP session. This means that the Edge Transport server verifies that the IP address of the SMTP server matches the registered domain name, which the server submits in the *HELO/EHLO* command. If the IP address doesn't match the resolved domain name, there's a good chance you're dealing with a spammer.

As you already know, an inbound message is assigned an SCL rating when the Content Filter is applied. This SCL rating is also analyzed by the Sender Reputation agent. The agent calculates statistics about a sender by looking at how many messages from that sender in the past had either a low or high SCL rating.

Lastly the Sender Reputation agent is capable of performing an open proxy test against the sender's IP address. If the connection is looped back to the Edge Transport server through known open proxy ports and protocols—more specifically, SOCKS 4 and 5, Wingate, Telnet, Cisco, HTTP CONNECT, and HTTP POST—the sending server is considered an open proxy. As you can see in Figure 7.48, you enabled this feature on the Properties page of Sender Reputation.

NOTE

For the Edge Transport server to perform an open proxy test against an external server, keep in mind that you need to open the required outbound ports in any firewall located between the Edge Transport server and the Internet. The following ports are used during an open proxy test: 1080, 1081, 23, 6588, 3128, and 80. If you're using a proxy server in your organization, you also need to configure the Sender Reputation agent to use the proxy server for open proxy tests. You do this using the *Set-SenderReputationConfig –ProxyServerName* CMDlet. For details on how to configure a proxy, type **Get-Help Set-SenderReputationConfig** in the EMS or refer to the Exchange Server 2007 Help file.

Depending on the results of these analyses and tests, the Sender Reputation agent assigns a sender reputation level (SRL) to the sender. As is the case with the SCL rating, this SRL can be a number between 0 and 9. The higher an SRL rating that is assigned to a sender, the more likely it is that the sender is a spammer. Under the Action tab, which also is found on the Sender Reputation Properties page, you can configure an SRL block threshold (see Figure 7.49), and when the threshold is exceeded, the sender is added to the IP Block list for a specified number of hours (the default is 24 hours).

Figure 7.48 The Sender Confidence Tab on the Sender Reputation Properties Page

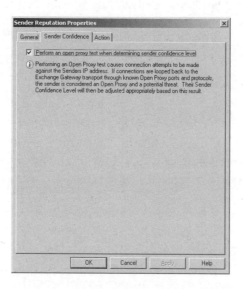

Figure 7.49 The Action Tab on the Sender Reputation Properties Page

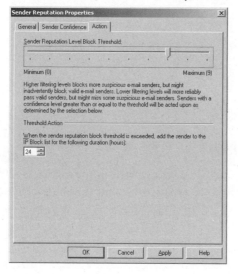

It's not in the hands of the Sender Reputation agent to decide how blocked messages are handled; this is instead controlled by the Sender Filter agent, which can be configured to block, reject, or stamp messages from blocked senders and continue processing.

> **NOTE**
>
> Senders that haven't yet been analyzed by Sender Reputation are assigned an SRL rating of 0. Only after the Edge Transport server has received 20 or more messages from a particular sender is an SRL calculated.

Antivirus Scanning

After a given message has been through the Attachment filter, it will be scanned by the antivirus product installed on the server, which could be ForeFront Security for Exchange Server 2007 (included in the Exchange 2007 Enterprise CAL) or a supported third-party product.

It should come as no surprise that the Edge Transport server role integrates perfectly with the ForeFront Security for Exchange Server 2007 product, but the server role also has rich support for partner antivirus providers. So you're not bound to use the ForeFront Security for Exchange Server product if you choose to deploy an Edge Transport server in your organization's perimeter network (DMZ or screened subnet).

Some of the third-party products that have shipped since Exchange Server 2007 was released in December 2006 are:

- Symantec
- Trend Micro
- GFI
- Kaspersky
- McAfee
- Sophos

All of these third-party providers participated in the Exchange 2007 Technology Adoption Program (TAP), so these products take full advantage of Exchange Server 2007 features.

> **NOTE**
>
> On February 8, 2005, Microsoft acquired the security software firm Sybari, the company behind the Exchange AntiGen product. The primary reason behind this purchase was to help enterprise customers become more secure. Since then Microsoft rebranded the AntiGen product series to ForeFront Security, which means that the old Exchange AntiGen product now is known as

ForeFront Security for Exchange Server. Not only has the product name changed, but Microsoft has also been busy improving the product as well as integrating it more tightly with Exchange Server 2007; now the product is recommended as *the* antivirus solution for the Edge Transport server. For more information about ForeFront Security for Exchange Server, see www.microsoft.com/forefront/default.mspx.

SOME INDEPENDENT ADVICE

As some of you might be aware, in 2004 Microsoft published a document called *The Coordinated Spam Reduction Initiative* (which can be downloaded from http://tinyurl.com/yxzsc5). Even today, it's an extremely interesting document that focuses on how you can reduce the amount of spam using different filters, mechanisms, and the like. Comparing the content of the document with the features included in the Edge Transport server role, you will notice that most of them have been implemented in Exchange Server 2007.

Outlook Junk E-Mail Filtering

When a message has been through all the filtering agents, the message will finally be send to the recipient mailbox, where the Outlook Junk E-Mail Filter will take the appropriate action, depending on the SCL rating of the message. If the message has an SCL rating that is equal to or greater than the SCL Junk E-Mail folder threshold, which is specified on the Content Filtering Properties page, it will be moved to the Junk e-mail folder in the recipient's mailbox. Details about the Outlook 2007 Junk e-mail filter are outside the scope of this book, but we can say that the filter has been improved even further since Outlook 2003.

Securing the Edge Server Using the Windows 2003 Security Configuration Wizard (SCW)

Because the Edge Transport server is located in the perimeter network (the DMZ or sub-screened network), it's much more vulnerable to potential attacks than the other Exchange 2007 server roles on the internal network. It's therefore highly recommended as well as a best practice to lock down the Edge Transport server role into as tight a state as possible.

You can lock down the Edge Transport server with the Security Configuration Wizard (SCW), a tool for reducing the attack surface of computers running Windows Server 2003 R2 or Windows 2003 server with Service Pack 1 (SP1) or higher applied. The SCW tool makes it a relatively easy and simple process to lock down the Edge Transport server, since you can do so using the SCW GUI wizard.

> **NOTE**
>
> The SCW can also be used to lock down the other Exchange 2007 server roles as well as Exchange 2003 front-end and back-end servers. Whether you want to do so depends on how aggressive the security policies are in your organization.

To lock down our Edge Transport server with the SCW, you first need to install the component. On the Edge Transport server, click **Start | Control Panel | Add or Remove Programs**. Now click **Add/Remove Windows Component**. Tick the **Security Configuration Wizard** component and click **Next** (see Figure 7.50). When the component has been installed successfully, click **Finish**.

Figure 7.50 Adding the Security Configuration Wizard Component

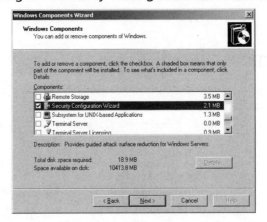

You now need to register the Exchange 2007 SCW extension file, which is located in the Scripts directory under C:\Program Files\Microsoft\Exchange (or whatever the path to your Exchange installation is). Since you need to do so using the *scwcmd register* command, open a command prompt window and type the following: **scwcmd register /kbname:MSExchangeEdge /kbfile: "C:\program files\Microsoft\Exchange Server\scripts\Exchange2007.xml."** Next, press **Enter**. See Figure 7.51.

Figure 7.51 Registering the Exchange 2007 SCW Extension File

Now that the Exchange 2007 SCW extension file has been properly registered, you can launch the SCW Wizard. This is done by clicking **Start | Administrative Tools | Security Configuration Wizard**. Then follow these steps:

1. On the **Welcome to Security Configuration Wizard** page, click **Next**.

2. Since you're going to create a new security policy, select **Create a new security policy** and click **Next** (see Figure 7.52).

Figure 7.52 Creating a New Security Policy

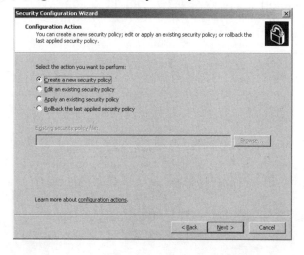

3. The NetBIOS name of the Edge Transport server will be pre-entered on the next page, and since you're going to apply the security policy to this, leave it like this and click **Next**.

4. When the security configuration database has been processed, click the **View Configuration Database** button.

    If the Exchange Server 2007 SCW extension file has been properly registered, you should see an entry for the Edge Transport server role as well as the other Exchange 2007 server roles in the **SCW Viewer,** as shown in Figure 7.53.

Figure 7.53 SCW Viewer

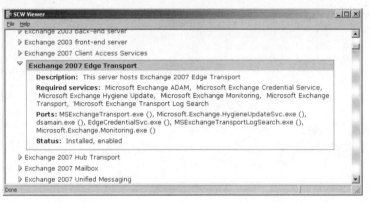

> **NOTE**
>
> If you don't see any entries for the Exchange 2007 server roles in the SCW Viewer, try running the SCW register command again. If it still doesn't show up, check the SCWRegistrar_log.xml file (located in the %*windir*%\security\msscw\logs directory) for any issues.

5. If you do see entries for the Exchange 2007 server roles in the SCW Viewer, close the viewer and click **Next**.

6. On the **Role-Based Service Configuration** page, click **Next**.

7. Now choose **Selected roles** in the drop-down box; uncheck all roles except **Exchange 2007 Edge Transport**, as shown in Figure 7.54; and click **Next**.

Figure 7.54 Selecting the Edge Transport Server Role

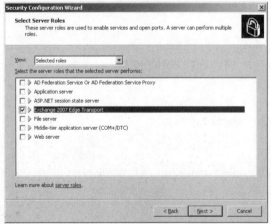

8. On the **Select Client Features** page, leave the default settings untouched (because you under normal circumstances don't need to change them, since they are configured based on the roles you chose in the beginning of the SCW). Click **Next**.

9. On the **Select Administration and Other Options** page, leave the default settings untouched. (As in Step 15, these are selected based on the role chosen in the beginning of the SCW.) Click **Next**.

10. Now you'll get a list of additional services found on the server while the SCW processed the security configuration database. When installing the Edge Transport server in a production environment, you should take your time and examine any services listed on this page, and then wisely decide whether they're required or not. If they're not required or you're unsure about this, I suggest that you uncheck them (you can always can enable them again, should they be required) and click Next.

11. You'll now need to decide how unspecified services (which basically are services not in the database yet) should be handled. You can choose to leave the startup mode as it is or have the service disabled. We recommend that you select **Disable the service** and then enable it manually should it be required. When you have decided how you would like unspecified services to be handled, click **Next**.

12. On the **Confirm Service Chances** page, verify that the service configuration for each service is set as expected, as shown in Figure 7.55 and click **Next**.

Figure 7.55 Confirming Service Changes

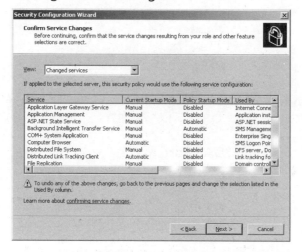

13. You have now reached the **Network Security** section of the SCW, which is where you'll configure inbound ports using the Windows firewall based on the

roles and administration options selected on the previous pages. In addition, this is where you can restrict access to ports and indicate whether port traffic is signed or encrypted using IPSec. It's very important that you configure this portion correctly, since answering the questions incorrectly might prevent the Edge Transport server from communication with the servers it's required to communicate with. Click **Next**.

14.   On the **Open Ports and Approve Applications** page, you need to pay special attention. As you read earlier in this chapter, the Edge Transport server will need to replicate data from Active Directory to the local ADAM store at a scheduled set of intervals. Because this is done using LDAP via port 50389 and 50636, you need to add both these ports on this page. To do so, click the **Add** button shown in Figure 7.56.

Figure 7.56 Adding the Respective Ports

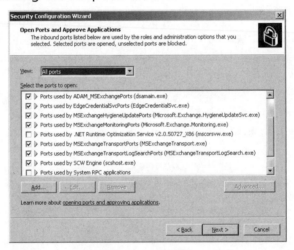

15.   On the **Add Port or Application** page, enter 50389 in the port number field, check **TCP,** and click **OK** (see Figure 7.57).

Figure 7.57 Adding the LDAP Port

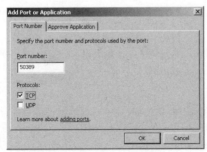

16.   Repeat **Step 15,** but enter port **50636** instead. Click **OK**.

NOTE

50389 and 50636 are default ports used for LDAP communication between Active Directory and ADAM, but if you for some reason should require so, you can change them using the ConfigureAdam.ps1 script located in the scripts directory under C:\Program Files\Microsoft\Exchange. This script invokes the *dsdbutil* command, which can be used to change the LDAP port, Secure LDAP port, log path, and the path of the directory database. To change the LDAP and Secure LDAP ports used by the Edge Transport server, you would need to open the EMS and navigate to the Scripts folder under the Exchange directory. Here you would need to type **ConfigureAdam.ps1 -ldapport:10389 -sslport:10636** and press **Enter**. This example would change the LDAP ports to 10389 and 10636, respectively. Although you would be able to manually change the port numbers directly using the registry editor, don't do so, since it will make the ADAM instance unavailable.

---

17.   Select the newly added port **50389** in the list and click the **Advanced** button.

18.   Click the **Local Interface Restrictions** tab and select **Over the following interfaces**. Check the network adapter connected to the internal network and click **OK**.

19.   Repeat **Steps 17** and **18** for port **50636**.

NOTE

If you have enabled and allowed Remote Desktop connections to the Edge Transport server, we also recommend that you do Steps 17 and 18 for 3389 (Remote Desktop Protocol). This will block any connection attempts on port 3389 from external sources.

---

20.   Now click **Next** and confirm the port configuration settings. Click **Next** again.

21.   You have now reached the **Registry Settings** section in the SCW, and since you can skip this section, check **Skip this section** and click **Next**. Do the same on the **Audit Policy** page and click **Next**.

22.   Now that you're through all the security configuration settings, it's time to save and apply the security policy. On the **Save Security Policy** page, click **Next**.

23. On the **Security Policy Filename** page, type a name for the policy and a description of the policy (this is optional). Click **Next** (see Figure 7.58).

Figure 7.58 Security Policy Filename

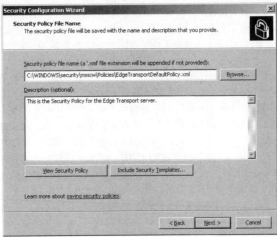

24. You will now be informed that applying this security policy to the selected server will require a reboot after the policy is applied. This is required for the configured applications or services to run properly. Click **OK,** select **Apply Now,** and click **Next** (see Figure 7.59).

Figure 7.59 Applying the Security Policy

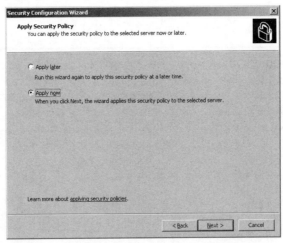

25. When the security policy has been applied, click **Next** and finally **Finish** to exit the SCW.

26. Reboot the server and verify that everything works as expected (mail flow, EdgeSync replication, Remote Desktop, and so on).

NOTE

If you're planning to deploy multiple Edge Transport servers in your perimeter network (DMZ or screened subnet), you can easily copy this Edge Transport server security policy XML file to the rest of the Edge Transport servers and apply it using the SCW.

Pointing Your MX Records to the Edge Transport Server

When the Edge Transport server has been fully deployed, the next step is to put it into production by routing incoming as well as outgoing messages through this server. To route incoming messages through it, you need to point the organization's MX or Mail Exchange record(s) to this server, unless you've got another Internet-facing SMTP server in front of your Edge Transport server, in which case you should just configure your Internet-facing SMTP server to forward all messages to the Edge Transport server.

To see the MX records for your domain, perform the following steps:

1. Open a **Command Prompt** window.

2. Type **Nslookup** and press **Enter**.

3. Now type **Set type=MX**.

4. Type your **SMTP domain** (such as *domain.com*) and press **Enter**.

This sequence of steps will list the MX records for your SMTP domain, similar to what is shown in Figure 7.60.

Figure 7.60 Pointing MX Records to the Edge Transport Server

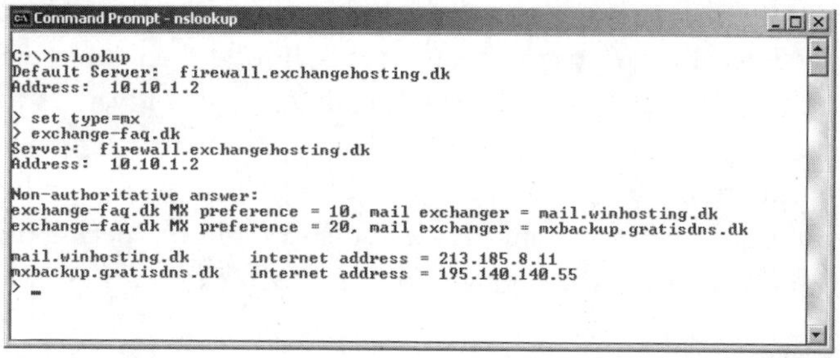

You can also use a Web-based service such as www.checkdns.net or www.dnsreport.com to retrieve your MX record information.

If you've got more than one MX record, the one with the lowest preference number is typically the one you should worry about, since any MX record with higher preference numbers are secondary MX record servers for your domain (that is, servers that will receive any messages, whereas for some reason your primary MX record doesn't respond to an *EHLO* or *HELO* command).

If you don't have an SMTP server in front of the Edge Transport server, you will need to change the MX record to point to your new server. This change will need to be done on the DNS server that hosts your SMTP domain (typically a DNS server located at your Internet service provider, or ISP).

TIP

In most cases, you make the MX record change yourself (via a Web-based administration panel), but if you are in doubt about how to make this change, ask your ISP/DNS provider to do it for you.

Depending on how your specific setup has been configured, there's also a chance that you simply need to change a rule in your ISA Server (or whatever firewall you have deployed in your organization) so that the rule points to the external IP address of the Edge Transport server.

In Chapter 12, which covers how you publish the different Exchange 2007 services and protocols through an ISA 2006 Server, we'll go through step-by-step instructions on how to publish your Exchange 2007 Server SMTP protocol, which is the same procedure for both an Edge Transport and a Hub transport server.

Deploying Multiple Edge Transport Servers in the Organization

If you're a messaging administrator or consultant working for a relatively large organization, deploying one Edge Transport server in the parameter network (DMZ or screened subnet) might not be sufficient. So your big question might be whether it's possible to deploy multiple Exchange 2007 Edge Transport servers, and if it is, how is the data in the ADAM store replicated between each Edge Transport server? Luckily you can answer yes to both of these questions; this section explains how to do exactly that.

You can deploy additional Edge Transport servers in your organization by cloning the configuration from the server that has already been deployed in the perimeter network. This is done by copying and exporting the configuration from an existing Edge Transport server (source server) to an XML file using the ExportEdgeConfig.ps1 script, which can be found in the Scripts directory under C:\Program Files\Microsoft\Exchange.

The ExportEdgeConfig.ps1 script exports all user-configured settings as well as data (except the EdgeSync subscription settings and the certificates that are used by the Microsoft Exchange EdgeSync service) to the XML file.

The configuration then needs to be copied and imported from the XML file to the newly installed Edge Transport server (target server), which is done using the ImportEdgeConfig.ps1, also found in the Scripts directory.

When you import the XML file on a new Edge Transport server using the ImportEdgeConfig.ps1, the script checks whether the configuration information and data exported from the source server are valid for the target server. If for some reason they aren't valid, the script will write the invalid setting(s) to an answer file that you can modify to specify the target server information that is used during the import configuration step.

Although you export all the configuration information except the EdgeSync subscription settings (including the configuration data in ADAM) from the source server and import it on the target server, you still must run the EdgeSync service on each Edge Transport server, since configuration data in ADAM cannot be replicated among the Edge Transport servers. This means that you need to run the EdgeSync subscription process after you have imported the cloned configuration.

When you have multiple Edge Transport servers deployed in the perimeter network, you can network and load-balance network traffic among the servers using the Domain Name System (DNS) round-robin mechanism. To use the round-robin mechanism, you need to enable the feature on the DNS server that resolves the names of the Edge Transport servers. When enabled, DNS uses round robin to rotate the order of resource record (RR) data returned in query answers where multiple records of the same type exist for a queried DNS domain name. This means that should one Edge Transport server be down, the Hub Transport server or the external SMTP server that tries to deliver an e-mail message to this Edge Transport server will retry, and then because of the rotation used by round robin, it will try to submit the e-mail message to another Edge Transport server in the perimeter network. The round-robin mechanism is enabled by default on servers running either Windows Server 2003 SP1 or later and Windows Server 2003 R2.

So to sum up, you need to perform the following steps in deploying additional Edge Transport servers in your perimeter network:

1. Install a clean Edge Transport server (following the guidelines in the beginning of this chapter).

2. Use the ExportEdgeConfig.ps1 script to export the source server's configuration information to an XML file. You do this by opening the **EMS**, where you navigate to **C:\Program Files\Microsoft\Exchange Server\Scripts;** typing **.\ExportEdgeConfig.ps1 −CloneConfigData:"C:\CloneConfigData.xml"**; and then pressing **Enter** (see Figure 7.61).

Figure 7.61 Cloning an Edge Transport Server

```
Machine: EDEX02 CWD: C:\Program Files\Microsoft\Exchange Server\Scripts
[PS] C:\Program Files\Microsoft\Exchange Server\Scripts>.\ExportEdgeConfig.ps1
CloneConfigData:"C:\CloneConfigData.xml"
Edge configuration is exported successfully to C:\CloneConfigData.xml
[PS] C:\Program Files\Microsoft\Exchange Server\Scripts>_
```

3. Now copy the **CloneConfigData.xml** file to the **target server**.

4. Before importing the XML file, you need to validate it using the ImportEdgeConfig.ps1 script. To do so, open the **EMS**; navigate to **C:\Program Files\Microsoft\Exchange Server\Scripts**; type **.\ImportEdgeConfig.ps1 –CloneConfigData:"C:\CloneConfigData.xml" -IsImport $false -CloneConfigAnswer:"C:\CloneConfigAnswer.xml"**; and press **Enter**.

5. You will now be informed that the answer file has been created successfully. Now open the **CloneConfigAnswer.xml** file in **Notepad**, and modify any settings that are reported invalid for the target server.

6. On the target server, use the ImportEdgeConfig.ps1 script to import the XML file. To do so, open the **EMS**; navigate to **C:\Program Files\Microsoft\Exchange Server\Scripts**; type **./ImportEdgeConfig –CloneConfigData:" C:\CloneConfigData.xml " -IsImport $true -CloneConfigAnswer:" C:\CloneConfigAnswer.xml"**; and press **Enter**.

You will now be informed that the import of the Edge configuration information succeeded.

The final step is to set up the EdgeSync service so that relevant configuration and recipient data are replicated from Active Directory to the ADAM store. Since we already went through these steps earlier in this chapter (in the "Creating and Importing an Edge Subscription File" section), we won't repeat them here.

The Edge Transport Rules Agent

Part of the new E-Mail Policy and Compliance feature set in Exchange Server 2007 is the edge transport rules agent, which is used to establish and enforce regulatory or corporate policies on e-mail messages sent to or received from the Internet.

Just as with the Hub Transport server, the transport rules agent on the Edge Transport server is capable of applying transport rules to messages flowing into and out of the organization, but although the transport rules agent looks very similar for both types of server roles, don't let it fool you. Although both server roles have a transport rules agent, several of the actions that are available for each server role are different. Actions such as applying message classification, appending disclaimer text, and sending bounced messages to senders with enhanced status code are all rules that are available on the Hub Transport server but not on the Edge Transport server.

For further information about the Hub Transport server-specific rules, see Chapter 6.

Delving into the inner details about each available transport agent rule actions and property sets available on the Edge Transport server is outside the scope of this book, but Table 7.4 lists all the available action properties and Table 7.5 all available property sets.

Table 7.4 Action Properties for Rules on the Edge Transport Server

Action Property	Expected Format	Description
Addresses	Array of Simple Mail Transfer Protocol (SMTP) addresses	On an Edge Transport server, *Addresses* accepts an array of SMTP addresses that are each enclosed in double quotation marks.
Classification	Single message classification object	*Classification* accepts a single message classification object. To specify a message classification object, use the *Get-MessageClassification* command. For example, use the following command to apply the *ExCompanyInternal* message classification to an action: *$Action.Classification = (Get-MessageClassification ExCompanyInternal).Identity*
EnhancedStatusCode	Single delivery status notification (DSN) code of 5.7.1, or any value between 5.7.10 and 5.7.999	*EnhancedStatusCode* specifies the DSN code and related DSN message to display to the senders of messages that are rejected by the *RejectMessage* transport rule action. The DSN message that is associated with the specified DSN status code is displayed in the user information portion of the NDR that is displayed to the sender. The specified DSN code must be an existing default DSN code or a customized DSN status code that you can create using the *New-SystemMessage* CMDlet.
EventMessage	Single string	*EventMessage* accepts a single string that is displayed in an event log, which is added to the Application event log on the local computer.

Continued

Table 7.4 continued Action Properties for Rules on the Edge Transport Server

Action Property	Expected Format	Description
FallBackAction	Single value with the choices of *Wrap, Ignore*, or *Reject*	
Font	Single value with the choices of *Arial, CourierNew*, or *Verdana*	*Font* specifies the font of the disclaimer text when the text is added to an e-mail message. The default font is *Arial*. Enclose the value in double quotation marks.
FontColor	Single value with the choices of *Black, Blue, Fuchsia, Gray, Green, Lime, Maroon, Navy, Olive, Purple, Red, Silver, Teal, White,* or *Yellow*	*FontColor* specifies the color of the font of the disclaimer text when the text is added to an e-mail message. The default color is *Gray*. Enclose the value in double quotation marks.
FontSize	Single value with the choices of *Smallest, Smaller, Normal, Larger,* or *Largest*	*FontSize* specifies the size of the font of the disclaimer text when the text is added to an e-mail message. The default size is *Smallest*. Enclose the value in double quotation marks.
HeaderValue	Single string	*HeaderValue* accepts a single string that is applied to the header specified using the *MessageHeader* action property. Enclose the string in double quotation marks.
Location	Single value with the choices of *Append* or *Prepend*	*Location* specifies where the disclaimer is inserted into the e-mail message. Append puts the disclaimer at the bottom of the e-mail message thread. *Prepend* puts the disclaimer at the start of the newest e-mail message. Enclose the value in double quotation marks.
MessageHeader	Single string	*MessageHeader* accepts a string that specifies which *MessageHeader* to add or modify. The string that is specified by the *HeaderValue* action property is inserted into the header that is specified by *MessageHeader*. Enclose the string in double quotation marks.

Table 7.4 continued Action Properties for Rules on the Edge Transport Server

Action Property	Expected Format	Description
Prefix	Single string	*Prefix* accepts a string that is prepended to the subject of the e-mail message. Enclose the string in double quotation marks.
RejectReason	Single string	*RejectReason* accepts a string that is used to populate the administrator information portion of the NDR that is returned to the e-mail sender if an e-mail message is rejected. Enclose the string in double quotation marks.
SclValue	Single integer	*SclValue* accepts a single integer from 0 to 9, which is used to configure the spam confidence level (SCL) of the e-mail message. Enclose the integer in double quotation marks.
Separator	Single value with the choices *WithSeparator* or *WithoutSeparator*	*Separator* specifies whether a separator is placed between the disclaimer and the e-mail message body. Enclose the value in double quotation marks.
Text	Single string	*Text* accepts a string that is used to populate the disclaimer message that is added to an e-mail message. Enclose the string in double quotation marks.

NOTE

Unlike the Hub Transport server, the Edge Transport server only allows you to specify an array of SMTP addresses. This is because the Edge Transport server doesn't have access to Active Directory, unlike the Hub Transport server, on which you can specify an array of Active Directory mailboxes, contacts, mail-enabled users, and distribution group objects.

Table 7.5 Supported Actions on the Edge Transport Server

Rule Action	Action Name	First Action Property	Additional Action Property	Rule Description
Log an event with message	LogEvent	EventMessage	Not applicable	LogEvent inserts an event into the Application log on the local computer.
Prepend the subject with string	PrependSubject	Prefix	Not applicable	PrependSubject prepends a string to the start of the e-mail message subject field.
Set the spam confidence level to value	SetScl	SclValue	Not applicable	SetScl configures the SCL on an e-mail message.
Set header with value	SetHeader	MessageHeader	HeaderValue	SetHeader creates a new message header field or modifies an existing message header field.
Remove header	RemoveHeader	MessageHeader	Not applicable	RemoveHeader removes the specified message header field from an e-mail message.
Add a recipient in the To field addresses	AddToRecipient	Addresses	Not applicable	AddToRecipient adds one or more e-mail addresses to the To address list of the e-mail message. The original recipients can see the additional address.
Copy the message to addresses	CopyTo	Addresses	Not applicable	CopyTo adds one or more e-mail addresses to the carbon copy (CC) field of the e-mail message. The original recipients can see the original address.
Blind carbon copy (BCC) the message to addresses	BlindCopyTo	Addresses	Not applicable	BlindCopyTo adds one or more e-mail addresses to the blind carbon copy (BCC) address list of the e-mail message. The original recipients aren't notified and can't see the additional address.

Continued

Rule Action	Action Name	First Action Property	Additional Action Property	Rule Description
Drop connection	*Disconnect*	Not applicable	Not applicable	*Disconnect* ends the connection between the sending server and the Edge Transport server without generating an NDR message.
Redirect the message to addresses	*RedirectMessage*	*Addresses*	Not applicable	*RedirectMessage* redirects the e-mail message to one or more e-mail addresses that are specified by the administrator. The message isn't delivered to the original recipient, and no notification is provided to the recipient or the sender.
Put message in quarantine	*Quarantine*	Not applicable	Not applicable	*Quarantine* redirects the e-mail message to the spam quarantine mailbox that is configured by using the *QuarantineMailbox* parameter on the *Set-ContentFilterConfig* CMDlet. *Note:* You must populate the *QuarantineMailbox* parameter with the *Set-ContentFilterConfig* CMDlet, and you need to make sure that the specified mailbox has been created. If the *QuarantineMailbox* hasn't been populated and a mailbox hasn't been created, any messages sent to this mailbox will be lost and an NDA will be generated!
Reject the message with status code and response	*SmtpRejectMessage*	*StatusCode*	*RejectReason*	*SmtpRejectMessage* deletes the e-mail message and sends a notification to the sender. The recipients don't receive the message or notification. This action enables you to specify a delivery status notification (DSN) code.
Silently drop the message	*DeleteMessage*	Not applicable	Not applicable	*DeleteMessage* deletes the e-mail message without sending a notification to either the recipient or the sender.

Creating Transport Rule

Creating a new edge transport agent rule can be done following these steps:

1. Log on to the Edge Transport server. Open the **EMC** and click the **Edge Transport work center node** in the **navigation tree**. Now select the Edge Transport server in the **Result pane.** In the **Work pane**, click the **Transport Rules** tab.

2. Now click **New Transport Rule** in the **Action pane** or, alternatively, right-click in the **Work pane** and select **New Transport Rule** in the context menu.

3. This will bring up the **New Transport Rule Wizard.** The first step is to specify a name that will match the purpose of the rule. In this example you want to send all messages with an attachment equal to or higher than 50MB to the Quarantine mailbox. Once you have entered the name and comment (optional), click **Next**.

4. You also have the option of having the rule enabled when it's created by checking **Enable Rule** (see Figure 7.62).

Figure 7.62 The New Transport Rule Wizard

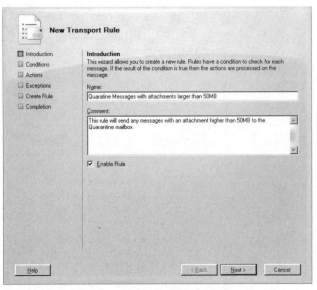

5. Next, select the condition(s) for the new rule. For the purpose of this example, you want to apply the rule to messages with an attachment equal to or larger than 50MB, so you'll check **When the size of any attachment is greater than or equal to limit**, set the value to **50000KB,** and click **Next** (see Figure 7.63).

Figure 7.63 Transport Rule Conditions

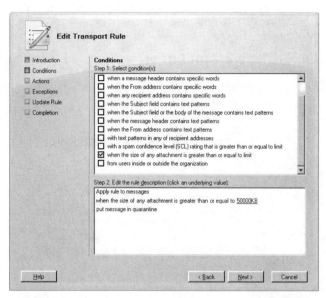

6. On the **Actions** page you can select the action(s) that should be taken for the messages matching the configured conditions. In this example, you check **Put message in quarantine** and click **Next** (see Figure 7.64).

Figure 7.64 Transport Rule Actions

7. On the next page you have the option of specifying one or more exceptions. In this example, you won't specify any exceptions, so just click **Next** (see Figure 7.65).

Figure 7.65 Transport Rule Exceptions

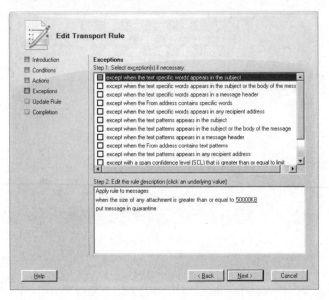

8. On the **Configuration Summary** page, click **New** to create the new rule.

9. Finally, click **Finish** to exit the New Transport Rule Wizard.

The newly created rule will now be listed in the Work pane, as shown in Figure 7.66, and you can at any time disable it or update it as required. If you have multiple rules, you can also change the priority among them.

The Address Rewrite Agent

The Edge Transport server also has an agent, called the *address rewrite agent*, which can be configured to enable modification of the SMTP addresses on both inbound as well as outbound e-mail messages. You might want to do this if, for example, your organization consists of multiple domains (perhaps after a merger or acquisition) and should be presented with a consistent appearance of e-mail addresses to external recipients on the Internet. The address rewrite agent can also be used if the organization uses third-party vendors to, for example, provide e-mail support and/or other services. In this situation the organization's customers would expect messages to come from your domain, not from a third-party vendor. Another purpose of the address rewrite agent could be to enable routing of inbound e-mail messages from outside the Exchange 2007 organization to the internal recipients.

Figure 7.66 The Transport Rule Listed in Exchange Management Console

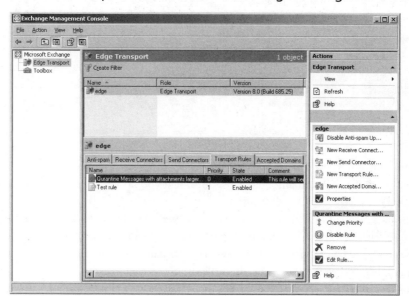

The address rewrite agent rewrites e-mail addresses by rewriting the SMTP headers in the e-mail messages, which flow in and out of the Edge Transport server. You can enable address rewriting on both inbound as well as outbound messages. The typical reason that you want to enable address rewriting on outbound messages is because you have multiple internal domains (for example, one root domain with multiple subdomains). With the address rewrite agent, you could then rewrite the SMTP header so that all outbound messages appear to come from the same domain instead of domain.com, subdomain1.domain.com, subdomain2.domain.com, and so on.

A reason that you would want to enable address rewriting on inbound messages could be because inbound e-mail messages would need to be routed to the intended recipients.

To create a new address rewriting entry on an Edge Transport server, you first need to make sure that either the address rewriting inbound agent and/or the address rewriting outbound agent is enabled. This should be the case on a newly installed Edge Transport server installation, but it's always a good idea to verify that this is the case. You can see whether these agents are enabled or disabled by opening the **EMS** and typing **Get-TransportAgent** (see Figure 7.67).

If the respective agent(s) are set to True, it means that the agent(s) is enabled. If the required agent is disabled (set to False), you will need to enable it by typing **Enable-TransportAgent –Identity "Address Rewriting Inbound Agent"** and/or **Enable-TransportAgent –Identity "Address Rewriting Outbound Agent"** depending on which agent you'll configure.

Figure 7.67 Checking Whether the Address Rewriting Agent Is Enabled

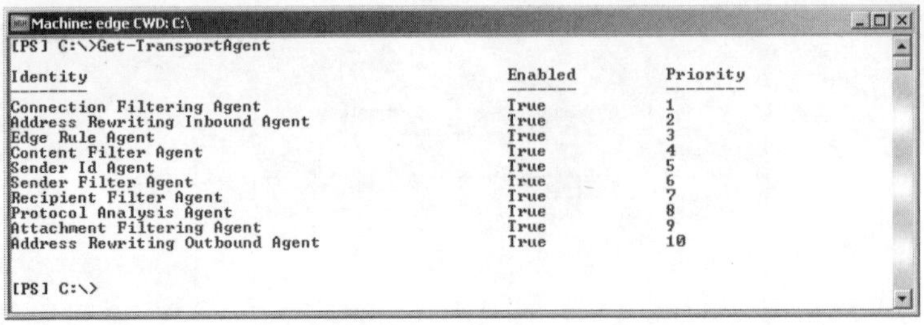

```
Machine: edge CWD: C:\
[PS] C:\>Get-TransportAgent

Identity                          Enabled      Priority

Connection Filtering Agent        True         1
Address Rewriting Inbound Agent   True         2
Edge Rule Agent                   True         3
Content Filter Agent              True         4
Sender Id Agent                   True         5
Sender Filter Agent               True         6
Recipient Filter Agent            True         7
Protocol Analysis Agent           True         8
Attachment Filtering Agent        True         9
Address Rewriting Outbound Agent  True         10


[PS] C:\>
```

For the purpose of this book, we'll only rewrite the headers for a single SMTP address and then a single SMTP domain, but this should give you an idea how the address rewrite agent works.

To create a new address rewriting entry for a single SMTP address, you need to use the *New-AddressRewriteEntry* CMDlet. For example, say that you want to rewrite the SMTP address henrik@exchangedogfood.dk to henrik@exchange-faq.dk. To do so you would need to create an *AddressRewriteEntry* using the following command: **New-AddressRewriteEntry –Name "Address rewrite entry for henrik@exchangedog-food.dk" –InternalAddress henrik@exchangedogfood.dk –ExternalAddress henrik@exchange-faq.dk** followed by pressing **Enter**.

If you wanted to create a new address rewriting entry for a single SMTP domain, you would need to use the following command: **New-AddressRewriteEntry –Name "Address rewrite entry for Exchangedogfood.dk" –InternalAddress exchangedog-food.dk –ExternalAddress exchange-faq.dk** followed by pressing **Enter**.

To read additional information about the address rewrite agent, consult the Exchange Server 2007 Help file.

Monitoring the Edge Transport Server

As is also the case with any of the other Exchange 2007 Server roles, you should make sure that you're always up to date with best practices relating to the Edge Transport server. We recommend that you run the Exchange Best Practices Analyzer tool on the box on a regular basis. In addition, you should monitor the server using Microsoft Operations Manager (MOM) 2005 or a similar product so that you can react proactively to any events or alerts generated by the Edge Transport server. MOM 2005 has its own Exchange Server 2007 Management Pack, which makes it possible to monitor activity such as messages per SCL level, total messages sent to quarantine, and rejected and/or deleted messages. You can also generate MOM reports showing you things such as hit rate for block lists, top spam-sending domain, top spam-sending IP address, and top targeted domain or individual recipient. All reports can, of course, be seen on a per-server basis.

Summary

In this chapter we focused on the Edge Transport server role included in the Exchange Server 2007 product. We went over the requirements of the server role as well as step-by-step instructions on how you deploy one or more Edge Transport server(s) in your perimeter network (DMZ or screened subnet). We then had a look at the available antispam filtering agents as well as how they are configured. Then we discussed how you properly secure an Edge Transport server using the Security Configuration Wizard (SCW). Lastly, we had a look at the transport rules agent and as well as the address rewriting feature, and we briefly discussed how you can and why you should monitor an Edge Transport server using a monitoring solution such as Microsoft Operations Manager (MOM) 2005.

Solutions Fast Track

Deploying the Edge Transport Server Role

- Remember that the Edge Transport server role should be isolated in the perimeter network (also called a DMZ or screened subnet), away from your Active Directory. The server role should therefore be installed in a workgroup on a standalone server.

- It's highly recommend that you install two network adapters in the server on which you're planning to install the Edge Transport server. One network adapter should be Internet facing; the other should be intranet facing. This way you can secure the Send and Receive connectors much more efficiently than would be the case with only a single network adapter.

- If your organization consists of multiple forests and you want to use the EdgeSync service in each of them, you must replicate all recipient addresses to one forest and then set up an edge subscription to that forest, because the EdgeSync service supports replication with only one forest at a time.

Enabling Name Resolution Lookups between the Edge Transport and Hub Transport Servers Suffix

- Bear in mind that to use several of the antispam features, you must use an edge subscription. This way, configuration as well as recipient data are replicated from Active Directory to the ADAM store using the EdgeSync service. It is possible to not use an EdgeSync subscription, but you will then not be able to use several of the antispam features on the Edge Transport server. In addition, you need to create all Send and Receive connectors manually.

■ If you're a small shop and cannot afford to have an additional Exchange 2007 server with the Edge Transport server role deployed in your DMZ, but you still want to take advantage of the antispam filtering agents to filter out spam in your organization, you're in luck, because you have the option of installing the antispam filtering agents on an Exchange 2007 server with the Hub Transport server role installed. To do so you need to run the install-AntiSpamAgents.ps1 script located in the Exchange scripts folder (by default, located under C:\Program Files\Microsoft\Exchange Server) on the Hub Transport server.

■ Since Microsoft played an important role in the invention of the Sender ID e-mail authentication technology, it's not surprising that Sender ID is supported in Exchange 2007, but some are wondering whether the DomainKeys e-mail authentication technology (which was invented by Yahoo, DomainKeys and Cisco) is supported in Exchange 2007. The answer is unfortunately not, but who knows—maybe they will implement DomainKeys support in a future service pack.

Installing the ADAM Component

■ When you deploy an Edge Transport server in your perimeter network (DMZ or screened subnet), it's very important that you secure it properly. The best way to lock it down is to use the Security Configuration Wizard (SCW).

■ One of the great things about using a one-way replication method from Active Directory to the Edge Transport server is that you only need to open one single inbound port in your intranet firewall, which is port 25 (SMTP). The respective LDAP port only needs to be allowed outbound.

Verifying That the EdgeSync Service Works as Expected

■ An important step in deploying an Edge Transport server in your DMZ is to change your MX records so that they point at the new Edge Transport server. If you don't host your own public DNS server, this is typically done on the public DNS server at your ISP. If, for example, you're using an ISA server to forward SMTP traffic to a server in your DMZ, you simply need to change the respective rule so that it points to your Edge Transport server instead.

■ You can see information about your MX records by using NSLookup, as shown in this chapter, but there are also several nice Web-based tools that can help you retrieve your MX records (and many other such things). Some of the best are dnsstuff.com and checkdns.net.

Manually Configuring the Required Connectors

■ Unlike the other Exchange 2007 Server roles, the Edge Transport server role uses Active Directory Application Mode (ADAM) to store configuration data. For this reason, you cannot recover an Edge Transport server using the *setup /m:recoverserver* switch as is the case with the other server roles in your organization. However, you can back up an Edge Transport server using the ExportEdgeConfig.ps1 script contained in the Exchange scripts folder, which by default is located under C:\Program Files\Microsoft\Exchange Server. To recover or clone an Edge Transport server, you can use the ImportEdgeConfig.ps1 contained in the same folder.

■ When you have multiple Edge Transport servers deployed in the perimeter network, you can network and load-balance network traffic among the servers using Domain Name System (DNS) round robin mechanism.

Pointing Your MX
Records to the Edge Transport Server

■ Part of the new E-mail Policy and Compliance feature set, in Exchange Server 2007, is the Edge Transport Rules agent, which is used to establish and enforce regulatory or corporate policies on e-mail messages sent to or received from the Internet. Just as with the Hub Transport server, the transport rules agent on the Edge Transport server is capable of applying transport rules to messages flowing into and out of the organization, but although the Transport Rules agent looks very similar for both types of server roles, don't let it fool you. Although both server roles have a transport rules agent, several of the actions that are available for each server role are different.

■ Unlike the Hub Transport server, the Edge Transport server only allows you to specify an array of SMTP addresses. This is because the Edge Transport server doesn't have access to Active Directory, as does the Hub Transport server, on which you can specify an array of Active Directory mailboxes, contacts, mail-enabled users, and distribution group objects.

The Address Rewrite Agent

■ If your organization consists of multiple domains (for example, after a merger or acquisition), you can use the address rewrite agent to provide a single consistent SMTP domain to the Internet.

■ Address rewriting can also be used to allow third-party vendors to provide support or other e-mail-based services using your SMTP domain. Because your customers and partners expect e-mail to come from your organization, this makes sense.

Deploying Multiple Edge Transport Servers in the Organization

■ If you use Microsoft Operations Manager (MOM) 2005 as the monitoring solution in your organization, you should install the Exchange 2007 MOM Management Pack and configure it to monitor the Edge Transport server(s) in your DMZ too. The Exchange 2007 MOM Management Pack can monitor your Edge Transport servers proactively as well as provide a wealth of reporting options, such as monitoring activity related to messages per SCL level, total messages sent to quarantine, and rejected and/or deleted messages. You can also generate MOM reports showing you things such as hit rate for block lists, top spam-sending domain, top spam-sending IP address, and top targeted domain or individual recipient. All reports can, of course, be seen on a per-server basis.

Frequently Asked Questions

The following Frequently Asked Questions, answered by the authors of this book, are designed to both measure your understanding of the concepts presented in this chapter and to assist you with real-life implementation of these concepts. To have your questions about this chapter answered by the author, browse to www.syngress.com/solutions and click on the "Ask the Author" form.

Q: I have deployed a single Exchange 2007 server with the Hub Transport, Client Access and Mailbox Server roles in my test environment. Although I've configured our firewall to forward SMTP traffic to the Exchange 2007 server, I cannot receive any messages from the Internet.

A: This behavior is actually by design. By default, an Exchange 2007 Hub Transport server is configured so that it doesn't accept anonymous e-mail from the Internet. Instead, Microsoft recommends that you deploy an Edge Transport server in your DMZ and have any inbound as well as outbound e-mail messages routed through this server. But if you cannot afford this or for some other reason don't want to deploy an Edge Transport server, you can configure your Hub Transport server to accept e-mail by configuring the default <servername> Receive connector to accept anonymous e-mail from the Internet. You do so by accessing the properties for the default Receive connector, which is located under **Server Configuration | Hub Transport** in the EMC. Here you select the **Permissions Groups** tab and enable **Anonymous users**.

Q: Is there any way I can test that the provider I have specified on my Edge Transport server's IP Block list feature works as expected?

A: Yes. You can use the *Test-IPBlockListProvider* CMDlet to test a provider. You must use the following format: **Test-IPBlockListProvider –IPAddress 192.168.1.10 –Provider ProviderName**.

Q: Since message queues are stored in an ESE database for either an Edge Transport or a Hub Transport server, I was wondering if it's possible to defragment the database used to store these message queues?

A: Yes, this is definitely possible. To defragment such a database, you must first stop the Microsoft Exchange Transport Service on the respective server. The database used to store message queues is mail.que, by default located under c:\program files\exchange server\TransportRoles\data\queue\mail.que. So to defragment the database, you must type **Eseutil /d c:\program files\exchange server\TransportRoles\data\queue\mail.que**.

Q: Can I see the message queues on an Edge Transport server using the Exchange Management Shell?

A: Yes. At any time you can have the queue listed by running the *Get-Queue* CMDlet, which displays information about existing queues on the Edge Transport server on which it's run. If you don't specify any parameters, the command queries all queues on the local server and returns a single page of results (1000 objects).

Q: Can I use an Edge Transport server as the SMTP gateway for a legacy messaging organization such as Exchange 2000 or 2003?

A: Yes. An Edge Transport server can be deployed as an SMTP relay and smart host server for your existing Exchange messaging infrastructure. However, keep in mind that you cannot take advantage of EdgeSync and therefore cannot use several of the attractive antispam features.

Chapter 8

High Availability for Exchange 2007 Mailbox Servers

Solutions in this chapter:

- **Managing the Local Continuous Replication Feature**

- **Managing a Cluster Continuous Replication-Based Setup**

- **Managing a Single Copy Cluster-Based Setup**

☑ **Summary**

☑ **Solutions Fast Track**

☑ **Frequently Asked Questions**

Introduction

The availability requirements for messaging and collaboration servers have increased drastically over the years, with the result that these servers are now among the most mission-critical servers in the datacenter. Several recent reports have concluded that e-mail is more important to end users than their phones. So it's not rocket science; it's in the interests of you as the Exchange Administrator to achieve as high an uptime as possible. Each of these facts played an important role when the Exchange Product Group developed Exchange Server 2007, so it's no surprise that when speaking of high availability as well as disaster recovery, we can find many improvements as well as new functionality in the Exchange Server 2007 product.

Exchange Server 2007 includes three primary high-availability solutions relating to the Mailbox Server role, although one of these features isn't really new at all but has instead changed name and been further improved since Exchange Server 2003. We're referring to the Single Copy Cluster (SCC) functionality, which is a clustered solution that uses a single copy of a storage group on storage that is shared between the nodes in a cluster. Those of you with just a little bit of Exchange cluster experience would say that the SCC solution is similar to a traditional Exchange 2000/2003 active/passive cluster setup, and you're right.

SOME INDEPENDENT ADVICE

With Exchange Server 2007, active/active clusters are no longer supported; only active/passive clusters are supported. If you have experience deploying Exchange 2000/2003 in an active/active cluster, most likely you understand why this was dropped in Exchange 2007. An Exchange cluster configured with two active nodes has never performed as well as one would have expected, since the failover causes the remaining node to take on additional processing operations. Constraints such as number of concurrent user connections per node and average CPU load per server limits also play an important role in the reason that active/active Exchange cluster setups have never been successful.

Then we have Local Continuous Replication (LCR), which is a solution that uses the new continuous replication technology introduced in Exchange 2007. LCR is a new functionality that uses built-in asynchronous log shipping and log replay technology to create and maintain a replica of a storage group on a second set of disks that are connected to the same server as the production storage group. As mentioned, the LCR solution uses log shipping and log replay and gives you the option of switching to the passive copy of the storage group in a matter of minutes, should the database in the active storage group become corrupted and shut down for one reason or another. The interesting thing about LCR is that this solution doesn't require more than a single Exchange 2007 server with the Mailbox Server role installed.

Finally, we have the Clustered Continuous Replication (CCR) solution, which, like LCR, uses the new Exchange 2007 continuous replication technology, but as the name implies, CCR is a clustered solution that eliminates the single point of failure that exists in traditional Exchange cluster setups today. This is done by maintaining a copy of the database on the active node; in the event of a database corruption, this allows both services and databases to fail over to the passive node. CCR can only be deployed in a two-node active/passive cluster.

Managing the Local Continuous Replication Feature

In this first section of the chapter we'll take a closer look at the architecture behind the new Local Continuous Replication (LCR) feature. We'll then go through the steps necessary to enable this feature; finally, we'll look at how we can take advantage of LCR should the database in the active copy of the storage group fail.

Local Continuous Replication under the Hood

The Exchange Product group developed the Local Continuous Replication (LCR) technology to provide a native data availability solution that can be used to recover an Exchange database on an Exchange 2007 standalone server in a matter of a few minutes. In Exchange 2003 as well as previous versions, you needed to recover the lost database by restoring it from backup, which, depending on the database size, could take up to many hours. With LCR, you will be able to switch over to an exact replica (that is, a fully updated copy) of the crashed database by running a simple Exchange 2007 task.

So how does this LCR magic work? As most of us know, the database type Exchange uses is Extensible Storage Engine (ESE). ESE employs transaction log files, which means that every time a modification is made, a transaction log file is generated (instead of the change being committed directly to the database). The reason is that when the ESE database is modified, the modification won't be made directly in the physical database but instead in memory of the respective Exchange 2007 Mailbox Server. This means that should the database for some reason become corrupted or shut down, Exchange always will be able to recover the lost data (which is held in memory, remember) by using the log files.

Each log file that is generated because of a modification in the database belonging to the active copy of the storage group is replicated (copied) from the source log folder (the log folder defined for the Storage Group containing the respective database) to a target log folder associated with the passive copy of the storage group. This isn't the entire truth, because each log file is first copied to an inspector log folder located beneath the target log folder, where it is inspected to make sure it is correct. (If it isn't correct, the log file will be recopied). Finally the file is copied to the target log folder and from there replayed into the database belonging to the passive copy of the storage group.

The target log folder also contains an IgnoredLogs folder that holds any valid log files that for some reason cannot be replayed. A typical reason is that the particular log is too old. In addition, the subfolder can contain an InspectionFailed and an E00OutofDate folder. The first is a folder that holds any log files that failed inspection. When this happens, an event 2013 will be logged in the application log. The E00OutofDate folder will hold any E00.log files that are present in the target log folder when a failover occurs.

A new Exchange 2007 service called the Microsoft Exchange Replication Service will be installed on any Exchange 2007 servers with the Mailbox Server role installed. These are responsible for replicating the log files to the target log folder. As you can see, we've tried to illustrate the basic architecture of LCR in Figure 8.1.

Figure 8.1 The Basic Local Continuous Replication Architecture

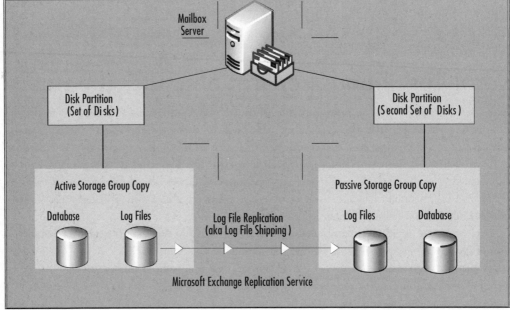

The log files that are replicated from the active copy to the passive copy of the storage group will be replayed in batches in order to provide the best performance possible.

Since LCR keeps an exact replica of the active copy of the storage group, the number of Exchange backups needed is also reduced drastically. But it's important to understand that LCR in no way eliminates traditional backups of the databases on your Exchange 2007 Mailbox servers; instead, it provides you with the option of taking weekly instead of daily backups, for example.

SOME INDEPENDENT ADVICE

Bear in mind that if you want to enable LCR for a storage group, the storage group may not contain more than one mailbox or public folder database. This is because LCR doesn't support multiple databases in the same storage group. Actually, you won't even be able to enable LCR on a storage group containing multiple databases. In addition, you cannot enable LCR for a storage group containing a Public Folder database if more than one Public Folder database exists in the organization. The reason is that LCR and Public Folder replication cannot run at the same time.

When you're partitioning the disks that should be storing the passive copies your storage groups, it is best practice to take advantage of mount points, because they will let you surpass the 26-drive-letter limitation that exists on a Windows 2003 server. If you end up in a situation where you need to switch to a passive copy of a storage group, using mount points will make the recovery process much more painless because you can quickly change drive letters and paths.

As has been the case with mailbox stores and log files in previous versions of Exchange, it's also recommended that you place the databases and log files for a passive copy of a storage group on separate disks, just as you do with active copies of storage groups.

You should, of course, also make sure that you partition the disks that are to be used for the passive copies of the storage groups, so they are at least the same size at the disks holding the active storage group copies. Finally, keep in mind that a Mailbox Server with LCR enabled will use approximately 30–40 percent more CPU and memory than a Mailbox Server on which LCR hasn't been enabled. These extra resources are primarily used by log file verification as well as log file replay.

TIP

LCR enables you to offload Volume ShadowCopy Service (VSS) backups from the active storage group to the passive storage group, which will preserve disk I/O on the disks on which the active storage group is located. This also means that you can perform restores from a passive copy of a storage group.

As you can understand, LCR is an ideal solution for small or medium-sized organizations because the functionality allows rapid recovery from database issues and requires only an extra set of disks for the database copies. LCR increases the availability of databases on an Exchange 2007 standalone server in an affordable way. For small shops that don't have a big fancy server with multiple sets of disks, it is possible to keep the LCR copy on an external USB disk.

Enabling Local Continuous Replication on a Storage Group

The LCR feature is enabled on a Storage Group level under the Mailbox subnode, located beneath the Server Configuration work center node in the left pane of the Exchange System Management Console, as shown in Figure 8.2.

1. To enable LCR for the First Storage Group, select it in the work pane, and click **Enable local continuous replication** in the Action pane.

Figure 8.2 The Local Continuous Replication Link in the Action Pane

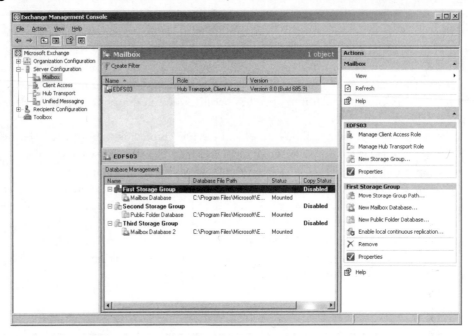

2. This will bring up the Local Continuous Replication Wizard's Introduction page, shown in Figure 8.3. As you can see, this page shows us the storage group as well as mailbox database name. Because there aren't many interactions on this page, simply click **Next**.

3. Now let's specify the path to the LCR files for the respective storage group (see Figure 8.4). For the purpose of this example, we're simply specifying the E: drive, which is a second set of disks on the server. When the location has been specified, we can click **Next**.

Figure 8.3 Enable Storage Group Local Continuous Replication

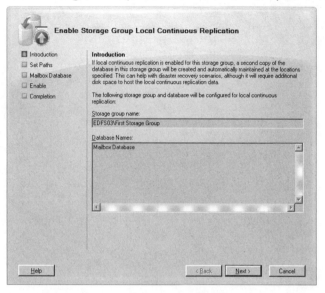

Figure 8.4 Specifying the Paths for the Replicated Log and System Files

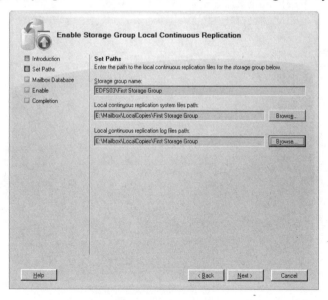

4.   On the Mailbox Database page, we have to specify the path to the location of the second copy of the database, as shown in Figure 8.5. When you have done so, click **Next**.

Figure 8.5 Specifying the Path for the Database Copy

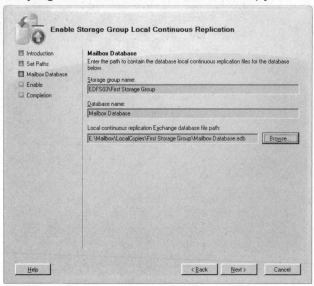

5. We have now reached the step where we enable LCR for the storage group, so let's do so by clicking **Enable** and see what happens. As shown in Figure 8.6, the Local Continuous Replication Wizard completed successfully. Click **Finish**.

Figure 8.6 The Local Continuous Replication Feature Was Enabled with Success

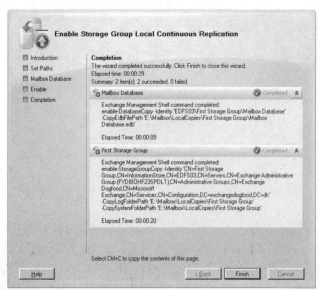

If you would rather enable LCR for a storage group via the EMS, you will have to do so using the *Enable-DatabaseCopy* and *Enable-StorageGroupCopy* CMDlets. To enable LCR for the First Storage Group, you would need to first run the following command:

```
Enable-DatabaseCopy -Identity "EDFS03\First Storage Group\Mailbox Database" -
CopyEDBFilePath:"E:\Mailbox\LocalCopies\First Storage Group\Mailbox Database.edb"
```

Then type:

```
Enable-StorageGroupCopy -Identity "EDFS03\First Storage Group"
-CopyLogFolderPath:"E:\ Mailbox\LocalCopies\First Storage Group"
-CopySystemFolderPath:"E:\ Mailbox\LocalCopies\First Storage Group"
```

NOTE

Even though we're dealing with a secondary copy of a production database, it's still a best practice to keep the log files and database separated on their own set of disks.

Now notice that the copy status for the First Storage Group has change to Healthy (see Figure 8.7).

Figure 8.7 The Copy Status for the Storage Group Is Healthy

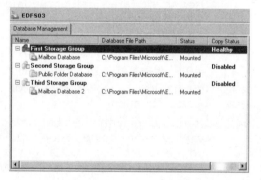

Viewing the Status for a Local Continuous Replication Copy

To view basic health and status information for an LCR copy, you can bring up the Properties page for the storage group on which LCR has been enabled. To do this, select the respective storage group and click the **Properties** link in the Action pane. On the Properties page, select the **Local continuous replication** tab, as shown in Figure 8.8. Here you can see the basic health for an LCR copy.

Figure 8.8 The LCR Status Properties Page

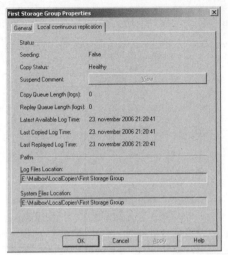

Table 8.1 lists the health and status information, with a short description of each.

Table 8.1 Local Continuous Replication Health and Status Information

Health/Status Information	Description
Seeding	Used to indicate whether seeding of the passive database occurs or not. Can have a status of True or False.
Copy Status	Used to indicate whether log file copying has started. Can have a status of Healthy, Suspended, or Broken.
Suspend Comment	Can be used to view *suspend* comment if LCR has been suspended.
Copy Queue Length (logs)	Used to display the number of log files that are waiting to be copied to the passive storage group's log file folder. Note that a copy is not considered complete until it has been inspected for corruption.
Replay Queue Length (logs)	Used to display the number of log files waiting to be replayed into the passive storage group's database.
Latest Available Log Time	Used to display the time stamp on the active storage group of the most recently detected new log file.
Last Copied Log Time	Used to display the time stamp on the active storage group of the last successful copy of a transaction log file.
Last Replayed Log Time	Used to display the time stamp on the passive storage group of the last successful replay of a log file.

In addition, you can see the path to the log file and system file location for the passive storage group copy.

If you want even more information about the health and status of an LCR copy, you can open the EMS and type **Get-StorageGroupCopyStatus –Identity** *<Storage Group>* **| FL**, as shown in Figure 8.9.

Figure 8.9 Retrieving LCR Status Information via the Exchange Management Shell

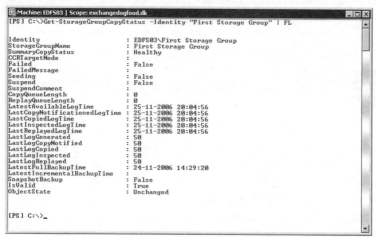

Going through each information field returned by the *Get-StorageGroupCopyStatus* CMDlet is outside the scope of this book, so if you want to dig deeper into these topics, we recommend that you refer to the Exchange 2007 Help file.

Switching to the Passive Storage Group Copy When Disaster Strikes

When disaster strikes and the database or log files in the active copy of the storage group have become corrupted and have shut down, you have the option to recover database availability by switching to the LCR copy (the passive copy of the storage group).

You can recover from corruption of either one or more log files or the database using a variety of methods, depending on whether you use mount points or not. One method is to run the *Restore-StorageGroupCopy* CMDlet with the *ReplaceLocations* parameter, which will activate the LCR copy as the active storage group copy in one step. To activate the LCR copy as the active storage group, you first need to make sure that the active database is dismounted, which should already be the case if it's corrupted. If this is not the case, you should dismount it now. When you have done so, we're ready to run the *Restore-StorageGroupCopy* CMDlet, which in the case of this example is done for the First Storage Group. So the command to run in the EMS is:

```
Restore-StorageGroupCopy -Identity "First Storage Group" -ReplaceLocations:$true
```

An integrity check will now be passed for the log files, and if it's completed without errors, the storage group copy switch will be completed and the production paths will be updated, as shown in Figure 8.10.

Figure 8.10 Switching to the LCR Copy Using the *Restore-StorageGroupCopy* CMDlet

All there is to do now is to mount the database using either the EMC or the EMS. Now notice that the Database File Path will have changed, as shown in Figure 8.11.

Figure 8.11 Database File Path Change

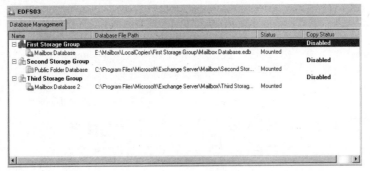

> **NOTE**
>
> When you have run the *Restore-StorageGroupCopy* CMDlet against a storage group, LCR for the respective storage group will be disabled. So remember to re-enable LCR for the particular storage group after you perform a switch to the LCR copy.

Although this method is straightforward and fully supported, Microsoft actually recommends that instead you use a method whereby you run the *Restore-StorageGroupCopy*

CMDlet without the *ReplaceLocations* parameter, to activate the copy in its current location, and then either move the files manually, change drive letters, or use mount point assignments to have the copy files reflected under the respective production paths so that the production database is maintained in the expected location. Following this method means that the active storage group copy will continue to have meaningful filenames that represent that they indeed are active production copies. Why is this the preferred method? Because Microsoft believes that using the *Restore-StorageGroupCopy* CMDlet with the *ReplaceLocations* parameter could lead to future confusion in distinguishing the active copy of the data from the passive copy of the data, and to be honest, we agree. That said, we cannot see why you shouldn't use the *ReplaceLocations* parameter if you know what you're doing; just make sure that you switch back to the original disk set again.

Let's examine an example of how you would use the recommend method. First, make sure that the production database is dismounted. Then open the EMS and type **Restore-StorageGroupCopy –Identity "First Storage Group"**.

This command will activate the copy and leave the path for the production storage group intact. Now you can choose between either moving the LCR copy files to the location of the original production database manually using Windows Explorer or using Xcopy or a similar tool. Just be sure to move or delete the files in the folder you move the files to first. When the files have been moved, you simply need to mount the database again, and that's it.

The second option available when using the *Restore-StorageGroupCopy* CMDlet without the *ReplaceLocations* parameter is to change the drive letter for the partition holding the LCR copy to the drive letter used by the production storage group. This can be done using either the Disk Management MMC snap-in or the Diskpart tool.

1. To do so using the MMC snap-in, click **Start | Run** and type **Diskmgmt.msc**. This will bring up the MMC snap-in shown in Figure 8.12. Now right-click the partition holding the production storage group and its database, then select **Change drive letter and paths** in the context menu.

2. In the Change Drive Letter and Paths For window, click **Change**, then specify an unallocated drive letter and click **OK**, as shown in Figure 8.13.

Figure 8.12 The Disk Management MMC Snap-in

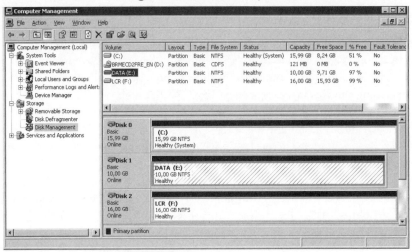

Figure 8.13 Specifying the Drive Letter for the Partition

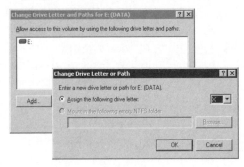

3. Click **OK** to the confirmation message and click **OK** to close the Change Drive Letter and Paths window.

4. Now change the drive letter for the partition holding your LCR copy to the drive letter that originally was assigned the partition that holds the production storage group, which in this example is **E:**.

It's important that the partition for which you change the drive letter for doesn't contain any other data used by other applications. If it does, you will most likely destroy functionality for the respective applications!

When you have changed the drive letter, all there is to do is to mount the database again, but remember, the paths for the active and passive storage groups must be the same on each partition.

NOTE

A restart of the server might be required for you to be able to assign the E: drive to the partition holding the LCR copy.

The last option available involves the use of mount points. A *mount point* is a feature with which you can surpass the 26-drive-letter limitation that exists in Windows 2003 Server. Using volume mount points, you can graft, or mount, a target partition into a folder on another physical disk. Since volume mount points are transparent to Exchange 2007 as well as most other programs, they are pretty popular, especially in deploying Exchange 2000/2003 cluster environments.

To use mount points to switch LCR storage group copies, you must already have configured the partitions holding the storage group copies to use them. If you haven't done so, the mount point option cannot be used. In this example, the Third Storage Group's folder as well as the LCR copy for this storage group, which is called Third Storage Group, point to an NTFS volume mount point.

You can see whether a particular folder in Windows Explorer is a mount point because the icon is represented as a disk and not the normal yellow folder icon (see Figure 8.14).

Figure 8.14 The Mount Point Icon in Windows Explorer

1. As is the case with the options we have covered, the first thing you should do before switching the storage group copies using NTFS volume mount points is to make sure that the database is in a dismounted state. If this is not the case, you should dismount it manually now. The next step is to open the EMS and type **Restore-StorageGroupCopy –Identity "Third Storage Group"** (which is the storage group used in this example).

2. Next open the Disk Management MMC snap-in, right-click the partition that is used as the NTFS volume mount point by the production storage group, then

select **Change Drive Letter or Paths** in the context menu. In the Change Drive Letter and Paths window, remove the existing path by highlighting it, then click the **Remove** button (see Figure 8.15).

Figure 8.15 Changing the NTFS Volume Mount Point Path

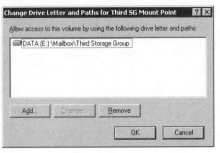

3. You now need to confirm that you want to remove the path. Click **Yes**.

4. Now remove the mount point for the partition used for the LCR copy, using the same steps. This is required to be able to use the LCR copy path as a mount point for the Production Storage Group copy.

5. We're now ready to mount the LCR copy to the Production Storage Group. We do so by right-clicking the partition that was used for the LCR copy, then choosing **Change Drive Letter or Paths** in the context menu. Now click **Add** and select **Mount** in the following empty NTFS folder. Click **Browse** and specify the path to the production storage group (see Figure 8.16). Finally, click **OK** twice and close the Disk Management MMC snap-in.

Figure 8.16 Specifying the New Path for the NTFS Volume Mount Point

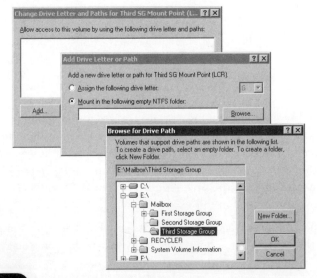

6. Now verify that the folder within Windows Explorer contains the expected data, and then mount the database again.

Is that cool or what?

Suspending Local Continuous Replication

On occasion, you might need to suspend LCR for a storage group. You need to suspend LCR should either the active or passive storage group copy for some reason become unavailable. Suspending LCR is also necessary if you need to seed the LCR copy (seeding is covered next in this chapter). Finally, you need to suspend LCR when you're performing an integrity check on the passive copy's transaction logs and database file, which is a recommended practice now and then.

> **NOTE**
>
> *Suspending LCR* means that all log file shipping as well as log file replaying is halted.
>
> Suspending LCR is a straightforward process; it's done by selecting the respective storage group in the EMC, then clicking **Suspend Local continuous replication** in the Action pane. When you click this link, you'll need to confirm that you really want to suspend LCR. In addition, you'll have the option of specifying why LCR was suspended. This comment can be viewed by clicking the **View Comment** button on the Properties page of the storage group (shown in Figure 8.17).

Figure 8.17 Suspending Local Continuous Replication

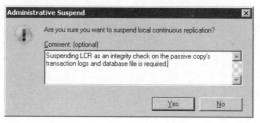

If you'd rather to suspend LCR for a storage group via the EMS, you'll need to do so using the *Suspend-StorageGroupCopy* CMDlet. To suspend LCR for the First Storage Group, where the comment shown in Figure 8.17 is specified, you should run the following command:

```
Suspend-StorageGroupCopy -Identity "First Storage Group" -SuspendComment
"Suspending LCR as an integrity check on the passive copy's transaction logs and
database file is required."
```

Again, you need to confirm that you really want to suspend LCR for the storage group. To do so, type **Y** for Yes and press **Enter**.

Resuming Local Continuous Replication

When the active or passive storage group is available again or when you have performed the integrity check or whatever type of maintenance you have completed, you need to resume LCR for the storage group. Again, this can be done via either the EMC or the EMS. To perform this task using the EMC, select the respective storage group and click **Resume local continuous replication** in the Action pane. When you do, the warning message shown in Figure 8.18 will appear. Click **Yes** and watch the Copy Status change to **Healthy** once again. Both log file shipping and log file replay have now been resumed.

Figure 8.18 Resuming Local Continuous Replication

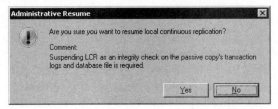

To resume LCR for a storage group via the EMS, type **Resume-StorageGroupCopy -Identity "First Storage Group"**.

Manually Seeding a Database Copy

Before we start talking about how to perform a manual seeding of a database copy, it would be a good idea to define the term *seeding* in terms of LCR. Seeding is the process whereby a database is added to a storage group copy. This can be a blank database or a copy of the database the storage group uses as the production database. When you enable LCR on a storage group using the EMC or via the EMS using the *Enable-DatabaseCopy* and *Enable-StorageGroupCopy* CMDlets, seeding normally takes place automatically. If it happens automatically, why should we even care about it, then? The answer is that there are a few situations in which manually seeding is required. The first is after you have performed an offline defragmentation of the production database belonging to the storage group for which you have enabled LCR. The second is if or when Exchange detects a corrupt log file, which the Microsoft Exchange Replication Service cannot replay into the database copy. The third is after a page scrubbing of a database on the active node in a Cluster Continuous Replication (CCR) setup occurs, and you then want to propagate these changes to the passive node in the CCR setup. Yes, you're right, the last one isn't really related to LCR but only continuous replication in clustered environments, where CCR is used. We'll talk much more about CCR later in this chapter.

Seeding a database copy manually can be done using the *Update-StorageGroupCopy* CMDlet in the EMS. Before doing so, you must suspend LCR for the respective storage group and then remove any .log, .chk, .jrs, and .edb files from the passive storage group's database copy, log files, and system files paths. To seed the database copy for the First Storage Group, you use the *Update-StorageGroupCopy* CMDlet and type **Update-StorageGroupCopy –Identity: "First Storage Group"**.

Running this command will create a temporary temp-seeding folder, and after a little while the seeding will take place, as shown in Figure 8.19.

Figure 8.19 Seeding a Mailbox Database Copy

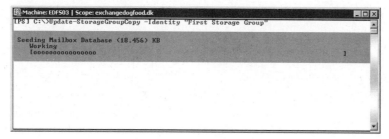

When seeding has taken place, the Microsoft Exchange Replication Service will start to replicate any .log, .chk, and .jrs files to the folder paths. When it's finished, you can resume LCR for the storage group, and you're back in business.

If you don't want to delete any .log, .chk, .jrs, and .edb files manually before running the *Update-StorageGroupCopy* CMDlet, you can tell the CMDlet to do it for you using the *DeleteExistingFiles* parameter. This method requires that you confirm the deletion of these files, as shown in Figure 8.20. The method you use is up to you, since they do the same thing.

Figure 8.20 Specifying That the *StorageGroupCopy* CMDlet Delete Any Existing Files

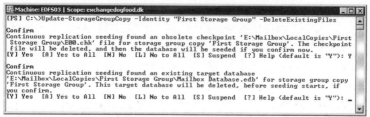

In addition, you can use the *ManualResume* parameter if you don't want replication to occur automatically on the storage group copy.

Another method available for seeding a database copy is to dismount the database in the EMC, suspend LCR for the storage group containing the database, and then copy the .edb file to the LCR copy folder using Windows Explorer. When the file has been copied, you then mount the database again using the EMC and resume LCR. Bear in mind that if you choose this method, your end users will be disconnected until the database is mounted. So unless there's a specific reason that you would use this method, we recommend that you use the *StorageGroupCopy* CMDlet.

Performing an Integrity Check of the Passive Copy Using Eseutil

It's a recommended best practice to periodically verify the integrity of the passive storage group copy to make sure neither the database copy nor any of the log files are corrupted. This is done by running a physical consistency check against both the database copy as well as the log files using Exchange Server Database Utilities (Eseutil.exe).

As mentioned earlier in this chapter, you need to suspend LCR on the storage group for which you want to verify the integrity of the passive database and log files.

To verify the physical integrity of the log files that have been replicated to the passive copy of the storage group, you'll need to open either a Command Prompt window or the EMS. In either the Command Prompt window or the EMS you should run Eseutil with the */k* switch followed by the log file prefix of the storage group.

The log file prefix for a storage group can be found under the General tab of the respective storage group, as shown in Figure 8.21.

Figure 8.21 Log File Prefix

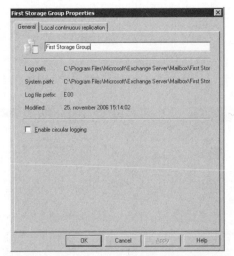

As you can see, the log file prefix for the First Storage Group typically is E00. To see the path for the log files, refer back to Figure 8.8. For the purpose of this example, the path is E:\Mailbox\LocalCopies\First Storage Group, so we'll need to type **Eseutil /k "E:\Mailbox\LocalCopies\First Storage Group\E00"**.

This will initiate checksum mode and start verifying each log file located under the specified path, as shown in Figure 8.22. If no corrupted log files are detected, the operation will complete successfully after a few seconds or minutes, depending on how many log files are contained in the respective folder.

Figure 8.22 Integrity Check of the LCR Log Files

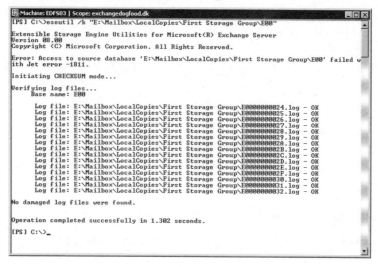

When the log files have been verified, we can move on to checking the integrity of the database copy. This is also done by running Eseutil with the /k switch but instead followed by the full path the database copy. In this example, we need to run the following command: **Eseutil /k "E:\Mailbox\LocalCopies\First Storage Group\Mailbox Database.edb"**.

Eseutil will once again initiate checksum mode and then create a temporary database so that the database copy can be checked for any errors (see Figure 8.23). Again, the time required for the integrity check depends on the size of the database.

When you have performed an integrity check of both the log files and the database copy (and hopefully Eseutil.exe hasn't found too many corrupted log files or issues with the database copy), you should make sure that LCR for the respective storage group is resumed again. Should you be so unlucky that Eseutil.exe finds one or more corrupted log files or corruption in the database copy, you need to disable LCR on the storage group, then remove the corrupted log files and/or database copy file. When the files have been removed, you can re-enable LCR, which will create a database copy and seed it as well as replicate any existing log files from the active copy of the storage group to the specified path.

Figure 8.23 Integrity Check of the LCR Database Copy

We'll bet that most of you understand the importance of during periodically integrity checks of both the log files as well as the database copy—right?

Disabling Local Continuous Replication on a Storage Group

There might come a time when you no longer want to have the LCR feature enabled for a particular storage group. Luckily, it's a painless process to disable this feature once it's enabled.

You can disable LCR for a storage group via either the EMC or the EMS. To disable LCR using the EMC, you need to select the Storage Group level under the Mailbox subnode, located beneath the Server Configuration work center node; you then click **Disable local continuous replication** in the Action pane, as shown in Figure 8.24.

Figure 8.24 Disable LCR Action Link

When we disable LCR for a storage group, we'll get the warning message shown in Figure 8.25, which tells us that LCR will be disabled for the replication database copy for the respective Storage Group. Since this is exactly what we want to do, click **Yes**.

Figure 8.25 Disabling Local Continuous Replication Confirmation

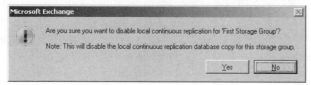

After we click Yes, believe it or not we'll get an additional warning message. This one informs us that we must delete the files (that is, the log files, EDB database, and so on) manually from the path (which in this example is E:\Mailbox\LocalCopies\First Storage Group) we specified when we originally enabled LCR (see Figure 8.26). Once you have clicked **OK** and deleted these files, LCR has been properly disabled.

Figure 8.26 Disabling Local Continuous Replication

If you want to disable LCR for a Storage Group via the EMS, you need to do so using the *Disable-StorageGroupCopy* CMDlet. To disable the LCR for the First Storage Group, type **Disable-StorageGroupCopy –Identity "First Storage Group"**. When you do, you'll get the same warning message as the one shown in Figure 8.25.

Local Continuous Replication Performance Objects and Counters

When the Exchange 2007 Mailbox Server role is installed, setup adds two LCR-related performance objects to the Windows 2003 Performance Monitor. To open the Performance Monitor, either click **Start | Run** and type **Perfmon** or click **Start | Administrative**

Tools and select **Performance**. This will bring up the Performance Monitor, shown in Figure 8.27.

Figure 8.27 The Performance Monitor

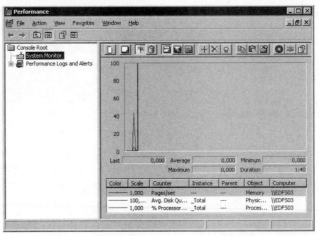

The first object is the MSExchange Replica Seeder performance object, which, as you can see in Figure 8.28, contains only one counter, called Seeding Finished %. This counter is used to show the progress of database seeding in percent. When you add this counter, you can choose which instance (in this case, the particular storage group) you want to view the database seeding for.

Figure 8.28 Continuous Replication Performance Objects

The MSExchange Replication performance object contains at least 14 different counters (see Table 8.2).

Table 8.2 Continuous Replication Performance Counters

Performance Counter	Description
Copy Queue Exceeds Mount Threshold (CCR only)	Copy Queue Exceeds Mount Threshold (CCR Only) is 1 if the copy queue length is larger than the Mount Threshold specified by the Auto Database Mount Dial. This counter is used only with CCR. It will always be 0 with LCR.
CopyGenerationNumber	Copy Generation Number is the generation of the last log file that has been copied.
CopyNotificationGeneration Number	Copy Notification Generation Number is the generation of the last log file the copier knows about.
CopyQueueLength	Copy Queue Length is the number of log generations waiting to be both copied and inspected successfully.
Failed	Failed is 1 if the replica instance is set to failed, otherwise 0.
InspectorGenerationNumber	Inspector Generation Number is the generation of the last log file that has been inspected.
ReplayBatchSize	Replay Batch Size is the number of log generations replayed together.
ReplayGenerationNumber	Replay Generation Number is the generation of the last log file that has been replayed successfully.
ReplayGenerationsComplete	Replay Generations Complete is the number of log generations already played in the current replay batch.
ReplayGenerationsPerMinute	Replay Generations Per Minute is the rate of replay in log generations per minute in the current replay batch.
ReplayGenerationsRemaining	Replay Generations Remaining is the number of log generations remaining to be played in the current replay batch.
ReplayNotificationGeneration Number	The generation of the last log file that replay knows about.
ReplayQueueLength	Replay Queue Length is the number of log generations waiting to be replayed.
Suspended	Suspended is 1 if the continuous replication is suspended. When the continuous replication is suspended, logs are not copied and replayed into the passive copy.

As you can see, all these counters can be used to determine how replication for an LCR-enabled storage group have progressed, but a high-availability feature such as LCR should really be monitored using a proactive and automated monitoring solution such as Microsoft Operation Manager (MOM) with the Exchange Server 2007 Management Pack installed.

Managing a Cluster Continuous Replication-Based Setup

Exchange Server 2007 introduces another new high-availability feature called Cluster Continuous Replication (CCR). This feature takes the new Exchange Server 2007 log file shipping and replay mechanisms (known as continuous replication) and combines them with the features that are available in a more traditional two-node Windows 2003 server active/passive cluster setup. A traditional two-node active/passive cluster has its benefits but has also always had one major drawback: You still have a single point of failure when it comes to the information stores. CCR provides redundancy for both Exchange Services and the information stores.

As is the case with traditional Exchange clusters, CCR uses Windows Clustering Services to provide virtual servers (which, in Exchange 2007, are called clustered mailbox servers) and failover capabilities. CCR has one big difference from traditional clusters, though, and that is that functionality doesn't require any kind of shared storage subsystem, because each node contains a local copy of the information stores. This eliminates the dependency on SAN technology in the cluster design, which makes CCR a more cost-efficient solution because you can use a storage option such as Direct Attached Storage (DAS) or Serial Attached SCSI.

With CCR, the transaction logs generated on the active node are replicated to the information store on the passive node using log file shipping. These replicated log files are then posted into the database(s) on the passive node using the log file replay technology. This means that should the active node or a database on this node fail or for some other reason go offline, an automatic failover to the passive node will occur. When the passive node becomes the active node, the replication of log files will happen from the new active node to the passive node.

Another thing worth mentioning about CCR is that the feature supports stretched clustering (called *geoclustering*), but bear in mind that the nodes must belong to the same subnet. This means that as the cluster is stretched between the locations, the subnet must be stretched, too.

TIP

When Exchange 2007 supports Longhorn server (which will be provided via a service pack when the Longhorn product has been released), we will be able to take advantage of stretched clustering spanning multiple subnets, both on the public as well as the private network (also called the heartbeat network).

Last but not least, you can reduce the frequency of backups and restores as well as perform backups of the databases on the passive node, and thereby not impact the performance of the active node. In Figure 8.29 you can see a basic CCR scenario.

Figure 8.29 A Basic Cluster Continuous Replication Scenario

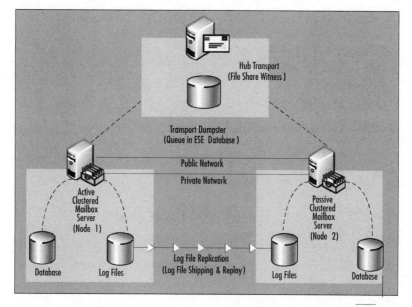

Prerequisites

To set up a CCR-based cluster, the following are required:

- A Windows 2003 Active Directory forest with at least one domain controller (raised to 2000 or 2003 forest functional level)

- Two Windows 2003 Server R2 Enterprise Editions or Windows 2003 Server SP1 Enterprise Editions

- One Windows File Share Witness, which is recommended to be an Exchange 2007 Hub Transport Server in the existing Exchange 2007 organization; note that CCR-based clusters don't use a shared quorum as traditional clusters do

- A Cluster Service Account in the Active Directory forest (we'll create this one later in this section)

You also need to apply the update mentioned in MS KB article 921181 to both servers that will act as nodes in the Exchange Server 2007 Clustered Mailbox setup. The update adds a new file share witness feature to the current Majority Node Set (MNS) quorum model. The file share witness feature lets you use a file share that is external to the cluster as an additional "vote" to determine the status of the cluster in a two-node MNS quorum cluster deployment, which is a requirement to use the CCR functionality in Exchange Server 2007.

To deploy CCR, the following hardware requirements must be met:

■ Two network interface cards (NICs) installed in each node—one for the public and one for the private cluster network (the heartbeat network)

■ Extra sets of disks or a DAS, SAN, or Serial SCSI solution to hold the database and transaction log files

In addition to the software and hardware requirements, you also should be aware of the following general requirements:

■ When dealing with CCR environments, you must and can only use one database per storage group.

■ You cannot create a public folder database in a CCR environment if you already have more than one public folder database in your organization.

■ In a CCR environment, Microsoft recommends that you create no more than 30 storage groups and databases (one database per storage group) on the clustered mailbox server.

■ The cluster on which Exchange 2007 is installed cannot contain Exchange Server 2000/2003 or any version of Microsoft SQL Server. Running Exchange 2007 in a cluster with any of these other applications is simply not supported.

SOME INDEPENDENT ADVICE

Some of you might wonder whether the licensing rules have changed regarding Exchange 2007 cluster setups. Unfortunately, this isn't the case; you still have to purchase an Exchange 2007 Enterprise Edition CAL for each node in your cluster (also any passive nodes). The reason is that the passive node still runs Exchange code although the node is the passive one.

Configuring the Network Interface for Each Node

When you start the servers that are to be the nodes in the cluster, begin by naming the machines EDFS07 and EDFS08 or whatever naming scheme you want to use. (These names have nothing to do with the Exchange server name that your clients will be configured to connect to later.) Now name the two network connections Public and Private (see Figure 8.30) for the external and the internal networks, respectively. Remember to do this on both nodes.

Figure 8.30 Network Connections

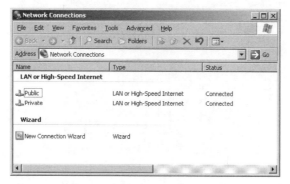

1. Click **Advanced | Advanced Settings**. If it's not already the case, make sure Public is listed first on the binding order list, then Private, and Remote Access Connections last. Also make sure that you clear the **File and Printer Sharing** check box for Microsoft Networks for the Private network connection, as shown in Figure 8.31.

Figure 8.31 Binding Order

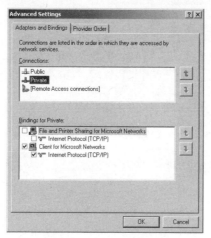

2. Now configure the **Public** network with the TCP/IP settings that should be used in your environment (see Figure 8.32).

Figure 8.32 Configuring the Public Network Interface

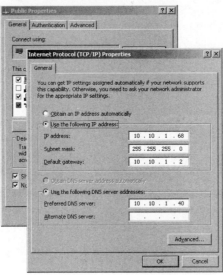

We also need to configure the Private network with an IP address and a subnet mask, as shown in Figure 8.33. Nothing else is required, since this network is used only for communication (heartbeats) between the nodes in the cluster.

Figure 8.33 Configuring the Private Network Interface

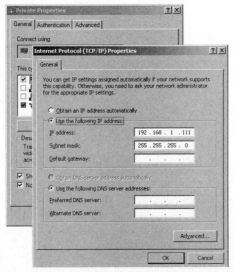

1. Click **Advanced**, then select the **DNS** tab. Here you should clear both the **Register this connection's addresses in DNS** and **Use this connection's DNS suffix** check boxes, as shown in Figure 8.34.

Figure 8.34 Configuring DNS Settings for the Private Network Interface

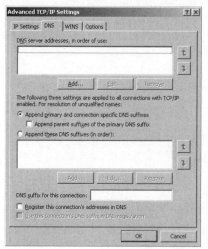

2. Click the **WINS** tab. Clear the **Enable LMHOSTS lookup** option and select **Disable NetBIOS over TCP/IP**, as shown in Figure 8.35.

Figure 8.35 Configuring WINS Settings for the Private Network Interface

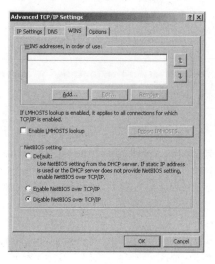

3. Click **OK** three times and close the Network Connections window.

Adding the Servers to the Active Directory Domain

Since a CCR setup requires both nodes to be part of the same Active Directory domain, now would be a good time to make this the case. You can add the nodes to the domain by right-clicking **My Computer** and selecting **Properties** in the context menu. Now click the **Computer Name** tab (see Figure 8.36), then the **Change** button, and specify the domain.

Figure 8.36 Adding the Nodes to the Domain

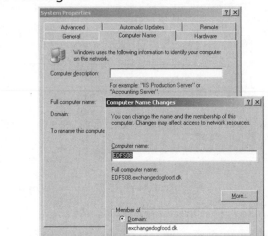

When you have added both servers to the domain as well as rebooted each, we can move on to creating the necessary cluster service account.

Creating a Cluster Service Account

Because each node belonging to the cluster needs to use the same account, we need to create a cluster service account.

The cluster service account must be a member of either the Exchange Server Administrators (ServerName) group or the Exchange Organization Administrators group. In addition, it must be a member of the local administrators group on each node in the cluster. For our purposes, we'll add it to the Exchange Organization Administrators group.

To create the cluster service account:

1. Log onto a domain controller in the respective Active Directory domain, then click **Start | Run** and type **DSA.msc** to open the Active Directory Users and Computers MMC snap-in. Now right-click the Organizational Unit (OU) in which you want the service account to be created, then choose **New | User** in the context menu. Give the account a meaningful name and user logon name (such as **Cluster Service Account** and **svc-cluster**), as shown in Figure 8.37. Now click **Next**.

Figure 8.37 Creating the Cluster Service Account

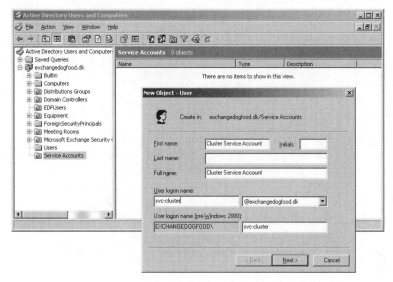

2. Give the service account a complex password and uncheck **User Must change password at next logon**, then check **Password never expires**, as shown in Figure 8.38. Click **Next**.

Figure 8.38 Specifying the Password for the Cluster Service Account

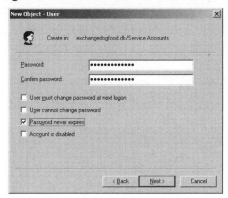

On the New User object completion page click Finish.

3.   Now we need to give the new cluster service account the appropriate permissions. To do so, open the **Properties** page for the user object and select the **Member Of** tab. Make sure it's the respective Active Directory domain that's shown in the **From this location** field, then click the **Add** button and type **Exchange Organization Administrators**, as shown in Figure 8.39. Click **OK**.

Figure 8.39 Adding the Cluster Service Account to the Exchange Organization Administrators Group

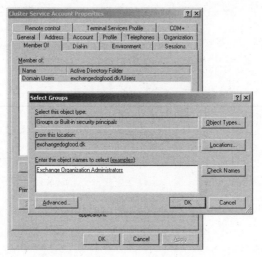

4.   Now switch over to the server that will be the first node in the cluster and click **Start | Run**. Type **compmgmt.msc**. Expand **Local Users and Groups** and select the **Groups** container. Open the **Properties** page for the Administrators group object in the right pane, then click the **Add** button. Make sure that the Active Directory domain is shown in the **From this location** field, as shown in Figure 8.40, and type **Cluster Service Account** (or whatever name you gave the account in your setup). click **Check Names** to verify that it resolves successfully. Click **OK** and close the Computer Management MMC snap-in.

Figure 8.40 Adding the Cluster Service Account to the Local
Administrators Group

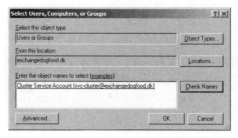

5. Repeat Steps 1–4 for the server that will be the second node in the cluster.

Creating and Configuring the Windows 2003 Server Cluster

Now that the two servers are ready to act as nodes in a Windows 2003 cluster, it's time to create the actual Windows 2003 Server Cluster. To do so:

1. Log onto EDFS07 with a domain admin account, then click **Start |**
   Administrative Tools | Cluster Administrator, and select **Create new**
   cluster in the drop-down box. Click **OK** and then click **Next**, as shown in Figure
   8.41.

Figure 8.41 Creating a New Cluster

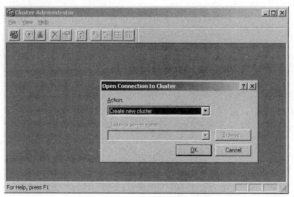

NOTE

You can also open a command prompt and type **Cluster.exe /create /wizard**
to start the Cluster Wizard.

2. Now specify the domain name as well as the cluster name (the name for the Windows 2003 cluster, *not* the Exchange cluster name to which the clients will connect) as shown in Figure 8.42, then click **Next**.

Figure 8.42 Specifying the Cluster Name and Domain

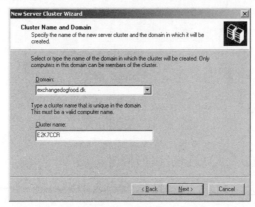

3. If it's not already entered, type the name of the Windows 2003 server that is to be the first node in the cluster (in this case, **EDFS07**), then click **Next** (see Figure 8.43).

Figure 8.43 Adding the First Cluster Node to the New Cluster

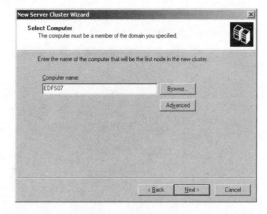

4. Let the Cluster Wizard determine the cluster configuration and click **Next**.

NOTE

You can ignore the two warnings shown in Figure 8.44, since the nodes in a cluster continuous replication-based mailbox server setup aren't going to share the same disk subsystem.

Figure 8.44 Analyzing Cluster Configuration

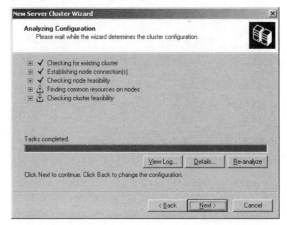

5.   Now enter the IP address that the cluster management tools should use to connect to the cluster (in this case, **10.10.1.218**) and click **Next** (see Figure 8.45).

Figure 8.45 Specifying the IP Address to Which the Cluster Management Tools Should Connect

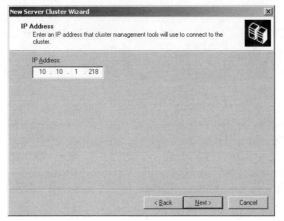

6. Enter the credentials of the cluster service account and click **Next** (see Figure 8.46).

Figure 8.46 Entering the Credentials of the Cluster Service Account

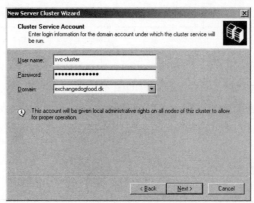

7. Now click **Quorum** and select **Majority Node Set** as the resource type, then click **OK** and **Next** (see Figures 8.47 and 8.48).

Figure 8.47 Proposed Cluster Configuration

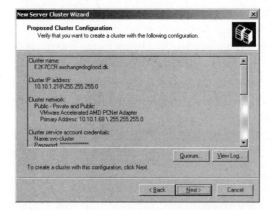

NOTE

The Majority Node Set resource type manages cluster configuration data that might or might not be on a cluster storage device. For example, the Majority Node Set resource type can manage cluster configuration data that is actually stored on multiple nodes in a cluster at the same physical location or in a geographically dispersed cluster. The Majority Node Set resource ensures that the cluster configuration data is kept consistent across the various nodes.

Figure 8.48 Setting Majority Node Set as the Resource Type

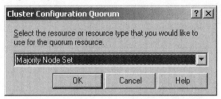

8. Now wait for the cluster to be configured, then click **Next** (see Figure 8.49).

Figure 8.49 Creating the Cluster

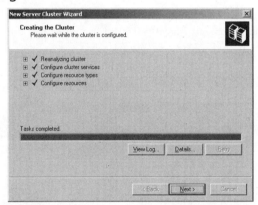

9. When the cluster has been completed successfully, you can click **Finish**.

We now have a full working Windows 2003 cluster running, but since there's only one node, it's not very fault tolerant. So let's add the second Windows 2003 server too. Do the following:

1. Right-click **EDFS07** in the left pane of the Cluster Administrator, then selecting **New | Node**, as shown in Figure 8.50.

Figure 8.50 Adding a Second Node to the Cluster

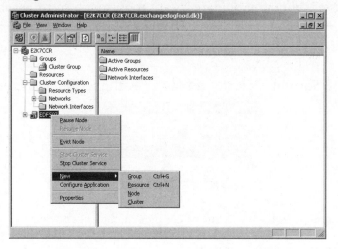

2.   The Add Nodes Wizard will launch and you can click **Next**. Enter the name of
     the server that is going to be the second node (for the purpose of this example,
     EDFS08), then click **Next** (see Figure 8.51).

Figure 8.51 Entering the Name of the Second Node

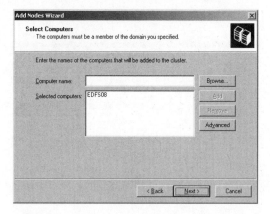

3.   Again, let the Add Notes Wizard determine the cluster configuration, then click
     Next (see Figure 8.52).

Figure 8.52 Analyzing Cluster Configuration

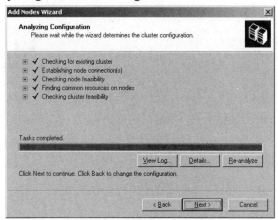

4   Enter the password for the cluster service account (in this case, **svc–cluster**, which we created earlier in the chapter), then click **Next** (see Figure 8.53).

Figure 8.53 Entering the Password for the Cluster Service Account

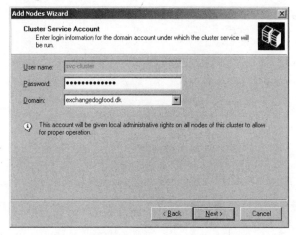

5.   When you are verified, you'll want to add the second node to the cluster with the configuration shown in Figure 8.54. Click **Next**.

6.   When the cluster has been configured properly without any errors or warnings (see Figure 8.55), click **Next**.

Figure 8.54 Proposed Cluster Configuration for Node Two

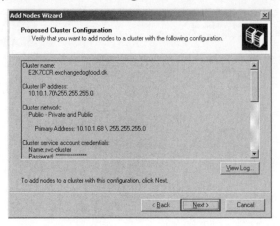

Figure 8.55 The Cluster Is Configured for the Second Node

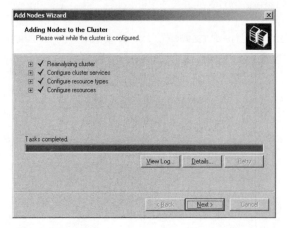

7. When the Add Notes Wizard has completed successfully, click **Finish**.

The second Windows server is now part of the cluster, as shown in Figure 8.56.

Figure 8.56 Cluster Administrator with Two Nodes

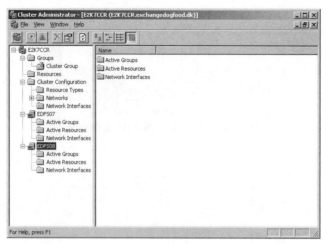

Installing the Necessary Windows Components

Before we move on to install the Exchange Server 2007 binaries, we need to make sure that the required Windows components have been installed. All types of Exchange Server 2007 installations (no matter what server role we're talking about) need the Microsoft .NET Framework 2.0 component installed.

If you have installed Windows Server 2003 Enterprise Edition with Service Pack 1 on the nodes, you need to download the Microsoft .NET Framework Version 2.0 Redistributable Package (x86) from Microsoft.com, since it's only a standard Windows component for Windows Server 2003 R2. If you're using Windows Server 2003 R2-based servers, you can install the component by clicking **Start | Control Panel | Add or Remove Programs | Add/Remove Windows Components**, checking the **Microsoft .NET Framework 2.0** check box as shown in Figure 8.57, then clicking **Next**.

Since we're deploying a clustered mailbox server, we also need to install the following IIS 6.0 components on each node:

- Enable network COM+ access
- Internet Information Services
- World Wide Web Service

Figure 8.57 Installing the Microsoft .NET Framework 2.0 Windows Component

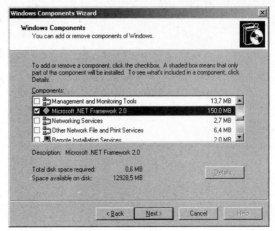

When you have done so, you can move on to configure the File Share Witness.

Configuring the Majority Node Set Quorum with File Share Witness

No doubt some of you are thinking: What the heck is a Majority Node Set quorum with File Share Witness? We can understand why; this is a completely new type of quorum model that is made available by installing the update (MS KB article 921181) mentioned in the beginning of this chapter section. The update makes it possible to use a file share witness that is external to the cluster as an additional "vote" to determine the status of the cluster in a two-node MNS quorum cluster deployment, which is a requirement for using the CCR functionality in Exchange Server 2007.

The file share for this file share witness can be located on any type of Windows server in your environment, but best practice is to use an Exchange 2007 Hub Transport server in the Active Directory server site containing the nodes in the respective cluster. We'll also use a Hub Transport server in this example.

The first thing you need to do is to create the file share on the Hub Transport server. You can do this either via the CLI or by using the GUI. In this example we'll use the GUI:

1. Log on to the Hub Transport server with a domain admin account, then open Windows Explorer and create a new folder called **MNS_FSQ_E2K7CCR** on the C: drive or wherever you want it to be created, as shown in Figure 8.58.

NOTE

It's recommended that you use the *MNS_FSQ_clustername* naming convention when you create this folder.

Figure 8.58 The Majority Node Set File Share Quorum Folder

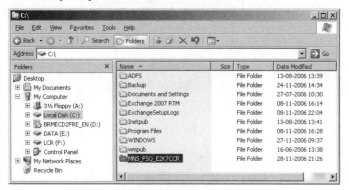

2. Now open the **Properties** page for the newly created folder and click the **Sharing** tab (see Figure 8.59).

Figure 8.59 The Majority Node Set File Share Quorum Folder Share

3.   Click **Permissions** and configure the share permissions so that only the Cluster Service Account is allowed access to this share (see Figure 8.60).

Figure 8.60 Share Permissions for the Majority Node Set File Share Quorum Folder

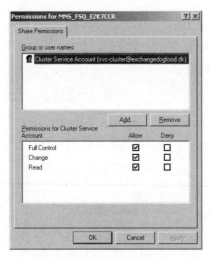

4.   Click **OK**, then select the **Security** tab. Here you should give Full Control to the local administrator and the cluster service account, as shown in Figure 8.61. Make sure you clear **Allow inheritable permissions from the parent to propagate to this object and all child objects** when doing so, then click **OK** twice and log off the server.

Figure 8.61 Security Permissions to the Majority Node Set File Share Quorum Folder

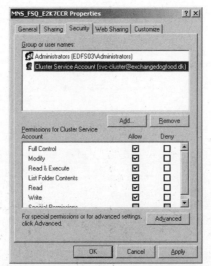

5. Back on EDFS07 or EDFS08, we now need to set the Majority Node Set Private Property attribute to point to the file share we just created. We do so by opening a command prompt, then issuing the command **Cluster res "Majority Node Set" /priv MNSFileShare=\\EDFS03\MNS_FSQ_E2K7CCR**.

NOTE

Make sure to replace the server name so that it matches the name of the Hub Transport server in your environment.

You will get a warning that all properties were stored but not all changes will take effect until the next time the resource is brought online, just as is shown in Figure 8.62.

Figure 8.62 Configuring the Majority Node Set on EDFS07

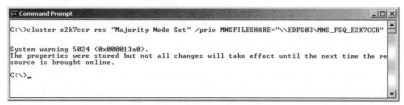

SOME INDEPENDENT ADVICE

In a couple of the CCR-based cluster deployments I've done, I have gotten an error message similar to the following when running the command *Cluster res "Majority Node Set" /priv MNSFileShare=\\EDFS03\MNS_FSQ_E2K7CCR*:
Too many command line parameters have been specified for this option.
See "CLUSTER RESOURCE /?" for correct syntax
Should you experience this error, too, you should be able to get going using the following command syntax instead:
Cluster <ClusterName> res "Majority Node Set" /priv MNSFileShare=UNCPath

6. To force all changes to take effect, we will move the cluster group from one node to the other (taking the cluster group offline and online again). Do this using the command **Cluster Group "Cluster Group" /Move**. When you have done so,

you will see that the cluster group is now online on E2K7Node2, as shown in Figure 8.63.

Figure 8.63 Moving the Cluster Group from One Node to the Other

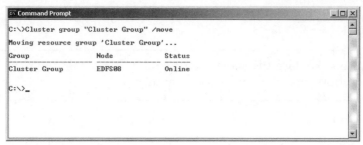

7. Now let's verify that the 7Priv property is set correctly. This can be done by issuing the command **Cluster Res "Majority Node Set" /Priv**.

As you can see in Figure 8.64, this property has been set correctly for the purposes of our example.

Figure 8.64 Verifying That the Property of *IPriv* Is Set Correctly

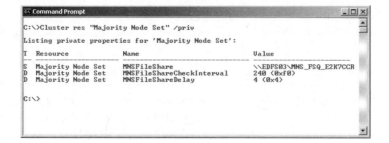

Configuring the Transport Dumpster

When deploying a CCR-based cluster in your environment, an important step is to enable the Transport Dumpster on the Hub Transport server.

The Transport Dumpster is a new feature of the Exchange 2007 Hub Transport server that can submit recently delivered mail after an unscheduled outage. For an e-mail message to be able to be retained in the Transport Dumpster, at least one of the message recipients must have his or her mailbox located on a CCR-based mailbox cluster server, because the Transport Dumpster works only with mailboxes located on a CCR-based mailbox server cluster. As mentioned earlier in this chapter, with CCR the replication of mailbox data from the active node to the passive node is *asynchronous*, which means that the passive node will always lag behind the passive node (although not by much). This means that should a failure of the active node occur, there's a chance that not all transaction log files will have been replicated to the passive node before this happens. This is where the Transport Dumpster comes into the picture. It can resubmit recently delivered mail and thereby constitute for the majority of the changes in the database(s). When a failure of the active node results in a lossy failover to the passive node, the cluster mailbox server will ask all the Hub Transport servers in the site to redeliver any lost mail.

> **NOTE**
>
> Should any of the messages that are being resubmitted to the cluster mailbox server be duplicates, the store is intelligent enough to discard any duplicates it finds.

The Transport Dumpster is enabled by default; you can see the default configured settings by running the *Get-TransportConfig* CMDlet.

Microsoft recommends that you configure the *MaxDumpsterSizePerStorageGroup* parameter, which specifies the maximum size of the Transport Dumpster queue for each storage group to a size that is 1.25 times the size of the maximum message that can be sent. For example, if the maximum size for messages is 10 megabytes (MB), you should configure the *MaxDumpsterSizePerStorageGroup* parameter with a value of 12.5 MB. In addition, Microsoft recommends that you configure the *MaxDumpsterTime* parameter, which specifies how long an e-mail message should remain in the Transport Dumpster queue, to a value of 07.00:00:00, which is seven days. This amount of time is sufficient to allow for an extended outage to occur without loss of e-mail. When you use the Transport Dumpster feature, additional disk space is needed on the Hub Transport server to host the Transport Dumpster queues. The amount of storage space required is roughly equal to the value of *MaxDumpsterSizePerStorageGroup* multiplied by the number of storage groups.

You use the *Set-TransportConfig* CMDlet to enable and configure the Transport Dumpster. So, for example, to configure the maximum size of the dumpster per storage group to 25 MB with a dumpster life of 10 days, you would need to run the command *Set-TransportConfig -MaxDumpsterSizePerStorageGroup 25MB -MaxDumpsterTime 10.00:00:00*.

To see the *MaxDumpsterSizePerStorageGroup* and *MaxDumpsterTime* configuration settings, you can type **Get-TransportConfig**, as shown in Figure 8.65.

Figure 8.65 Transport Configuration Settings

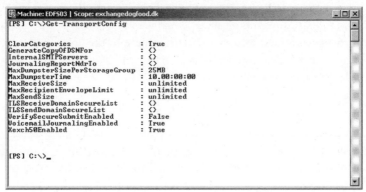

Installing Exchange 2007 on the Active Node

It's time to install the Exchange Server 2007 binaries on each node. We'll start with EDFS07, which is the active node. To do so:

1. Double-click **Setup.exe** on the network share or the DVD media containing the Exchange 2007 setup files.

2. The Exchange Server 2007 Installation Wizard splash screen will launch, and as you can see in Figure 8.66, Step 1: Install .NET Framework 2.0, Step 2: Install Microsoft Management Console (MMC), and Step 3: Install Windows PowerShell have already been completed.

Figure 8.66 The Exchange Server 2007 Splash Screen

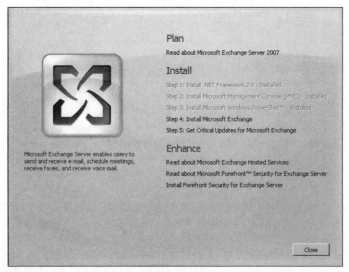

NOTE

If you have installed Windows Server 2003 with Service Pack 1 on each node, you need to download Microsoft Management Console (MMC) 3.0 and install it manually (by following the link in Step 2). But since I'm using Windows 2003 R2 Servers in my environment, the MMC 3.0 is installed by default.

Click **Step 4: Install Microsoft Exchange**. Then click **Next** and accept the **License Agreement**. Click **Next** once again. Decide whether you want to enable error reporting or not (it's a good idea to enable this function, since the Exchange Product Group will receive any obscure errors you should experience in your CCR setup), then click **Next**.

3. Now select **Custom Exchange Server Installation** (see Figure 8.67) and click **Next**.

Figure 8.67 Selecting a Custom Exchange Server Installation

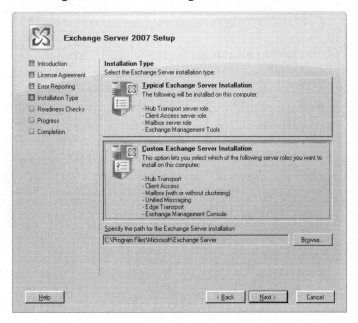

4. Check **Active Clustered Mailbox Role** as shown in Figure 8.68 and click **Next**.

Figure 8.68 Selecting to Install an Active Clustered Mailbox Role

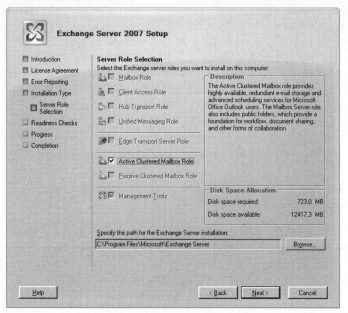

5. Now select **Cluster Continuous Replication**, then specify a name for the mailbox server (the name you want your Outlook clients to connect to) and a unique IP address on your public network. Finally, specify the path for the clustered mailbox server database files (which in the example is **E:**) or use the default path (see Figure 8.69).

    If you're installing CCR in a production environment, you should keep the transaction log files and database on separate disks, but if you're deploying CCR in a test environment, you simply use the default path.

6. Let the readiness check complete, and if no issues are found, click **Next** to begin the installation.

Figure 8.69 Selecting to Install a Cluster Continuous Replication Cluster and Specifying the Name and IP Address of the Clustered Mailbox Server

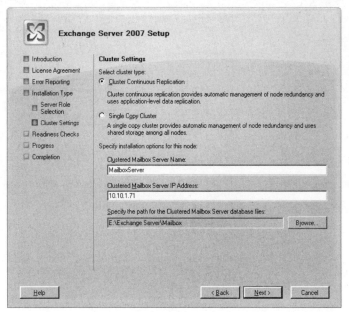

The Exchange Server 2007 Installation Wizard will now copy the needed Exchange files, install and configure the Mailbox Role, and finally create and configure the clustered mailbox server resources locally and create the object in Active Directory. After all steps have been completed, untick **Exit Setup** and open Exchange System Manager (yes, this will be corrected in a later build), then click **Finish**. We don't want to open the EMC just yet; we'll install Exchange on the second node first.

Installing Exchange 2007 on the Passive Node

Log on to EDFS08 with a domain admin account and do the same steps as we did when installing Exchange Server 2007 on EDFS07. The only difference is that you should select **Passive Clustered Mailbox Role** instead of Active Clustered Mailbox Role, as shown in Figure 8.70.

Figure 8.70 Installing the Passive Clustered Mailbox Role on the Second Node

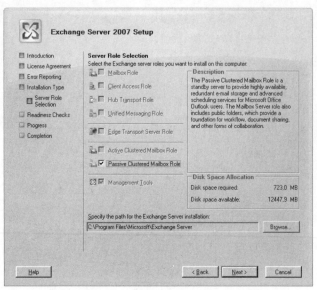

Testing the Functionality of the Clustered Mailbox Server

It's time to verify that our Exchange 2007 clustered mailbox server is working as expected. Let's first open the Cluster Administrator and check whether the respective Exchange resources have been created. If you take a look at Figure 8.71, it looks good; we have both nodes listed in the left pane and all Exchange resources have been created and are currently owned by EDFS07.

Try to open the EMS by clicking **Start | All Programs | Microsoft Exchange Server 2007 | Exchange Management Shell** on one of the nodes, then type **Get–ClusteredMailboxServerStatus –Identity MailboxServer**. As you can see in Figure 8.72, the status of the clustered mailbox server is Online, and EDFS7 is currently the active node.

Figure 8.71 Listing All Exchange Cluster Resources in the Cluster Administrator

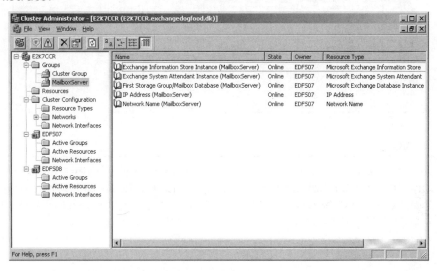

Figure 8.72 Requesting the Online Status of the Clustered Mailbox Server

Now that we have verified that the clustered mailbox server is online, let's try to move the Exchange resources from node one to node two using the *Move-ClusteredMailboxServer* CMDlet. In the environment used in this chapter, we do so by issuing the command *Move-ClusteredMailboxServer -Identity:MailboxServer -TargetMachine:EDFS08 -MoveComment:"Verifying the Move Clustered Mailbox Server Functionality!"*

You're then asked to confirm this action. Type **Yes**, then press **Enter**. After a while the clustered mailbox resources will have been moved to the second node (EDFS08), as shown in Figure 8.73.

Figure 8.73 Moving the Clustered Mailbox Resources to the Second Node

WARNING

Even though it's possible to move the cluster resource groups between nodes using the Cluster Administrator console, you should *always* do so using the *Move-ClusteredMailboxServer* CMDlet, because the Move Group task in the Cluster Administrator console isn't Exchange 2007 aware.

Viewing the Clustered Mailbox Server From Within the Exchange Management Console

Let's take a look at the clustered mailbox server in the EMC. To do so, click **Start | All Programs | Microsoft Exchange Server 2007 | Exchange Management Console**, then drill down to **Server Configuration | Mailbox**. Notice that the clustered mailbox server we named MailboxServer is listed in the Results pane and that it's recognized as a cluster server, as shown in Figure 8.74.

Figure 8.74 Viewing the Clustered Mailbox Server in the Exchange Management Console

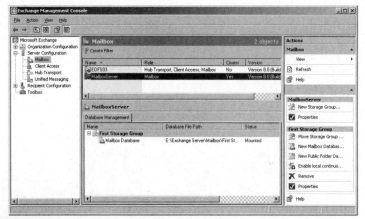

Simulating a Failover from One Node to the Other

Now let's try to simulate a failover from EDFS08 (currently the active node) to EDFS07 so that we can see what will happen from the Outlook client perspective. To switch from one node to the other, we'll issue the CMDlet we used earlier in the chapter: *Move-ClusteredMailboxServer -Identity:MailboxServer -TargetMachine:EDFS07 -MoveComment:"Simulating a failover from one node to the other, seen from the end-user perspective"*.

When a manual move or a failover occurs, the balloon shown in Figure 8.75 will appear because all services need to be stopped on EDFS07 before they can be moved and brought online on EDFS08.

Figure 8.75 Connection to the Exchange Server Has Been Lost

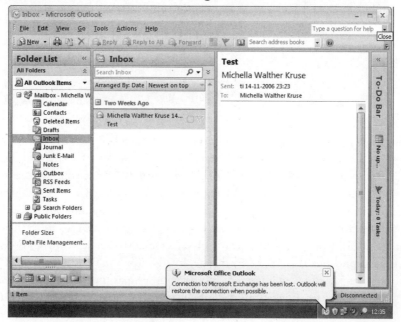

Depending on the number as well as the size of the databases in your Cluster Continuous Replication setup, this will take somewhere between 10 seconds to a couple of minutes, which shouldn't cause panic for the end users in the organization.

When EDFS08 has taken over, the end users will be notified that the connection to the Exchange Server has been restored (see Figure 8.76).

Figure 8.76 Connection to the Exchange Server Has Been Restored

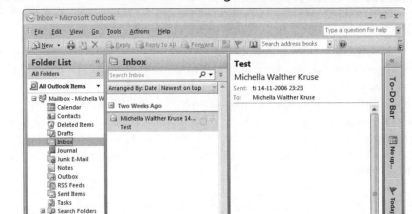

As you have seen you throughout this chapter, you benefit from several advantages when you choose to install the Exchange 2007 Mailbox Server role in a Cluster Continuous Replication setup in your organization. The primary benefit is that you no longer have a single point of failure in regard to the Mailbox/Public Folder databases. Should the database on one node crash, an automatic failover to the other node containing the secondary database will be completed. This also means that you no longer need to use a shared storage system in the CCR setup, as is the case with Exchange 2007 Single Copy Clusters as well as cluster setups in previous versions of Exchange. In addition, the two nodes in the CCR setup can even be placed in two different locations, as long as they belong to the same subnet. Not only that, the installation of the Exchange 2007 cluster has also been further simplified over previous versions. Since the CCR setup uses log file shipping and replay to a secondary database, you also don't have to do full online backups as often as was the case in Exchange 200x and earlier versions. Last but certainly not least, the failover process has been improved in several areas now that the new file share witness model has been introduced.

Backup Choices in a CCR Setup

When you deployed a cluster with Exchange 2003, the only option available when the stores were going to be backed up was to take a backup of the stores running on the production servers. With CCR (and LCR), you have the option of taking a backup of the database copies on the passive node, thereby eliminating any heavy load on the active node, both in terms of I/O to the disk spindles as well as CPU usage.

Keep in mind, though, that you can only perform a backup on the passive node using VSS, which means that Windows Backup cannot be used for this purpose. Instead you need to use Microsoft Data Protection Manager version 2 (DPM v2) or a third-party backup application that supports VSS backups.

It's also worth mentioning that any backups performed via the passive node will be backups of the database copies, not the databases on the active node. So, you might wonder, what will happen to the transaction log files on the active node? When the backups have been performed on the passive node, all log files associated with the respective storage group on the active node will be truncated. In addition, the database header on the active node will be modified, and this will generate a log file that will be replicated to the passive node and then modify the database header on the passive node afterward.

To read more about how you back up the databases in Exchange 2007, see Chapter 10.

Managing a Single Copy Cluster-Based Setup

In addition to the CCR type of setup, Exchange 2007 supports the Single Copy Clusters (SCC) type, which, as mentioned in the beginning of the chapter, is more or less identical to the traditional active/passive clusters we know from previous versions of Exchange. This means that a SCC-based cluster only provides service failover and still has a single point of failure when it comes to the databases, unless a shared storage solution that provides redundancy in other means is used in the environment. An SCC-based cluster using a fault-tolerant SAN is just as good as a CCR-based cluster in terms of data availability, but such a solution is much more expensive than a CCR solution.

An SCC is basically a clustered mailbox server that consists of two or more servers (known as *nodes*) that share the same storage (for databases and log files). The shared storage subsystem is typically a SAN. In Figure 8.77 you can see what the architecture behind a typical SCC scenario looks like.

Figure 8.77 A Basic Single Copy Cluster Scenario

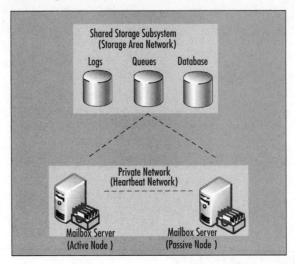

NOTE

We know we mentioned it in the beginning of this chapter, but because it's important that you understand this concept, we repeat: Exchange Server 2007 no longer supports active/active clusters. Only active/passive clusters are supported in Exchange 2007.

The primary benefit of an SCC is that it provides high availability of server resources because one node takes over should the active node be taken offline or fail for some reason. In addition, you can apply hotfixes, service packs, and the like to the nodes without having any downtime of your mission-critical mailbox servers. However, bear in mind that an SCC is susceptible to failure of the shared storage subsystem. This means that no matter how many nodes are part of your cluster, you'll always have a single point of failure when you're using SCC opposite a CCR-based cluster, which, as we demonstrated, provides storage group failover via the new log file shipping and replay functionality.

Since most of you don't have the necessary hardware for a cluster, before you actually decide to deploy one in your environment, we thought it would be a clever idea to show you how to install an SCC in a Virtual Server 2005 R2 environment. Pretty much all the steps in this section can be used to install the SCC on real hardware, too.

SOME INDEPENDENT ADVICE

Some of you might wonder whether standby blusters are supported in Exchange 2007, just as they were in Exchange 2003. A *standby cluster* is a Windows cluster that matches a production Exchange cluster in terms of hardware and software configuration, including Windows and Exchange versions and any updates or hotfixes that have been applied. In addition, a standby cluster has the Exchange program files installed but has not yet been configured with any Exchange Virtual Servers (EVS). Lastly, a standby cluster can only be used when all Exchange Virtual Servers on the production cluster are offline.

So, is a standby cluster supported in Exchange 2007? The answer is no, but then it's really not that useful anymore, since Exchange 2007 gives us the ability to recover an Exchange 2007 cluster using the new *Exsetup /RecoverCMS* switch (which is similar to the */DisasterRecovery* switch we know from previous versions of Exchange). Even better, the */RecoverCMS* switch can be used to recover both Exchange 2007 CCR and SCC-based cluster setups. We'll take a closer look at the */RecoverCMS* switch in Chapter 10.

Prerequisites

To follow the steps throughout this section, you need the following:

- One physical machine running Virtual Server 2005 R2. Since this product is free to download from the Microsoft Web site, getting it shouldn't be a problem. You can download Virtual Server 2005 R2 from the following link: www.microsoft.com/windowsserversystem/virtualserver/software/default.msp.

- A Windows 2003 Active Directory forest with at least one domain controller (raised to 2000 or 2003 forest functional level).

- At least one existing Exchange 2007 Hub Transport/Client Access server already installed in the aforementioned forest.

- Two virtual guests running Windows 2003 R2 or Windows 2003 SP1 Enterprise Edition with at least 512MB RAM and two virtual NICs each—one for the Public network and one for the Private network (the heartbeat network). This means that you need to create an additional virtual network on the virtual host server; None (Guest Only) is sufficient for this network.

NOTE

To install a Exchange 2007 Single Copy Cluster, you also need to install the cluster hotfix mentioned in MS KB article 898790, which at the time of this writing can be requested by contacting Microsoft Product Support Services. Microsoft is working on making it public.

Configuring the Network Settings for each Network Interface

In this example, we'll create an SCC consisting of two active/passive clusters that will be part of the same Exchange organization as the CCR-based cluster we discussed previously in this chapter. This means that you will need to install two NICs in each node (which we recommend you call *public* and *private* so that you can see what belongs to which network) and then configure the private and public interfaces for each of the two nodes identically to the network interfaces we configured on the two nodes in the CCR-based cluster setup. The only difference would be the IP addresses, since using the same ones would result in IP conflicts, but everything from the binding order, WINS, DNS, and so on should be the same for each interface. So instead of going through all the steps again, refer back to the "Configuring the Network Interfaces for Each Node" subsection of the "Managing a Cluster Continuous Replication-Based Cluster Setup" section of this chapter.

Creating the Shared Cluster Disks

As those of you with cluster experience are aware, a Windows cluster requires a quorum cluster disk. This quorum disk is used to store cluster configuration database checkpoints and log files that help manage the cluster as well as maintain consistency. Since we're dealing with a virtual environment, we need to create this disk in the Virtual Server 2005 R2 Web console. This is done by following these steps:

1.   Open the **Virtual Server Manager**, then click **Create | Fixed Size Virtual Hard Disk** under **Virtual Disks**, as shown in Figure 8.78.

Figure 8.78 Creating a Fixed-Size Virtual Hard Disk

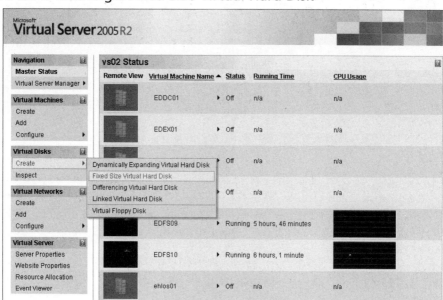

2. Place the virtual hard disk file (.VHD) in the folder containing your two virtual Windows 2003 Servers, then set the size to **500MB** (or less if you're low on disk space). Then click **Create** (see Figure 8.79).

Figure 8.79 Specifying the Virtual Hard Disk Filename and Size

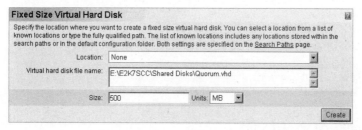

3. We now need to add the virtual quorum disk to each of the two virtual Windows 2003 Servers. Let's add it to EDFS09 first. We do this by clicking **Master Status | EDFS09 | Edit Configuration**. Since this disk needs to be shared between the nodes, we need to click **SCSI Adapters**, then **Add SCSI Adapter** (see Figure 8.80). Under the new SCSI adapter, check **Share SCSI Bus for Clustering**, then set the SCSI adapter ID to **6** (or whatever SCSI adapter ID is unused in your environment). Click **OK**.

Figure 8.80 Adding an Additional Shared SCSI Adapter

4. We now need to make the new disk visible on each node, so click **Hard disks |
   Add disk**, then select **SCSI 1 ID 0** in the **Attachment** drop-down menu.
   Finally, specify the path to the virtual Quorum disk, which in this example is
   E:\E2K7SCC\Shared Disks\Quorum.vhd, as shown in Figure 8.81. Click
   OK.

Figure 8.81 Adding a Virtual Hard Disk

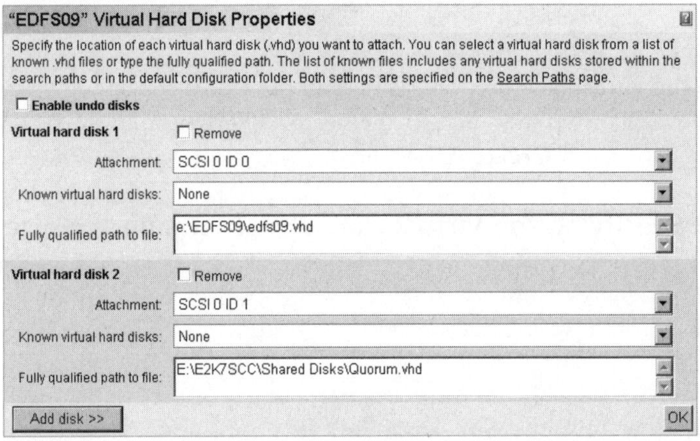

SOME INDEPENDENT ADVICE

If you're installing the SCC in a Virtual Server 2005 R2 environment like I do
in this example, you need to create a virtual SCSI adapter for each disks you
want to share between the nodes. Since you should place the databases and
log files on share disks as well, I recommend you create two additional virtual
fixed sized disks more, one called Logs.vhd and one called Databases.vhd.
When these have been created you need to add two additional virtual SCSI
adapters on each virtual guest, and since the two disks should be shared
between the nodes this should have Share SCSI bus for clustering enabled
and configured with SCSI adapter ID 6 like the adapter for the quorum disk

we already created. When you have done so, you will be able to add the two disks under Virtual Hard Disk Properties on each node respectively.

---

5. We now need to partition the Quorum disk in the Disk Management console on EDFS09, so start the virtual machine, log on using a domain admin account, click **Start | Run**, and type **Compmgmt.msc**. Under **Storage**, click **Disk Management** (see Figure 8.82). Click **Next** three times in the Initialize and Convert Disk Wizard that appears, then click **Finish**.

6. The detected disk now needs to be partitioned. To do so, right-click the unallocated space then select **New partition**.

7. Click **Next** three times and select the drive letter **Q** (for quorum), then click **Next** again. Use **NTFS** as the file system type and type **Quorum** in the Volume label field. To speed up the formatting process, it's a good idea to tick **Perform a quick format**.

Figure 8.82 Partitioning the Shared Disks and Assigning Drive Letters

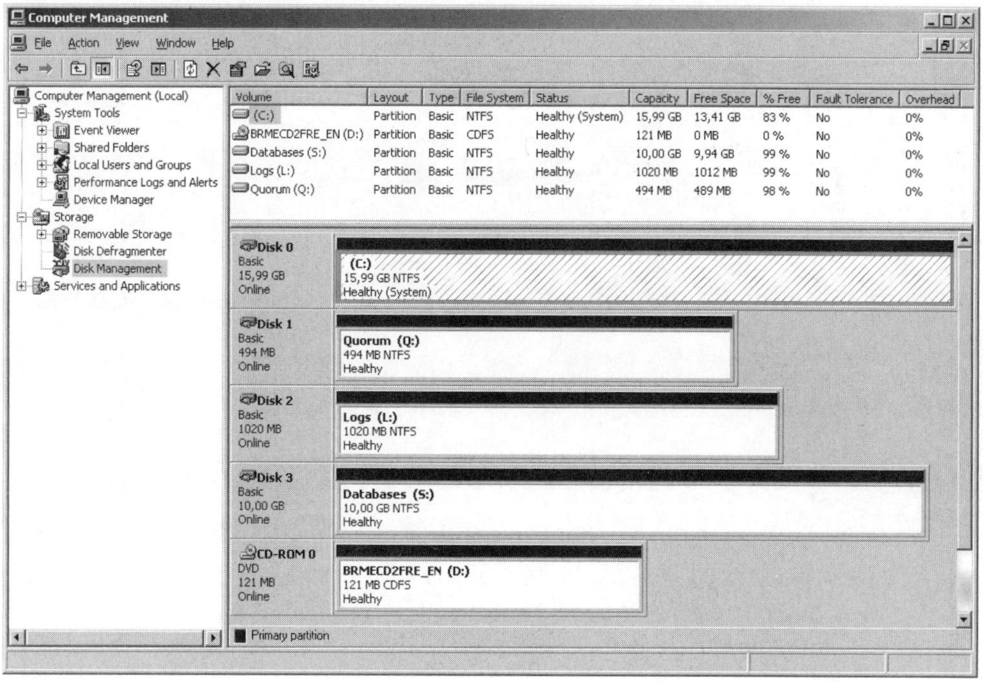

8. Now turn off EDFS09, then turn on EDFS10 and log on to the server with a domain admin account. Again, click **Start | Run** and type **Compmgmt.msc**.

Under **Storage**, click **Disk Management Mark the Quorum disk (disk 1) active** and assign it the drive letter **Q** (see Figure 8.83).

Figure 8.83 Allocating Drive Letters to the New Partitions on the Second Node

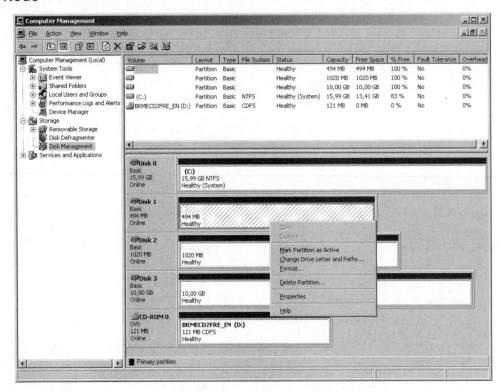

Now verify that you can access the Q: drive from Windows Explorer. Also try to create a test file on each server and make sure you can see it both ways.

Creating the Windows Server 2003 Cluster

We have reached the point where we can create the actual Windows 2003 cluster. To do so:

1. Turn off EDFS10, then log on to EDFS09 with a domain admin account. Now click **Start | Administrative Tools | Cluster Administrator**, then select **Create new cluster** in the drop-down box and click **OK**, then click **Next**.

2. If it's not already the case, specify the domain in which the two Windows 2003 Servers are members, then type the name of the cluster (in this case, **E2K7SCC**), then click **Next**.

3. If it's not already entered, type the name of the Windows 2003 Server, which will be the first node in the cluster (in this case, **EDFS09**), then click **Next**.

4. The Cluster Wizard will now determine the cluster configuration, and after a while you should get a check mark in each checked configuration step. We can now click **Next**.

5. Now enter an IP address that cluster management tools will use to connect to the cluster and click **Next**.

6. Enter the cluster service account and password, then click **Next**.

7. You now see a screen with the proposed cluster configuration. Click the **Quorum** button and make sure that the cluster configuration quorum is set to **Disk Q**, as shown in Figure 8.84. Then click **Next**.

Figure 8.84 Selecting the Resource Type Used for the Quorum Resource

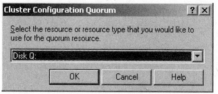

8. The cluster will now be created. Again, you need to wait for each step to complete, then click **Next | Finish**.

We have created the cluster itself, but since it consists of only one node, we'll need to add the other Windows server as well. To do so:

1. Turn on EDFS10 and log in with a domain admin account. Now click **Start | Administrative Tools | Cluster Administrator**. Select **Add nodes to cluster** in the drop-down menu, then specify the cluster name in the **Cluster or server name** box and click **OK**.

2. Click **Next** in the Add Nodes Wizard.

3. Type **EDFS10** (or whatever you named the second server), then click **Add** and click **Next**.

4. When the configuration has been analyzed, click **Next**.

5. Enter the password for the cluster service account (in this case, the administrator account), then click **Next**.

6. Verify that you want to add the node to the cluster with the configuration shown on the proposed cluster configuration page, then click **Next**.

7. After a short period, the node will be added to the cluster. If it's not, you might want to expand the respective task as well as view the log. If each task has com-

pleted successfully, click **Next | Finish** and verify that none of the nodes contains
an error icon in the Cluster Administrator (see Figure 8.85).

Figure 8.85 The Cluster Administrator Will Cluster Resources Listed and
Online

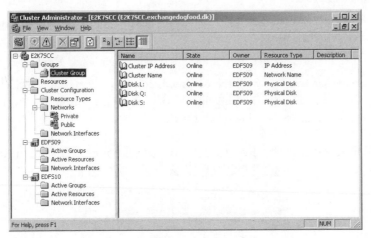

8. There's one last thing you want to do before moving on, and that is to right-click
    and select **Properties** for the Private network in the left pane. Since the sole pur-
    pose of the Private network is to be used for communication between the internal
    cluster nodes, you should select **Internal cluster communications only (pri-
    vate network)**, as shown in Figure 8.86, then click **OK**. Do the same for the
    Public network, but set it to **Client access only (public network)**.

Figure 8.86 Changing the Cluster Role for the Private Network

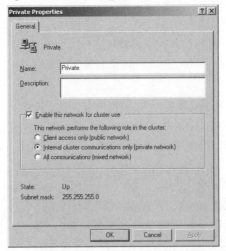

We now have a fully operational two-node active/passive Windows cluster up and running.

Installing the Necessary Windows Components

Before we move on and try to install the Exchange Server 2007 Beta 2 bits, we need to make sure that the required Windows components have been installed. All types of Exchange Server 2007 installations (no matter what server role we're talking about) need the Microsoft .NET Framework 2.0 component installed.

> **NOTE**
>
> If you have installed Windows Server 2003 Enterprise Edition with Service Pack 1 on the nodes, you need to download the Microsoft .NET Framework Version 2.0 Redistributable Package (x86), since it's only a standard Windows component for Windows Server 2003 R2.

Since we're installing the Mailbox Server role in the cluster, we also need to install the following IIS 6.0 components:

- Enable network COM+ access
- Internet Information Services
- World Wide Web Service

> **NOTE**
>
> Remember to install these components on both cluster nodes.

Installing Exchange Server 2007 on the Active Node

It's time to install the Exchange Server 2007 binaries on each node. Let's start with EDFS09. We'll do this using the GUI, so do the following:

1. Navigate to the network share or DVD media that contains the Exchange 207 binaries, and double-click **Setup.exe**.

2. On the Exchange 2007 Setup splash screen, click **Step 4: Install Microsoft Exchange**. Then click **Next**. Accept the **License Agreement** and then click **Next** once again. Decide whether you want to enable error reporting or not (it's a good idea to enable this functionality since the Exchange Product Group will receive any obscure errors you should experience in your cluster setup), then click **Next**.

3. Now select **Custom Exchange Server Installation**, then click **Next**.

4. Check **Active Clustered Mailbox Role** and click **Next**.

5. Now select **Single Copy Cluster**, then specify a name for the mailbox server (the name you want your Outlook clients to connect to) and a unique IP address on your public network. Finally, specify the path for the clustered mailbox server database files (the virtual shared database disk you created earlier), then click **Next** (see Figure 8.87).

Figure 8.87 Specifying the Name and IP Address of the Clustered Mailbox Server

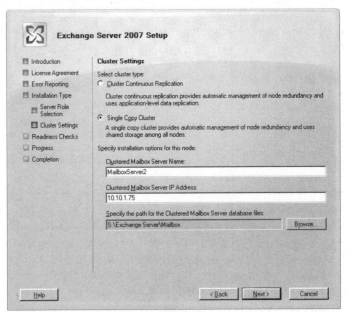

> **NOTE**
>
> To set the path for the clustered mailbox server database files, it's important that the cluster group containing the shared disks is owned by EDFS09. The reason for this is that you aren't allowed to use the shared disks if the cluster group is currently owned by EDFS10.

6. Let the readiness check complete, and if no issues are found, click **Next** to begin the installation.

7. The Exchange Server 2007 Installation Wizard will now copy the needed Exchange files, install and configure the Mailbox role, then create and configure the clustered mailbox server resources locally and create the object in Active Directory. When each step has been completed, clear the **Exit Setup and open Exchange System Manager** check box, then click **Finish**. We don't want to open the EMC just yet; we'll install Exchange on the second node first.

8. Log on to EDFS10 with a domain admin account and perform the same steps we did in installing Exchange Server 2007 on EDFS09. The only difference is that you should check **Passive Clustered Mailbox Role** instead of **Active Clustered Mailbox Role**.

When you have installed the Exchange Clustered Mailbox Role on the second node, we can move on to the next section, where we verify that the functionality of the clustered mailbox server works as expected.

Testing the Functionality of the Single Copy Cluster

It's time to verify that our Exchange 2007 clustered mailbox server is working as expected. Let's first open the Cluster Administrator and check whether the respective Exchange Resources have been created. If you take a look at Figure 8.88, it looks good; we have both nodes listed in the left pane and all Exchange resources have been created and are currently owned by EDFS09.

Figure 8.88 Listing All Exchange Cluster Resources in the Cluster Administrator

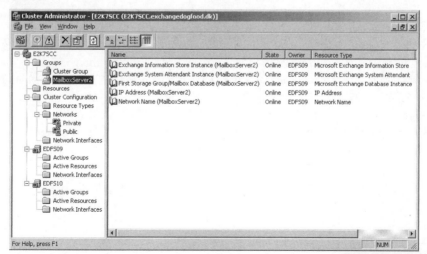

If you look closer at Figure 8.88, though, you can see that two cluster groups exist: one containing the cluster IP, name, and the shared disks, and one created by Exchange 2007 setup containing the Exchange Information Store, System Attendant, Storage Groups, and Database instances as well as the Exchange virtual server IP address and network name. WE recommend that you move all shared resources from the cluster group to the MailboxServer2 group (or whatever you called it); otherwise, you will have problems mounting the database when moving the clustered mailbox server from one node to the other (which we'll do in just a moment).

In addition, if you have assigned a shared disk specifically for the transaction log files, remember to change the path for these files. You can do so by selecting the respective storage group under **Server Configuration | Mailbox node** in the EMC, then click the **Move Storage Group** link in the Action pane. In the Move Storage Group Wizard, change the path for the log files to the **L:** drive or whatever drive you assigned them.

Now try to open the EMS by clicking **Start | All Programs | Microsoft Exchange Server 2007 | Exchange Management Shell** on one of the nodes, then type **Get-ClusteredMailboxServerStatus**. As you can see in Figure 8.89, the status of the clustered mailbox server is Online, and EDFS09 is currently the active node. This just keeps getting better and better, doesn't it?

Figure 8.89 Verifying That the Cluster Is Online

Now that we have verified that the clustered mailbox server is online, let's try to move the Exchange resources from node one to node two using the *Move-ClusteredMailboxServer* CMDlet. In the test environment we're using, we do so by issuing the command *Move-ClusteredMailboxServer -Identity:MailboxServer2 -TargetMachine:EDFS10 -MoveComment:"Testing the Move Clustered Mailbox functionality!"*.

You're then asked to confirm this action. Type **Yes**, then press **Enter** (see Figure 8.90). After a while the clustered mailbox resources will be moved to the second node.

Figure 8.90 Moving the Clustered Mailbox Resources to the Second Node

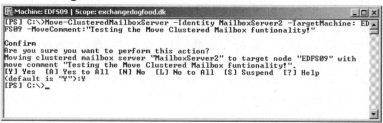

!WARNING

Although it's possible to move the cluster resource group between the nodes using the Cluster Administrator console, you should always do so (just as is the case with CCR-based clusters) using the *Move-ClusteredMailboxServer* CMDlet because the Move Group task in the Cluster Administrator console isn't Exchange 2007 aware.

Let's also take a look at the clustered mailbox server in the EMC. To do so, click **Start | All Programs | Microsoft Exchange Server 2007 | Exchange Management Console**, then drill down to **Server Configuration | Mailbox**. Notice that the clustered mailbox server we named MailboxServer is listed in the Results pane and that it's recognized as a cluster server (see Figure 8.91). Also notice that the Mailbox Database for this server points to the S: drive, exactly as we specified during the installation of the Active Clustered Mailbox role.

Figure 8.91 Viewing the Clustered Mailbox Server in the Exchange Management Console

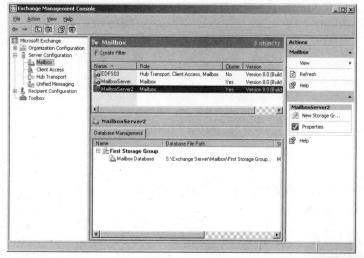

Summary

In this chapter we focused on the Mailbox server-related high-availability features included in Exchange Server 2007. First we took a look at how the Local Continuous Replication (LCR) feature works, and then we covered how it's implemented as well as managed. We then moved on to the new Cluster Continuous Replication (CCR) functionality, which makes it possible to deploy a mailbox server cluster, providing not only service availability but also database availability, which means that no single point of failure exists when using this type of cluster. We covered how to deploy a CCR-based cluster step by step as well as showed you how to manage it once deployed. Finally, we took a close look at the Single Copy Cluster (SCC) feature, which is similar to the traditional active/passive clusters we know from Exchange 2000 and 2003. We showed you the steps involved in deploying this type of cluster in a virtual server environment so that you can decide whether this is the type of cluster you want to use in your production environment.

Solutions Fast Track

Managing the Local Continuous Replication Feature

☑ The Exchange Product Group developed the Local Continuous Replication (LCR) technology to provide a native data availability solution that can be used to recover an Exchange database on an Exchange 2007 standalone server in a matter of a few minutes.

☑ Since LCR keeps an exact replica of the active copy of the storage group, the number of Exchange backups needed is also reduced drastically. But it's important to understand that LCR in no way eliminates traditional backups of the databases on your Exchange 2007 Mailbox servers; instead, it provides you with the option of taking weekly instead of daily backups, for example.

☑ As you can understand, LCR is an ideal solution for small or medium-sized organizations because the functionality allows rapid recovery from database issues and only requires an extra set of disks for the databases copies. LCR increases the availability of databases on an Exchange 2007 standalone server in an affordable way. For small shops that don't have a big fancy server with multiple sets of disks, it is possible to keep the LCR copy on an external USB disk.

☑ When disaster strikes and the database or log files in the active copy of the storage group become corrupted and shut down, you have the option of recovering database availability by switching to the LCR copy (the passive copy of the storage group).

☑ It's a recommended best practice to periodically verify the integrity of the passive storage group copy to make sure that neither the database copy nor any of the log files are corrupted. This is done by running a physical consistency check against both the database copy as well as the log files using Exchange Server Database Utilities (Eseutil.exe).

☑ When the Exchange 2007 Mailbox Server role is installed, setup adds two LCR-related performance objects to the Windows 2003 Performance Monitor.

Managing a Cluster Continuous Replication-Based Setup

☑ Exchange Server 2007 introduces a new high-availability feature called Cluster Continuous Replication (CCR). This feature combines the new Exchange Server 2007 log file shipping and replay mechanisms (known as continuous replication) with the features that are available in a more traditional two-node Windows 2003 server active/passive cluster setup.

☑ With CCR, the transaction logs generated on the active node are replicated to the information store on the passive node using log file shipping. These replicated log files are then posted into the database(s) on the passive node using the log file replay technology. This means that should the active node or a database on this node fail or for some other reason go offline, an automatic failover to the passive node will occur.

☑ A Majority Node Set (MNS) quorum with File Share Witness is a completely new type of quorum model that is made available by installing the update (MS KB article 921181) mentioned in this chapter. The update makes it possible to use a file share witness that is external to the cluster as an additional "vote" to determine the status of the cluster in a two-node MNS quorum cluster deployment, which is a requirement to use the CCR functionality in Exchange Server 2007.

☑ The Transport Dumpster is a new feature of the Exchange 2007 Hub Transport server that can submit recently delivered mail after an unscheduled outage. For an e-mail message to be able to be retained in the Transport Dumpster, at least one of the message recipients must have his or her mailbox located on a CCR-based mailbox cluster server, because the Transport Dumpster works only with mailboxes located on a CCR-based mailbox server cluster.

☑ Moving the Exchange resources from node one to node two should be done using the *Move-ClusteredMailboxServer* CMDlet. In the environment used in this chapter, we did so by issuing the cmdlet *Move-ClusteredMailboxServer -Identity:MailboxServer -TargetMachine:EDFS08 -MoveComment:"Verifying the Move Clustered Mailbox Server Functionality!"*.

☑ When we deployed a cluster with Exchange 2003, the only option available when the stores were going to be backed up was to take a backup of the stores running on the production servers. With CCR (and LCR), you have the option of taking a backup of the database copies on the passive node, thereby eliminating any heavy load on the active node related to both I/O to the disk spindles as well as CPU usage.

Managing a Single Copy Cluster-Based Setup

☑ Exchange 2007 supports the Single Copy Clusters (SCC) type, which is more or less identical to the traditional active/passive clusters we know from previous versions of Exchange. This means that a SCC-based cluster only provides service failover and still has a single point of failure when it comes to the databases, unless a shared storage solution that provides redundancy via other means is used in the environment. An SCC-based cluster using a fault-tolerant SAN is just as good as a CCR-based cluster in terms of data availability, but such a solution is much more expensive than a CCR solution.

☑ Exchange Server 2007 doesn't support active/active clusters anymore; only active/passive clusters are supported in Exchange 2007.

☑ Although it's possible to move the cluster resource group between the nodes using the Cluster Administrator console, you should always do so (as is the case with CCR-based clusters) using the *Move-ClusteredMailboxServer* CMDlet because the Move Group task in the Cluster Administrator console isn't Exchange 2007 aware.

Frequently Asked Questions

The following Frequently Asked Questions, answered by the authors of this book, are designed to both measure your understanding of the concepts presented in this chapter and to assist you with real-life implementation of these concepts. To have your questions about this chapter answered by the author, browse to **www.syngress.com/solutions** and click on the **"Ask the Author"** form.

Q: Why would I want to deploy CCR instead of SCC?

A: Deploying CCR instead of SCC has several advantages. First, you no longer have a single point of failure regarding databases. Second, unlike SCC, CCR doesn't require a shared storage subsystem such as a SAN, because the nodes in a CCR don't share the same disks. Third, you have the option of spanning the CCR between two locations (although they must be on the same subnet, which means the subnet has to be stretched).

Q: You mentioned that it was possible to back up the passive copy of the databases in a CCR using a backup application with VSS support for Exchange databases. Is this also possible when we use LCR on a single Exchange 2007 box?

A: Yes, this is also supported on a single box with LCR enabled for one or more storage groups.

Q: How should I proceed when implementing storage design for a CCR-based setup?

A: To achieve storage resiliency, it is recommended that the passive copy be placed on a storage array that is completely isolated from the active copy's storage array. Isolating the arrays from one another also provides the flexibility to use a variety of storage solutions. If the storage solutions used by the active copy and the passive copy are isolated from each other, your storage solutions don't even need to be the same type or brand.

Q: Should I use an identical set of disks for the database copies in a CCR or LCR setup?

A: It's a best practice to size the active and passive storage solutions equivalently. The storage solution used by the passive copy should be sized in terms of both performance and capacity to handle the production load in the event of a failure.

Q: How many databases can I have in each storage group when I'm using either LCR or CCR?

A: You can only have one database in each storage group when you use either LCR or CCR. In addition, you cannot have more than one Public Folder database in the organization if you want to replicate a Public Folder database using continuous replication technology.

Q: Why would I want to use continuous replication technology in my Exchange environment?

A: Continuous replication provides service availability and service continuity for an Exchange 2007 mailbox server, without the cost and complexity of a shared storage cluster.

Chapter 9

Disaster Recovery with Exchange Server 2007

Solutions in this chapter:

- Backing Up Exchange 2007 Using Windows 2003 Backup

- Restoring Exchange 2007 Storage Groups and Databases Using Windows 2003 Backup

- Repairing a Corrupt or Damaged Exchange 2007 Database Using Eseutil

- Restoring Mailbox Data Using the Recovery Storage Group Feature

- Recovering an Exchange 2007 Server Using the RecoverServer Switch

- Recovering an Exchange 2007 Cluster Using the RecoverCMS Switch

- Restoring Mailbox Databases Using the Improved Database Portability Feature

Introduction

As mentioned in the previous chapter, the messaging and collaboration servers are mission critical, being perhaps the most vital servers in our datacenters today. It's therefore of the utmost importance that these servers be up and running all the time. Most service level agreements today require more than 99.99 percent uptime when it comes to the messaging and collaboration servers in the organization. In the previous chapter we showed you some of the options available to provide high availability of the Exchange 2007 mailbox Servers. But even if you have HA solutions such as CCR-based mailbox servers available, a disaster can still strike in your environment, and if this happens, you better be prepared since downtime typically means lost productivity and revenue. In this chapter, we'll go through the steps necessary to back up the different Exchange 2007 Server roles in your organization, and, just as important, look at how you restore Exchange 2007 servers and data should it be required.

Backing Up Exchange 2007 Using Windows 2003 Backup

Frequent backups of the Exchange 2007 servers in an organization are important operational tasks that, though a bit trivial, should be taken very seriously. We can only imagine one thing worse than a complete failure of an Exchange 2007 server, and that's a complete failure of an Exchange 2007 server without any backups to restore from. In the first section of this chapter, we'll take a look at what you must back up, depending on which Exchange 2007 Server roles were deployed in your organization.

Backing Up an Exchange 2007 Mailbox Server

One of the most important things to back up regarding Exchange 2007 Mailbox Servers are the databases, which hold user mailboxes and public data. As you saw in the previous chapter, Exchange 2007 provides a new continuous replication functionality that keeps a second copy of one or more databases in a storage group in sync with the active versions of the databases using log file shipping and replay. This provides an extra level of protection for Mailbox and Public Folder databases. However, although the new functionality allows you to make less frequent backups of your databases, it doesn't eliminate the *need* for database backups. In this section, we'll show you how to perform a backup of the databases on an Exchange 2007 server.

SOME INDEPENDENT ADVICE

Another reason why it's crucial to conduct frequent full backups of your Exchange databases with an Exchange-aware backup application is to commit and delete any transaction log files generated since the last full backup. If these log files aren't committed, they will take up more and more space on your disks, and when there's no more disk space for the log files, the database will be dismounted.

Since Exchange 2007 databases still use ESE, you can (just as with previous versions of Exchange), back them up using the Exchange-aware native Windows 2003 backup tool. Exchange 2007 supports two different backup methods. The first is a legacy streaming backup method based on the ESE application programming interface (API), which allows you to back up one or more storage groups at the same time. However, only one backup job can run against a specific storage group. Most of us are familiar with this type of backup since it's the one we have used for ages when referring to Exchange databases. The ESE API backup method is supported by the Windows 2003 backup tool, as well as most third-party backup products.

Then we have the Volume Shadow Copy Service (VSS) backup method, which some of you may know from Exchange 2003 where it was first introduced. The interesting thing about VSS is that this method, in addition to what the legacy streaming backup method offers, can also make an online backup of the copy database when using either Local Continuous Replication or Cluster Continuous Replication in your setup. This means you can schedule the backup windows anytime you want since taking a backup of the database copy has no performance-related impact on the active database. Unfortunately, this method isn't supported by the Windows 2003 backup tool when speaking Exchange databases (only file level backups), and Microsoft doesn't offer any products capable of using VSS, at least not at the time of this writing.

NOTE

The Data Protection Manager (DPM) v2 product will support VSS backups, however. DPM is a server software application that enables disk- and tape-based data protection and recovery for file servers, servers running Microsoft Exchange, and servers running Microsoft SQL Server in an Active Directory Domain Services (AD DS) domain. DPM performs replication, synchronization, and recovery point creation to provide reliable protection and rapid recovery of data for both system administrators and end users.

Let's go through the steps necessary to back up an Exchange 2007 Mailbox and Public Folder database on an Exchange 2007 Mailbox Server. The first thing you need to do is launch the Windows 2003 backup tool, which can be done by clicking **Start** | **Run** and typing **NTBackup**. Now click **Switch to Advanced Mode** and then click the **Backup** tab shown in Figure 9.1.

Figure 9.1 Windows 2003 Backup Tool

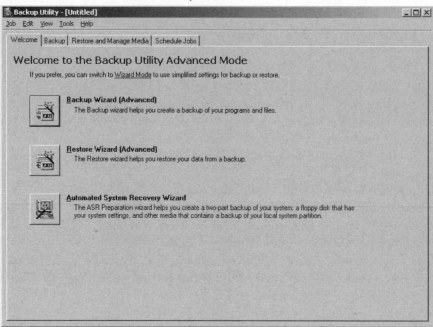

Under the **Backup** tab expand **Microsoft Exchange Server** | **Mailbox Server** | **Microsoft Information Store** and check the storage group(s) containing the **Mailbox** and **Public Folder** database (Figure 9.2). Now specify the backup media or filename you want to perform the backup to, and then click **Start Backup**.

As you can see in Figure 9.3, you now have the option of entering a description for the respective backup job, as well as specify whether the backed-up data should be appended to an existing backup. In addition, you can create a scheduled backup job so it runs, let's say, every day at midnight. By clicking the **Advanced** button, you also have the option of having the backed-up data verified when the job completes.

Figure 9.2 Selecting the Storage Groups to Be Backed Up

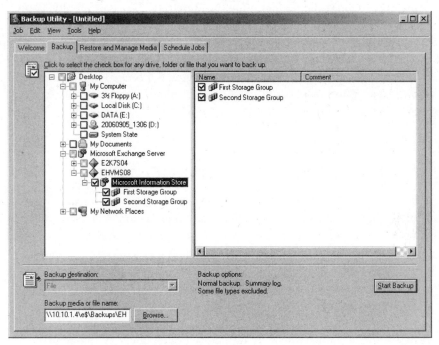

Figure 9.3 Backup Job Information

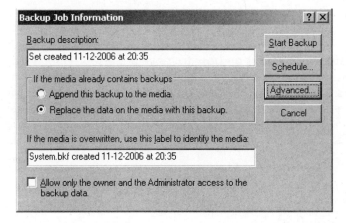

Typically, you should set up an automated backup job schedule, but for the purpose of this example we'll just choose to back up the databases once. When ready, click **Start Backup**.

When the backup job has completed, you can view a report, which will contain any warnings or errors that might occur during the backup.

That's how you back up the Mailbox and Public Folder databases, as well as commit and delete any existing transaction log files using the Windows 2003 Backup tool. Sounds simple, right?

Some of you might wonder whether there isn't anything else you need to back up on an Exchange 2007 Mailbox Server? The answer is no critical files at least since you can always recover an Exchange 2007 Mailbox Server using the *Setup /Mode:RecoverServer* command (shown later in the chapter), but it's always a good idea to back up the System State of the respective server as well.

Backing Up an Exchange 2007 Hub Transport Server

Since an Exchange 2007 Server with the Hub Transport Server role installed was designed to store all configuration data in the Active Directory configuration container, not much needs to be backed up on a server with this role installed either. But just as with the Mailbox server role, you should back up the System State.

Some of you may be wondering why I haven't mentioned anything about backing up the message queues stored in an ESE database on an Exchange 2007 Hub Transport Server… Well, there shouldn't be any need to do so since you can mount the message queues on another existing, or newly installed, Hub Transport server if required. You just need to retrieve the mail.que (which, by default, is located under C:\Program Files\Microsoft\Exchange Server\TransportRoles\data\Queue) from the failed Hub Transport server.

> **NOTE**
>
> Step-by-step instructions on how to move a message queue from a failed Hub Transport server to another Hub Transport server in the organization is outside the scope of this book, but you can find information on the topic by searching under "Working with the Queue Database on Transport Servers" in the Exchange 2007 Documentation Help file.

One thing you might want to back up regarding an Exchange 2007 Hub Transport Server is the Message Tracking and Protocol logs which, by default, are located under C:\Program Files\Microsoft\Exchange Server\TransportRoles\Logs. These files can be backed up using a file level backup.

As is the case with a Mailbox Server, you can recover a Hub Transport server using the *Setup /Mode:RecoverServer* command.

Backing Up an Exchange 2007 Client Access Server

When using Exchange 2007 Server with the Client Access Server role installed, there are several files you should back up. The first, and perhaps most important, to back up is the IIS Metabase, which among other things is used to store OWA Virtual Directory configuration data. You can back up the IIS configuration on a CAS using the following command:

get-owavirtualdirectory "owa (default web site)" | export-clixml owa.xml – depth 1

In order to restore the IIS configuration from the owa.xml file, you need to use a Windows PowerShell script similar to the following (save it as Restore-OWA.PS1 or use some other meaningful name):

```
$ErrorActionPreference = 'stop'
$savedprops = @(
'DirectFileAccessOnPublicComputersEnabled',
'DirectFileAccessOnPrivateComputersEnabled',
'WebReadyDocumentViewingOnPublicComputersEnabled',
'WebReadyDocumentViewingOnPrivateComputersEnabled',
'ForceWebReadyDocumentViewingFirstOnPublicComputers',
'ForceWebReadyDocumentViewingFirstOnPrivateComputers',
'RemoteDocumentsActionForUnknownServers',
'ActionForUnknownFileAndMIMETypes',
'WebReadyFileTypes',
'WebReadyMimeTypes',
'WebReadyDocumentViewingForAllSupportedTypes',
'AllowedFileTypes',
'AllowedMimeTypes',
'ForceSaveFileTypes',
'ForceSaveMimeTypes',
'BlockedFileTypes',
'BlockedMimeTypes',
'RemoteDocumentsAllowedServers',
'RemoteDocumentsBlockedServers',
'RemoteDocumentsInternalDomainSuffixList',
'LogonFormat',
'ClientAuthCleanupLevel',
'DefaultDomain',
'FormsAuthentication',
'BasicAuthentication',
'DigestAuthentication',
```

```
'WindowsAuthentication',
'GzipLevel',
'FilterWebBeaconsAndHtmlForms',
'NotificationInterval',
'DefaultTheme',
'UserContextTimeout',
'ExchwebProxyDestination',
'VirtualDirectoryType',
'RedirectToOptimalOWAServer',
'DefaultClientLanguage',
'LogonAndErrorLanguage',
'UseGB18030',
'UseISO885915',
'OutboundCharset',
'CalendarEnabled',
'ContactsEnabled',
'TasksEnabled',
'JournalEnabled',
'NotesEnabled',
'RemindersAndNotificationsEnabled',
'PremiumClientEnabled',
'SpellCheckerEnabled',
'SearchFoldersEnabled',
'SignaturesEnabled',
'ThemeSelectionEnabled',
'JunkEmailEnabled',
'UMIntegrationEnabled',
'WSSAccessOnPublicComputersEnabled',
'WSSAccessOnPrivateComputersEnabled',
'ChangePasswordEnabled',
'UNCAccessOnPublicComputersEnabled',
'UNCAccessOnPrivateComputersEnabled',
'ActiveSyncIntegrationEnabled',
'AllAddressListsEnabled',
'InternalUrl',
'ExternalUrl'
)

$vdir = import-clixml $args[0]

'Recreating "' + $vdir.name + '"' + ' owa version: ' + $vdir.owaversion
if ($vdir.owaversion -eq 'Exchange2007') {
```

```
new-owavirtualdirectory -website $vdir.website -internalurl
$vdir.internalurl -externalurl $vdir.externalurl
}
else {
new-owavirtualdirectory -website $vdir.website -owaversion $vdir.
owaversion -name $vdir.displayname -virtualdirectorytype $vdir.
virtualdirectorytype
}
$new = get-owavirtualdirectory $vdir.name
'Restoring properties'
foreach ($prop in $savedprops) {
if ($prop -eq 'ExchwebProxyDestination' -or $prop -eq
'VirtualDirectoryType') {
continue
}
$new.$prop = $vdir.$prop
}
$new | set-owavirtualdirectory
```

To restore the IIS configuration data that were saved in the owa.xml file, type **Restore-OWA.PS1 owa.xml**.

In addition to the IIS metabase, you should back up the System State and the files listed in Table 9.1.

Table 9.1 Files Needed to Restore the IIS Configuration

Data	Location
Microsoft Office Outlook Web Access Web site, and Web.config file	C:\ProgramFiles\ Microsoft\Exchange Server\ ClientAccess\Owa
IMAP4 and POP3 protocol settings	C:\Program Files\Microsoft\ Exchange Server\ClientAccess\
Availability service	Active Directory configuration container and file system, including the Web.config file C:\Program Files\Microsoft\ Exchange Server\ClientAccess\ exchweb\ews
Autodiscover	IIS metabase

Continued

Table 9.1 continued Files Needed to Restore the IIS Configuration

Data	Location
Exchange ActiveSync	Active Directory configuration container File system, including the Web.config file in the \ClientAccess\Sync folder IIS metabase
Outlook Web Access virtual directories	Active Directory configuration container and file system C:\Program Files\Microsoft\ Exchange Server\ClientAccess\
Web services configuration	IIS metabase

Like a Mailbox or Hub Transport Server, a Client Access Server can be restored using the *Setup /Mode:RecoverServer* command.

Backing Up an Exchange 2007 Unified Messaging Server

Exchange 2007 servers with the Unified Messaging (UM) role installed store most of the configuration data in the Active Directory, which means it's very limited what you need to back up on the UM server itself.

Table 9.2 lists the files you need to back up.

Table 9.2 Files to Back Up on Unified Messaging Server

Data	Location
Custom audio prompts: Custom audio files (.wav) for UM Dial Plans and UM Auto Attendants Custom audio files (.wav) for telephone user interface (TUI) or Voice Access	C:\Program Files\Microsoft\ Exchange Server\UnifiedMessaging\ Prompts
Incoming calls: .eml and .wma files for each voicemail	C:\Program Files\Microsoft\ Exchange Server \ UnifiedMessaging\temp

In addition, you should back up the System State.

The rest of the configuration data is, as mentioned previously, stored in Active Directory, which makes it possible to restore using the *Setup /Mode:RecoverServer* command.

Backing Up an Exchange 2007 Edge Transport Server

An Exchange 2007 Server with the Edge Transport Server role installed can be restored by using a Cloned Configuration (employing the ImportEdgeConfig.ps1 script). For step-by-step instructions on how you deal with clone configuration, see Chapter 7. In addition to cloned configuration, you should back up System State as well as the Message Tracking and protocol logs, which are located in C:\Program Files\Microsoft\Exchange Server\ TransportRoles\Logs. The message queues that are stored in an ESE database just like message queues on a Hub Transport server can be mounted on another Edge Transport server.

Restoring Exchange 2007 Storage Groups and Databases Using Windows 2003 Backup

So now that you have seen how to back up Mailbox and Public Folder databases, you should of course also be aware of how you restore these databases properly should you experience a database corruption or find them unusable in some other way. In this section, I'll show you how to perform a restore of a Mailbox database from the backup set we created earlier in this chapter. When you restore a Mailbox or Public Folder database from a backup set, any associated transaction log files are restored as well. It's important you understand that a restore of a Mailbox database will copy the database file (.EDB) into its original location on the disk, and thereby overwrite any existing .EDB file. In addition, any transaction log files will be copied to a temporary location, which can be specified when doing the actual restore. Upon the restore's completion (hopefully without any serious warnings or errors!), the log files will be replayed into the restored version of the database. In addition to the log files, a file called Restore.env will also be copied to the specified temporary folder. This file keeps control of which storage group the log files belong to, as well as the database paths and range of log files that have been restored.

In order to restore the aforementioned Mailbox database, we need to perform the following steps. First, open the **Exchange Management Console**, expand **Server Configuration**, and then select the **Mailbox** subnode. Now choose the respective Mailbox server in the **Result** pane, and then dismount the Mailbox database, as shown in Figure 9.4.

Figure 9.4 Dismounting the Mailbox Database

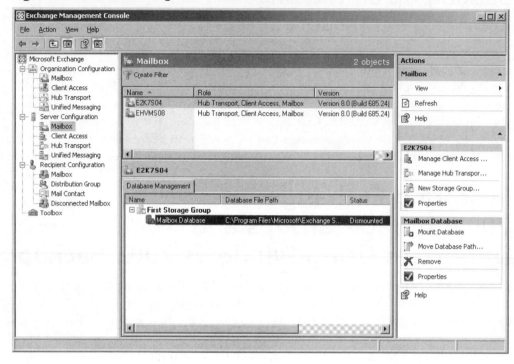

Now open the properties page for the Mailbox database. Check **This database can be overwritten by a restore** (Figure 9.5) and click **OK**.

Figure 9.5 Allowing the Mailbox Database to Be Overwritten by a Restore

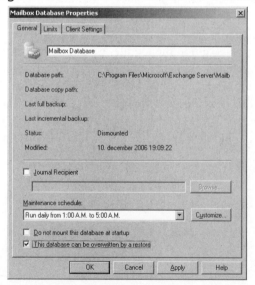

We're now ready to restore the databases using the Windows 2003 Backup tool, so let's launch this tool by clicking **Start | Run** and typing **NTBackup**, and then selecting the **Restore and Manage Media** tab. Expand the desired media item and backup set, then check the **log files** and **mailbox database**, as shown in Figure 9.6. We can then click **Start Restore**.

Figure 9.6 Restoring the First Storage Group

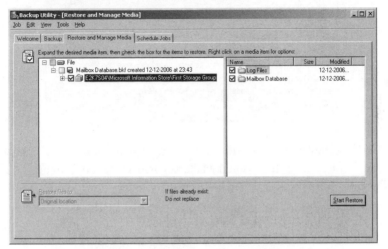

You'll be faced with a screen similar to the one shown in Figure 9.7. Here, you need to specify the server you want to restore the database to (the local server on which the Windows 2003 Backup tool is run is typically pre-entered here), and the temporary location for log and patch files. In addition, you need to specify whether the restore you're performing is the last restore set. If you select this option, all the restored log files will be replayed automatically into the database after the restore has completed. You typically want to do this if you don't have any incremental or differential backups of the database's log files you need to restore after this restore. Finally, you have the option of specifying that the database should be mounted automatically after the restore has occurred. When you have made your selections, click **OK**.

The restore will now begin. Depending on the size of the database, it will take some time to complete. Since the database in this example is under 11MB, the restore took less than a second, as you can see in Figure 9.8. When the restore has completed, you can click the **Report** button to see a detailed log of the restore process. When ready, click **Close**.

Figure 9.7 Restoring Database Store Options

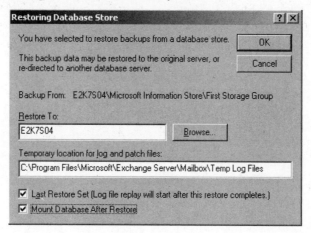

If your restore completed successfully, you can now switch back to the Exchange Management Console, where the restored Mailbox database should have been mounted automatically, and we can call the restore a success.

Figure 9.8 Restore Completed Successfully

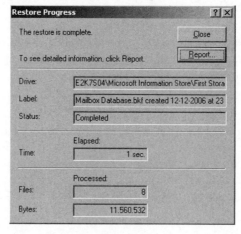

NOTE

It's beyond the scope of this book to show the steps necessary to restore a database to its last good known state using a combination of a full backup set and incremental or differential backups.

Repairing a Corrupt or Damaged Exchange 2007 Database Using Eseutil

There may be situations where you either don't have a proper backup set to restore a particular database from, or perhaps you found out that the database you just restored to replace a corrupt or damaged database is also corrupt or damaged. This is where Extensible Storage Engine Utilities for Microsoft Exchange Server (Eseutil) comes in. Eseutil is a command-line utility that can be used to perform a range of database tasks including repair, offline defragmentation, and integrity checks. Eseutil hasn't changed much from Exchange 2003 since Exchange still uses ESE databases when speaking Exchange 2007. This means that pretty much all of the switches and parameters available in Eseutil are the same as in previous versions. Since there are plenty of books and online documentation describing how you should approach fixing a corrupt database using Eseutil, I won't include comprehensive information on how to use this utility in this book. Instead, I'll provide you with the most common Eseutil switches, as well as a few examples.

Eseutil, as in previous versions, is located in the Bin folder under your Exchange installation path, which in Exchange 2007, by default, is C:\Program Files\Microsoft\Exchange Server. However, you no longer need to run the tool from that path; you can just open a Command Prompt window and type **Eseutil**, as shown in Figure 9.9.

Figure 9.9 Eseutil Modes

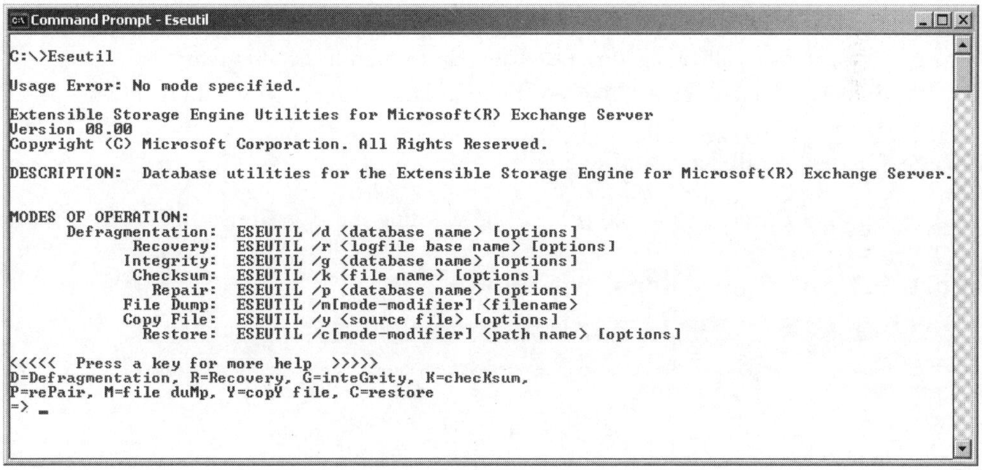

```
C:\>Eseutil

Usage Error: No mode specified.

Extensible Storage Engine Utilities for Microsoft(R) Exchange Server
Version 08.00
Copyright (C) Microsoft Corporation. All Rights Reserved.

DESCRIPTION:   Database utilities for the Extensible Storage Engine for Microsoft(R) Exchange Server.

MODES OF OPERATION:
     Defragmentation:   ESEUTIL /d <database name> [options]
           Recovery:   ESEUTIL /r <logfile base name> [options]
          Integrity:   ESEUTIL /g <database name> [options]
           Checksum:   ESEUTIL /k <file name> [options]
             Repair:   ESEUTIL /p <database name> [options]
          File Dump:   ESEUTIL /m[mode-modifier] <filename>
          Copy File:   ESEUTIL /y <source file> [options]
            Restore:   ESEUTIL /c[mode-modifier] <path name> [options]

<<<<<  Press a key for more help  >>>>>
D=Defragmentation, R=Recovery, G=inteGrity, K=checKsum,
P=rePair, M=file duMp, Y=copY file, C=restore
=> _
```

NOTE

You can also run Eseutil directly from the Exchange Management Shell.

Before we move on, we want to stress that it's very important you always try to restore your databases from a backup if possible, since there's a good chance you will lose some data when performing a repair of a database. The reason for this is that Eseutil often needs to discard rows from tables or even entire tables. In addition, you should have a repaired database running in your production environment only for a temporary period, which means that after you have repaired a database, you should move all mailboxes from the database to a new one. Needless to say, you should also be sure to make a copy of the database before performing a repair using Eseutil.

NOTE

Did you know that when a database corruption occurs, 99.9 percent of the time it's caused by the underlying hard disk drive subsystem? Yes, it's true! This means there's a pretty good chance the database corruption experienced is caused by an I/O issue on the disk set in your Exchange 2007 server. You should therefore always examine the Application and System logs, searching for any events that might indicate this to be the problem.

Eseutil /P can, in addition to the Mailbox and Public Folder databases, also be run against the ESE database-based message queues on either a Hub Transport or Edge Transport server in your Exchange 2007 organization.

To repair a corrupted or otherwise damaged database, run Eseutil with the /P switch. So, to repair a database called Mailbox Database.edb located in E:\Program Files\Microsoft\Exchange Server\Mailbox\First Storage Group, you would need to type:

Eseutil /P "E:\Program Files\Microsoft\Exchange Server\Mailbox\First Storage Group\Mailbox Database.edb"

After pressing **Enter**, you would receive the warning message shown in Figure 9.10.

Figure 9.10 An Eseutil Repair Warning

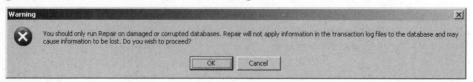

NOTE

You must have the necessary amount of free space (equal to 110 percent of the database file size) on the disk containing the database before you can run Eseutil /P and Eseutil /D.

Click **OK** to proceed, and then wait until Eseutil has repaired the database. If the database is completed successfully, it's highly recommended you perform a full backup of the database, since restoring a backup made before the repair would roll the database back to the state it was in at the time of the backup, which wouldn't be very smart.

After you have run Eseutil /P against a database, also run Eseutil /D in order to fully rebuild indexes and defragment the database. In order to run Eseutil /D against the database, type:

Eseutil /D "E:\Program Files\Microsoft\Exchange Server\Mailbox\First Storage Group\Mailbox Database.edb"

When an offline defragmentation has been completed, there's one additional thing to do: repair the database at the application level (repair information and relationships between mailboxes, folders, items, and attachments) by running the Information Store Integrity Checker (Isinteg) utility with the *-fix* parameter. Figure 9.11 shows the parameters and syntaxes available for the Isinteg utility.

Figure 9.11 Isinteg Switches

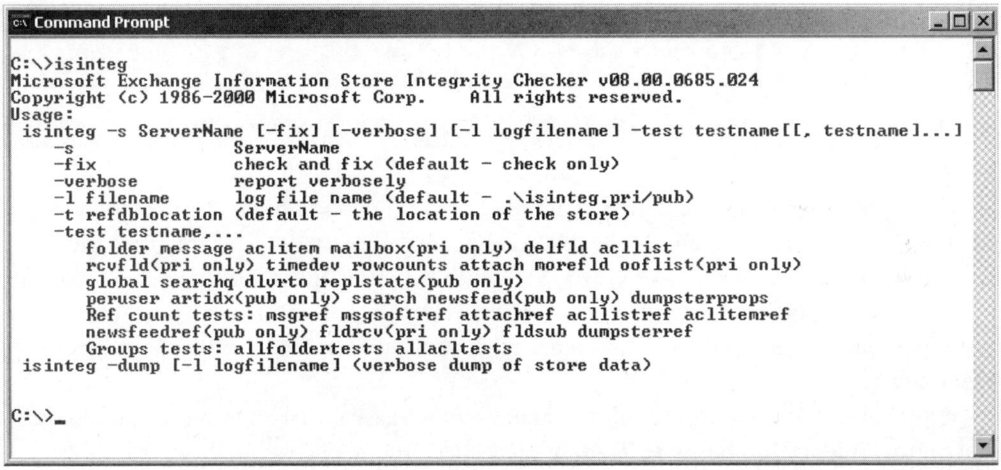

```
C:\>isinteg
Microsoft Exchange Information Store Integrity Checker v08.00.0685.024
Copyright (c) 1986-2000 Microsoft Corp.    All rights reserved.
Usage:
 isinteg -s ServerName [-fix] [-verbose] [-l logfilename] -test testname[[, testname]...]
    -s              ServerName
    -fix            check and fix (default - check only)
    -verbose        report verbosely
    -l filename     log file name (default - .\isinteg.pri/pub)
    -t refdblocation (default - the location of the store)
    -test testname,...
        folder message aclitem mailbox(pri only) delfld acllist
        rcvfld(pri only) timedev rowcounts attach morefld ooflist(pri only)
        global searchq dlvrto replstate(pub only)
        peruser artidx(pub only) search newsfeed(pub only) dumpsterprops
        Ref count tests: msgref msgsoftref attachref acllistref aclitemref
        newsfeedref(pub only) fldrcv(pub only) fldsub dumpsterref
        Groups tests: allfoldertests allacltests
 isinteg -dump [-l logfilename] (verbose dump of store data)

C:\>_
```

If you aren't comfortable running the Eseutil and Isinteg utilities manually on your databases, you also have the option of performing a repair using a wizard-driven interface. This is where the new Disaster Recovery Management tool, a sibling of tools such as the Exchange Best Practices Analyzer Tool (ExBPA), comes into play. To invoke this tool, click the **Toolbox** work center node in the navigation tree in the **Exchange Management Console**, then open the tool by selecting it in the Result pane and clicking **Open Tool** in the **Actions** pane (Figure 9.12).

Figure 9.12 Disaster Recovery Management Tool

The tool will now check if there is any tool or configuration file updates available on Microsoft.com, and if so, apply them without requiring a restart. Once any updates have been applied, click the **Go to Welcome Screen** link, then enter an identifying label for the activity, and click **Next**. When the tool has connected to the Active Directory, you will be presented with the task list shown in Figure 9.13. Here, you should select the **Repair Database** task.

Now select the storage group that contains the database you wish to repair, click **Next**, and on the **Select Databases to Repair** page, check the respective database, as I did in Figure 9.14. Then, click **Next**.

Figure 9.13 Exchange Troubleshooting Assistant Tasks

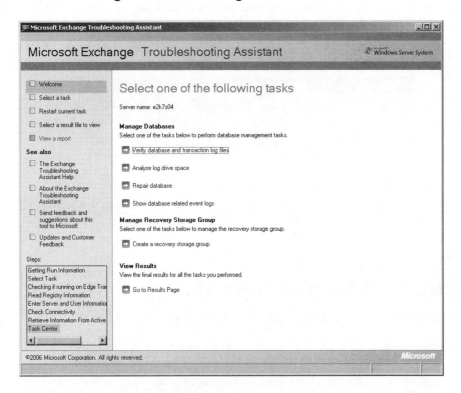

Figure 9.14 Selecting the Database to Repair

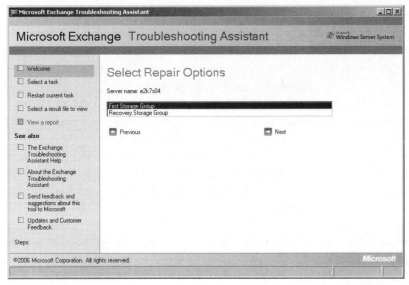

You will now need to read a repair task warning. I suggest you read it carefully. When you have done so, choose **Continue to Perform Repair Task**, and then click **OK** in the confirmation dialog box shown in Figure 9.15.

Figure 9.15 ExTRA Confirmation

The tool will now run Eseutil /P and then Eseutil /D, followed by Isinteg –fix –test all-tests against the respective database, just like we did manually earlier in this section. After a while, depending on the size of the database, you will be taken to a Report Repair Results page where you can see if the actions completed without any issues, and if not, it will show an explanation why it didn't.

Restoring Mailbox Data Using the Recovery Storage Group Feature

The Recovery Storage Group (RSG) feature, which was originally introduced back in Exchange 2003, gives you, the Exchange administrator, the option of mounting a second copy of a mailbox database (typically a mailbox database restored from backup) so you can extract data from one or more mailboxes in the respective database during working hours without affecting the production databases.

Depending on how much you have used the new Exchange 2007 Management Console (EMC), you may have noticed you can no longer create an RSG from within the EMC. With Exchange 2007, this is instead done using the new Database Recovery Management tool, which as you saw in the previous section, is found under the Exchange Toolbox work center, or by using the Exchange Management Shell (EMS).

When mounting a copy of a Mailbox database to an RSG, you can extract the data from a mailbox and then merge the data with another mailbox located in a mailbox database in a production storage group. You can also extract the data and copy it to a specific folder in another mailbox. With Exchange 2003 RTM, the data was extracted, copied, and merged with another mailbox or mailbox folder using the Microsoft Exchange Server Mailbox Merge Wizard (ExMerge) tool, but in Exchange 2003 SP1 the process was integrated into the Exchange 2003 System Manager GUI.

There are a few things you should be aware of when dealing with RSGs. First, they cannot be accessed by any protocols other than MAPI, and although they can be accessed using MAPI, this doesn't mean you can connect to a mailbox stored in a recovery database using an Outlook MAPI client. MAPI is strictly used to access mailboxes using the Exchange Troubleshooting Assistant and the respective Exchange Management Shell cmdlets. In addition, you should be aware that you still cannot use RSGs to restore Public Folder data, only mailbox data. It's also worth mentioning that even though you can create up to 50 storage groups on an Exchange 2007 Enterprise edition server, you're limited to one RSG per server. However, it's supported to add multiple mailbox databases to an RSG as long as all databases belong to the same storage group. Finally, you should note that although it's possible to add a restored mailbox database to an RSG on another Exchange 2007 server, it's important you understand that the Exchange 2007 server must belong to the same Active Directory forest.

With the preceding in mind, let's move on and see how you manage RSGs.

Managing Recovery Storage Groups Using the Exchange Troubleshooting Assistant

You can create a Recovery Storage Group (RSG) either by using the Disaster Recovery Management tool, which is based on the Microsoft Exchange Troubleshooting Assistant (ExTRA), or by running the *New-StorageGroup* cmdlet with the *–Recovery* parameter in the Exchange Management Shell.

To create the RSG using the Disaster Recovery Management tool, you should first launch it from beneath the Toolbox work center in the navigation tree of the Exchange Management Console (EMC). Let the tool check for any tool or configuration file updates available, and then click the **Go to Welcome** screen link. Enter an identifying label for this activity (such as Create RSG), and then click **Next**. In the **Tasks** list that appears, click **Create a Recovery Storage Group**, and then select the storage group you want to link with the recovery storage group, as shown in Figure 9.16. Then, click **Next** once again.

Figure 9.16 Selecting the Storage Group to Link with the RSG

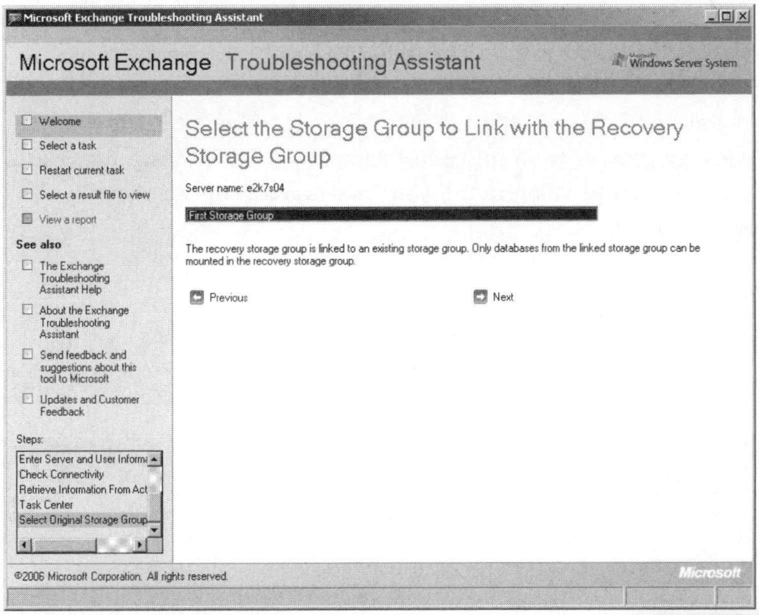

Now it's time to create the RSG, but before doing so you need to give it a name (the default name is Recovery Storage Group, which should be okay in most situations). When you have entered an appropriate name, click **Create the recovery storage group** (Figure 9.17).

Figure 9.17 Creating the RSG

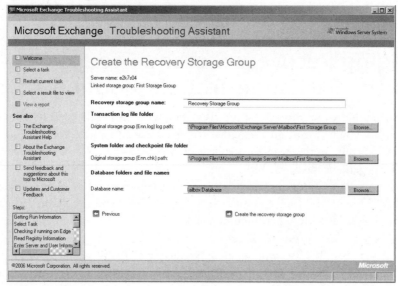

After a little while, you will be presented with a screen similar to the one in Figure 9.18, and the RSG for the respective Mailbox database has now been created.

With the RSG created, we can move, copy, or restore database and transaction log files to the recovery storage group paths. To see the path for the recovery storage group log and database files, click **Show Create Recovery Storage Group Information**. By default, the path is C:\Program Files\Microsoft\Exchange Server\Mailbox\<Storage Group>\RSG*xxxxxxxxx*, as you can see in Figure 9.19. The RSG*xxxxxxxxx* folder will appear empty in Windows Explorer until you have moved, copied, or restored the database and transaction log files to it.

Figure 9.18 RSG Result

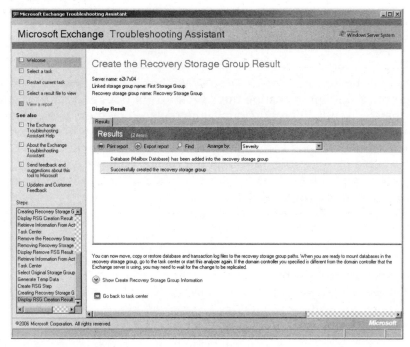

Figure 9.19 Storage Group and Recovery Storage Group Paths

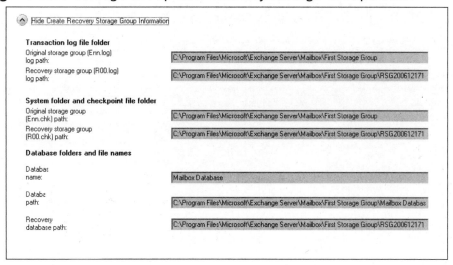

For the purpose of this example, we will restore a Mailbox database from a backup using the Windows 2003 Backup tool. So let's launch the Windows 2003 Backup tool in advanced mode, and then click the **Restore and Manage Media** tab. Here we need to select the

Mailbox database and log files we want to restore. When you have done so, click the **Start Restore** button.

> ### NOTE
>
> Note that the Restore Files To: Drop-Down box is set to Original Location. Also notice we cannot change this selection. But does that mean the Mailbox database currently in production will be replaced by the one we restore from backup? No, this is not the case. First, we haven't dismounted the production Mailbox database, and second, we haven't enabled the *This Database Can Be Overwritten By A Restore* option on the Mailbox database property page. Because of this, the Mailbox database will be restored to the recovery storage group we just created.

Now specify the Exchange Server to which you want to restore the respective Mailbox database, and then enter a temporary location for the log and patch files. Lastly, check **Last Restore Set** (Log File Replay will start after this restore completes) since this is the last restore set. When you are done, click **OK** and wait for the restore job to complete. Then, click the **Close** button.

The respective files have now been restored to the RSG*xxxxxxxxx* folder, as you can see in Figure 9.20.

Figure 9.20 The Restored Mailbox Database in Windows Explorer

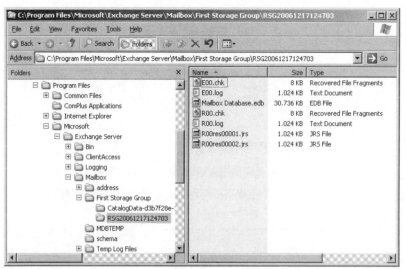

Since we didn't check the *Mount Database After Restore* option, the Mailbox database will now be in a dismounted state. With this in mind, let's switch back to the ExTRA Task Center. As shown in Figure 9.21, we now have several new recovery storage group–related tasks available. Since the Mailbox database needs to be mounted before we can extract data from it, we have to click **Mount or dismount databases in the recovery storage group**.

On the **Mount or Dismount Database** page, check the respective Mailbox database and click **Mount selected database** (Figure 9.22).

Figure 9.21 Selecting Mount or Dismount Databases in the Recovery Storage Group

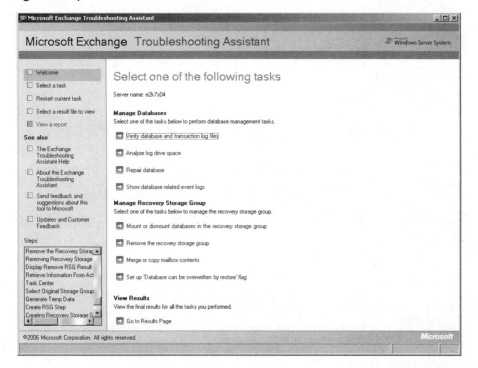

Once the Mailbox database has been mounted, click **Go back to task center**, and then select **Merge or copy mailbox content**. This will bring us to a screen similar to the one shown in Figure 9.23, here you should just make sure the Mailbox database you wish to extract data from is selected, and then click **Gather merge information**.

Figure 9.22 Mounting the Mailbox Database Using the ExTRA Tool

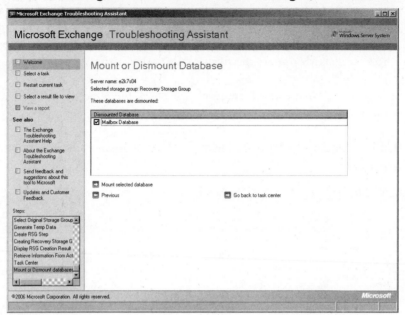

Figure 9.23 Selecting a Mounted Database in the Recovery Storage Group

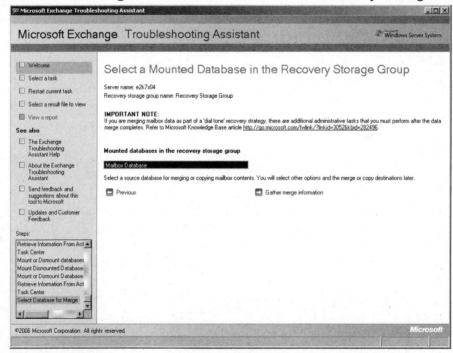

We now have the option of swapping the Mailbox database mounted to the RSG and the linked production Mailbox database (a recommended step if you're performing a dial-tone database restore) by checking Swap Database Configurations, as can be seen in Figure 9.24. Since this option will swap the two databases, both of them need to be dismounted, which will affect mail service to the end users whose mailboxes are stored in the respective database.

Figure 9.24 The Database Swap Option

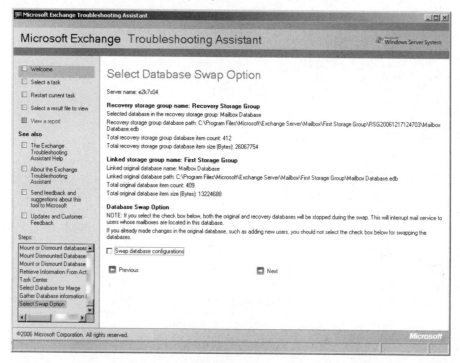

Since we aren't dealing with a dial-tone database restore in this example, just click **Next**. On the **Select Merge Options** page, click **Perform pre-merge tasks** (Figure 9.25).

> **NOTE**
>
> Note that you have the option of clicking Show Advanced Options. Under the Advanced options, we can specify different match and filtering options, as well as the bad item limit. This is also the place where you specified whether all merge mailbox data should be merged to the respective mailboxes in the production Mailbox database, or whether they should be copied to a single target mailbox.

Figure 9.25 Specifying Merge Options

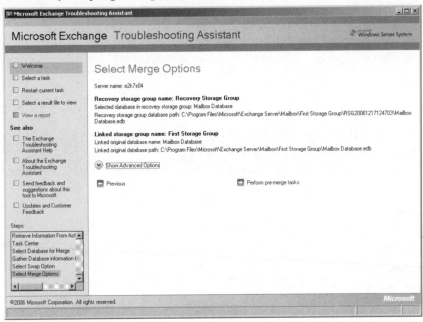

The final step is to select the mailboxes you want to merge. You do this by checking the box to the left of each user name in the list, as shown in Figure 9.26.

Figure 9.26 Selecting the Mailboxes to Merge

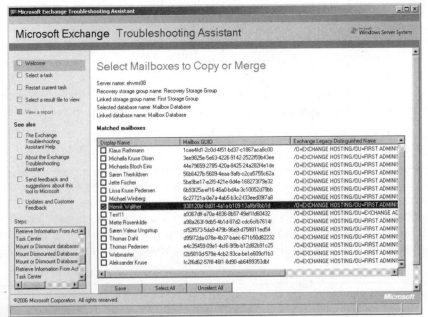

Now wait for the tool to merge the mailbox data from the Mailbox database in the recovery storage group for the selected mailbox. When the mailbox data merge has completed, you should be able to see the content deleted from the production Mailbox database. You don't even need to restart the Outlook or OWA client for the restored data to appear!

When you have merged or copied the required Mailbox data, you can use ExTRA to dismount and then remove the recovery storage group. Be sure you delete the files in the RSG*xxxxxxxxx* folder after you have removed it so the files don't take up valuable disk space.

Managing Recovery Storage Groups Using the Exchange Management Shell

As mentioned earlier in this chapter, you can also manage an RSG using the Exchange Management Shell (EMS). If you know your cmdlets, restoring mailbox data from a Mailbox database in a recovery storage group can be done a lot faster than when you're using ExTRA.

The first step is to create the RSG. In order to create an RSG via the EMS, you need to run the *New-StorageGroup* cmdlet with the *−Recovery* parameter. So, to create an RSG for the first storage group on a server named E2K7S04, type:

New-StorageGroup −Server E2K7S04 −LogFolderPath "E:\Program Files\Microsoft\Exchange Server\Mailbox\First Storage Group\RSG −Name "Recovery Storage Group" −SystemFolderPath "E:\Program Files\Microsoft\Exchange Server\Mailbox\First Storage Group\RSG" −Recovery

The *LogFolderPath* and *SystemFolderPath* parameters are used to specify where the RSG-related files should be located. As you can see, we specified they should them to be restored to a subfolder called RSG under E:\Program Files\Microsoft\Exchange Server\Mailbox\First Storage Group\RSG. If you intend to do the same, please make sure there's sufficient disk space available for the Mailbox database you're restoring from backup.

To see if a respective storage group is a recovery storage group (as well as many other types of information), you can use the *Get-StorageGroup <storage group name> | FL* command. If the storage group is a recovery storage group, it will say True under Recovery, as shown in Figure 9.27

The next step is to add a recovery database (either moved, copied, or restored from backup) to the RSG, this is done by running the *New-MailboxDatabase* cmdlet with the *MailboxDatabaseToRecover* parameter. So, to add a recovery database to the recovery storage group on a server named E2KS04 with the edb file path pointing to E:\Program Files\Microsoft\Exchange Server\Mailbox\First Storage Group\RSG, type:

New-MailboxDatabase −MailboxDatabaseToRecover "Mailbox Database" −StorageGroup "E2K7S04\Recovery Storage Group" −EDBFilePath "E:\Program Files\Microsoft\Exchange Server\Mailbox\First Storage Group\RSG\Mailbox Database.edb"

Figure 9.27 Full List of Recovery Storage Group Information

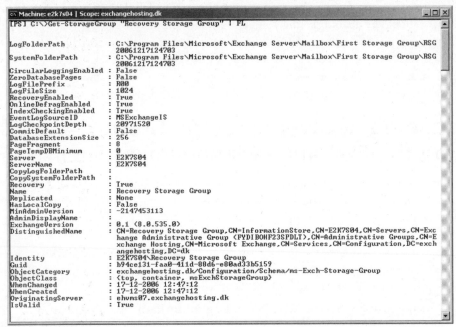

With the Mailbox Database created in the recovery storage group, we now need to con-figure it to allow overwrites by running the *Set-MailboxDatabase* cmdlet with the *−AllowRestore* parameter. To allow file restores for the recovery database just created, type:

Set-MailboxDatabase -Identity "E2K7S04\Recovery Storage Group\Mailbox Database" -AllowFileR
estore $true

Now that we have created a recovery database in the recovery storage group and allowed it to be overwritten by a file restore, it's time to restore the mailbox database version from which you want to extract and copy or merge data to the mailbox database in produc-tion. To do so, launch the Windows 2003 Backup tool and restore the respective Mailbox database version using the same steps as we did when we used the ExTRA to recover Mailbox data.

We now need to mount the restore Mailbox database using the *Mount-Database* cmdlet. In order to do so, type:

Mount-Database −Identity "E2K7S04\Recovery Storage Group\Mailbox Database"

With the Mailbox database mounted, we can now extract Mailbox data from it. For example, if you want to merge the mailbox data of an existing user in the recovery database to the production Mailbox database, you need to type:

Restore-Mailbox –Identity \<username\> -RSGDatabase "servername\RSG name\database name"

In Figure 9.28, we recovered mailbox data for a user called Test User 1 on a server named E2K7S04.

Figure 9.28 Restoring Mailbox Data from a Mailbox in a Recovery Storage Group

```
Machine: e2k7s04 | Scope: exchangehosting.dk                              _ □ ×
[PS] C:\>Restore-Mailbox -Identity "TestUser1" -RSGDatabase "e2k7s04\Recovery Storage Group\Mailbox
Database"

Confirm
Are you sure you want to perform this action?
Recovering mailbox content from the mailbox 'Test User 1' in the recovery database
'E2K7S04\Recovery Storage Group\Mailbox Database' into the mailbox for 'Test User 1
<Testuser1@exchangehosting.dk>'. The operation can take a long time.
[Y] Yes  [A] Yes to All  [N] No  [L] No to All  [S] Suspend  [?] Help (default is "Y"):
```

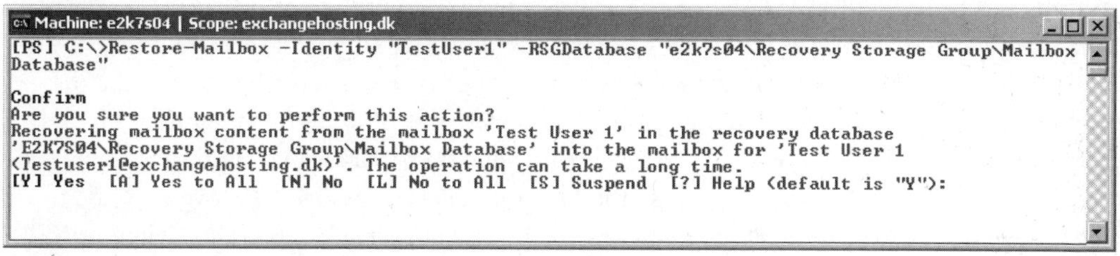

> **NOTE**
>
> Depending on the size of the mailbox to be recovered, this merging process can take a long time.

If you need to recover mailbox data for all users in the RSG, you would need to use the following command:

Get-MailboxStatistics -Database "Recovery Storage Group\Mailbox Database" | Restore-Mailbox

Let's suppose the mailbox in the recovery database that you want to recover data from has in the meantime been deleted from the production Mailbox database. In this case, you have the option of recovering the mailbox data to a target folder in another mailbox by using the following command:

Restore-Mailbox –RSGMailbox "Test User 1" -RSGDatabase "servername\RSG name\database name" –Identity "Test User 2" –TargetFolder "Test User 1 Recovered data"

Just as with recovering data using the ExTRA tool, when using the Exchange Management Shell you should remember to remove the RSG after the required data has been recovered. To do so, first run the command to remove the recovery database:

Remove-MailboxDatabase –Identity "E2K7S04\Recovery Storage Group\Mailbox Database"

Click **Yes** to the confirmation warning, and then type the following command in order to remove the RSG:

Remove-StorageGroup –Identity "E2K7S04\Recovery Storage Group"

Finally, delete the RSG folder manually using Windows Explorer.

Recovering an Exchange 2007 Server Using the RecoverServer Switch

What could be worse than facing one or more seriously corrupted Exchange 2007 mailbox databases? Yes, you guessed right: facing a completely dead Exchange 2007 Server. In this section, I'll shine some light on the steps necessary to restore an Exchange 2007 Server that has experienced a major hardware failure causing a complete loss of data. As is the case with Exchange 2000 and 2003, you can recover an Exchange 2007 Server in a fairly straightforward way. As you probably know, we could use the DisasterRecovery switch to recover a dead Exchange 2000 or 2003 Server on new hardware, but with Exchange 2007 this switch no longer exists. Instead, it has been replaced by the new RecoverServer switch, which is similar to the DisasterRecovery switch. The interesting thing about the RecoverServer switch is that it can be used to recover all types of Exchange 2007 Server roles, except the Edge Transport Server role, which uses ADAM and not the Active Directory to store configuration data.

> **NOTE**
>
> To recover a server with the Edge Transport Server role installed, you must use the cloned configuration tasks to export and import configuration information. You can read more about the cloned configuration tasks in Chapter 7.

When you run Setup with the RecoverServer switch on a new Windows 2003 Server that is configured with the same name as the one that has crashed or is permanently down for some reason, Setup will read the configuration information for the respective Exchange 2007 server from the Active Directory. In addition to applying the roles and settings stored in Active Directory, Setup will, as is the case when installing an Exchange 2007 Server role without the RecoverServer switch, install the Exchange files and services required for the respective Exchange 2007 server role(s). This means that local customizations done on the server (such as Mailbox databases, Receive connectors, custom OWA settings, SSL certificates, and so on) need to be re-created or recovered manually afterward.

In this section, we'll go through the steps necessary to recover an Exchange 2007 server with the Hub Transport, Mailbox Server, and Client Access Server roles installed.

Restoring and Configuring the Operating System

When you have received a replacement server or replacements for the failed hardware components, it's important you configure and partition the disk sets in the new server so they are identical to the way they were configured in the failed server. When the hardware is configured according to the documentation you wrote for the failed Exchange 2007 (which you did write, right?), we can begin installing the operating system from the Windows 2003 Server 64-bit media. When Windows 2003 Server has been installed, it's important you install the Windows Components required by the Exchange Server 2007 Server roles, as well as any service packs and Windows updates that were applied on the failed server. For details about which Windows components are required for each server role, refer back to Chapter 2.

In addition to that already mentioned, you should also make sure you name the new server with the same server name. Before doing so, however, it's important the failed Exchange 2007 server be turned off. In addition, you should add the server to the respective Active Directory domain, first resetting the computer account for the respective Exchange 2007 server. In order to reset the computer account, you must follow these steps.

1. Log on to a domain controller or another server with the Adminpak installed in the Active Directory domain, and then open the **Active Directory Users and Computers (ADUC) MMC** snap-in.

2. In the ADUC MMC snap-in, navigate to the organizational unit (OU) containing your computer accounts (by default, the Computers OU), right-click the computer account that should be reset, and then select **Reset Account**, as shown in Figure 9.29.

Figure 9.29 Resetting the Computer Account in the ADUC MMC Snap-in

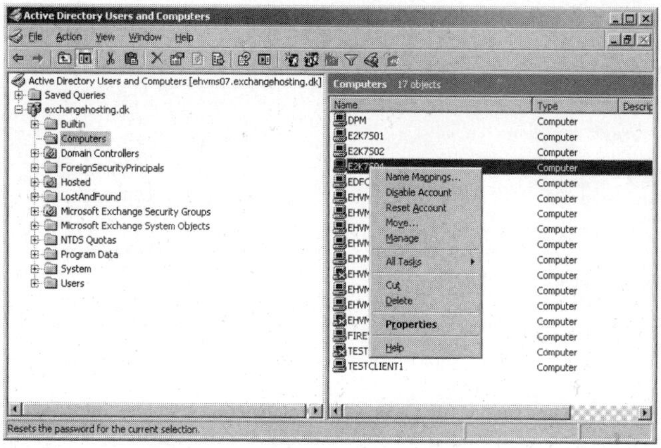

3. Click **Yes** to the warning in the dialog box that appears, and then click **OK**.

We can now join the new server to the domain without issues. Do so and perform the required reboot.

Installing Exchange 2007 Using the RecoverServer Switch

Now that Windows 2003 has been installed properly, we can move on and start installing Exchange 2007 by running Setup.exe with the RecoverServer switch. In order to do so, perform the following steps:

1. Click **Start | Run** and type **CMD**. Then, press **Enter**.

2. Change to the directory or media containing your Exchange 2007 Setup files, and then type **Setup.com /M:RecoverServer**. As can be seen in Figure 9.30, Exchange 2007 Setup will now prepare the Exchange 2007 setup, and then perform the mandatory prerequisite checks. Finally, it will begin to copy the Exchange files and then configure each Exchange 2007 Server role by reading the required configuration information from Active Directory.

Figure 9.30 Recovering an Exchange 2007 Server Using the RecoverServer Switch

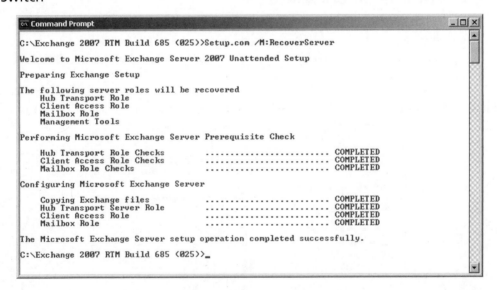

NOTE

If you're recovering an Exchange 2007 server with the Hub Transport Server role installed, and this is the only Exchange 2007 server with this role installed, its recommended you run Setup.com /M:RecoverServer with the /DoNotStartTransport syntax since there's a few post-recovery steps that should be completed before this role is made active.

When the Exchange setup has completed each phase successfully, we're close to calling the server recovery a success. However, there are a few post-recovery steps that need to be finished, depending on what Exchange 2007 Server roles are installed on the server. It's obvious a recovered server with the Mailbox Server role must have the respective Mailbox database and Public Folder database restored from backup, or copied back from the disks on the old server (if possible). If the Public Folders are replicated with other Exchange 2000/2003 or 2007 servers in the Exchange organization, you don't need to restore it since an empty Public Folder database will be backfilled from the other Public folder server(s).

NOTE

If you need to restore one or more Mailbox and/or Public Folder databases to the recovered server using the Windows 2003 Backup tool, note that you must catalog the respective backup (.BKF). This is done by selecting the **Restore and Manage Media** tab, and then clicking **Tools | Catalog** a backup file in the menu.

If the Hub Transport Server role is installed on the recovered Exchange 2007 server, you may also need to restore any saved message queue databases (which in Exchange 2007 are stored in an ESE database and not in the NTFS file system as was the case with Exchange 2000 and 2003) and place them in the right folder (should be done while the Microsoft Exchange Transport service is stopped, which is why it's a good idea to run the RecoverServer switch with the /DoNotStartTransport syntax if you're recovering an Exchange 2007 server with the Hub Transport Server role installed), as well as reconfigure any Receive connectors since these are stored locally on the Hub Transport Server and not in Active Directory, as is the case with Send Connectors. In addition, you may need to restore the Client Access Server settings (custom OWA files and/or virtual directories). Custom virtual folder settings can be restored by using the script method mentioned earlier in this chapter.

SOME INDEPENDENT ADVICE

Although it should be the most comprehensive, as well as fastest, way to recover a server using the RecoverServer switch, it's worth mentioning that it's fully supported to restore an Exchange 2007 Server by restoring the System State as well as all the Exchange installation files. Bear in mind, however, that this method requires you restore Exchange 2007 on the same hardware.

Recovering an Exchange 2007 Cluster Using the RecoverCMS Switch

To finish off this chapter, we wanted to talk a little about how you can recover an Exchange 2007 clustered mailbox server (both CCR and SCC) by using the *ExSetup.exe* command with the RecoverCMS switch. Since we're talking about restoring a cluster, many of you may think the tasks involved are terribly complex. As a matter of fact, it's a relatively simple task. The biggest challenge is rebuilding the Windows 2003 cluster itself, which as you learned in Chapter 8, is a rather harmless process. Once you have rebuilt the Windows 2003 cluster on new hardware, you need to install the Passive Clustered Mailbox Role on one of the Windows 2003 cluster nodes, navigate to the Exchange Bin folder (which, by default, is located under C:\Program Files\Microsoft\Exchange Server\), and then run the following command:

ExSetup.exe /RecoverCMS /CMSName:<name of the clustered mailbox server> /CMSIPAddress:<IP address of the clustered mailbox server>

When the clustered mailbox server has been recovered successfully (if the recovered clustered mailbox server is based on a CCR), you need to enable replication as replication, which, by default, will be in a suspended state after recovery using the RecoverCMS switch. In addition you must (both when recovering a CCR and SCC) start the Exchange System Attendant service manually since it will stop right after the clustered mailbox server has been recovered.

The next step is to restore the respective Mailbox and/or Public Folder databases that existed on the failed clustered mailbox server from backup, or move/copy them from their respective locations.

NOTE

If you're recovering a Single Copy Cluster (SCC) and stored the Mailbox and Public Folder databases on a storage area network (SAN), you won't need to restore the databases from backup as long as each node points to the same shared storage subsystem that the failed clustered mailbox server did.

When any required Mailbox and/or Public Folder databases have been restored, you should now install the Passive Clustered Mailbox Role on the second node (and if recovering an SCC, any additional nodes). If you recovered a clustered mailbox server that is based on SCC, we can now call the recovery of the clustered mailbox server a success, but if you use CCR, there's one final task to complete, and that is to reseed the replica and resume replication. To reseed the second copy of the database(s), you should run the following command in the Exchange Management Shell:

Update-StorageGroupCopy –Identity: <Servername\Name of StorageGroup>

When the storage group(s) have been reseeded, you can resume replication by running:

Resume-StorageGroupCopy –Identity:<Servername>\Name of Storage Group>

So, this was not as difficult as you had imagined it, right?

Restoring Mailbox Databases Using the Improved Database Portability Feature

As those of you with plenty of disaster recovery experience from Exchange 2003 might be aware, Mailbox database portability (that is mounting a Mailbox database to an alternative Exchange Server) was rather limited in this version of Exchange, actually the only options available were to mount the respective Mailbox database into a recovery storage group (RSG), into a storage group on a server with the same name as the failed server, or into the storage group on an Exchange Server in the same administrative group. Although mailbox databases were portable between Exchange 2003 servers (on the same service pack level) in the same administrative group, certain tasks were involved with this procedure. You had to rename the Mailbox databases appropriately, as well as re-link each mailbox in the database to an Active Directory user account before the mailbox could be accessible to an end user. In addition, several other issues might exist if the Mailbox database contained a System Attendant mailbox. Finally, depending on what type of third-party applications were running on the particular Exchange server, it was also best practice to reboot the server once the Mailbox database move was completed.

With Exchange 2007, the Mailbox database portability feature has been improved drastically. Now you can port and recover a Mailbox database to any server in the Exchange 2007 organization, and because of the new Autodiscover service (which we discussed in Chapter 5), all Outlook 2007 clients will be redirected to the new server automatically the first time they try to connect after the Mailbox database has been mounted on another Exchange 2007 server.

NOTE

Since only Outlook 2007 clients can take advantage of the new Autodiscover service introduced in Exchange 2007, any legacy clients (Outlook 2003 and earlier) won't be redirected to the new server automatically.

Some of you might wonder if Exchange 2007 (unlike Exchange 2003) allows you to port or recover a Public Folder database to another server. The answer is no. Doing so is still not supported since it will break Public Folder replication. The proper method for moving a Public Folder database to another server is to add the respective server to the Public Folder replica list.

Okay, now that you have heard how cool the new Mailbox database portability improvements in Exchange 2007 are, let's take a look at the steps needed they entail:

First, it's important you make sure the Mailbox database you wish to port or recover to another server is in a clean shutdown state. If not, you must perform a soft recovery of the database, which is done by running Eseutil /R <ENN> against it. ENN is the prefix of the storage group to which you want to commit any existing transaction log files. One method you can use to find this prefix is to open the property page of the respective storage group containing the Mailbox database you wish to port or recover to another Exchange 2007 server (see Figure 9.31).

Figure 9.31 The Transaction Log Files Prefix

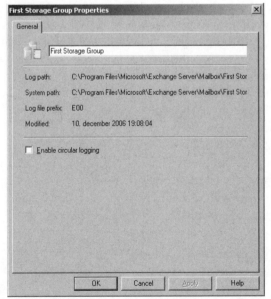

Once the Mailbox database is in a clean shutdown state, the next step is to move the Mailbox database (.EDB file, transaction log files, and Exchange Search catalog) to the system path folder of the respective storage group on the other server, and then create a new Mailbox database in the storage group using the following command:

New-MailboxDatabase –StorageGroup <Servername>\<Name of Storage Group> -Name <Name of Mailbox Database>

In this example, you will mount a database named Mailbox database to the Third Storage Group on an Exchange 2007 Server called EHVMS08. Therefore, the command we need to run is shown in Figure 9.32.

Figure 9.32 Creating a New Mailbox Database in the Third Storage Group

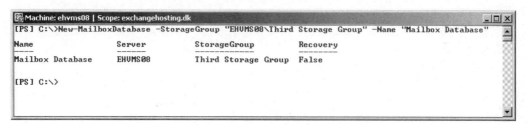

Because Exchange 2007 won't create an .EDB file for a newly created Mailbox database before it's mounted for the first time, using the *New-MailboxDatabase* cmdlet to create a new Mailbox database, while the Mailbox Database.edb file is placed in the folder of the Third Storage Group will not conflict in any way. Actually, you can just move ahead and mount the ported Mailbox database.

NOTE

It's important that the name of the new Mailbox database you create using the *New-MailboxDatabase* cmdlet matches the name of the Mailbox database you ported or recovered from the old Exchange 2007 Server; otherwise, you won't be able to mount it.

To mount the Mailbox database, you can use the Mount-Database "Mailbox Database" or the Exchange Management Console. When the Mailbox database has been mounted appropriately, there's only one more task to complete, and that is to modify (re-link) the Active Directory user account objects associated with a mailbox in the Mailbox database that we ported to a new server, so they point to the correct server. This can be done by using the following command:

Get-Mailbox –Database "E2K7S04\Mailbox Database" | Move-Mailbox –TargetDatabase "EHVMS08\Mailbox Database" –ConfigurationOnly: $True

You then must confirm that you wish to perform this operation. Type **Y** for Yes, and press **Enter**.

NOTE

If you receive an error when trying to run this command, check to make sure the Mailbox database is mounted on the old Exchange 2007 server.

Now would be a good time to access a few mailboxes (using Outlook 2007 or OWA 2007) stored in the Mailbox database we ported so you can verify the end users still have mailbox connectivity.

Summary

In this chapter, we took a look at how to properly back up the different server roles in Exchange 2007. We then went through how you restore an Exchange 2007 Server with one or more server roles installed, as well as how you can restore a corrupt Mailbox or Public Folder database using the Windows 2003 Backup tool, and if this isn't an option, how you can repair a corrupt database using Eseutil. We also had walked through how you can recover mailbox data using the improved Recovery Storage Group (RSG) feature. In addition, I showed you how it's possible to recover a failed Exchange 2007 server using the RecoverServer and RecoverCMS switches. Lastly, we talked about the improvements that have been made regarding database portability in Exchange 2007.

Solutions Fast Track

Backing Up Exchange 2007 Using Windows 2003 Backup

☑ Frequent backups of the Exchange 2007 servers in an organization are important operational tasks, which perhaps can be a bit trivial, but should be taken very seriously. I can only imagine one thing that's worse than a complete failure of an Exchange 2007 server, and that's a complete failure of an Exchange 2007 server without having any backups to restore from.

☑ One of the most important things to back up regarding Exchange 2007 Mailbox Servers are the databases that hold user mailboxes and public data.

☑ Since Exchange 2007 databases still use ESE, you can (just as with previous versions of Exchange) back them up using the Exchange-aware native Windows 2003 backup tool.

☑ Exchange 2007 supports two different backup methods. The first is a legacy streaming backup, which is a backup method based on the ESE application programming interface (API) that allows you to back up one or more storage groups at the same time. However, only one backup job can run against a specific storage group. Then we have the Volume Shadow Copy Service (VSS) backup method, which some of you may know from Exchange 2003, where it was first introduced. The interesting thing about VSS is that this method, in addition to what the legacy streaming backup method offers, can also take an online backup of the copy database when using either Local Continuous Replication or Cluster Continuous Replication in your setup.

Restoring Exchange 2007 Storage Groups and Databases Using Windows 2003 Backup

☑ It's important you understand that a restore of a Mailbox database will copy the database file (.EDB) into its original location on the disk, and thereby overwrite any existing .EDB file.

☑ Once a restore has completed, the log files will be replayed into the restored version of the database. In addition to the log files, a file called Restore.env will also be copied to the specified temporary folder, and this file is the one that keeps control of which storage group the log files belong to, as well as the database paths and range of log files that have been restored.

Repairing a Corrupt or Damaged Exchange 2007 Database Using Eseutil

☑ There may be situations where you either don't have a proper backup set to restore a particular database from, or perhaps you have found out that the database you just restored, in order to replace a corrupt or damaged database, is corrupt or damaged itself. In such situations, you have the option of repairing the database using Extensible Storage Engine Utilities for Microsoft Exchange Server (Eseutil).

☑ Eseutil hasn't changed much from Exchange 2003 since Exchange still uses ESE databases when speaking Exchange 2007. This means that pretty much all of the switches and parameters available in Eseutil are the same as in previous versions.

☑ As in previous versions, Eseutil is located in the Bin folder under your Exchange installation path, which in Exchange 2007, by default, is C:\Program Files\Microsoft\Exchange Server.

☑ When a database corruption occurs, 99.9 percent of the time it's caused by the underlying hard disk drive subsystem.

Restoring Mailbox Data Using the Recovery Storage Group Feature

☑ The Recovery Storage Group (RSG) feature, which was originally introduced back in Exchange 2003, gives you (the Exchange administrator) the option of mounting a second copy of a mailbox database (typically a mailbox database restored from backup). This way, you can extract data during work hours from one or more mailboxes in the respective database without affecting the production databases.

☑ With Exchange 2007, the RSG feature is accessed using the new Database Recovery Management tool, which is found under the Exchange Toolbox work center. You can also work with RSGs using the Exchange Management Shell (EMS).

☑ When you have merged or copied the required Mailbox data, you can use ExTRA to dismount and then remove the Recovery Storage Group. Be sure you delete the files in the RSG*xxxxxxxxx* folder again after you have removed it so the files don't take up valuable disk space.

Recovering an Exchange 2007 Server Using the RecoverServer Switch

☑ Just as with Exchange 2000 and 2003, you can recover an Exchange 2007 Server in a fairly straightforward way. As you perhaps know, we could use the DisasterRecovery switch to recover a dead Exchange 2000 or 2003 Server on new hardware, but with Exchange 2007 this switch no longer exists. Instead, it has been replaced by the new RecoverServer switch, which is similar to the DisasterRecovery switch.

☑ The RecoverServer switch can be used to recover all types of Exchange 2007 Server roles except for the Edge Transport Server role, which uses ADAM and not the Active Directory to store configuration data.

☑ If you're recovering an Exchange 2007 Server with the Hub Transport Server role installed, and this is the only Exchange 2007 Server with this role installed, it's recommended you run Setup.com /M:RecoverServer with the /DoNotStartTransport syntax since there's a few post-recovery steps that should be completed before this role is made active.

☑ When you run Setup with the RecoverServer switch on a new Windows 2003 Server that is configured with the same name as the one that has crashed or is permanently down for some reason, Setup will read the configuration information for the respective Exchange 2007 server from the Active Directory. In addition to applying the roles and settings stored in Active Directory, Setup will (just as when installing an Exchange 2007 Server role without the RecoverServer switch) install the Exchange files and services required for the respective Exchange 2007 server role(s).

Recovering an Exchange 2007 Cluster Using the RecoverCMS Switch

☑ You can recover an Exchange 2007 clustered mailbox server (both CCR and SCC) by using the *ExSetup.exe* command with the RecoverCMS switch.

☑ If you're recovering a Single Copy Cluster (SCC) and have stored the Mailbox and Public Folder databases on a storage area network (SAN), you won't need to restore the databases from backup as long as each node points to the same shared storage subsystem as the failed clustered mailbox server did.

Recovering Mailbox Databases Using the Improved Database Portability Feature

☑ With Exchange 2007, the Mailbox database portability feature has been improved drastically. Now you can port and recover a Mailbox database to any server in the Exchange 2007 organization, and because of the new Autodiscover service (which we discussed in Chapter 5), all Outlook 2007 clients will be redirected to the new server automatically the first time they try to connect after the Mailbox database has been mounted on another Exchange 2007 server.

☑ It's important that the name of the new Mailbox database you create using the *New-MailboxDatabase* cmdlet matches the name of the Mailbox database you ported or recovered from the old Exchange 2007 Server. Otherwise, you won't be able to mount it.

Frequently Asked Questions

The following Frequently Asked Questions, answered by the authors of this book, are designed to both measure your understanding of the concepts presented in this chapter and to assist you with real-life implementation of these concepts. To have your questions about this chapter answered by the author, browse to **www.syngress.com/solutions** and click on the **"Ask the Author"** form.

Q: Now that we have Local Continuous Replication (LCR) and Cluster Continuous Replication (CCR), should you still take regular backups of the Exchange 2007 databases using a backup application?

A: It's important to understand that LCR and CCR aren't replacements for traditional regular backups. Instead, they are meant to serve as the primary fast recovery solution in case one or more of your production databases shuts down. But with LCR or CCR, you can change your backup schedule from daily to weekly backups.

Q: I heard you can take backups of the passive databases when using LCR or CCR, but I don't have the option of choosing the passive database in Windows 2003 Backup?

A: You're right in that LCR or CCR gives you the option of performing the backup of the passive database(s), but although the Windows 2003 Backup tool supports Volume Shadow Copy Service (VSS) backups, this is only the case when performing file-level–based backups of the databases. In order to perform a backup of the passive databases, you must use a third-party backup solution that supports VSS backups or Microsoft's Data Protection Manager version 2 (DPM v2), which at the time of this writing is still a beta product.

Q: How do you create and manage a Recovery Storage Group (RSG) in the Exchange 2007 Management Console?

A: You don't. With Exchange 2007, the RSG feature cannot be managed using the Exchange Management Console, as was the case in Exchange 2003. Instead, you must create and manage RSGs using the Database Recovery Management tool (which can be found beneath the Toolbox work center node) or the Exchange Management Shell.

Q: Is it possible to restore a Public Folder database to a Recovery Storage Group (RSG) in Exchange 2007?

A: No. Unfortunately, the RSG feature is still limited to Mailbox databases only.

Q: Can I recover all types of Exchange 2007 Server roles using the new RecoverServer switch?

A: Yes, almost. The only Exchange 2007 Server role that cannot be recovered using the RecoverServer switch is the Edge Transport server since this server doesn't belong to the Active Directory. To recover an Edge Transport server, you must instead use the cloned configuration method, which you can read more about in Chapter 7.

Chapter 10

Transitioning from Exchange 2000 or 2003 to Exchange 2007

Solutions in this chapter:

- **Preparing the Environment for a Transition to Exchange Server 2007**

- **Exchange 2003 and Exchange 2007 Coexistence**

- **Replicating Public Folders to Exchange 2007**

- **Pointing Internet Clients to the Client Access Server**

- **Moving Legacy Mailboxes to Exchange 2007**

- **Redirecting Inbound Mail to the Exchange 2007 Server**

- **Decommissioning the Exchange Legacy Server**

Introduction

Since only the Exchange 2007 64-bit version is supported in a production environment, and because previous versions of Exchange (2000 and 2003) exist only in 32-bit versions, an in-place upgrade from Exchange 2000 or 2003 to Exchange Server 2007 isn't a supported scenario. Instead you must do a transition from these legacy Exchange Server(s) to Exchange 2007. A *transition* is the process in which you perform an upgrade to Exchange 2007—that is, you move data from any legacy Exchange servers in your Exchange organization to new Exchange 2007 servers, after which you decommission the legacy Exchange servers. A transition should not be confused with a migration; unlike a transition, a *migration* is the process in which you move data from a non-Exchange messaging system (such as GroupWise, Lotus Notes or SendMail) to an Exchange organization, or move data from a legacy Exchange organization in an existing Active Directory Forest to an Exchange organization in a new Active Directory Forest.

In this chapter we'll look more closely at performing a transition from a legacy Exchange organization consisting of a single Exchange 2003 server to an Exchange 2007 server, which will be installed as a typical Exchange Server installation.

The purpose of this chapter is to give you insight into how you perform a simple transition for legacy Exchange servers to an Exchange 2007 server in the same organization. Migrations from non-Exchange messaging systems as well as cross-forest transitions are outside the scope of this book.

Preparing the Environment for a Transition to Exchange Server 2007

Before we begin deploying the Exchange 2007 Server in our legacy Exchange organization, there are several preliminary requirements that we must complete. We need to prepare the Active Directory forest, the existing Exchange organization, and the server on which we plan to install Exchange Server 2007. In the following sections, we'll go through each preliminary requirement that must be completed before we even start to think about deploying Exchange Server 2007.

Preparing the Active Directory Forest

First we must make sure that the domain controller that is the schema master in the Active Directory forest runs Windows Server 2003 with at least Service Pack 1 applied. This is also true for any Global Catalog servers in each Active Directory site in which you plan to deploy Exchange 2007. We recommend that you run Windows Server 2003 with Service Pack 1 applied on all domain controllers in the Active Directory forest, since this version supports Exchange 2007 service notifications, allows users to browse the address book in Microsoft Outlook Web Access, and provides the ability to look up distribution list membership in a more efficient manner than in Windows 2000 Server.

NOTE

If you have any non-English domain controllers in your Active Directory Forest, you should also be sure you apply the hotfix mentioned in MS KB article 919166 (http://support.microsoft.com/kb/919166) to the respective domain controller; otherwise you can experience issues accessing the address book when you're using OWA 2007.

Although Exchange 2007 supports 32-bit-based Global Catalog servers, you should seriously consider replacing them with 64-bit-based servers instead. An organization with 20,000 Active Directory objects or more will gain a significant increase in performance by doing so. Actually, you can expect a 64-bit Global Catalog server with 14 GBs of RAM installed to handle the workload of up to 11 32-bit Global Catalog servers. Talk about an improvement that saves you a lot of money on hardware in the long term as well as patch management!

Finally, Exchange 2007 requires that the domain functional level is set to Windows 2000 Server or Windows Server 2003. You do this by following these steps:

1. Open the Active Directory Users and Computers MMC snap-in on a domain controller in your Active Directory, then right-click the **domain** and choose **Raise Domain Functional Level** in the context menu. Now change the domain functional level to **Windows Server 2003**, as shown in Figure 10.1, then click **Raise**.

Figure 10.1 Raising the Domain Functional Level to Windows Server 2003

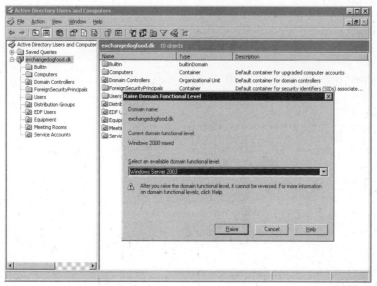

2. You will now receive an informational note similar to one shown in Figure 10.2. If you're dealing with a large topology that contains many domain controllers, you should keep this information in mind, but if you have only a couple of domain controllers deployed, you can safely ignore this information. Click **OK**.

Figure 10.2 Raise Domain Functional Level Information

Preparing the Legacy Exchange Organization

Since Exchange Server 2007 requires the legacy Exchange organization to run in native mode, we need to decommission any pre-Exchange 2000 servers (that is, Exchange 5.5 Servers and previous versions) that exist in the Exchange organization. Does this mean that you cannot do a transition directly from Exchange 5.5 to Exchange 2007 in the same Active Directory forest? Yes, that is correct! Those of you, hopefully few, who still have an Exchange 5.5 organization and want to move to Exchange 2007 must first upgrade to 2000 or 2003 and then do the transition from Exchange 2000 or 2003 to Exchange 2007.

You must also make sure that any Exchange 2000 servers in your Exchange organization run with Exchange 2000 Service Pack 3 and that any Exchange 2003 servers have Service Pack 2 applied. In addition, you should note that if you plan to keep at least one Exchange 2000 or 2003 server in the Exchange organization, the following services are unsupported by Exchange Server 2007:

- Novell GroupWise connector (Exchange 2003 Service)
- Microsoft Mobile Information Server (Exchange 2000 Service)
- Instant Messaging Service (Exchange 2000 Service)
- Exchange Chat Service (Exchange 2000 Service)
- Exchange 2000 Conferencing Server (Exchange 2000 Service)
- Key Management Service (Exchange 2000 Service)
- cc:Mail connector (Exchange 2000 Service)
- MS Mail connector (Exchange 2000 Service)

NOTE

At the time of this writing, the Exchange Product Group is working on an Exchange 2007 version of the Novell GroupWise connector.

When you're ready to switch your Exchange organization to native mode, you do so by following these steps:

1. Open the Exchange 2003 System Manager. Right-click the **Exchange Organization** node and select **Properties** in the context menu. Now click the **Change Mode** button, as shown in Figure 10.3.

Figure 10.3 Switch the Exchange Organization to Native Mode

2. You will now receive a warning message similar to the one shown in Figure 10.4. Click **Yes**, click **OK,** and then close the Exchange 2003 System Manager.

Figure 10.4 Switch the Exchange Organization to Native Mode

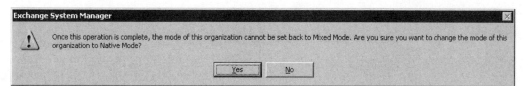

SOME INDEPENDENT ADVICE

If it's not already the case, we also recommend that you check **Display routing groups** and **Display administrative groups** (refer back to Figure 10.3) because we'll need to verify the existence of the routing and administrative groups created by Exchange 2007 Setup later in this chapter.

If you're unsure whether your environment is ready for the deployment of the first Exchange 2007 server, it's a good idea to run the latest version of the Exchange Best Practices Analyzer (ExBPA) to see if there's anything you need to do before you can proceed. The latest version of ExBPA, version 2.7, which you can download at www.exbpa.com, includes an Exchange 2007 Readiness Check option, as shown in Figure 10.5.

Figure 10.5 Exchange 2007 Readiness Check Option in ExBPA 2.7

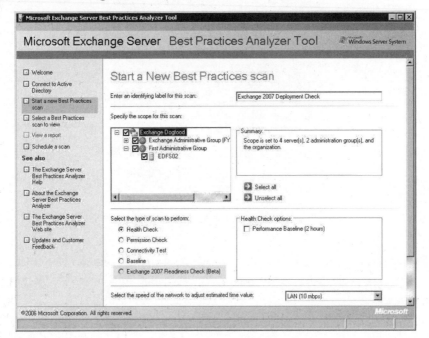

Suppressing Link State Updates

Depending on your topology, Link State updates must be suppressed on any Exchange 2000 or 2003 servers in the Exchange legacy organization when you're deploying an Exchange 2007 Server. Bear in mind, however, that this is required only if you're planning to establish more than one routing group connector in the organization.

To suppress Link State updates on any Exchange 2000 or 2003 servers in your organization:

1. Log onto the respective servers, then open the registry editor by clicking **Start | Run** and typing **regedit** followed by pressing **Enter**.

2. Now navigate to **HKEY_LOCAL_MACHINE\System\CurrentControlSet\Services\RESvc \Parameters** and right-click on **Parameters**, then select **New | DWORD**. Type **SuppressStateChanges** as the name value for the new DWORD. Finally, double-click **SuppressStateChanges** and enable it by entering **1** in the data value field, as shown in Figure 10.6.

Figure 10.6 Suppressing Link State Updates

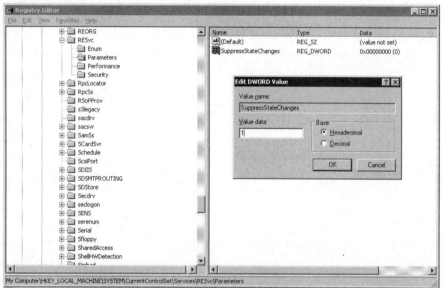

When the *SuppressStateChanges* key has been created, close the registry editor, then restart the Simple Mail Transfer Protocol (SMTP) service, the Microsoft Exchange Routing Engine service, and Microsoft Exchange MTA Stacks service so that the change takes effect.

For the purpose of this book, we're deploying a single Exchange 2007 server into a legacy Exchange organization consisting of a single Exchange 2003 server, which means we don't need to suppress Link State updates. But as mentioned, this is a required step on all legacy Exchange servers if you're planning to establish more than one routing group connector in your Exchange organization. Keep this in mind if you're planning to move from a multiple Exchange 2000 or 2003 scenario to Exchange 2007.

Extending the Active Directory

With all prerequisites fulfilled, we can move on and prepare the Active Directory using the respective Exchange 2007 Setup.exe switches. Exchange 2007 Setup includes several switches; in this section we'll go through each of those related to preparing the Active Directory.

WARNING

Each of the switches we discuss here will run automatically during the deployment of the first Exchange 2007 server in the Exchange legacy organization (if the account you're logged on with has Schema and Enterprise Admin rights!), so it's not mandatory that you run them before installing Exchange 2007. However, depending on the size as well as the topology of your environment, it might be wise to prepare the Active Directory first using these switches before you start the actual deployment process.

Prepare Legacy Exchange Permissions

The first thing we need to do in deploying an Exchange 2007 into a legacy Exchange organization is to run *Setup.com /PrepareLegacyExchangePermissions*, to grant specific Exchange permissions in the Active Directory domain(s) in which one or more Exchange 2000 or 2003 Servers exists or where Exchange 2000 or 2003 *DomainPrep* has been executed. The reason we must run *Setup.com /PrepareLegacyExchangePermissions* is that the Exchange 2003 or Exchange 2000 Recipient Update Service won't otherwise function correctly after the Active Directory schema has been updated with Exchange 2007-specific attributes.

TIP

For a detailed explanation of why *Setup.com /PrepareLegacyExchangePermissions* must be run in an Active Directory domain in which one or more Exchange 2000 or 2003 Servers exists or where Exchange 2000 or 2003 *DomainPrep* has been executed, search for "preparing legacy Exchange permissions" in the Exchange 2007 Documentation found at www.microsoft.com/technet/prodtechnol/exchange/e2k7help.

To run *Setup.com /PrepareLegacyExchangePermissions*, you must open a Command Prompt window and navigate to the directory, network share, or DVD media containing your Exchange 2007 Setup files, then simply type **Setup.com /PrepareLegacyExchangePermissions** followed by pressing **Enter**, as shown in Figure 10.7. Bear in mind that the account you're logged on with must be a member of the Enterprise Admins group.

Figure 10.7 Preparing Legacy Exchange Server Permissions

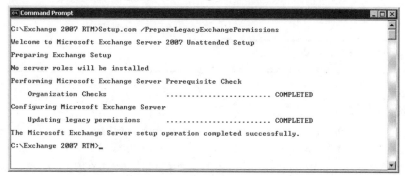

SOME INDEPENDENT ADVICE

Some of you might be in a situation where you want to prepare the Active Directory domain before you install the x64-bit version of Windows Server 2003 on a server in the Active Directory forest, and therefore you cannot run *Setup.com /PrepareLegacyExchangePermissions* using the 64-bit version of Exchange 2007 because you don't have any x64-bit Windows 2003 Servers deployed yet. But fear not—using the 32-bit version of Exchange 2007 to *prepare* your production Active Directory environment is fully supported. As mentioned in the introduction to this chapter, the 32-bit version of Exchange 2007 is not supported in a production environment except for management tasks, and preparing the Active Directory is considered a management task.

Prepare Schema

The next command to run to prepare the environment is *Setup.com /PrepareSchema*, which will connect to the domain controller schema master and import LDAP files to update the schema with Exchange 2007-specific attributes. To do so, open a Command Prompt window and type **Setup.com /PrepareSchema** followed by pressing **Enter**, as we did with the previous switch. Setup will now update the schema as necessary, as shown in Figure 10.8. To run this command, the account you're logged on with must be a member of both the Enterprise and Schema Admins groups.

Figure 10.8 Running Setup.com with the *PrepareSchema* Switch

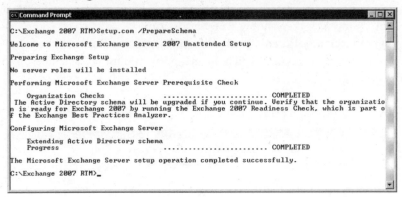

Prepare AD

The *Setup.com /PrepareAD* command is used to configure global Exchange objects in Active Directory, create the Exchange Universal Security Groups (USGs) in the root domain, and prepare the current domain. The global objects reside under the Exchange organization container. In addition, this command creates the Exchange 2007 Administrative Group, which is named Exchange Administrative Group (FYDIBOHF23SPDLT), as well as creating the Exchange 2007 Routing Group, called Exchange Routing Group (DWBGZMFD01QNBJR).

You can run the *Setup.com /PrepareAD* command before running */PrepareLegacyExchangePermissions* and */PrepareSchema,* as shown in Figure 10.9. Doing so will run the */PrepareLegacyExchangePermissions* and */PrepareSchema* commands automatically. Running this command requires you log on with an account that is a member of the Enterprise Admins group.

Figure 10.9 Running Setup.com with the *PrepareAD* Switch

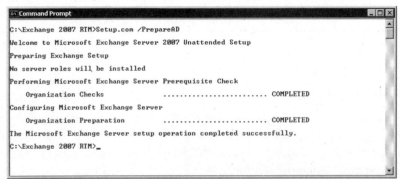

As you might be aware, Exchange 2007 doesn't use Routing Groups and Administrative Groups, as Exchange 2000 or 2003 did. Administrative Groups have been dropped completely, and message routing in Exchange 2007 is based on Active Directory sites. But for Exchange 2007 to c-exist with Exchange 2000 or 2003, Exchange must create the mentioned Administrative Group and Routing Group, which can only be viewed via an Exchange 2000 or 2003 System Manager or by using ADSI Edit, as shown in Figures 10.10 and 10.11.

Figure 10.10 Exchange 2007 Administrative and Routing Group in the Exchange 2003 System Manager

Figure 10.11 Exchange 2007 Administrative and Routing Groups in ADSI Edit

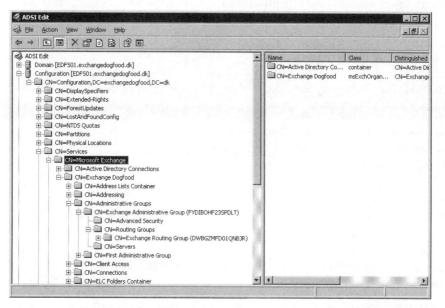

SOME INDEPENDENT ADVICE

Okay, with all these boring switches, it's time for a little fun! Did you know that although coding a product such as Exchange 2007 is a lot of hard work, the Exchange Product Group always has time for a little humor? To prove it, let's take the GUID of the Administrative Group shown in Figure 10.10 and shift each letter upward. Now do the same for the GUID of the Exchange Routing Group shown in Figure 10.11, but do it downward. Did you manage to see what it translates to? Yes, it's EXCHANGE12ROCKS!

For those who don't know, "Exchange 12" was the codename for Exchange Server 2007 until the product got a real name in April 2006.

PrepareDomain and *PrepareAllDomains*

It's also possible to prepare a local domain or all domains in the Active Directory using the *Setup.com /PrepareDomain* and *Setup.com /PrepareAllDomains*, respectively. These switches will set permissions on the Domain container for the Exchange servers, Exchange Organization Administrators, Authenticated Users, and Exchange Mailbox Administrators; create the Microsoft Exchange System Objects container if it does not exist; set permissions on this container for the Exchange servers, Exchange Organization Administrators, and Authenticated Users; and in the current domain, create a new domain global group called Exchange Install Domain Servers. In addition, it will add the Exchange Install Domain Servers group to the Exchange Servers USG in the root domain.

Like the commands we've already been through, these commands also need to be run from a Command Prompt window, as shown in Figure 10.12.

Figure 10.12 Running Setup.com with the *PrepareDomain* Switch

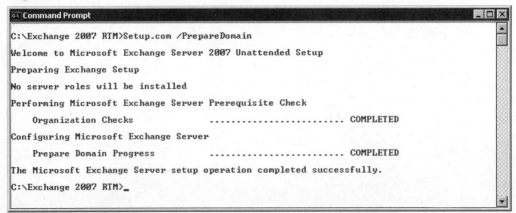

```
C:\Exchange 2007 RTM>Setup.com /PrepareDomain
Welcome to Microsoft Exchange Server 2007 Unattended Setup
Preparing Exchange Setup
No server roles will be installed
Performing Microsoft Exchange Server Prerequisite Check
    Organization Checks         ...................... COMPLETED
Configuring Microsoft Exchange Server
    Prepare Domain Progress     ...................... COMPLETED
The Microsoft Exchange Server setup operation completed successfully.
C:\Exchange 2007 RTM>_
```

Preparing the Exchange 2007 Server

When our environment has been prepared for Exchange Server 2007, the next step is to prepare the server on which you plan to install Exchange 2007 and then begin the actual Exchange installation. Since all these steps were covered intensely in Chapter 2, we won't repeat them here, but we will quickly mention a couple of things that are different in installing Exchange 2007 into a legacy Exchange organization. During the installation, you're given the option of creating a routing group connector between the administrative group containing the legacy Exchange server(s) and the Exchange 2007 administrative group, as shown in Figure 10.13.

Figure 10.13 Preparing the Exchange 2007 Routing Group Connector

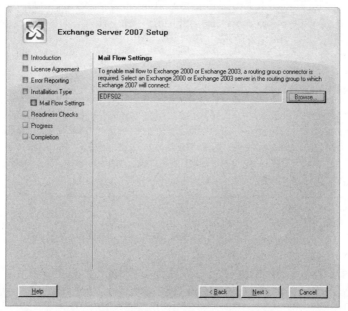

This routing group connector is created in both directions and needs to be created to establish mail flow between the servers in the legacy routing group and the Exchange 2007 routing group. In addition, the Exchange 2007 Setup Wizard won't ask you whether a Public Folder database to support legacy Outlook clients should be created but will instead do so automatically. The reason behind this behavior is probably that the Exchange Product Group took for granted that all organizations that will make a transition to Exchange 2007 still have legacy Outlook clients deployed in the organization.

When Exchange 2007 has been installed successfully, you should remember to complete the tasks listed under the Deployment tab on the Microsoft Exchange node, or at least the tasks relevant to your environment. You should also skim through the optional tasks list on the End-to-End Scenario tab. Again, refer to Chapter 2 for further information.

Exchange 2003 and Exchange 2007 Coexistence

It should come as no surprise that there are several things you should be aware of when you're dealing with a coexistence environment consisting of Exchange or 2003 and Exchange 2007. Most of the management-related tasks (creating and moving mailboxes and administering public folders) were mentioned in Chapter 3, but there are also a few things you should be aware of when it comes to organization wide or global settings.

When the first Exchange 2007 server has been deployed in the legacy Exchange organization, most of the Global Settings that originally were configured on an Exchange 2000 or 2003 server will be transferred to the Exchange 2007 Server automatically, since global Exchange settings are stored in Active Directory. This means that recipient policies, Internet Message Formats, SMTP connectors, and Exchange delegation permissions are applied to user mailboxes stored on the Exchange 2007 as well.

SOME INDEPENDENT ADVICE

Any Exchange ActiveSync (EAS) device policy settings you have enabled on an Exchange 2003 SP2 server will not be transferred to Exchange 2007. This means that you must make sure that you enable any EAS polices you created on the Exchange 2007 server for the legacy mailboxes you move to the Exchange 2007 server.

Figure 10.14 shows you the default policy originally created on our Exchange 2003 server.

Figure 10.14 The Exchange 2003 Default Policy

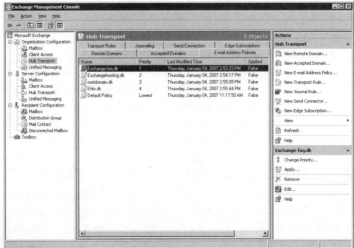

Also note that when the Exchange 2007 server has been deployed in the legacy Exchange organization, any of the organization-level settings should be managed using Exchange 2007 Management tools (EMC or EMS) during the coexistence period.

Replicating Public Folders to Exchange 2007

When you deploy an Exchange 2007 server with the Mailbox Server role installed into a legacy Exchange organization, Exchange Setup will create one Mailbox database and one Public Folder database on the server by default, as shown in Figure 10.15.

Figure 10.15 Exchange 2007 Mailbox and Public Folder Databases

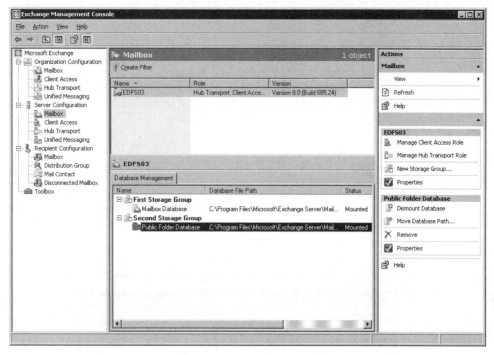

The Public Folder database is created so that you can replicate any Public Folder data stored on your legacy Exchange servers to Exchange 2007. Even if you don't use Public Folders to store data in your environment, there's one other reason you might want to keep the Public Folder database mounted on your Exchange 2007 server. As you might know, Exchange 2007 no longer uses a Public Folder (or more specifically, a System Folder named SCHEDULE+ FREE BUSY in your Public Folder hierarchy) to store free/busy information for the mailbox users in the organization. Instead, free/busy information is stored directly in each user's mailbox and retrieved using a new Web-based service called the

Availability service. The advantage of this new approach is that there are no longer any 15-minute delays when free/busy time for a user is updated. Instead, the update happens instantly. So why would we want to keep the Public Folder database on our Exchange 2007 server if free/busy information is retrieved using this new method? If you still have legacy Outlook clients (that is, Outlook 2003 and earlier versions) running in your organization, these clients still need to use the Public Folder method to retrieve free/busy information, since only Outlook 2007 supports the new Availability service.

If you don't use Public Folders to store data and only have Outlook 2007 clients deployed in your organization, you can safely remove the Public Folder database because you don't have anything to use it for. This also means you can skip the following steps.

Okay, let's get going with setting up a replica for the Public Folders on our Exchange 2003 server that should be replicated with the new Exchange 2007 Public Folder database. To do so, we must use either the Exchange 2003 System Manager or the EMS. For the purpose of this example, we'll use the Exchange 2003 System Manager.

> **NOTE**
>
> Managing Public Folders using the EMC is not possible in Exchange 2007 RTM but will be integrated into Exchange 2007 Service Pack 1.

To add the Exchange 2007 Public Folder database to the replica list on the Exchange 2003 server, do the following:

1. Open the Exchange 2003 System Manager, then expand **Administrative Groups | First Administrative Group | Folders | Public Folders**, as shown in Figure 10.16.

Figure 10.16 Public Folders in the Exchange 2003 System Manager

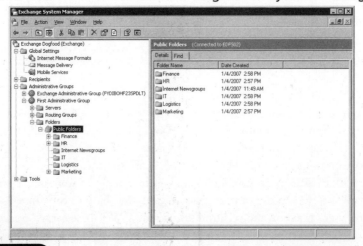

2. Now open the **Properties** page of each public folder, then click the **Replication** tab and add the **Exchange 2007 server** to the replica list, as shown in Figure 10.17.

Figure 10.17 Public Folder Replication Tab

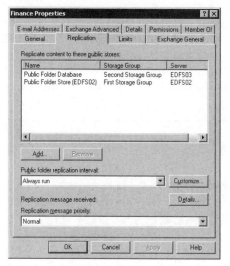

> **NOTE**
>
> Exchange 2003 Service Pack 2 introduced a new Public Folder Settings Wizard that makes it a breeze to add servers to replica lists. So if you have a lot of Public Folders in your Public Folder tree, we highly recommend that you use this wizard, which you can read more about in one of the author's article at MSExchange.org (www.msexchange.org/tutorials/Public-Folder-Improvements-Exchange-2003-Service-Pack-2.html). If you have thousands of Public Folders, you might want to use the Public Folder replica scripts located in the Exchange Scripts folder (which can be found under C:\Program Files\Microsoft\Exchange Server).

Even if you have legacy Outlook clients in your organization, you don't need to set up a replica for the SCHEDULE+ FREE BUSY or the OFFLINE ADDRESS BOOK system folder, since this will be done automatically when you deploy an Exchange 2007 server in a legacy Exchange organization.

When all Public Folders have been replicated to the Exchange 2007 server, you should remove the old Exchange 2000 or 2003 server(s) from the replica lists. When any Public Folder data has been removed from the respective Public Folder instances, you can dismount the old Public Folder stores (E2k3 SP2 won't let you remove the Public Folder store until the data is gone and it won't get gone while it's dismounted). You should verify that your clients still are capable of seeing Public Folder data as well free/busy information and accessing the offline address book before you delete it, though. If this is not the case, we recommend that you wait a little longer so that you're sure the replication has occurred properly.

SOME INDEPENDENT ADVICE

Unlike previous versions of Outlook Web Access (OWA), OWA 2007 doesn't include a GUI for accessing Public Folders. This means that to access Public Folders using Internet Explorer, you must open a separate browser window and type **https://FQDN/public**. It's important that you're aware of this missing feature.

Pointing Internet Clients to the Client Access Server

Now would be a good time to point any Internet client that is OWA, EAS, or RPC over HTTP (now called Outlook AnyWhere) in your organization to the client access server running on the Exchange 2007 server. If you're using a firewall such as ISA Server (which you do, right?), this change is done at your ISA Server firewall. If for some reason you don't use an ISA Server in your DMZ but perhaps a Check Point FireWall-1 or another "firewall" such as a Cisco PIX, you should do the redirection there. If you don't have a firewall, you should make the change on the external DNS server hosting your Internet domain.

NOTE

If your ISA server is configured to preauthenticate your OWA users, you must change the Authentication method for the OWA virtual directory under **Server Configuration | Client Access** in the EMC to **Basic** authentication, since it's configured to use forms-based authentication by default.

So, you ask, will any users with a mailbox on my Exchange 2000 or 2003 server still be able to use OWA, Exchange ActiveSync, or Outlook AnyWhere (formerly known as RPC over HTTP) to access their mailboxes? Yes, this will work just fine, since the client access server is backward compatible and will redirect the clients to the respective legacy mailboxes on the Exchange 2000 or 2003 server.

NOTE

When you make these changes, your users will no longer be able to access their mailboxes using Outlook Mobile Access (OMA), because OMA has been discontinued in Exchange 2007.

Moving Legacy Mailboxes to Exchange 2007

Now we have reached the point at which we're going to move our legacy mailboxes from Exchange 2000 or 2003 Server to Exchange 2007. Doing so is a straightforward process and can be done using either the Move Mailbox Wizard in the EMC or the *Move-Mailbox* CMDlet in the EMS. For the purpose of this book, we'll use the EMC. Do the following:

1.   If it's not already open, launch the EMC, then expand the **Recipient Configuration** work center and click the **Mailbox** subnode. Now highlight all the legacy mailboxes, as shown in Figure 10.18, and then click the **Move Mailbox** task in the Action pane.

Figure 10.18 Selecting Legacy Mailboxes in the Exchange Management Console

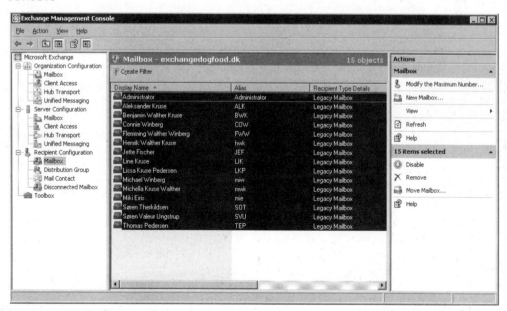

2. This will launch the Exchange 2007 Move Mailbox Wizard, where you need to specify the destination server, storage group, and mailbox database. Select the **Exchange 2007 Server** in the drop-down box (see Figure 10.19), and then click **Next**.

Figure 10.19 Specifying the Exchange 2007 Server as the Destination Server

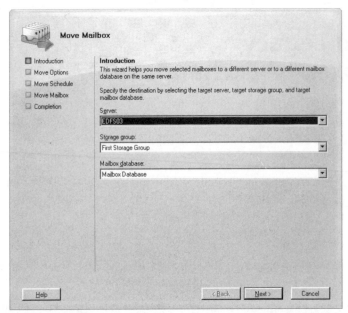

3. On the Move Option page, specify how you want to manage any corrupted messages found in a mailbox, then click **Next**. This will bring us to the Move Schedule page, where we can specify whether we want to move the mailboxes immediately or at a scheduled time. In addition, we have the option of cancelling the Move Mailbox job after X number of hours. When you have made your selections, click **Next**, then click **Move** on the Move Mailbox page to begin moving the mailboxes to the Exchange 2007 server, as shown in Figure 10.20.

    As is the case with the Move Mailbox Wizard in Exchange 2003, the Exchange 2007 Move Mailbox Wizard can move four mailboxes at a time, and only one instance of the wizard can run on a server.

Figure 10.20 The Move Mailboxes Summary Page

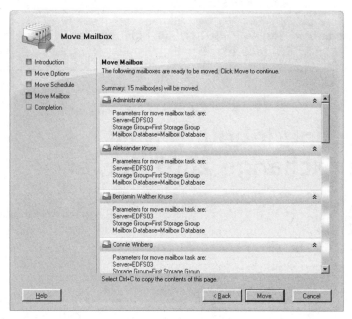

4. When all the mailboxes have been moved to the Exchange 2007 server, click **Finish** to exit the Move Mailbox Wizard, and then check to make sure that mail flow between the Internet and the mailboxes on the Exchange 2007 server works as expected in both directions.

If you will be running in a coexistence environment for a period of time, it's important to understand that mailboxes stored on an Exchange 2007 server must not be managed using the Active Directory Users and Computers (ADUC) MMC snap-in but instead must be managed using the EMC or the EMS. However, Exchange 2003 mailboxes can still be managed using ADUC.

NOTE

If you want to move the mailboxes using the EMS, do so using the *Move-Mailbox* CMDlet. Using the *Move-Mailbox* CMDlet gives you a set of advanced options, among which the most interesting one is the option of specifying the number of mailboxes to be moved at a time (as you read earlier, the Move Mailbox Wizard is limited to four).

If you wanted to move all mailboxes from a legacy Exchange server named EDFS02 to the default Mailbox database on an Exchange 2007 server named EDFS03, you could use one of the below commands:

Get-Mailbox | Where-Object {$_.servername –eq "EDFS02"} | Move-Mailbox –TargetDatabase:"EDFS03\Mailbox Database"
   or
   Get-mailbox –Server EDFS02 | Move-Mailbox –TargetDatabase "EDFS03\Mailbox Database"

Redirecting Inbound Mail to the Exchange 2007 Server

When all legacy mailboxes have been moved to the Exchange 2007 server, we can point SMTP traffic (port 25/TCP) directly to the Exchange 2007 server so that inbound messages are routed directly to it. It's recommended to deploy an Edge Transport server in your perimeter network (DMZ) and let this server route inbound messages to the Exchange 2007 server on your internal network. For instructions on how to deploy an Edge Transport server, see Chapter 7.

If you don't want to deploy an Edge Transport server, you should bear in mind that you need to change the Permission Groups settings on the Default <server> receive connector under the Server Configuration work center node | Hub Transport subnode in the EMC so that Anonymous users are allowed to connect to the Exchange 2007 server, as shown in Figure 10.21. Otherwise you won't be able to receive e-mail messages from other SMTP servers on the Internet.

Figure 10.21 Permission Groups Settings on the Default Receive Connector

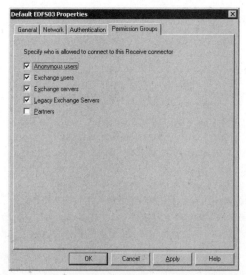

In addition, you should make sure that any Send connector on the Organization Configuration | Hub Transport | Send Connector tab is configured properly so that it can send outbound mail (using either a smart host or DNS MX), as shown in Figure 10.22.

Figure 10.22 Permission Groups Settings on the Default Receive Connector

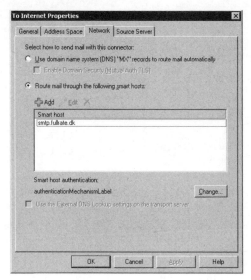

When the necessary changes have been made, we can delete the routing group connector that was set up to establish mail flow between the Exchange 2003 and 2007 routing groups. To do so:

1. Expand **Administrative Groups | First Administrative Group | Routing Groups | Connectors** and right-click the respective **Routing Group Connector**, then select **Delete** in the context menu, as shown in Figure 10.23.

2. Since the routing group connector won't be deleted at both ends, you also need to delete it under the **Exchange Administrative Group (FYDIBOHF23SPDLT) | Exchange Routing Group (DWBGZMFD01QNBJR) | Connectors**.

Figure 10.23 Deleting the Routing Groups Connector

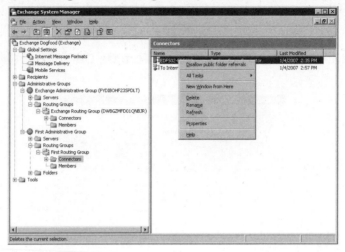

Officially the correct way of deleting the routing group connectors is to use the Remove-RoutingGroupConnector cmdlet, but since Exchange 2003 version blocking doesn't block deletes, you can use the Exchange 2003 System Manager as well.

Decommissioning the Legacy Exchange Server

The final step is to decommission the Exchange 2000 or 2003 server and we can consider the transition done. The Exchange 2003 server should be removed using the Exchange 2003 Setup program, which can be launched via Add or Remove Programs (see Figure 10.24).

Figure 10.24 Add or Remove Programs

Before we begin uninstalling the Exchange 2003 server, we first need to assign the Recipient Update Service (RUS) to our Exchange 2007 server. We do this not because RUS should be used (in fact, Exchange 2007 no longer uses RUS) but because the Exchange 2003 Setup program won't let us uninstall Exchange 2003 before RUS has been assigned to another server. To assign RUS to the Exchange 2007 Server:

1. Open the Exchange 2003 System Manager, then expand the **Recipients** node and select **Recipient Update Services**. Now open the **Properties** pages for both Recipient Update Service (Enterprise Configuration) and Recipient Update Service (domain), then click the **Browse** button under the Exchange Server text box and specify the **Exchange 2007 Server** instead. Click **OK** twice and close the System Manager, as shown in Figure 10.25.

Figure 10.25 Assigning the Recipient Update Service to the Exchange 2007 Server

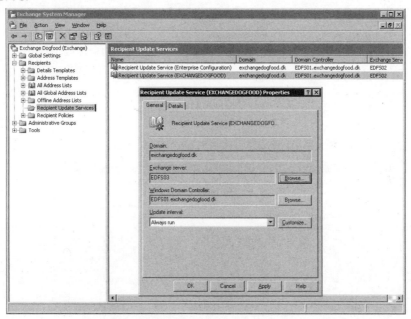

Microsoft will release an Exchange 2003 hotfix, which will prevent one from reassigning the RUS to an Exchange 2007 server, sometime in the future. This reason being this really is an invalid setting that should be blocked. Instead the recommendation will be to use ADSIedit to remove the enterprise RUS object.

2. Now we can continue uninstalling the server, so select **Microsoft Exchange**, then click the **Change/Remove** button.

3. The Exchange 2000 or 2003 Wizard will appear. Click **Next**, then select **Remove** in the Action drop-down box, as shown in Figure 10.26. Click **Next**.

Figure 10.26 Exchange 2003 Installation Wizard Component Selection Page

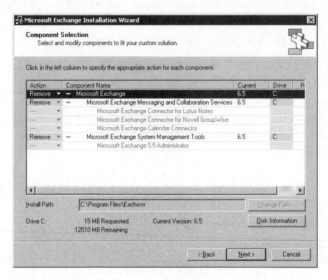

4. On the Installation Summary page, click **Next**, and wait for the Exchange 2003 uninstall process to complete (see Figure 10.27).

Figure 10.27 The Exchange 2003 Uninstall Process

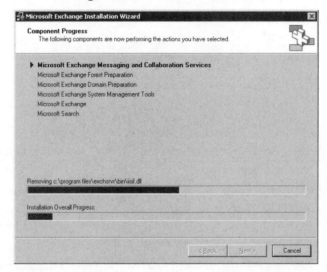

NOTE

If the Exchange 2000 Setup files aren't located on an accessible drive or network share, you will be prompted to insert the Exchange 2003 CD media during the uninstallation process.

5. When the uninstall process has completed, click **Finish** to exit the Exchange 2003 Setup Wizard (see Figure 10.28).

Figure 10.28 Exchange 2003 Successfully Uninstalled

NOTE

If the Exchange 2003 uninstallation fails for some reason, it could be necessary to remove the Exchange 2003 server by deleting the Server object in the Exchange System Manager, or if you're unsuccessful doing this, too, then by using ADSI Edit.

Summary

As you saw throughout this chapter, making a transition from an Exchange 2000 or 2003 server to Exchange 2007 in the same Active Directory forest is a straightforward process, and since Exchange 2007 coexists just fine with legacy Exchange servers, you can do the transition at your own pace. Coexistence support is laudable, since a transition process typically happens in several phases. First, you redirect your Internet clients to the client access server (CAS), then move the legacy mailboxes to the Mailbox server, and finally, point inbound mail to the Hub Transport server.

Solutions Fast Track

Preparing the Environment for a Transition to Exchange Server 2007

☑ The domain controller that is the schema master in the Active Directory forest should run Windows Server 2003 with at least Service Pack 1 applied.

☑ Any Global Catalog servers in each Active Directory site in which you plan to deploy Exchange 2007 should run Windows Server 2003 with at least Service Pack 1 applied.

☑ For any non-English domain controllers in your Active Directory forest, apply the hotfix mentioned in MS KB article 919166 (http://support.microsoft.com/kb/919166).

☑ Exchange 2007 requires that the domain functional level is set to Windows 2000 Server or Windows Server 2003.

☑ Since Exchange Server 2007 requires that the legacy Exchange organization is running in native mode, we need to decommission any pre-Exchange 2000 servers (that is, Exchange 5.5 servers and previous versions) that exist in the Exchange organization.

☑ Depending on your topology, Link State updates must be suppressed on any Exchange 2000 or 2003 servers in the Exchange legacy organization when you're deploying an Exchange 2007 Server. Bear in mind that this is required only if you're planning to establish more than one routing group connector in the organization.

Exchange 2003 and Exchange 2007 Coexistence

☑ There are several things you should be aware of in dealing with a coexistence environment consisting of Exchange or 2003 and Exchange 2007. Most of the management-related tasks (creating and moving mailboxes and administering public folders) were mentioned in Chapter 3.

☑ Most of the Global Settings that originally were configured on an Exchange 2000 or 2003 server will be transferred to the Exchange 2007 server automatically, since global Exchange settings are stored in Active Directory. This means that recipient policies, Internet Message Formats, SMTP connectors, and Exchange delegation permissions are applied to user mailboxes stored on the Exchange 2007 as well.

☑ Any Exchange ActiveSync (EAS) device policy settings you have enabled on an Exchange 2003 SP2 server will not be transferred to Exchange 2007. This means that you must make sure that you enable any EAS polices you created on the Exchange 2007 server for the legacy mailboxes you move to the Exchange 2007 Server.

Replicating Public Folders to Exchange 2007

☑ Managing Public Folders using the EMC is not possible in Exchange 2007 RTM but will be integrated with Exchange 2007 Service Pack 1.

☑ Even if you don't use Public Folders to store data in your environment, there's one other reason that you might want to keep the Public Folder database mounted on your Exchange 2007 server. As you might know, Exchange 2007 no longer uses a Public Folder (or more specifically, a System Folder named SCHEDULE+ FREE BUSY in your Public Folder hierarchy) to store free/busy information for the mailbox users in the organization. Instead, free/busy information is stored directly in each user's mailbox and retrieved using a new Web-based service called the Availability service.

☑ If you don't use Public Folders to store data and only have Outlook 2007 clients deployed in your organization, you can safely remove the Public Folder database because you don't have anything to use it for.

☑ Unlike previous versions of Outlook Web Access (OWA), OWA 2007 doesn't include a GUI for accessing Public Folders. This means that to access Public Folders using Internet Explorer, you must open a separate browser window and type **https://FQDN/public**. It's important that you're aware of this missing feature.

Pointing Internet Clients to the Client Access Server

☑ When the CAS has been deployed, you should point any Internet client that is OWA, EAS, or RPC over HTTP (now called Outlook AnyWhere) in your organization to the client access server running on the Exchange 2007 server. If you're using a firewall such as ISA Server, this change is done at your ISA Server firewall. If for some reason you don't use ISA Server in your DMZ but perhaps a Check Point FireWall-1 or a wannabe firewall such as a Cisco PIX, you should do the redirection there.

☑ When you have pointed your Internet clients to the CAS, your users will no longer be able to access their mailboxes using Outlook Mobile Access (OMA), because OMA has been discontinued in Exchange 2007.

Moving Legacy Mailboxes to Exchange 2007

☑ Moving legacy mailboxes to an Exchange 207 Mailbox server is a straightforward process and can be done using either the Move Mailbox Wizard in the EMC or the *Move-Mailbox* CMDlet in the EMS.

☑ If you will be running in a coexistence environment for a period of time, it's important to understand that mailboxes stored on an Exchange 2007 server must not be managed using the Active Directory Users and Computers (ADUC) MMC snap-in but instead must be managed using the EMC or the EMS. However, Exchange 2003 mailboxes can still be managed using ADUC.

☑ If you want to move the mailboxes using the EMS, do so using the *Move-Mailbox* CMDlet. Using the *Move-Mailbox* CMDlet gives you a set of advanced options, among which the most interesting one is the option of specifying the number of mailboxes to be moved at a time (the Move Mailbox Wizard is limited to four).

Redirecting Inbound Mail to the Exchange 2007 Server

☑ When all legacy mailboxes have been moved to an Exchange 2007 server, we can point SMTP traffic (port 25/TCP) directly to the Exchange 2007 server so that inbound messages are routed directly to it.

☑ It's recommended to deploy an Edge Transport server in your perimeter network (DMZ) and let this server route inbound messages to the Exchange 2007 server on your internal network.

☑ If you don't want to deploy an Edge Transport server, you should bear in mind that you need to change the Permission Groups settings on the Default <server> receive connector under the Server Configuration work center node | Hub Transport subnode in the EMC so that Anonymous users are allowed to connect to the Exchange 2007 server.

Decommissioning the Exchange Legacy Server

☑ Exchange 2003 server should be removed using the Exchange 2003 Setup program.

☑ Before uninstalling the Exchange 2003 server, we first need to assign the Recipient Update Service (RUS) to our Exchange 2007 server.

☑ Before uninstalling the Exchange 2003 server, we first need to delete the routing group connector assigned to the Exchange 2003 Server.

☑ If the Exchange 2000 Setup files aren't located on an accessible drive or network share, you will be prompted to insert the Exchange 2003 CD media during the uninstall process.

☑ If the Exchange 2003 uninstallation for some reason should fail, it might be necessary to remove the Exchange 2003 server by deleting the Server object in the Exchange System Manager, or if you're unsuccessful doing this, too, then by using ADSI Edit.

Frequently Asked Questions

The following Frequently Asked Questions, answered by the authors of this book, are designed to both measure your understanding of the concepts presented in this chapter and to assist you with real-life implementation of these concepts. To have your questions about this chapter answered by the author, browse to **www.syngress.com/solutions** and click on the **"Ask the Author"** form.

Q: Can I do an in-place upgrade from Exchange Server 2000 or 2003 to Exchange 2007?

A: No. An in-place upgrade from an Exchange 2000 or 2003 server to Exchange 2007 is not supported. To upgrade from any of these Exchange legacy servers to Exchange 2007, you must perform a transition, meaning that you'll deploy Exchange 2007 into the existing Exchange organization and then move Exchange data and settings to Exchange 2007.

Q: Can I do a transition from Exchange 5.5 to Exchange 2007?

A: No. A transition from Exchange 5.5 or earlier versions is not supported. To move from Exchange 5.5 to Exchange 2007, you must first upgrade to Exchange 2000 or 2003 and then move to Exchange 2007 from there.

Q: In which order should I deploy Exchange 2003 Server roles when doing a transition from Exchange 2000 or 2003 to Exchange 2007?

A: In a scenario where you will install the different Exchange 2007 Server roles on different hardware, you should first deploy the CAS, then moved on and deploy the Edge Transport server in your DMZ. After you have deployed the Edge Transport server, you can deploy the Hub Transport server and then finally the Mailbox server. If you plan to use Unified Messaging (UM) in your organization, you should deploy this server role after the Mailbox Server roles have been properly deployed.

Q: How should I decommission any legacy Exchange servers (Exchange 2000 or 2003) when I've deployed Exchange 2007 in my Exchange organization?

A: First, you should make sure that you have deleted any routing group connector assigned to the respective Exchange 2000 or 2003 server. Then you should assign RUS to the Exchange 2007 server (because an Exchange server responsible for RUS cannot be uninstalled). You can then open the Exchange 2000 or 2003 Setup program and remove each Exchange component in the Setup menu.

Q: How do I establish a mail flow between the legacy Exchange servers and Exchange 2007 server in the organization?

A: Because of the routing topology changes in Exchange 2007, you must set up a routing group connector between the legacy routing group and the Exchange 2007 routing group. You have the option of doing this during setup, but it can also be accomplished afterward using the *New-RoutingGroup* CMDlet in the EMS.

Q: When I try to uninstall an Exchange 2000 or 2003 server using the Exchange Setup program, I receive an error message and cannot proceed. How should I remove the legacy Exchange server?

A: If you have moved all mailboxes from the legacy Exchange server, deleted any routing group connectors associated with it as well as assigned RUS to another server. (If you only have one legacy Exchange server, you can assign it to an Exchange 2007 server because it isn't used in Exchange 2007.) If you still receive an error message when trying to uninstall, you have two other options. You can either delete the respective server object using the Exchange System Manager, or if this isn't possible, use ADSI Edit.

Q: Will I lose all my global Exchange settings when I've finished the transition from Exchange 2000 or 2003 to Exchange 2007?

A: No. Global Exchange settings such as recipient policies, Internet Message Formats, SMTP connectors, and Exchange delegation permissions will be transferred to the Exchange 2007 server automatically, since global Exchange settings are stored in Active Directory.

Chapter 11

Introduction to Exchange Server 2007 Unified Messaging

Solutions in this chapter:

- What Is Exchange 2007 Unified Messaging?
- Exchange 2007 Unified Messaging Features
- The Unified Messaging Infrastructure
- The Unified Messaging Mailbox Policies

☑ Summary

☑ Solutions Fast Track

☑ Frequently Asked Questions

Introduction

Unified Messaging is the integration of voice, fax, and e-mail messages into the user's Inbox. Exchange Server 2007 Unified Messaging connects Exchange Server with the existing telephony network infrastructure to provide access to different kinds of messages in a single location. After reading this chapter, you will have a thorough understanding of Unified Messaging and the way it is integrated into Exchange 2007. Furthermore, you will know the different Unified Messaging components and features that make up the Exchange 2007 Unified Messaging service.

Bear in mind that this chapter is an introduction to the feature set provided by the Unified Messaging server role, and not a comprehensive chapter on how to configure and integrate UM with your existing PBX infrastructure.

What Is Exchange 2007 Unified Messaging?

Unified Messaging brings voice, fax, and e-mail messages together into one mailbox that is accessible by telephone or e-mail on a computer or mobile device.

Normally, you would manage your voicemail and fax messages in a different way than you would manage your e-mail. It usually requires various clients and methods to acquire these different messages. E-mail is read on a computer with something like Outlook or a Web mail client, voicemail messages are obtained through the telephone, and fax messages come to—and are sent from—physical fax machines, or they are integrated into a messaging system through a third-party application. Besides the different access methods, the process also results in separate address lists for each of the three messaging types, making it hard to keep all of the address lists straight.

SOME INDEPENDENT ADVICE

Once you have implemented Exchange 2007, you will find Unified Messaging a valuable extra service. Calculate the costs of maintaining your current voicemail, auto attendant, and fax servers and compare it with the costs of a Unified Messaging service that probably provides more functionality than all of your current systems combined. In most cases, you will see that Unified Messaging is not only more useful, but also costs less.

To install the Unified Messaging role, there must be a mailbox server, client access server, and a Hub Transport server available. The Unified Messaging role can be installed on the same server as the other roles (except the Edge Transport server role), and can also be installed on a dedicated server.

You can select the feature in the custom installation screen, as shown in Figure 11.1

Figure 11.1 Exchange Setup Wizard Custom Installation

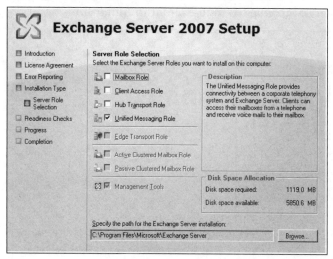

Unified Messaging brings the different message types together and provides a single point of access to these messages, resulting in a better user experience. To provide this, Exchange Server 2007 contains the following core features:

- Call answering
- Fax receiving
- Outlook Voice Access (OVA)
- Automated Attendant

These features are discussed in more detail in the next section.

> **NOTE**
>
> Consolidate sites and systems by implementing Exchange 2007 Unified Messaging. All voicemail and fax systems in branch offices can be consolidated into one Unified Messaging server. Replacing individual offices' voice mail systems with a single centralized system can drastically lower support and maintenance costs for the voicemail system by eliminating the most expensive component: legacy voice mail hardware.

NOTE

For more information, read the Unified Messaging whitepaper at www.microsoft.com/exchange/evaluation/um.mspx.

Exchange 2007 Unified Messaging Features

Exchange 2007 gives users Unified Messaging features such as call answering, fax receiving, Outlook voice access, and an Auto Attendant.

Call Answering

The Call Answering feature consists of functions to answer incoming calls on behalf of the mailbox owner, play their personal greeting, record a voicemail message, and submit the recorded voicemail message from a caller to the mailbox as an attachment to an e-mail message. The voicemail messages are attached to e-mail messages as WMA-files which can be played from within the Outlook client or on a phone by clicking the "play on phone" link in the e-mail message (see Figure 11.2). The name of the sender of the message that contains the voicemail is determined by using Caller-ID and the global address list and contacts. To set a personal greeting, the mailbox owner has to gain access to their mailbox by using a phone. The feature that provides phone access to the mailbox is called Outlook Voice Access, which will be covered later in this section. As all messages are routed through the Hub Transport server, voicemail messages are also routed through this server. This way, transport rules can be applied to these messages.

Figure 11.2 An Example Exchange Voice Mail Message

NOTE

Use the Outlook 2007 client which is part of the Office 2007 suite. For Unified Messaging, the advantage of using the Outlook 2007 client with Exchange 2007 is that users can change their Unified Messaging settings from within their Outlook client.

The interaction with the Outlook Voice Access system is based on automatic speech recognition (ASR), but it is also possible to perform many actions by using Touch-Tone dialing. Unified Messaging language packs are available that allow the OVA system to speak additional languages to callers. These packs contain pre-recorded prompts like "Welcome. You are connected to Microsoft Exchange," in the selected language. They also enable text-to-speech so content can be read to the caller in the language the message was written in.

Auto Attendants are replacements for human operators. Auto Attendants can provide anonymous incoming calls with a series of voice prompts that help them locate the appropriate department or employee and place a call to that number. The Auto Attendant consists of voice prompts (WAV files) that callers get to hear instead of a human operator. This feature can also be used with Touch-Tone or speech inputs. The Auto Attendants are completely customizable so as to meet the business needs of any organization.

SOME INDEPENDENT ADVICE

Install Unified Messaging language packs for all languages in which you will receive e-mail. To provide a great user experience, make sure the text-to-speech module can read all the messages in a correct manner.

NOTE

Unified Messaging language packs can be downloaded at www.microsoft.com/downloads/details.aspx?familyid=A59E41BD-5760-45EF-8299-1DC57601D9BD&displaylang=en.

The Unified Messaging Infrastructure

Because the Unified Messaging component of Exchange Server 2007 connects with telephony and fax systems, you should be familiar with basic telephony concepts and terminology.

- **Private Branch eXchange (PBX)** A PBX is a device that acts as a switch for switching telephony calls. This device is used to provide internal telephone connections and offer access to telephone numbers through shared outside lines to make calls external to the company. Additional communication devices can be connected to a PBX besides telephones—such as fax machines, voice mail systems, and others. Calls from outside the company are transferred to the appropriate extension or forwarded by a human operator.

- **IP-PBX** An IP-PBX is a PBX that operates with Internet Protocol (IP). This simplifies the infrastructure because telephones can be connected to the same local area network (LAN) as the computers and servers. The IP-PBX switches calls to the appropriate phone by using the IP address of the telephone. For using IP-based telephony, all telephones must support the IP protocol. A hybrid IP-PBX supports IP phones, but is also able to connect traditional analog and digital telephones.

- **Voice over Internet Protocol (VoIP)** This technology enables the use of IP-based networks as the infrastructure for telephone calls.

- **IP or VoIP gateway** IP/VoIP gateways are hardware devices that can be used to connect legacy PBX systems to local area networks to provide IP-based telephony services. These gateways convert the legacy protocols from the PBX to VoIP-based protocols like SIP and RTP. For an up-to-date list of supported gateways, see the link in the shortcut area of this section.

- **Dial plan** The dial plan is a set of rules that is used by the PBX to determine which action to take when it receives a call. For example, a 0 is often used to get to the public telephone network. When the first number is not a 0, the PBX knows it will be an internal call, but then needs to know how many more numbers to wait for before taking action. Within the Unified Messaging server, the dial plan creates a link between an Exchange Server 2007 recipient's phone extension in the Active Directory and the recipient's Unified Messaging–enabled mailbox. After a dial plan is configured, a Unified Messaging server must be added to the plan. This links the dial plan and the server and enables the server to accept and handle incoming calls.

- **Hunt group** A hunt group is a set of extensions shared by users. When a PBX receives a call for a number that is assigned to a hunt group, it searches through the connected extensions to find an available phone. Hunt groups are often used to distribute calls among members of support or sales departments. Customers call one number for the support team, and the call could be routed to any member of the team who is not currently on the phone. Within the Unified Messaging con-figuration, a hunt group is a logical representation of an existing PBX or IP-PBX hunt group. This provides Unified Messaging possibilities for the pilot number (shared telephone number of the hunt group).

An Exchange 2007 Unified Messaging component connects with the existing telephony infrastructure to create a Unified Messaging infrastructure. Figure 11.3 shows an example of a Unified Messaging infrastructure.

Figure 11.3 Unified Messaging Infrastructure

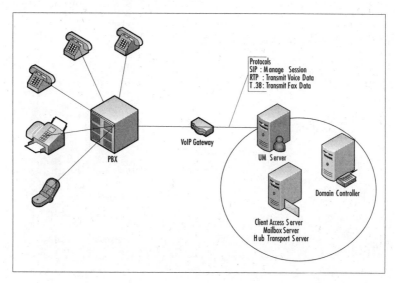

This Unified Messaging infrastructure consists of the following components:

- **PBX and connected phones** The PBX is connected to the external telephone system using one or more lines. The telephones are directly connected to the PBX system. Incoming calls are routed by the PBX to the appropriate phone.

- **VoIP gateway** The PBX system is attached to the VoIP gateway. The VoIP gateway, meanwhile, is connected to the PBX with a fixed number of ports; this depends on the gateway's capabilities. Whenever there's no answer or a "do not disturb" signal on a user's phone, the call is routed to the VoIP gateway with infor-mation about the destination phone number and the ID of the caller. The PBX also forwards calls made to specific telephone numbers—for example, when users call the telephone number to access the Automated Attendant services on the Unified Messaging server. When using an IP-PBX, it's not always necessary to use a VoIP or IP gateway. Figure 11.4 shows the wizard that configures the connection between the Unified Messaging server and the VoIP gateway.

■ **Exchange 2007 Unified Messaging server** The VoIP gateway is attached to the server. This Unified Messaging server takes calls from the IP gateway and handles the requests. The Unified Messaging server uses the SIP protocol and listens for requests on the default SIP port 5060 tcp. For speech processing, the server depends on the Microsoft Speech Server (MSS) component. This component is installed as part of the Unified Messaging role and runs as the MS Exchange Speech Engine service.

■ **Domain controllers** The domain controllers provide directory information, enabling the Unified Messaging server to route the incoming calls. Within the directory, all the Unified Messaging–enabled users have a phone extension number attribute. This attribute is used by the Unified Messaging server to find the appropriate user and route the message to their mailbox.

Figure 11.4 UM IP Gateway Wizard

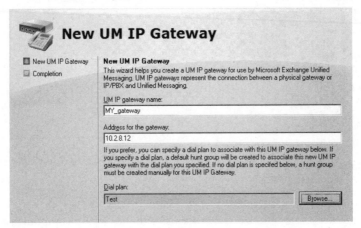

> **NOTE**
>
> Obtain assistance of a Unified Messaging specialist to make sure there is a smooth transition to Exchange 2007 Unified Messaging from a legacy voice mail system.

The Unified Messaging server uses three IP protocols for Unified Messaging communications:

■ **(SIP) Session Initiation Protocol** SIP is a real-time signaling protocol and is used to maintain the communication session. TLS can be used to secure the SIP traffic. Exchange Server 2007 Unified Messaging uses only SIP over tcp.

- **(RTP) Real-Time Transport Protocol** RTP is the protocol used for the transport of voice traffic between the VoIP gateway and the Unified Messaging server. RTP provides high-quality, streaming voice connections. RTP traffic can also be secured by using TLS.

- **T.38 (Real-Time Facsimile)** This protocol is the fax transport protocol used by the Unified Messaging server. The Unified Messaging server assumes that all incoming calls are voice, so a fax call originates as a voice call using the RTP protocol. When the Exchange Unified Messaging server detects the fax tone, the call is switched to the T.38 protocol.

Some Independent Advice

If you are thinking about replacing your current PBX, take a look at systems that can be directly connected to Exchange 2007 Unified Messaging. One of the few is Cisco Call Manager 5.x. Using a system that can be directly connected eliminates the need for an extra gateway device.

Note

For information on IP-PBX and PBX support to http://technet.microsoft.com/en-us/library/aa996831.aspx. For information on IP/VOIP gateway support, visit http://technet.microsoft.com/en-us/library/bb123948.aspx. To find Unified Messaging partners, go to http://directory.microsoft.com.

The Unified Messaging Mailbox Policies

When a new Exchange 2007 recipient is created, it is not UM-enabled. Once you enable a user for Unified Messaging, you can manage, modify, and configure the UM-related properties for the user. You can then view and modify UM-related settings such as the associated UM dial plan, the associated UM mailbox policy, and the extension number for the user.

UM-related settings are stored for a user in two places: the recipient's mailbox and the user's Active Directory object. When you enable a recipient for Unified Messaging, you are setting a specific property on the user's mailbox.

Using Unified Messaging mailbox policies enables you to apply and standardize Unified Messaging configuration settings for Unified Messaging–enabled users. You can create Unified Messaging mailbox policies and then add the policy to a collection of Unified Messaging–enabled mailboxes to apply a common set of policies or security settings. Unified Messaging mailbox policies are required before you can enable users for Unified Messaging.

The default Unified Messaging mailbox policy is generated when you create the first dial plan, but you can establish additional mailbox policies based on your business's needs. With a Unified Messaging mailbox policy, you can configure the following settings:

- Dial plan (required)

- Maximum greeting length

- Number of unsuccessful login attempts before the password is reset

- Minimum number of digits required in a PIN

- Number of days until a new PIN is required

- Number of previous passwords disallowed

- Restrictions on international calling

Figure 11.5 shows the General tab of a Unified Messaging mailbox policy.

Figure 11.5 A Unified Messaging Mailbox Policy

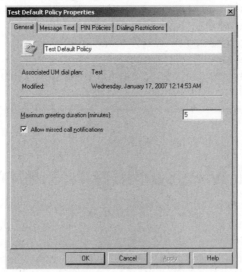

Each mailbox can be linked to only one Unified Messaging mailbox policy.

NOTE

Try to reduce the number of Unified Messaging mailbox policies to simplify administration. For more information on managing Unified Messaging mailbox policies, visit http://technet.microsoft.com/en-us/library/aa996341.aspx.

When you enable a user account for Unified Messaging, you must specify a mailbox policy and an extension, and you must assign a PIN or configure the system to generate the initial PIN for the user. When the user is Unified Messaging–enabled, Exchange Server sends the user an e-mail message indicating that the user's account has been enabled; the message also contains the PIN.

NOTE

Implement strong PIN requirements for Unified Messaging users. This can be enforced by creating Unified Messaging PIN policies that require six or more digits for PINs, and increasing the level of security for your network. You can also enhance the level of security of your network by reducing the number of failed logon attempts for UM-enabled users.

Summary

This chapter focused on the Unified Messaging server (included in Exchange Server 2007) and its role. This server role provides a connection between PBX systems and the e-mail system. Installing this role requires the other Exchange roles to be installed (except for the Edge server role). Unified Messaging offers voicemail and fax messages in your mailbox and provides telephone access to that mailbox. The embedded speech recognition enables users to navigate through their mailbox by using voice commands.

Solutions Fast Track

What Is Exchange 2007 Unified Messaging?

☑ Unified Messaging is the combination of voice, fax, and e-mail messages.

☑ Unified Messaging centralizes access to different types of messages at one location.

☑ Unified Messaging allows users to access their mailbox through an ordinary phone.

Exchange 2007 Unified Messaging Features

☑ The Exchange Unified Messaging server provides a voice mail and fax system.

☑ The Auto Attendant provides a customizable, speech-enabled service that answers phone calls and automates dialing through directory integration, acting as a switchboard application.

☑ Outlook voice access lets users access their mailbox by using a phone and voice commands.

The Unified Messaging Infrastructure

☑ The Exchange 2007 Unified Messaging server can be connected directly to some IP-PBX systems. Other PBX systems can be connected by implementing a gateway device between the PBX and the Unified Messaging server.

☑ Domain controllers provide the necessary information for finding the correct mailbox for each incoming call.

☑ The communication used between the telephony system and the Unified Messaging server is based on standard protocols.

Frequently Asked Questions

The following Frequently Asked Questions, answered by the authors of this book, are designed to both measure your understanding of the concepts presented in this chapter and to assist you with real-life implementation of these concepts. To have your questions about this chapter answered by the author, browse to **www.syngress.com/solutions** and click on the **"Ask the Author"** form.

Q: Is it possible to test the Unified Messaging service of Exchange 2007 without a PBX?

A: It is possible to try out the server by using a soft phone (telephone emulator). Instructions can be found at http://technet.microsoft.com/en-us/library/aa998254.aspx.

Q: What languages are supported by the automated speech recognition (ASR) system?

A: Currently, only English is supported.

Q: Which gateways of PBX does Exchange 2007 support?

A: Exchange 2007 currently supports VoIP gateways from Intel (PIMG and TIMG gateways) and AudioCodes (MediaPack and Mediant2000). With these gateways, it is possible to connect Exchange 2007 UM to a large range of PBX systems. The Cisco Call Manager 5.x is tested and can be connected directly to Exchange 2007 UM.

Q: How does a PBX forward WMA files to the exchange server? What format is used, and where is this configured in Exchange 2007?

A: The PBX does not create the file. The PBX forwards the call to the Unified Messaging server where it is recorded, saved as a sound file, and mailed to the appropriate mailbox. By default, the server uses wma encoding. This is configured in the dial plan on the Settings tab.

Index

Syngress: *The Definition of a Serious Security Library*

Syn·gress (sin–gres): *noun, sing.* Freedom from risk or danger; safety. See *security*.

Syngress: *The Definition of a Serious Security Library*

Syn·gress (sin-gres): *noun, sing.* Freedom from risk or danger; safety. See *security*.

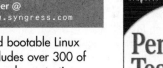

Syngress: *The Definition of a Serious Security Library*

Syn·gress (sin–gres): *noun, sing.* Freedom from risk or danger; safety. See *security*.

Syngress: *The Definition of a Serious Security Library*

Syn·gress (sin–gres): *noun, sing.* Freedom from risk or danger; safety. See *security*.

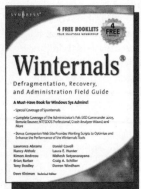

Syngress: *The Definition of a Serious Security Library*

Syn·gress (sin–gres): *noun, sing.* Freedom from risk or danger; safety. See *security.*

How to Cheat at Designing Security for a Windows Server 2003 Network

Neil Ruston, Chris Peiris

While considering the security needs of your organiztion, you need to balance the human and the technical in order to create the best security design for your organization. Securing a Windows Server 2003 enterprise network is hardly a small undertaking, but it becomes quite manageable if you approach it in an organized and systematic way. This includes configuring software, services, and protocols to meet an organization's security needs.

ISBN: 1-59749-243-4

Price: $39.95 US $55.95 CAN

How to Cheat at Designing a Windows Server 2003 Active Directory Infrastructure

Melissa Craft, Michael Cross, Hal Kurz, Brian Barber

The book will start off by teaching readers to create the conceptual design of their Active Directory infrastructure by gathering and analyzing business and technical requirements. Next, readers will create the logical design for an Active Directory infrastructure. Here the book starts to drill deeper and focus on aspects such as group policy design. Finally, readers will learn to create the physical design for an active directory and network Infrastructure including DNS server placement; DC and GC placements and Flexible Single Master Operations (FSMO) role placement.

ISBN: 1-59749-058-X

Price: $39.95 US $55.95 CAN

How to Cheat at Configuring ISA Server 2004

Dr. Thomas W. Shinder, Debra Littlejohn Shinder

If deploying and managing ISA Server 2004 is just one of a hundred responsibilities you have as a System Administrator, "How to Cheat at Configuring ISA Server 2004" is the perfect book for you. Written by Microsoft MVP Dr. Tom Shinder, this is a concise, accurate, enterprise tested method for the successful deployment of ISA Server.

ISBN: 1-59749-057-1

Price: $34.95 U.S. $55.95 CAN

SYNGRESS®

Syngress: *The Definition of a Serious Security Library*

Syn·gress (sin‑gres): *noun, sing.* Freedom from risk or danger; safety. See *security*.

Configuring SonicWALL Firewalls

Chris Lathem, Ben Fortenberry, Lars Hansen

Configuring SonicWALL Firewalls is the first book to deliver an in-depth look at the SonicWALL firewall product line. It covers all of the aspects of the SonicWALL product line from the SOHO devices to the Enterprise SonicWALL firewalls. Advanced troubleshooting techniques and the SonicWALL Security Manager are also covered.

ISBN: 1-59749-250-7

Price: $49.95 US $69.95 CAN

Perfect Passwords:
Selection, Protection, Authentication

Mark Burnett

User passwords are the keys to the network kingdom, yet most users choose overly simplistic passwords (like password) that anyone could guess, while system administrators demand impossible to remember passwords littered with obscure characters and random numerals. Author Mark Burnett has accumulated and analyzed over 1,000,000 user passwords, and this highly entertaining and informative book filled with dozens of illustrations reveals his findings and balances the rigid needs of security professionals against the ease of use desired by users.

ISBN: 1-59749-041-5

Price: $24.95 US $34.95 CAN

SYNGRESS

Syngress: *The Definition of a Serious Security Library*

Syn·gress (sin–gres): *noun, sing.* Freedom from risk or danger; safety. See *security.*

SYNGRESS®

Syngress: *The Definition of a Serious Security Library*

Syn·gress (sin-gres): *noun, sing.* Freedom from risk or danger; safety. See *security*.

How to Cheat at Managing Windows Server Update Services

AVAILABLE NOW
order @
www.syngress.com

Brian Barber

If you manage a Microsoft Windows network, you probably find yourself overwhelmed at times by the sheer volume of updates and patches released by Microsoft for its products. You know these updates are critical to keep your network running efficiently and securely, but staying current amidst all of your other responsibilities can be almost impossible. Microsoft's recently released Windows Server Update Services (WSUS) is designed to streamline this process. Learn how to take full advantage of WSUS using Syngress' proven "How to Cheat" methodology, which gives you everything you need and nothing you don't.

ISBN: 1-59749-027-X

Price: $39.95 US $55.95 CAN

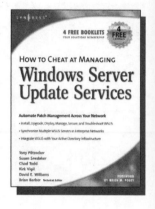

AVAILABLE NOW
order @
www.syngress.com

How to Cheat at IT Project Management

Susan Snedaker

Most IT projects fail to deliver – on average, all IT projects run over schedule by 82%, run over cost by 43% and deliver only 52% of the desired functionality. Pretty dismal statistics. Using the proven methods in this book, you'll find that IT project you work on from here on out will have a much higher likelihood of being on time, on budget and higher quality. This book provides clear, concise, information and hands-on training to give you immediate results. And, the companion Web site provides dozens of templates for managing IT projects.

ISBN: 1-59749-037-7

Price: $44.95 U.S. $64.95 CAN

SYNGRESS®

Syngress: *The Definition of a Serious Security Library*

Syn·gress (sin–gres): *noun, sing.* Freedom from risk or danger; safety. See *security*.

Managing Cisco Network Security, Second Edition

Offers updated and revised information covering many of Cisco's security products that provide protection from threats, detection of network security incidents, measurement of vulnerability and policy compliance, and management of security policy across an extended organization. These are the tools that you have to mount defenses against threats. Chapters also cover the improved functionality and ease of the Cisco Secure Policy Manager software used by thousands of small-to-midsized businesses, and a special section on Cisco wireless solutions.

ISBN: 1-931836-56-6
Price: $69.95 USA $108.95 CAN

How to Cheat at Managing Microsoft Operations Manager 2005

Tony Piltzecker, Rogier Dittner, Rory McCaw, Gordon McKenna, Paul M. Summitt, David E. Williams

My e-mail takes forever. My application is stuck. Why can't I log on? System administrators have to address these types of complaints far too often. With MOM, system administrators will know when overloaded processors, depleted memory, or failed network connections are affecting their Windows servers long before these problems bother users. Readers of this book will learn why when it comes to monitoring Windows Server System infrastructure, MOM's the word.

ISBN: 1-59749-251-5
Price: $39.95 U.S. $55.95 CAN

SYNGRESS®

Syngress: *The Definition of a Serious Security Library*

Syn·gress (sin–gres): *noun, sing.* Freedom from risk or danger; safety. See *security.*

SYNGRESS